DARWIN, LITERATURE AN
RESPECTABILI

The success of Charles Darwin's evolutionary theories in mid-nineteenth-century Britain has long been attributed, in part, to his own adherence to strict standards of Victorian respectability, especially in regard to sex. Gowan Dawson contends that the fashioning of such respectability was by no means straightforward or unproblematic, with Darwin and his principal supporters facing surprisingly numerous and enduring accusations of encouraging sexual impropriety. Integrating contextual approaches to the history of science with recent work in literary studies, Dawson sheds new light on the well-known debates over evolution by examining them in relation to the murky underworlds of Victorian pornography, sexual innuendo, unrespectable freethought and artistic sensualism. Such disreputable and generally overlooked aspects of nineteenth-century culture were actually remarkably central to many of these controversies. Focusing particularly on aesthetic literature and new legal definitions of obscenity, Dawson reveals the underlying tensions between Darwin's theories and conventional notions of Victorian respectability.

GOWAN DAWSON is Lecturer in Victorian Literature at the University of Leicester. He is co-author of *Science in the Nineteenth-Century Periodical: Reading the Magazine of Nature* (Cambridge, 2004).

CAMBRIDGE STUDIES IN NINETEENTH-CENTURY
LITERATURE AND CULTURE

General editor

Gillian Beer, *University of Cambridge*

Editorial board

Isobel Armstrong, *Birkbeck, University of London*
Kate Flint, *Rutgers University*
Catherine Gallagher, *University of California, Berkeley*
D. A. Miller, *Columbia University*
J. Hillis Miller, *University of California, Irvine*
Daniel Pick, *Birkbeck, University of London*
Mary Poovey, *New York University*
Sally Shuttleworth, *University of Oxford*
Herbert Tucker, *University of Virginia*

Nineteenth-century British literature and culture have been rich fields for interdisciplinary studies. Since the turn of the twentieth century, scholars and critics have tracked the intersections and tensions between Victorian literature and the visual arts, politics, social organization, economic life, technical innovations, scientific thought – in short, culture in its broadest sense. In recent years, theoretical challenges and historiographical shifts have unsettled the assumptions of previous scholarly synthesis and called into question the terms of older debates. Whereas the tendency in much past literary critical interpretation was to use the metaphor of culture as 'background', feminist, Foucauldian, and other analyses have employed more dynamic models that raise questions of power and of circulation. Such developments have reanimated the field. This series aims to accommodate and promote the most interesting work being undertaken on the frontiers of the field of nineteenth-century literary studies: work which intersects fruitfully with other fields of study such as history, or literary theory, or the history of science. Comparative as well as interdisciplinary approaches are welcomed.

A complete list of titles published will be found at the end of the book.

DARWIN, LITERATURE AND VICTORIAN RESPECTABILITY

GOWAN DAWSON

CAMBRIDGE
UNIVERSITY PRESS

CAMBRIDGE UNIVERSITY PRESS
Cambridge, New York, Melbourne, Madrid, Cape Town, Singapore,
São Paulo, Delhi, Dubai, Tokyo

Cambridge University Press
The Edinburgh Building, Cambridge CB2 8RU, UK

Published in the United States of America by Cambridge University Press, New York

www.cambridge.org
Information on this title: www.cambridge.org/9780521128858

First published 2007
Reprinted 2008
This digitally printed version 2009

A catalogue record for this publication is available from the British Library

ISBN 978-0-521-87249-2 Hardback
ISBN 978-0-521-12885-8 Paperback

For my mother and in memory of my father

Contents

Figures

Acknowledgements

Many friends and colleagues have contributed greatly to this book, and I would like to offer my sincere thanks for the support and generosity shown to me during the period I have been researching and writing it. My greatest thanks are to Sally Shuttleworth who, as an exemplary supervisor, supported the project from its very inception, and has continued, throughout its various permutations, to respond to my ideas with both critical acumen and unstinting kindness. I am also extremely grateful to Bernard Lightman and Gregory Radick for reading and commenting on manuscript drafts of various chapters. The book has benefited greatly from the suggestions and comments of Samuel Alberti, Laurel Brake, Daniel Brown, Janet Browne, Geoffrey Cantor, Marysa Demoor, Frank James, Alexandra Karl, Jack Morrell, Lynda Nead, Richard Noakes, Joan Richards, Joanne Shattock, Peter Shillingsburg and Jonathan Topham. At Cambridge University Press, my thanks go to Gillian Beer, Linda Bree and Maartje Scheltens, as well as an anonymous referee whose generous and insightful report on the manuscript enabled me to make numerous improvements to the final draft.

Various institutions have played an important role in the book's generation, and I would like to thank the staff of the British Library, City University Library, Leeds University Library, Musée provincial Félicien Rops, Senate House Library, University of Leicester Library and University of Sheffield Library. I am also very grateful to those libraries and archives which allowed me access to unpublished manuscript material in their possession: the Bradlaugh Papers are used by courtesy of the Bishopsgate Institute; the Darwin Manuscript Collection is used with the permission of the Syndics of Cambridge University Library; the Huxley Papers are used by permission of the Archives, Imperial College London; the Tyndall Papers are used by courtesy of the Royal Institution of Great Britain; the Pearson, Robertson and UCL Council Papers are used by courtesy of University College London Library Services. Both the Science in the Nineteenth-Century

Periodical (SciPer) project at the Universities of Leeds and Sheffield and the Department of English at the University of Leicester provided me with extremely supportive and stimulating working environments whilst I was writing the book, and I am particularly grateful to the University of Leicester for granting me a period of study leave which enabled me to prepare the final draft.

A portion of chapter one appeared in *Victorian Poetry* 41 (2003), and earlier versions of parts of chapters two and five have been published in *Unmapped Countries: Biological Visions in Nineteenth-Century Literature and Culture*, ed. by Anne-Julia Zwierlein (London: Anthem Press, 2005), and *Science Serialized: Representations of the Sciences in Nineteenth-Century Periodicals*, ed. by Sally Shuttleworth and Geoffrey Cantor (Cambridge, MA: MIT Press, 2004). Permission to reprint is gratefully acknowledged.

Finally, I thank my family and friends for their support, and not least their patience, during the long time in which this book has gradually taken shape. Helen Wilkinson in particular has given me all the encouragement, love and good counsel that I could ever have expected. Similarly, my parents, Stefanie and Paul, have always offered the unfailing support, both emotional and material, that has enabled me to follow my own particular path, and it is to them that the book is dedicated.

CHAPTER I

Introduction: Darwinian science and Victorian respectability

At a meeting of the Geological Society of London in November 1856, Richard Owen, the foremost comparative anatomist and perhaps the most eminent man of science in mid-Victorian Britain, reached the conclusion of an address on the newly discovered jawbone of an early prehistoric mammal. Turning aside from the structural specifics of the *Stereognathus ooliticus*, he took the opportunity to issue an urgent warning against the irreligious scientific doctrines that had been promulgated in Paris earlier in the century and were now being adopted by a 'small and unfruitful minority' of naturalists in London. Despite their vaunted modernity, these heretical views, Owen insisted, derived originally from the demeaning 'tenets of the Democritic and Lucretian schools' that were formulated in ancient Greece and Rome. Owen was particularly concerned with the potential consequences of such antiquated axioms for nineteenth-century scientific education, and while averring that those 'concerned in the right conception and successful modes of studying organized structures by the Young have little to fear', he nevertheless admonished his audience that the 'insinuation and masked advocacy of the doctrine subversive to a recognition of the Higher Mind . . . call for constant watchfulness and prompt exposure'. Recent exponents of such specious doctrines were, Owen proclaimed, not 'healthy' or 'normal', and, afflicted with 'some, perhaps congenital, defect of mind', they might corrupt the otherwise wholesome minds of others, and the impressionable and conspicuously capitalized 'Young' especially.[1]

The principal aim of Owen's address was to condemn the use of empirical deduction rather than functional correlation – which pointed to the existence of an intelligent creator – in palaeontological reconstructions, and he delivered it, as Joseph Dalton Hooker remarked, with 'cool deliberation & emphasis & pointed tone'. Throughout, Owen's glowering gaze was fixed on one particular member of the elite audience at the Geological Society: the headstrong tyro and advocate of deduction Thomas Henry Huxley. In the ensuing debate, Huxley appeared discomfited and, unable to muster his usual acerbic wit, 'did not defend himself well (though with temper)' against Owen's refutation of his views on palaeontological method.[2] In the following month, moreover, he went on to express an uncharacteristic desire to foster a 'nobler tone to science' without such 'petty personal controversies'.[3] Huxley usually relished his bitter feuds with rival naturalists, and even Owen's strident and authoritative attack on his understanding of palaeontology, in which Huxley actually had little practical experience, seems unlikely to have prompted such a muted response.[4]

What perhaps put Huxley on the back foot in this particular confrontation was the peculiarly moralistic tone of the warning which Owen issued in the peroration to his highly technical palaeontological discourse. After all, he deliberately identified modern scientific approaches like Huxley's which repudiated the role of a higher designing intelligence with the ancient atomistic philosophies of Democritus and Lucretius, who for centuries had been denounced as dangerous pagan sensualists. Owen himself was certainly aware of the strategic potential of such insidious associations with the moral corruption of the ancient world, having earlier condemned his anatomical opponents, in *On the Nature of Limbs* (1849), for sinking into an 'Epicurean slough of despond' from which 'every healthy mind naturally recoils'.[5] Still worse, in his imperative demands for a 'constant watchfulness and prompt exposure' on behalf of vulnerable youngsters, Owen also invoked a distinctive rhetoric of moral anxiety and furtive surveillance which closely resembled the language of numerous contemporary treatises on the dangers of juvenile masturbation. In the nineteenth century, as Thomas W. Laqueur has noted, 'parents were urged by many a guidebook to exercise the utmost vigilance' in order to 'stop the depredations of the supposedly secret vice'.[6] Even Owen's characterization of the supporters of Lucretian scientific views as 'unfruitful', and with unhealthy and defective minds, accorded with prevalent nineteenth-century medical assumptions that the unproductive emission of semen would leave those who indulged in masturbation dangerously depleted and potentially infertile. The 'masked advocacy' of subversive and originally pagan scientific doctrines, Owen's strategic rhetoric implied, was the intellectual equivalent of onanism and required a similarly scrupulous vigilance from society's ethical guardians to prevent its iniquitous effects from spreading.

Owen, of course, drew upon a long, well-worn tradition connecting materialism and unbelief with moral corruption and debauchery, including the entwinement of pornography and materialist philosophies in the Enlightenment.[7] In any case, his particular insinuations at the Geological Society were carefully calculated to remain sufficiently oblique to avoid contravening the gentlemanly standards of the mid-nineteenth-century scientific community, and they seem only to have temporarily discomfited his most persistent and ferocious adversary.[8] Significantly, though, the bitter and protracted palaeontological dispute between Owen and Huxley during the mid-1850s is generally regarded as a precursor to the larger controversy prompted by the publication of *On the Origin of Species* at the end of the decade, which Owen savaged in an anonymous notice for the *Edinburgh Review*.[9] Similarly malevolent and disreputable accusations would become one of the most persistent – if hitherto least acknowledged – aspects of the long-running debates over Charles Darwin's evolutionary theories.

Darwin's particular conception of organic evolution, as many historians have observed, quickly became part of a wider political campaign, which Frank Miller Turner has famously termed 'scientific naturalism', to wrest the last vestiges of intellectual and cultural authority away from the monopolistic Anglican Church establishment, as well as the gentlemanly amateurs who represented its interests in the scientific world.[10] Scientific naturalism instead sought to establish a new secular understanding of both nature and society that could be interpreted correctly only by an emergent cadre of scientific professionals. The metropolitan leaders of this nascent intellectual order, who from 1864 met regularly at meetings of the exclusive and politically influential X-Club, adopted Darwin's competitive, evolutionary view of the natural world, along with the similarly naturalistic principles of the conservation of energy and the uniformity of nature, as a valuable weapon in the wider struggle between Nonconformist Dissenters, with their meritocratic and reformist aspirations, and the established Church, which, through its control of pulpits, schools and universities, remained the chief systematizer of national culture.[11]

In a society already fissured by the shift from a hierarchical clerical culture to a more socially amorphous urban industrialism, it was essential for scientific naturalism to provide a new secular theodicy which might reconcile the expectations of a growing population with the changed realities of the nascent social order. Rather than being simply discarded, traditional religious values were instead naturalized, with law and uniformity supplanting theology as the guarantors of order in both the natural world and human society.[12] Darwin's theories, as part of this wider agenda of scientific naturalism, had to be urgently sequestered from any hostile associations that might tarnish them in the eyes of the various audiences for science in Victorian Britain and consequently undermine the political aspirations of dissident secular intellectuals, who, as Adrian Desmond and James Moore have put it, were busy 'selling themselves to the public as . . . a respectable white-collar body'.[13] The endeavours to dissociate Darwinism from ideologically sensitive epithets such as 'materialism' or 'atheism', and to purge transmutationism of its earlier connotations of scurrilous political radicalism, have, in recent years, received a great deal of historiographic consideration.[14] But, as this book will argue, from the late 1860s attention shifted increasingly from general concerns with political propriety to specific anxieties over sexual respectability, and it was actually Darwin's surprisingly recurrent connection with sexual immorality, in various sectors of the period's burgeoning print culture, which emerged as perhaps the most significant impediment to establishing a naturalistic worldview as a morally acceptable alternative to earlier theological outlooks. These iniquitous associations, moreover, would prove remarkably difficult to shake off.

This aspect of the reception of Darwin's evolutionary theories also reflected wider cultural changes in Britain during the 1860s and 1870s which did much to switch attention from the relatively quiescent political scene to new concerns with sexual and moral transgression. The authority of middle-class norms of respectability, which, shaped by early nineteenth-century evangelicism, had long sought to regulate behaviour in relation to drinking, gambling and sex, was widely perceived to have become markedly weaker in this period, and with regard to the latter in particular.[15] There is, as Michael Mason has argued, 'evidence that the 1860s saw a considerable relaxing of [sexual] codes, especially among young middle class people' which helped establish a 'new environment for sexual reform'.[16] But such changing attitudes towards sex were inevitably accompanied by various anxieties regarding their potentially invidious effects on wider areas of Victorian society and culture. Most notably, the introduction of new legislation on obscenity in the mid-1850s, and the largely adverse critical response to the emergence, during the following decade, of the aesthetic or art for art's sake movement, made the regulation of licentious mass urban culture as well as of studiedly amoral avant-garde art and literature matters of urgent public solicitude. In both cases, it was specific concerns with the regulation of representations of sexuality that, more than ever before, were the central issue. As Martin Myrone has recently contended: 'Lord Campbell's [Obscene Publications] Act of 1857 did not simply represent a tightening of the laws regarding obscenity, but a crucial turning-point in which sexuality is isolated as a cause of social disorder, rather than as something to be treated as part of a wider public order issue.'[17] This separation of sexuality from other forms of disorder inevitably increased its visibility as a social problem, and, as in Michel Foucault's famous thesis of regulation as a mode of production, actually prompted exaggerated fears that polite society was being overwhelmed by an inexorable proliferation of obscene images and other forms of sexual depravity.[18]

In the early 1870s the Scottish critic and poet Robert Buchanan certainly expressed an almost hysterical revulsion upon returning from his native Highlands to the 'great Sodom or Gomorrah' of London and finding 'photographs of nude, indecent, and hideous harlots, in every possible attitude that vice can devise, flaunt[ed] from the shop-windows'. The 'female Leg' in particular was unavoidable in the depraved popular culture of the metropolis; 'Walk along the streets,' Buchanan warned, the 'shop-windows teem with Leg. Enter a music-hall – Leg again, and (O tempora! O mores!) the Can-Can.' While those responsible for such 'matter or prints suggestive of indecency' were, according to Buchanan, 'at last being taken in hand' by recent legislation on obscenity and the prosecutions launched by the Society for the Suppression of Vice, even these were not sufficient to cope adequately with the deluge of material of an 'obscene and vulgar nature' with which the 'streets are full'.[19] Nor, significantly, was the high art and literature produced by members of the aesthetic movement immune from similar imputations, for Buchanan explicitly identified the 'Sensualism' expressed in recent avant-garde poetry by Algernon Charles Swinburne and Dante Gabriel Rossetti as the moral 'cancer of all society', and he insisted that 'all the gross and vulgar conceptions of life . . . emanate from this Bohemian class' with its amoral 'critical theory that art is simply the method of getting most sweets out of one's living sensations'.[20] It is notable that, according to the *Oxford English Dictionary*, the cultural categories 'aestheticism' and 'pornography' were coined within two years of each other during the mid-1850s, and while Buchanan's derisive comments were characteristically hyperbolic, their sentiments were evidently far from uncommon. Instead, they articulate widespread concerns with the increasing prominence of sex in various aspects of modern culture.

What Peter Bailey has termed the 'sexualisation of everyday life' in the final decades of the nineteenth century can be seen to have had some extremely important consequences for the Victorian disputes over evolution.[21] Indeed, as this book will show, it was regularly avowed that the growing licentiousness of modern culture, and the alleged excesses of aestheticism especially, actually gave warning of the repulsive direction in which society was being taken by the increasingly influential doctrines of Darwinism. Such lurid accusations were prompted in part by *The Descent of Man*, published at the beginning of 1871, in which Darwin himself identified sexual desire and reproduction as the driving forces of the whole evolutionary process. In the same book, Darwin also contended that man's moral feelings of right and duty were not innate but had been evolved over time by the natural selection of sympathetic social instincts. It was claimed by his critics that by negating the metaphysical criterion for morality – which, according to many, was the very basis of the civic order – the overtly naturalistic science of Darwin and his inner circle of friends and colleagues threatened to unleash a torrent of immorality and corruption that would surpass the scandalous vices of even the pagan world. These allegations, as will be seen, were generally much more explicit than Owen's rather furtive insinuations concerning paganism in his Geological Society address at the end of 1856.

Several historians have recently challenged stereotypical notions of Victorian prudery and respectability, demonstrating that sexual moralism was not expressed consistently across the nineteenth century nor uniformly adhered to amongst all social groups.[22] The many charges made against Darwinian science were nevertheless potentially extremely damaging in the light of the indubitable emphasis on respectability and sexual restraint maintained in specific sectors of society in this period. In particular, the 'primacy of morality', according to Stefan Collini, remained a defining feature of Victorian intellectual life.[23] In order to neutralize the charges of encouraging sexual immorality, the proponents of evolutionary theory, attempting to forge their own naturalistic social theodicy, had to shield Darwinism equally vigorously from any such invidious connections, in part by distinguishing a self-proclaimed 'pure' science – drawing on all senses of that overdetermined adjective – from the less reputable aspects of nineteenth-century general culture.

Like stereotypes of Victorian prudery, the familiar concept of the 'Darwinian Revolution' in the mid-nineteenth century has also increasingly been questioned in recent historical scholarship, which has instead proposed that the simplistic notion of a triumphant epochal shift instigated by a single individual be replaced by a more nuanced emphasis on what James A. Secord has recently termed 'the debates that took place after the publication of a series of printed books'.[24] This book explores precisely these debates over works such as *The Descent of Man* and Huxley's *Evidence as to Man's Place in Nature* (1863), but, for the very first time, it examines them in relation to the murky underworlds of Victorian pornography, sexual innuendo, unrespectable freethought and artistic sensualism. In so doing, it sheds important new light even on those evolutionary controversies which have already been the subject of extensive scholarship, and contends that such disreputable and generally overlooked aspects of nineteenth-century culture were actually remarkably central to many of

these debates. The book integrates contextualist approaches to the history
of science with recent work in nineteenth-century literary and cultural history, situating the Victorian disputes over Darwin's scientific theories in
a wider set of contexts and material cultures, and those emerging from
aestheticism and new legal definitions of obscenity in particular. Such an
approach extends dramatically the range of participants actively involved
in debates over evolution, from pornographic engravers and clandestine
authors of freethinking treatises on sexuality to conservative literary critics
and the ostensibly demure wives of prominent men of science, as well as
the spaces and formats in which such issues were discussed and contested.[25]
Notably, the book provides extensive new evidence of how even Darwin
himself became implicated in the attempts of radical freethinkers to challenge both the legitimacy of the recently passed Obscene Publications Act
and conventional taboos over issues like birth control and prostitution.

It also offers, amongst other things, a new way of understanding the
relations between science and literature in an intellectual milieu of perpetually disputed boundaries. The frequently problematic interconnection of
Darwinian science and aesthetic literature considered in this book suggests
that the prevalent 'One Culture' model of literature and science scholarship,
which implicitly celebrates discursive interchanges between scientific and
literary modes of writing as invariably creative and mutually advantageous,
has been much too sanguine in its approach to the interrelations of science and literature in the Victorian period.[26] Rather than examining how
scientific concepts have informed various aspects of works of literature, or
even how science has borrowed different rhetorical structures and tropes
from literary forms of writing, the book instead focuses on how the actual
interconnection of the two was itself, between the late 1860s and mid-1890s,
regularly exploited and manipulated for a variety of strategic reasons. Those
seeking to discredit the cultural authority of evolutionary science identified
it with the alleged sensual indulgence of aestheticism, while those attempting to establish it as a respectable secular theodicy denied such a connection
and instead emphasized links with more reputable literary writers.

Drawing on a broad range of sources including journalism, scientific
books and lectures, sermons, radical pamphlets, aesthetic and comic verse,
novels, law reports, illustrations and satirical cartoons, as well as less traditional formats such as the gossip and hearsay recorded in private letters,
the book reveals the unscrupulous and often extremely effective strategies
employed by a variety of different critics, both scientific and otherwise,
to undermine Darwinism. While focusing principally on Darwin himself,
it also examines how many of his leading allies and followers, including

Huxley, John Tyndall, William Benjamin Carpenter and William Kingdon Clifford, were similarly implicated in disputes over their apparent espousal of immorality, although even long after his death in April 1882 it was Darwin who remained the dominant figure in various controversies concerning science and sexual respectability. Significantly, the book shows that the opposition to various aspects of evolutionary science was often much stronger and more potent than has generally been recognized in accounts that adhere to the model of the so-called 'Darwinian Revolution' rather than emphasize the more complex and considerably less one-sided debates of the period. Darwinian men of science, to take only one example, were constrained significantly by the allegations made by antagonists such as Owen, and often had no choice but to fashion their model of professional scientific authority, as well as their public personas, in accordance with the standards of respectability laid down by their most bitter adversaries. While much recent scholarship has been alert to what James E. Strick has termed the 'intense desire to be "respectable"' of figures like Darwin and Huxley, this book makes clear that the fashioning of such respectability was by no means a straightforward or unproblematic endeavour.[27] Maintaining an unsullied personal reputation, vitally important in an age when much of the intellectual credibility of science relied upon the virtuous character of its leading individual exponents, was often an extremely precarious process, even for such an apparent model of scientific propriety as Darwin himself.

THE INDECENCY OF THE PROCESS

Only four months before Owen's insidious remarks at the Geological Society regarding the potentially immoral tendency of scientific doctrines that renounced the role of a divine intelligence, Huxley had responded with mischievous ribaldry to a question from Darwin concerning the peculiar reproductive mechanisms of hermaphrodite jellyfish. In the summer of 1856, Darwin, wrapped up in writing his 'Preliminary Essay' on species and eager to verify the improvement of jellyfish by cross-fertilization, asked ingenuously 'whether the ciliograde acalephes could not take in spermatozoa by the mouth'. Unable to resist, Huxley, a considerably more worldly man and with a taste for scurrilous mordancy, responded that the 'indecency of the process is to a certain extent in favour of its probability, nature becoming very *low* in all senses amongst these creatures'.[28] Huxley's incisive riposte was particularly striking because, as Lisa Z. Sigel has shown, in Victorian Britain fellatio was considered amongst the most 'offensive' of 'foreign practices', stretching the 'capacity for open discussion to its limits' even amongst gentlemanly collectors of erotica like Henry Spencer Ashbee.[29] Such sexual dissipation, as Huxley's lewd but not necessarily unscientific observation intimated, was actually found much more readily in nature than a corresponding continence. Similar sentiments concerning the intrinsic unseemliness of the natural world were expressed elsewhere in the nineteenth century, with the French historian and sceptic Ernst Renan declaring, in his autobiographical *Souvenirs d'enfance et de jeunesse* (1883), that 'la nature ne tient pas du tout à ce que l'homme soit chaste,' which Matthew Arnold translated as 'Nature cares nothing for chastity.'[30] In response, Arnold observed primly that 'few things have ever struck me more than M. Renan's dictum', and he insisted that rather than watching 'with amused indulgence the worship of the great goddess Lubricity, let us stand fast, and say that it is against nature, human nature, and that it is ruin'.[31] Darwin, on the other hand, appeared to be neither perturbed nor at all shocked by Huxley's vulgar levity.

In fact, Darwin at once relayed his younger colleague's lewd remark to their mutual friend Hooker, evidently considering it a choice epigram to be swapped amongst discerning male friends, before reflecting, in his now legendary and much-quoted ironical synopsis of the impending *On the Origin of Species*, 'What a book a Devil's chaplain might write on the clumsy, wasteful, blundering low & horribly cruel works of nature!'[32] This sardonic and permissive attitude towards such profane topics, even when expressed exclusively in private correspondence, certainly contravened conventional standards of middle-class respectability, which, according to Mike J. Huggins, ensured that the 'contents of mid-Victorian diaries or private letters often seem dictated by rules of propriety and lacking in spontaneity, with few . . . mentions of non-respectable behaviour'.[33] Instead, both Huxley's remark and Darwin's untroubled response accord with the 'convivial fraternalist discourse' and 'tolerant cosmopolitanism' which Hannah and John W. Gay have identified as characteristic of the 'masculine culture' of nineteenth-century science.[34]

Rebecca Stott has likewise noted how at the time of Darwin's lengthy researches on cirripedia during the 1850s, 'in letters to scientific colleagues he seems to be interested *only* in barnacle sexuality, presenting the barnacle as a figure of sexual comedy' consisting, in one case, of 'nothing but a tremendously long penis coiled up'.[35] Inevitably, such bawdy scientific anecdotes were not generally divulged to wives or other female family members, and Darwin's almost obsessive concern with the peculiarities of barnacle sexuality was much less evident in his four volumes of published writings on

cirripedia than in his private letters. Nevertheless, this rather risqué sexualization of the natural world, which would later torment writers like Arnold,
was not only the source of the earthy and unashamed ribaldry which frequently characterized Darwin's correspondence with Huxley and others,
but was also absolutely integral to his early evolutionary speculations on
contentious topics like asexuality, cross-fertilization and the superabundant
fecundity that was the main prerequisite of natural selection.

Yet it is one of the oldest axioms of scholarship on Darwin that, in the
words of J. W. Burrow, with 'infidelity and materialism . . . generally associated with immorality . . . It was of great importance [to the success of *On
the Origin of Species*] that Darwin and Huxley were gentlemen and family
men of complete financial, political and sexual respectability.'[36] Similarly,
Michael Ruse has contended that the '"respectability" that evolutionism
gained after the *Origin* was in large part due to the respectability of the
Darwinians themselves . . . To a man, they were exemplars of the most
boring Victorian respectability . . . good family men of impeccable sexual
propriety.'[37] Writing in the 1960s and 1970s respectively, Burrow and Ruse
made no attempt to explain how such sexual respectability was actually
achieved, assuming that Darwin's privileged class position and cosy domestic situation were sufficient to account for his apparently exemplary personal
reputation, and, still more presumptuously, inferring that supporters like
Huxley invariably enjoyed similar social advantages.

More recently, historians have acknowledged that this respectability was
not necessarily intrinsic to Darwin and evolutionary science and have examined some of the strategies by which it was achieved, with Strick noting how
'Darwin and his supporters . . . followed . . . [a] respectable model of scientific behaviour' which eschewed the disreputable forms of science, including
mesmerism and earlier versions of progressive development, practiced by
atheists and medical radicals.[38] The issue of spontaneous generation, Strick
contends, was a 'particularly explosive one for the status of evolution as
respectable science' and was consequently expunged from the scientific
agenda of Darwin and his closest colleagues.[39] Adrian Desmond has similarly made it clear that a 'crucial need for quiet respectability dominated
Darwin's life' and necessitated his careful avoidance of any connection with
scientific or political radicalism.[40] The explanation for the famously long
delay before the eventual publication of the *Origin*, Desmond suggests,
was simply that 'Darwin was frightened for his respectability' during the
incendiary period of the 1840s.[41]

While it has done much to advance our understanding of the nineteenth-
century debates over evolution, this emphasis on the contingent nature

of Darwin's respectability, and the strategies by which it was achieved and maintained, has generally focused on the containment of earlier threats from the 1830s and 1840s such as the unrespectable evolutionism of Robert Chambers's anonymous blockbuster *Vestiges of the Natural History of Creation* (1844), which, as Secord has shown, was considered 'in bad taste' by many of its readers.[42] The relative neglect of parallel concerns later in the nineteenth century implies that once such problematic associations had been neutralized, the simultaneous and interconnected projects of, in Strick's words, 'professionalization and respectability' could be rapidly consolidated, ensuring that the propriety of Darwinian science became as unproblematic and implicitly irreproachable as Burrow and Ruse had earlier assumed it to be.[43]

Even long after the *Origin*'s publication, though, the moral probity of Darwinism was by no means so assured, and its principal exponents continued to struggle to maintain their respectability throughout the later decades of the nineteenth century. At meetings of the pro-Darwinian X Club, the mathematician Thomas Archer Hirst remarked in 1864, 'there is perfect outspokenness . . . amongst ourselves', and his comment that the gatherings were also 'very pleasant and "jolly"' perhaps suggests a continuation of the kind of lewd drollery that was so often a feature of the private correspondence between Darwin's inner circle in the previous decade.[44] But, at almost exactly the same time, it became increasingly necessary to expunge even the slightest hint of similar vulgarity from the published writings of those associated with Darwinism. Reading through the proofs of Huxley's *Man's Place in Nature* in the summer of 1862, the elderly geologist Charles Lyell warned that a passage attacking opponents such as Owen as '*emasculate* monks' was 'not in good taste & will do no good', while another reference to 'Uncircumcised Judaizers' was likewise 'disagreeable & will not tell'.[45] On reflection, Huxley agreed with Lyell 'about the "emasculate" and "uncircumcised"' and removed both of the disreputable terms from the published version of the book, although he insisted, with faux righteousness, that it was a 'great piece of self-denial to abstain from expressing my peculiar antipathy to the people indicated, and I hope I shall be rewarded for the virtue'.[46] Even with these discreet textual amendments, however, *Man's Place in Nature* was still considered somewhat distasteful by many of its original readers, and, as will be seen in chapter four, it continued to have its respectability impugned into the following decade.

Far from being an isolated example of such self-denial, Huxley's removal of potentially unseemly sexual references from the proofs of *Man's Place in Nature* was actually merely one of numerous occasions on which some of the most celebrated evolutionary texts of the nineteenth century were extensively bowdlerized. Darwin's own *The Descent of Man* was significantly altered on the grounds of avoiding any hint of indecency or offensiveness, while many of his closest friends and colleagues, including Carpenter, Tyndall and Clifford, were also compelled to change aspects of their published writings for similar considerations. Even as late as 1890, the Finnish anthropologist Edward Westermarck was warned by Edward Burnett Tylor that his evolutionary account of *The History of Human Marriage* was 'too sexual for even a special public' and required that the 'words . . . be a little toned down'.[47] Alfred Russel Wallace similarly advised that the book should 'be as reticent as possible', with the term '"marriage" [used] in place of "sexual intercourse"' in the chapters likely to 'be the most read'.[48] Nor was such circumspection unwarranted, for following the passing of the Obscene Publications Act in the mid-1850s the precise legal status of many avowedly scientific works that dealt with otherwise unmentionable sexual subjects was brought into question at various levels of the judicial system. Both Darwin's *The Descent of Man* and Westermarck's *The History of Human Marriage* were invoked by impertinent freethinking radicals as elite scientific texts that, like their own illicit publications, might contravene existing legal definitions of obscenity.[49] As the regular bowdlerization of prominent evolutionary texts and similar anxieties over the remit of recent obscenity legislation make clear, the respectability of Darwinian science was not necessarily assured even in the final decades of the nineteenth century, and the maintenance of a reputation for sexual propriety required perpetual vigilance, not only from the authors of scientific books, but also from circumspect proofreaders, editors and publishers.

Despite these concerns, the second half of the nineteenth century has been identified as a period in which science itself was increasingly discussed in terms of its intrinsic morality and potentially beneficial effects on ethical character. The very designation 'man of science', which was employed much more frequently in this period than the newly coined and more neutral 'scientist', emphasized, as Ruth Barton has pointed out, the 'nature of the person rather than the activity undertaken; it alluded to the qualities of mind and character supposedly needed for and formed by the practice of science', in particular self-renunciation and moral character.[50] The methodological practices of science also had important implications for morality, with Lorraine Daston and Peter Galison proposing that mechanical means of achieving objective representations such as photography were part of a 'profoundly moralized vision, of self-command triumphing over the temptations and frailties of flesh and spirit' in which 'nineteenth-century objectivity aspired to the self-discipline of saints'.[51] This new model of the scientific renunciation of subjective interpretation in favour of patience, honesty and self-abnegation evidently verged towards an ideal of bodily as well as mental asceticism, persistently eliding empirical exactitude with sexual restraint.

Significantly, this abstemious scientific epistemology was also closely connected, according to Daston and Galison, with the growing social and cultural authority of scientific naturalism in mid-Victorian Britain:

> By ringing the changes on the resonant cultural themes of self-purification through self-abnegation, scientists persuaded others of their worthiness to assume priestly functions in an ever more secularized society. Sometimes this ambition to become the new clerisy was laid bare for all to see, as in the cases of . . . T. H. Huxley and John Tyndall in Britain.[52]

Developing Daston and Galison's influential argument, George Levine has similarly contended that for supporters of evolution and usurpers of the erstwhile Anglican elite the 'power to observe accurately becomes a moral as well as an epistemological virtue', affording the ability to withstand the consequences of finding that the universe was not designed for man's benefit.[53] An insistence on the ethical propriety enjoined by scientific method was certainly integral to the polemical agenda of many of those proselytizing of behalf of an evolutionary worldview, with Huxley boldly proclaiming that 'natural knowledge, in desiring to ascertain the laws of comfort, has been driven to discover those of conduct, and to lay the foundations of a new morality', and Clifford insisting that the 'duty of intellectual honesty, of carefully testing every belief' was the fundamental 'rule of right conduct'.[54] It was Darwin himself, ensconced in domestic seclusion in rural Kent and sufficiently wealthy to remain untrammelled by the pursuit of narrowly professional or commercial interests, who was persistently portrayed as the exemplar of the purity and propriety instilled by the disinterested study of empirical facts.[55] The rigorous self-control required by the epistemology of nineteenth-century science also ensured that other advocates of Darwinism could similarly claim to be the moral superiors – in terms of both intellectual and bodily discipline – of even the most otherworldly of their clerical adversaries.

In the seventeenth century, Steven Shapin has proposed, micro-social factors like gentlemanly manners and morality were integral to the acceptance of certain empirical claims about the natural world over others by groups such as the Royal Society; in fact, as Shapin claims, 'truth might be made subservient to civility' with the 'relevant maxim, pervasive in the civil conversations of early modern gentlemanly society . . . "believe those whose manner inspires confidence".[56] While rupturing the erstwhile relation between such gentlemanly civility and scientific authority was at the fore of the reformist agenda of Huxley and other Darwinian men of science, the nineteenth century's new scientific ideal of self-denying asceticism nevertheless ensured that a similarly propositional form of moral propriety remained highly significant in the various forums in which science was discussed in Victorian Britain.

The cultivation of a reputation for unimpeachable respectability was thus crucial to establishing the scientific credibility of Darwinism, no less than its social and cultural authority, and it was imperative for its main proponents to exhibit – or at least be seen to do so – extremely high standards of personal morality. An evangelical conception of moral character, with its 'vision of life as a perpetual struggle in which one's ability to resist temptation . . . needed to be subject to constant scrutiny', extended, as Collini has argued, across every sector of Victorian intellectual life, including secular thinkers, and this self-abnegating ideal of character was, Collini suggests, something to be 'possessed and enjoyed in public view'.[57] Concerns with private character and public intellectual authority were closely intertwined in scientific debates throughout the nineteenth century, but, significantly, the demonstration of ethical propriety by the leading exponents of Darwinian science became particularly urgent in the light of the numerous accusations of moral turpitude and sexual indecency made against them between the late 1860s and the mid-1890s that are examined in this book.

GOOD POETRY WAS NEVER WASTED ON A WORSE SUBJECT

If these accusations of immorality were so prevalent, and apparently so significant for various aspects of evolutionary science, it might be asked why there has been so little consideration of them in the extensive scholarship on Darwin over the last few decades. The connection of science with sexual scandal is, after all, hardly unheard of, and episodes such as the ribald response to Joseph Banks's botanical explorations in the Pacific during the late eighteenth century have become a staple of popularizing works of history of science.[58] But, while Desmond has acknowledged that 'there were concerted efforts to discredit Huxley's rival naturalist morality' by the exponents of a religious code of ethics during the final decades of the nineteenth century, there has been little historiographic attention to how this strategy was actually pursued. Indeed, Desmond himself provides only a very limited number of examples of those who attempted to discredit Huxley's moral agenda, mentioning merely the High Church Tory William Hurrell Mallock and the Catholic lawyer William Samuel Lilly.[59] The reason for this relative lack of attention to attempts to undermine the moral propriety of Darwinism from even the most assiduous and resourceful historians of science is perhaps that the principal strategy for tarnishing the respectability of evolutionary science in late Victorian Britain, employed frequently by both Mallock and Lilly as well as many others, was to associate it with the purported immorality of avant-garde art and literature. This connection of Darwinian science with aestheticism has not generally been recognized by contextualist historians of science examining nineteenth-century evolutionism, or even, for that matter, by literary critics concerned with the interrelations between science and literature in the period.

Certainly, science and aestheticism might, at first, seem an odd pairing considering the latter's assertion of art's autonomy from extra-aesthetic concerns. However, the contemporaneous disputes over the sensualism and blasphemy of modern literature and the alleged materialism and unbelief of Darwinian science can be seen to frequently overlap and interact with each other. In 1880 an article in the *Contemporary Review* even averred that 'Science, culture, and aesthetics, or their best advertised professors, are at present united by a joint cupidity, founded on a common atheism; or, let us say, agnosticism', and this underlying conceptual unity, it was claimed, had resulted in an 'appeal so eagerly made by artistic immoralists to science, begging her, on the ground of a common atheism, to come down and deliver them from virtue'.[60] The abhorrently amoral creeds of aestheticism, as the *Contemporary* article implied, found their justification in the naturalistic doctrines of contemporary science and were an inevitable consequence of the disavowal of supernatural religion implicit in the evolutionary views advanced by Darwin and his followers.

The publication of the first two volumes of John Ruskin's *Modern Painters* in 1843 and 1846 had given a new emphasis to the consideration of aesthetics in the mid-Victorian period, although the group of avant-garde writers who first came to prominence in Britain during the late 1860s, including Swinburne, Rossetti (previously known only as an artist), William Morris and Walter Pater, had little sympathy with Ruskin's conception of the moral and religious functions of art and the perception of beauty. Instead, they adhered to the French aesthetic doctrine 'l'art pour l'art', promulgated since the 1830s by Victor Cousin and Théophile Gautier, which insisted on the separation of art from all social or moral concerns and urged that the cultured and sensuous experience of artistic beauty was vastly more

important than the quotidian affairs of everyday life. Such aesthetic appreciation, moreover, required that certain individuals be absolved from the
ordinary limitations of society. Even while it did not necessarily espouse
actual immorality, this provocatively amoral and unapologetically elitist
credo, which promoted the cultivation of subjective perception as well
as an egotistic individualism and a self-indulgent openness to new experiences, ran directly counter to the stern injunctions to self-restraint and
disinterestedness that were central to what Collini has termed the Victorian
'"culture of altruism" that particularly flourished between the 1850s and the
1880s'.[61] Inevitably, it provoked a storm of protest from both critics and
theologians, with Pater's articulation of the central tenets of aestheticism
in the 'Conclusion' to *Studies in the History of the Renaissance* (1873) widely
denounced as an inducement to self-indulgent hedonism and other forms
of moral turpitude.

The poetry of Swinburne, according to numerous critics, exhibited both
disturbing stylistic excesses and a preoccupation with blasphemy and illicit
sensuality which made clear exactly what kind of artistic works would
be produced under the banner of the depraved aesthetic philosophy. Still
worse, the allegedly dissolute personal lives of Swinburne and Rossetti, as
well as rumours of the heterodox erotic propensities of Swinburne and
Pater, ensured that, long before the better-known indiscretions of Oscar
Wilde, aestheticism was widely connected with various forms of societal and
sexual transgression, and, most particularly, with the unmanly disruption
of conventional gender distinctions.[62] In its main principles and leading
preoccupations, aesthetic art and literature stood in an overtly antagonistic
relation to both the altruistic selflessness and the restrained manliness that
were the most fundamental attributes of the Victorian ethos of morality
and character.[63]

Although the advocates of aestheticism were a rather inchoate grouping,
both artistically and politically, they were immediately assumed to constitute a cohesive and sinister coterie, bent on importing a corrupt Gallic
philosophy that would undermine the traditional relationship, established
as far back as Plato's *Republic* and central to Victorian attitudes towards
culture, between artistic beauty, ethics and religious truth.[64] Nor was this
presumed cabal of heterodox and immoral subversion confined merely
to the proponents of art's autonomy from moral and social considerations.
Looking back at the late 1860s and early 1870s, John Morley, then the editor
of the fledgling *Fortnightly Review*, remarked that 'our miscellany of writers
and subjects was soon taken by prejudiced observers to disclose an almost
sinister unity in spirit and complexion'.[65] Under Morley's editorship, which

lasted from 1867 to 1882, the *Fortnightly* regularly published essays and verse by prominent aesthetic writers, including Pater, Swinburne, Rossetti and Morris, and Morley actually lent the journal's support to their contentious artistic doctrines in his own editorial columns.[66]

But, significantly, the *Fortnightly* was even more conspicuous as the periodical of choice for Huxley, Tyndall, Clifford and many other leading exponents of evolution and scientific naturalism, and, as Morley's reminiscence suggested, there were many who perceived a unity – whether sinister or otherwise – between the two groups. Morley himself certainly discerned important connections between them at the time, and, as Edwin Mallard Everett has written:

The faith of the *Fortnightly* in the . . . science of Huxley and Tyndall . . . was based upon a 'forward-looking' social philosophy, and by forward-looking the review usually meant non-theological. And because they were non-theological Morley opened his review to Swinburne, Rossetti, Morris, and Pater, some of whose works were characterised by an imposing aesthetic paganism. The *Fortnightly Review*, even in the sixties, could detect the relation between paganism and the modern spirit.[67]

The *Fortnightly*, Morley noted at the end of his editorship, had fostered 'a certain undefinable concurrence among writers coming from different schools and handling very different subjects' that encompassed both evolutionary science and aesthetic literature, and this shared mode of publication evidently emphasized the areas of potential similarity between them.[68]

Perhaps the clearest indication of this putative concurrence between Darwinism and aestheticism, as well as the *Fortnightly*'s role in drawing attention to it, was that they were attacked by their respective opponents in extremely similar ways, and often in the same rival periodicals. So, while the publication of Swinburne's controversial *Poems and Ballads* in August 1866 famously prompted widespread charges of sensuality and immorality, as well as paganism and blasphemy, these accusations corresponded almost exactly with the iniquitous insinuations of pagan sensualism and moral defectiveness that Owen, as was seen earlier, had made against Huxley's palaeontological emphasis on empirical deduction at the Geological Society a decade before. In fact, Swinburne himself later compared his predicament following an impertinent attack on his literary merits in the philistine *Quarterly Review* to the situation 'if the late Mr. Darwin or the living Mr. Huxley had found himself the object of a most vehement attack . . . in the columns of the *Church Times*', and he implied that his aesthetic approach to literature was just as liable to misrepresentation in the conservative press as the evolutionary views of Darwin or Huxley.[69]

Alongside such mutative allegations of paganism and immorality, the slippery signifier materialism affords a particularly striking instance of how certain critical terms shifted across the ostensibly different contexts of debates over science and literature, constantly adding insidious new meanings to their linguistic overdeterminacy. With the bloody horrors of the French Revolution widely blamed on the godless philosophy of Enlightenment Encyclopedists such as Baron d'Holbach, materialism carried extremely dangerous connotations in Victorian Britain. Huxley had long endeavoured to dissociate himself from any hint of this offensive designation, but his scientific outlook was nevertheless regularly condemned as, in the words of the *Edinburgh Review*, 'a revival, under a more ingenious form' of the 'extravagant' views of 'the French encyclopédistes' and the 'doctrines of [d'Holbach's] "System de la Nature"', which deserved to be called 'harsh names' because it was 'indistinguishable from . . . absolute materialism, and even tends to atheism'.[70] As an exasperated Herbert Spencer remarked in a letter to Huxley, the proponents of Darwinism were for ever being told by their opponents: 'You *shall* be materialists whether you like it or not.'[71] Such imputations of materialism, though, were by no means confined to purely scientific controversies, and began to be deployed equally commonly in the rhetoric of the literary disputes over aestheticism.

In Buchanan's infamous attack on the so-called 'Fleshly School of Poetry', launched in the *Contemporary* in October 1871, the derogatory epithet 'Fleshly' served as a signifier for an abnormally intense concern with the sensuous world that was virtually indistinguishable from materialism. Buchanan had actually appropriated the term from Swinburne's own writing, where it appeared in poems like 'Before Dawn' (1866) as well as in various critical essays, and Swinburne himself often used it interchangeably with materialism, complaining, for instance, of the ghosts in many Renaissance plays that the 'quaint materialism of these realistic and too solid spectres' rendered them insufficiently distinct from the 'fleshly fellows of the scene'.[72] Now Buchanan contended that, in his own overly sensuous verse, Swinburne, along with Rossetti, sought to 'extol fleshliness as the distinct and supreme end of poetic and pictorial art; to aver that poetic expression is greater than poetic thought, and by inference that the body is greater than the soul'.[73] Buchanan's hyperbolic revulsion at the prominence of sex in metropolitan popular culture was noted earlier, and the aesthetic emphasis on the material articulated in Swinburne's and Rossetti's poetry was, according to him, likewise grossly sexual, exhibiting 'so sickening a desire to . . . convey mere animal sensations, that we merely shudder at the shameless nakedness'.[74] The latent materialism of this incessantly carnal verse was also conjoined with the complete eschewal of religious belief: 'the walking gentlemen . . . bare their roseate bosoms and aver that *they* are creedless.'[75] The acute attention to specific tangible details which was a leading characteristic of both Swinburne's and Rossetti's aesthetic verse advanced a sensuous materialist epistemology which, Buchanan insisted, encouraged sordid animalism and disavowed the supernatural basis of religion.

Other critics also aligned aesthetic poetry with both materialism and unbelief, and William John Courthope contributed an anonymous notice to the *Quarterly* in 1872 which berated recent works by Swinburne, Rossetti and Morris for exhibiting precisely these attributes. In the same vein as Buchanan, he proclaimed:

We call them a school, because, though differing from each other in their choice of subjects and in their style . . . an atmosphere of what is called materialistic feeling pervades the poetry of all three. Atheism, which is directly avowed by one, is passionately professed by another, not as the supplanter of superstition, but as the rival of Christianity.[76]

Buchanan, however, went even further in the following years by explicitly connecting the prioritization of the material in aesthetic poetry with the alleged materialism of contemporary science. In a signed article for the *New Quarterly Magazine* in April 1876 entitled 'Lucretius and Modern Materialism', he contested the conclusions that Tyndall had advanced less than two years earlier in his Presidential Address to the British Association for the Advancement of Science at Belfast. In this notorious Address, Tyndall had remonstrated against 'the restrictions of Materialism' while at the same time 'discern[ing] in . . . Matter . . . the promise and potency of all terrestrial Life' and insisting on 'the mysterious control of Mind by Matter'.[77] In the controversy which inevitably ensued Tyndall was widely denounced for promoting a dangerously materialist view of existence.

Buchanan was, of course, principally a poet and critic of literature, and he examined Tyndall's scientific doctrines by considering the poetry of Lucretius, whose understanding of the universe, he declared, was 'entirely at one with Professor Tyndall'.[78] In his Address, Tyndall, as will be discussed in chapter three, had controversially drawn a parallel between modern science and the atomism advanced by classical writers such as Lucretius. Buchanan now made clear the similarly close correspondence between the latest works of lubricious contemporary poets and the ancient verse of Lucretius, who, he noted, was 'as explicit in his physiological explanations as Walt Whitman', the controversial American poet whose verse was often linked to that of Swinburne and whose principal advocate in Britain was Rossetti's elder brother William Michael. In fact, while Rossetti's own salacious sonnets had put 'on record for other full-grown men to read, the most secret mysteries of sexual connection', Lucretius's verse, Buchanan insisted, likewise 'treats very physiologically of the nature of love and desire'.[79] According to Buchanan, moreover, the sensuous Roman poet Lucretius was 'just, in fine, such a singer as our own Tyndall would be, if the Professor would only put his ornate periods into the flowery fetters of rhyme'.[80] Significantly, in this perspective, Tyndall's materialistic science becomes merely another version of the fleshly creed promulgated in the verse of Rossetti, Swinburne and their coterie of licentious companions.

Throughout 'Lucretius and Modern Materialism', Buchanan considered Victorian science as if it were another form of poetry, and voiced complaints against Tyndall's Lucretian doctrines which very closely resembled his earlier admonition of the immoral fleshliness of aesthetic verse. In the expanded pamphlet version of his original 'Fleshly School' article, he opined: 'we have had a little too much of the Body . . . since so many centuries of Sexuality have done so little for poetry, it might be advantageous to give Spirituality a trial, and to see if *her* efforts to create a literature are equally unsuccessful.'[81] In 'Lucretius and Modern Materialism', he made an almost identical appeal for a poetic form that would express the spiritual side of human existence, only this time substituting materialism for carnal sexuality in the structure of his argument. Apropos of Lucretius's atomism, he contended that 'good poetry was never wasted on a worse subject, and . . . if this is the best poetic solution of Creation that MATERIALISM has to offer us, we shall feel ourselves justified, *pace* Professor Tyndall, in resuscitating some Poet of SPIRITUALISM as soon as possible!'[82] It was the eighteenth-century Christian mystic Emmanuel Swedenborg whose fortunes Buchanan sought to revive, contending that his prose poems depicted the existence of an external spiritual realm which was far more certain than the actuality of the material world that neither Swinburne's and Rossetti's fleshly verse nor Tyndall's materialist science were able to pass beyond.

Sexual debauchery, aesthetic approaches to literature, unbelief and naturalistic forms of science were all, in Buchanan's critical writing during the mid-1870s, elided in a single pejorative term: materialism. Swinburne had long parodied the coarse physicality of many Christian doctrines and he responded to such charges by insisting that it was actually the Church's own communion rituals that were most redolent of materialism.[83] Any 'creed . . . sustained on theophagy', he observed, made itself 'laughably insupportable . . . when its advocates denounce or deride their antagonists as – of all opprobrious names upon earth – materialists'.[84] Despite Swinburne's satirical impudence, however, accusations of materialism were rarely a laughing matter, and, having originally been used in debates over science, the offensive term moved swiftly from scientific to poetic controversies. Perturbingly, it then leached back into the language of scientific disputes, such as the opprobrium provoked by Tyndall's Belfast Address, with new and even more insidious associations, including lubricious artistic immorality, now added to its range of meanings.

METAPHORS DERIVED FROM SCIENCE

This association of prominent advocates of evolutionary science with the immoral sensualism that was widely ascribed to aesthetic art and literature was clearly extremely problematic for attempts to uphold Darwinism's reputation for moral probity. With Darwinian scientific professionals endeavouring to establish both their cultural authority and respectability in a period in which many aspects of evolution still retained connotations of scurrilous political radicalism, these more recent pejorative associations needed to be urgently refuted. One response, as will be seen with the case of Tyndall in chapter three, was simply to reiterate the scrupulous standards of personal morality exhibited by scientific practitioners, as well as the strict discipline and moral propriety instilled – and indeed required – by empirical methods of experimentation and observation. Another, again employed by Tyndall, was to emphasize the already existing connections between the leading advocates of scientific naturalism and older and more reputable literary writers, most notably the Poet Laureate Alfred Tennyson and the conservative Sage of Chelsea Thomas Carlyle. Carlyle in particular embodied an ethos of manliness, heroic self-improvement and selfless hard work, which was the very antithesis of the effeminacy and hedonistic self-indulgence that was regularly attributed to aesthetic writers like Swinburne and Pater.[85] Historians of science such as Barton and Paul White have recently called attention to the fashioning of specific self-identities amongst Victorian men of science, whose rhetoric often stressed attributes such as self-sacrifice and a disinterested love of truth, and the cultivation and deliberate flaunting of particular literary connections, as well as the refutation of others, can be seen as an integral part of this scientific self-fashioning.[86]

Tyndall and Huxley had established close friendships with both Tennyson and Carlyle during the 1850s and 1860s, and in the following decades they regularly offered profuse praise for their work and especially its relevance to modern scientific concerns. As Tyndall observed of Carlyle in *The Times* in 1881, 'In physical subjects I never encountered a mind of stronger grasp and deeper penetration than his', while Huxley similarly commended Tennyson's 'insight into scientific method' and acclaimed him as the 'only modern poet . . . to understand the work and tendency of modern science'.[87] Tyndall particularly insisted on the empirical rigour of their literary engagement with science, remarking of Carlyle in an 1890 article for the *Fortnightly* that the 'scientific reader of his works must have noticed the surprising accuracy of the metaphors he derived from Science', and later telling Tennyson's son Hallam that 'in regard to metaphors drawn from science, your father, like Carlyle, made sure of their truth.'[88]

However, this insistence on literature's indebtedness to science was not an entirely disinterested judgement and instead had important strategic advantages for Tyndall's own scientific position. Indeed, while, as was seen earlier, critics like Buchanan implied that Tyndall's materialistic views were a scientific counterpart of the fleshly creed allegedly advanced in the aesthetic verse of Rossetti and Swinburne, Tyndall himself drew attention to how the more renowned writings of Carlyle and Tennyson were actually closer literary equivalents of his own disciplined and meticulous approach to science, aligning the scientific aspiration for verifiable truth with the faithful metaphors deployed by such eminent literary figures. Even when there was no evident admiration for these writers, self-conscious allusions to Tennyson's epic verse, like that of Darwin in *The Descent of Man* examined in chapter two, could still be used to imbue the discussion of contentious issues like human evolution with both cultural gravitas and tacit respectability. Unlike the problematic association with aestheticism, these more reputable literary connections evidently had considerable strategic value in establishing the appropriate cultural credentials of naturalistic forms of science.

The extremely close relationship between men of science like Tyndall and Huxley and literary figures such as Tennyson and Carlyle has been much discussed in scholarship on science in the Victorian period, with Turner remarking that 'Carlyle's idealist concepts and moral doctrines' allowed 'contemporaries of a rationalistic and naturalistic bent of mind . . . to accept secular society with good conscience and a finite universe without spiritual regret', thereby easing the 'transition from a religious apprehension of the universe to a scientific and secular one'.[89] Paradoxically, however, many of Carlyle's writings expressed a fervent antagonism towards almost every aspect of nineteenth-century science, and its apparent materialism and godlessness most of all. Even Tyndall's own Belfast Address, according to Carlyle, articulated a squalid 'philosophy fit for dogs'.[90] Tennyson's verse similarly expressed a profound ambivalence regarding the religious implications of many modern scientific developments. The reservations concerning science expressed by both Carlyle and Tennyson are, of course, extremely well known, but even Carlyle's insistence on the sublime grandeur of the naturalistic, but nonetheless spiritually and morally uplifting, universe – in which Tyndall and Huxley famously claimed to discern a reflection of their own secular sense of the higher meaning of the natural world – did not, as Turner appears to assume, necessarily accord with the emergent values of scientific naturalism.

The interpretation of Carlyle's deliberately contradictory concept of '"Natural Supernaturalism" as a secularization' rather than an affirmation of 'extra-ecclesiastical spirituality', Janis McLarren Caldwell has recently argued, does not 'adequately . . . take into account the incessantly metaphysical quality of Carlyle's thought'. Instead, as Caldwell proposes, it is possible that the 'scientific publicists wilfully misread Carlyle' and 'adapted his thought to their own purposes'.[91] In any case, the transcendentalism which dominated Carlyle's thinking actually had, according to Caldwell, much more in common with the idealist approach of the Darwinian's *bête noire* Owen, whose 'transcendental anatomy', she claims, 'not only sounds like Carlyle's natural supernaturalism', but is 'at bottom the same doctrine'.[92] While the proposal that Huxley and Tyndall might have deliberately misinterpreted Carlyle's work for their own particular purposes remains merely a speculative possibility, it nevertheless suggests that, for scientific naturalists eager to emphasize their connection with such a reputable literary figure in the wake of widespread associations with aestheticism during the 1870s and 1880s, the strategic value of his writing could have been just as significant as its actual content. Tyndall was certainly willing to similarly reinterpret the ostensible meaning of Tennyson's anti-materialist poem 'The Ancient Sage' (1885) in order, as will be seen at the end of chapter three, to negate its implicit critique of his own views and instead emphasize his essential congruity with its revered author.

It was the concerns of aesthetic writers that were, in reality, often much closer to those of the exponents of Darwinian science than the interests of either Carlyle or Tennyson. Pater's early essays for the *Westminster Review* and *Fortnightly* self-consciously invoked both the ideas and vocabulary of the scientific articles that appeared in the same liberal journals, drawing, for example, on Tyndall's account of an experiment on radiant heat in which he brought 'invisible rays to a focus' with 'sufficient heat at the focus to set London on fire' in his metaphorical description of the moment of poetic epiphany in which the aesthetic writer must 'define in a chill and empty atmosphere the focus where rays, in themselves pale and impotent, unite and begin to burn'.[93] Notably, this metaphor derived from science, which appeared in Pater's sensuous and overtly homoerotic appreciation of the German art critic Johann Winckelmann, was one that Tyndall himself would never have dared even to acknowledge. The infamous 'Conclusion' to Pater's *Studies in the History of the Renaissance*, moreover, accepted without demur the 'tendency of modern thought' to reduce 'physical life' to both a 'combination of natural elements to which science gives their names' and a sequence of 'processes which science reduces to simpler and more elementary forces'.[94] Pater continued to exhibit a marked enthusiasm for scientific issues such as 'organism and environment, or protoplasm perhaps, or evolution' even in his final book *Plato and Platonism* (1893), and his concern with various aspects of nineteenth-century science has long been acknowledged in scholarship on his work.[95]

Swinburne's verse similarly celebrated an evolutionary pantheism that was remarked upon by several reviewers as well as some members of Darwin's circle of supporters. In contrast to Carlyle's extravagant disdain, Swinburne also expressed intense admiration for 'Tyndall's magnificent address' at Belfast in 1874, applauding its vision of 'science so enlarged and harmonized' and insisting that his own 'habit of mind is not (I hope) unscientific, though my work lies in the field of art instead of science'.[96] When, in the early 1880s, a Society for the Suppression of Blasphemy was founded, it proposed to 'get up cases, as our funds will allow, against Professor Huxley, Dr Tyndall, Herbert Spencer, Swinburne . . . and others, who by their writings have sown widespread unbelief'.[97] Although Swinburne himself expressed ironic surprise at the existence of an 'association for prosecuting and suppressing the circulation of the works of Tyndall, Huxley . . . *and* A. C. Swinburne', the short-lived society's connection of his name with those of men of science such as Huxley and Tyndall – whose heretical essays were, after all, being published alongside Swinburne's profane verse in the pages of the *Fortnightly* – indicates that the links between aestheticism and evolutionary science were very evident to many in late Victorian Britain.[98]

Yet, as will be shown throughout this book, these conspicuous connections were disavowed strenuously by the proponents of Darwinism, even when this involved deliberately refashioning aspects of the posthumous reputation of Clifford, who, unlike his more circumspect colleagues, expressed an admiration for Swinburne in his public writings. The adamant refusal of such a connection finally took the form, by the 1880s and 1890s, of the pathologization of aestheticism as a dangerous agent of cultural and mental degeneration requiring urgent medical attention. Meanwhile, literary allusions to more reputable writers like Tennyson and Carlyle, as well as to revered figures in literary history such as Shakespeare, were used, in part, to associate naturalistic scientific theories with a more acceptable set of values, even when these writers were actually much less sympathetic to the direction of modern science than members of the aesthetic movement like Pater and Swinburne.

The diverse literary allusions which pervaded nineteenth-century scientific writing, from John Milton to Walt Whitman, have been discussed at great length in studies of literature and science over the last few decades. They are generally viewed as either merely decorative or as a means by which scientific authors, who often had an extensive knowledge of literary culture, could address the concerns of audiences outside a specific professional group.[99] Perhaps more significantly, however, they could also be used to signify the decency and respectability – or otherwise – of particular scientific theories and practices in relation to wider Victorian culture, with allusions to, say, Tennyson's epic verse lending an air of grandeur to discussions of man's evolutionary ascent, and references to Swinburne's more controversial poetry linking scientific writing with sexual transgression, blasphemous iconoclasm and even republican politics. These competing literary allusions played an extremely significant role in the reception of Darwinism in Victorian Britain, and especially the endeavours to establish it as a respectable and morally acceptable secular theodicy, although it is one that has not hitherto been considered in the extensive scholarship on the subject. Only by combining the approaches of contextualist history of science with literary and cultural studies, as this overtly interdisciplinary book attempts to do, can the full implications and importance of these literary connections be recovered, adding a significant new dimension to the much-studied nineteenth-century debates over Darwin's evolutionary theories.

CHAPTER 2

Charles Darwin, Algernon Charles Swinburne and sexualized responses to evolution

In October 1869 the opening number of the *Academy* carried a small item of literary gossip announcing the imminent completion of a new work by Charles Darwin in which 'the main conclusions arrived at in his *Origin of Species* . . . will be applied to Man'. The 'difficult question of the gradual development of the characteristic moral and intellectual attributes of man from lower types' would 'also be briefly considered' in Darwin's new book, which, the *Academy*'s exclusive preview noted, was 'to be published next year'.[1] The *Academy*, an eclectic but uncompromisingly highbrow monthly review, was the latest addition to the stable of periodicals, also including the *Quarterly Review*, owned by John Murray. Murray, who had been the publisher of *On the Origin of Species* in 1859, was now similarly engaged in the preparation of its successor, and the *Academy*'s advance notice was a convenient means of whetting the public's appetite for Darwin's latest evolutionary opus. But Darwin, fatigued by overwork and afflicted with his customary ill-health, did not deliver the completed manuscript until more than a year later, and the two volumes of *The Descent of Man, and Selection in Relation to Sex* finally appeared on the shelves of bookshops only at the end of February 1871. By this time, Murray had relinquished control of the loss-making *Academy*, and the opportunity to once more trail Darwin's new monograph in its pages had been lost. The *Academy*'s mistimed puff, however, was not to be the only difficulty to emerge from the *Descent*'s delayed publication.

Darwin had famously postponed publication of the *Origin* for more than two decades because of fears over the response to his evolutionary theories, and now in the much briefer interval before the appearance of the *Descent* he again grew anxious about how the book would be received. In the summer of 1870, when still confident that the *Descent* would be out by the autumn, Darwin forecast that 'many will decry [it] as very wicked', and, after completing the final proofs early in the next year, he expressed fear that it would 'aggravate' even close friends and wondered despondently 'whether the book is worth publishing' at all.[2] More significantly, the prolonged gestation of the *Descent* also gave an opportunity to Darwin's opponents, who had grown in numbers and authority during the last years of the 1860s, to pre-emptively undermine his new findings, as well as to offer their own rival accounts of human origins.[3] Indeed, the most sustained attack on the theories articulated in the *Descent*, St George Mivart's carping but technically expert *On the Genesis of Species*, actually appeared a month earlier than Darwin's own book. Even worse, just as copies of the *Descent* finally went on sale, Paris was overrun by the Prussian armies that had been besieging the French capital for the last six months, prompting a complete breakdown of civic order and a period of brutal civil war. The interminable delays in its publication seemed, at least to Darwin, to have already doomed the prospects of the *Descent* amongst both specialists and a wider reading public unnerved by events across the Channel.

But the critical onslaught that Darwin feared never occurred. The initial reception of the *Descent* was in fact largely positive, and, as Darwin soon acknowledged, not only had the 'book . . . sold wonderfully' but also it was equally 'wonderful that there has been no abuse'.[4] The *Descent's* much anticipated application of evolutionary theory to humans, as historians have long argued, failed to provoke anything like the same controversy as the *Origin*. Adrian Desmond and James Moore have observed that 'the subject was less bad news than old news', while Janet Browne has recently noted: 'Faced with a new book about descent in 1871, journalists seemed to find little to say. They and their readers had become accustomed to the idea of evolution.'[5] Certainly, works such as Charles Lyell's *The Antiquity of Man* and Thomas Henry Huxley's *Evidence as to Man's Place in Nature*, both published in 1863, had already drawn much of the sting from the idea of human evolution, and, rather than inciting intense theological controversy, Darwin's so-called 'man book' was, according to the *Edinburgh Review*, instead 'competing with the last new novel' in the drawing-rooms of middle-class families.[6] Darwin was nevertheless apprehensive that though he had received 'no abuse as yet' he would 'not escape' censure entirely, and he remained convinced that 'some, no doubt, will come, strong enough'.[7] Most of the critical notices which, as Darwin predicted, the *Descent* did receive have tended to be disregarded by historians as the outpourings of 'cranks' whose harsh words 'could no longer hurt' him, and only the more specialist reviews penned by the likes of Mivart and Alfred Russel Wallace have received much historiographic attention.[8]

There was, however, one particular vein of criticism of the *Descent* which was articulated in both the highbrow reviews of Mivart and others as well as in more popular responses, including cartoons and other visual images, and which seems to have troubled Darwin deeply. Notwithstanding the exemplary personal reputation of its author, a surprisingly large number of critics claimed that the *Descent* transgressed Victorian standards of respectability, as well as the acceptable boundaries of nineteenth-century scientific publishing. Its reductive account of man's moral and spiritual faculties, and especially the prominence given throughout to sexuality, not only made the book highly distasteful, but might potentially even encourage vice and immoral depravity. Far from leaving him unaffected, such lurid imputations in fact became increasingly perturbing to Darwin and his supporters, and, despite the frequently hyperbolical rhetoric of these accusations, they give an insight into how concerns with sexual immorality became integral to the opposition to Darwinism in the 1870s.

While critics of the *Descent* generally acknowledged the possibility that man's physical form had evolved from lower organisms, they strenuously denied Darwin's assertion that the human capacity for moral action was similarly evolved, and different only in degree, not kind, from the self-sacrificing acts of intelligent dogs and monkeys. Reviews in the *Quarterly*, the *Edinburgh* and *The Times* even hinted ominously that such speculations might have extremely deleterious consequences. The sinister insinuations of these staid but nonetheless influential organs of establishment opinion furtively associated the theories expressed in Darwin's book with the contemporaneous collapse of civic and moral order in France, long regarded as a hotbed of similarly heretical sentiments. Such invidious parallels are well known to historians, but what has not previously been noted is that the delayed publication of the *Descent* also coincided with the release of Algernon Charles Swinburne's latest collection of verse, *Songs Before Sunrise*. Darwin's book became increasingly implicated not only with Swinburne's own political radicalism, but also, and potentially much more harmfully, with the infamous poet's notoriety for aesthetic sensualism and flagrant sexual depravity.

In the light of these damaging associations, the suitability of the *Descent* for a family audience also became a matter of concern, even though Darwin and Murray had actually paid scrupulous attention, during the book's production, to avoiding anything that might be considered indelicate. At the same time, the familiar images of apes comically exhibiting their kinship with humans that had been a mainstay of the popular response to evolutionary theory in the 1860s took on a more troubling, sexualized aspect in the following decade. Despite Darwin's customary diffidence, such imputations of peddling an immoral and potentially corrupting view of human existence, made in specialists books and highbrow periodicals just as much as in more demotic publications, could not continue to be simply disregarded.

In 1874, three years after the appearance of the *Descent*, Darwin was finally forced to take precipitate action following an allegation, made in an article in Murray's *Quarterly*, that members of his own family, as well as his school of supporters, actively advocated a return to the immoral lusts of the pagan world. The anonymous author of the offending *Quarterly* article was Mivart and the bitter controversy that it provoked, during which the former Darwinian anatomist was ostracized by his erstwhile colleagues, has long been recognized as one of the most ferocious and personal confrontations of the entire evolutionary debates of the nineteenth century. This chapter, by examining the wider context of the earlier allegations made against the *Descent* of encouraging sexual immorality, offers, amongst other things, a new understanding of just what was at stake during this crucial and highly revealing exchange.

SENTENCES LIABLE TO THE IMPUTATION OF INDECENCY

Although, as is well known, man was conspicuously absent from *On the Origin of Species*, humans had been part of Darwin's evolutionary speculations since at least the notebook on 'Man, Mind and Materialism' which he began in the late 1830s. The writing of the *Descent* some thirty years later, as Darwin told Alphonse de Candolle, was prompted partly by his 'having been taunted that I concealed my views' on the subject in the *Origin*.[9] Now, man was to take centre stage in Darwin's published writing, as he had long ago in his private notebooks and correspondence, as well as in the fervid debates prompted by the *Origin*. By the early 1870s, though, the comparison of human anatomy with the structures of lower animal forms – the evidence bearing on the origin of man with which the *Descent* begins – was no longer particularly contentious. Unlike Huxley in *Man's Place in Nature*, moreover, Darwin did not begin the *Descent* with any potentially threatening images of manlike apes. Instead, one of the first specific pieces of evidence for human transmutation that the book provided were the tiny folds of the human ear, which, as Darwin claimed, were a 'vestige of formerly pointed ears' that man shared with his simian forebears.[10] By focusing initially on such an apparently innocuous, as well as entertainingly droll, detail of human anatomy, Darwin gave his readers an opportunity to experience for themselves the evidence for man's evolution in a way that was unthreatening by simply examining their own ears. Even Murray, who remained equivocal about his bestselling author's theories, could joke that Darwin's book would 'cause men to prick up what little has been left them of *ears*'.[11] Far from provoking indignation, Darwin's demonstration of the homological structures of humans and the lower animals could instead provide an amusing diversion at middle-class dinner parties.

There were, however, aspects of Darwin's account of human evolution which remained highly controversial, most notably the correspondence drawn between man's moral faculties and the inherited instincts of animals. When writing the *Descent*, Darwin had adopted the suggestion of his friend Joseph Dalton Hooker that 'morals . . . would be very interesting if discussed like any branch of natural history', claiming, in the published book, that the method was entirely original: 'as far as I know, no one else has approached it exclusively from the side of natural history' (1:71).[12] While he readily agreed with the majority of his mid-Victorian contemporaries that the 'moral sense' was 'the most noble of all the attributes of man', Darwin's natural historical perspective led him to conclude that man's exalted moral feelings of right and duty had been evolved by the natural selection of sympathetic social instincts (1:70). As the human mind became increasingly evolved, Darwin contended, such instinctual responses were then overtaken by a reflective consciousness that, in allowing civilized man to recognize even the 'remote consequences of his actions', had ensured that 'self-regarding virtues, such as temperance, chastity, etc.' had 'come to be highly esteemed or even held sacred' (1:165). In the *Descent*, Darwin extolled exactly the same ethical values already venerated in mid-Victorian bourgeois culture, differing from more traditional conceptions of morality and respectability only by locating their origins in natural rather than spiritual processes. Indeed, evolution, as Darwin assured his readers, meant that 'virtue would be triumphant' (1:104). But such a sanguine teleology could not mask certain problematic aspects of Darwin's evolutionary account of morality.

While Darwin adopted David Hume's conviction that social sympathies were instinctive in man, thereby parting company with the likes of John Stuart Mill, he did not accept that any higher forms of virtue were similarly innate to humans. Such virtues were instead an attribute only of highly evolved, civilized members of the species. Throughout the *Descent*, Darwin drew on the anthropological findings of John McLennan and Sir John Lubbock, as well as his own experiences during the voyage of HMS *Beagle*, to furnish examples of the startling 'immorality of savages', whose sympathetic instincts and powers of reasoning remained insufficiently evolved to support moral feelings (1:96–7). Infanticide, blood sacrifices and other 'unnatural crimes' made clear the 'utter licentiousness' of both those savages still existing in the nineteenth century and the earliest primitive humans (1:96). Although, as will be discussed later, Darwin did not necessarily include sexual promiscuity amongst these unspecified crimes against nature, his descriptions of savage immorality in the *Descent* invoked the same 'rhetoric of "unspeakability"', in which the 'reader is asked to fill in the blank with imagined customs more horrible than cannibalism and infanticide', that Patrick Brantlinger has recently identified in nineteenth-century missionary accounts of Polynesia, which, paradoxically, were both overtly moralistic and at the same time potentially titillating.[13]

Elsewhere in the *Descent*, Darwin insisted that morality constituted 'by far the most important . . . of all the differences between man and the lower animals' (1:70). Nevertheless, at the same time as revealing the moral deficiency of more primitive members of the human species, he also acknowledged that it was 'in a high degree probable' that a 'moral sense or conscience' equivalent to man's could be similarly evolved by 'any animal whatever' endowed with social instincts and sufficient intelligence (1:71). Paradoxically, moreover, the *Descent* abounded with charmingly anthropo-morphic examples of animals, like the 'heroic little monkey' described in the book's conclusion, whose incipient sense of virtue far exceeded that of savage humans (2:404). Morality, in Darwin's contradictory chronology of ethical evolution, was not only not innate to man, but could also be found more readily in the instinctual behaviour of the lower animals than in the savage practices of primitive humans.[14]

Even when it did exist in humans, morality was not, in strict evolu-tionary terms, an absolute *a priori* category. Instead, it was a relative form of sentiment and behaviour which had prevailed merely because it had been advantageous to the survival of a particular society. The 'hatred of indecency', as Darwin explained in the *Descent*, 'appears to us so natu-ral as to be thought innate', but it was in fact only a 'modern virtue, appertaining exclusively . . . to civilised life', and was not necessary – and might possibly even prove detrimental – to the success of less civilized forms of human society (1:96). In such a view, no form of behaviour could be reproached as intrinsically wrong or sinful. An 'intelligent Kandyan chief' from a society which practiced polygamy could, in an example that Darwin took from Lubbock's *Prehistoric Times* (1869), be 'perfectly scandal-ized at the utter barbarism of living with only one wife' (2:363). Although the *Descent* obviously placed modern civilization at the apex of human-ity's developmental scale, and much of Darwin's language in the book was overtly teleological, there remained an implicit relativism in its account of morality which would enable hostile critics like Mivart to cast suspicion on the practical implications of Darwin's naturalistic understanding of human origins.

At the same time, Darwin's application of the theory of sexual selection to human reproductive behaviour would also give rise to similarly adverse insinuations. Sexual selection, which Darwin had touched upon only briefly in the *Origin*, was actually the principal subject of the *Descent*, taking up far more of the book's two volumes than the discussion of human origins. Darwin offered copious evidence, drawn from across the animal world, of the physical combat and aesthetic competition by which the males of a species struggled for female mates.[15] Such sexual selection, as Darwin explained to Wallace, had 'always been a subject which has interested me much', but from the early 1860s it became increasingly central to his understanding of human evolution, and racial and sexual differences in particular (Wallace, though, remained unconvinced).[16] As a consequence, in the *Descent* Darwin included man in his wide-ranging account of the workings of sexual selection, noting that the 'whole process of . . . the reproduction of the species, is strikingly the same in all mammals', even down to 'the act of courtship by the male', who, whether baboon or human, responded similarly to the smell and appearance of the opposite sex (1:13).

The potentially provocative inclusion of human sexual behaviour alongside that of other species was moderated by the anthropomorphic – and decidedly Victorian – assumptions which Darwin brought to descriptions of the mating habits of widely different animals, such as the instinctually connubial canaries, which, even when bred with five separate females, invariably returned to the first, who was 'alone treated as the wife' with the others merely 'treated as concubines' (1:271). Such anthropomorphism was not, of course, unique to Darwin; in the eighteenth century Linnaeus's system of botanical classification had depicted plant reproduction as a marriage, an analogy developed by Darwin's own grandfather Erasmus in *The Loves of the Plants* (1789), while in *The Variation of Animals and Plants under Domestication* (1868), published whilst he was writing the *Descent*, Darwin had noted Virgil's advice to ancient agriculturists regarding which cattle to 'reserve for husband of the herd'.[17] Along with this projection of conjugal fidelity onto the natural world, the ways in which human courtship resembled that of the lower animals were likewise depicted in romanticized images, most likely arising from Darwin's well-known taste for sentimental domestic fiction, of 'young rustics at a fair, courting and quarrelling over a pretty girl, like birds at one of their places of assemblage' (2:122). In later editions of the *Descent*, moreover, Darwin also added a reference to Arthur Schopenhauer's wistful remarks on the 'comic or tragic' potential of 'all love intrigues'.[18] In fact, as Ruth Yeazell has pointed out, in the *Descent* Darwin 'implicitly deferred the representation of sex in order to dwell on the story of choosing' in precisely the same way that the nineteenth-century English novel 'quietly subordinated the erotic impulses that drove its courtship plot'.[19] The more disquieting implications of rooting human sexuality in animal behaviour, however, could not be elided entirely by Darwin's cosy anthropomorphism and lush romantic rhetoric.

As with genteel novelistic conventions for portraying courtship, Darwin also insisted that in sexual selection, at least in the case of humans, the initial act of choosing was invariably the prerogative of the male, who, being 'more powerful in body and mind than woman', had 'gained the power of selection' (2:371). Unlike the 'lower animals', and even some 'utterly barbarous tribes', for whom the 'females are the selectors' and who respond to 'those males which excite or charm them most', more highly evolved women remained decorously passive, their principal concern being merely 'decorating themselves with all sorts of ornaments' in order to attract the attentions of male selectors (2:371–2). Darwin, though, had earlier confessed in a letter to Francis Galton that he was 'very doubtful about the share males & females play in sexual selection', and elsewhere in the *Descent* he acknowledged the existence of the 'opposite form of selection, namely, of the more attractive men by the women' amongst the most highly evolved humans, proposing, contradictorily, that 'in civilised nations women have free or almost free choice', before again reverting to his usual emphasis on male selection (2:356).[20] This rather muddled reversal of the usual role of females as selectors in the allegedly 'exceptional' case of humans did exempt Darwin from having to consider the invidious prospect of powerful and sexually excitable women and maintained the conventional nineteenth-century sexual double standard that attributed erotic desires only to men and assumed that women always remained passively aloof (2:371). However, as Gillian Beer has noted, Darwin's clumsy volte-face also created 'crucial difficulties' for the theory of sexual selection (not least its abandonment of Darwinism's characteristic rejection of human exceptionalism), and, as will be seen, was either frequently ignored, or was itself conspicuously reversed, by many of the *Descent*'s initial readers.[21]

Sexual selection, Darwin told Wallace in 1867, was 'growing into quite a large subject', and this increasing concern with reproductive behaviour would come to dominate the *Descent* four years later.[22] Indeed, it was sex and procreation, rather than death and extinction, that were now depicted as the driving forces in the evolutionary process; 'Sex and sexual congress', as Beer has pointed out, were 'central to Darwinian evolutionary theory'.[23]

Far from there being any possibility that the book's overriding focus on sex might further degrade humanity, however, Darwin claimed that the central role of sexual selection in man's evolution could actually challenge the far more demeaning assertions of nineteenth-century anthropologists that the sexual relations of primitive humans were entirely promiscuous, or, even worse, polyandrous. Both McLennan and Lubbock contended that amongst early humans 'all the men and women in the tribe are husbands and wives to each other', but sexual selection, in Darwin's view, could not operate if the 'pairing of man . . . is left to chance', and required instead that the strongest males actively selected attractive females and then defended them against rivals in what was, at least temporarily, a monogamous union (2:358).

The anthropological evidence amassed by McLennan and Lubbock notwithstanding, the *Descent* implied that the evident impact of sexual selection on human development must indicate that 'when men had only doubtfully attained the rank of manhood, they would probably have lived . . . as monogamists' (2:367). At some later point in his development, Darwin conceded, man had 'pass[ed] through a stage of promiscuous intercourse' brought on by a lack of eligible females, although he insisted that this had probably only been a temporary phase, and observed that amongst nineteenth-century savages 'many tribes practise some form of marriage' (2:363). Even while it contradicted the *Descent*'s earlier emphasis on the immorality of insufficiently evolved savages, the theory of sexual selection seemed to offer an evolutionary rationale for patriarchal sexual respectability, just as the associated theory of 'pangenesis', which proposed that the germ cells essential to hereditary transmission were emitted from all over the body and could leave vital organs dangerously depleted if over-produced, apparently gave biological backing to the necessity of limiting masturbation.[24]

In the *Descent*, Darwin nevertheless acknowledged that, from a purely evolutionary point of view, such outward sexual respectability needed only to be very short-lived: 'As far as sexual selection is concerned, all that is required is that choice should be exerted before the parents unite, and it signifies little whether the union lasts for life or only for a season' (2:360). He had, moreover, long recognized that the potential for immoral reproductive behaviour extended well beyond just primitive humans. In 1863 Darwin had discussed sexual morality in nineteenth-century Scotland with John Brodie Innes, the erstwhile curate of Down, who had told him that north of the border 'illegitimate children are in swarms' with the 'proportion of bastards . . . larger than in any country in Europe and the morals in this respect tally exactly'.[25] Later, McLennan would similarly inform Darwin that the very same promiscuity exhibited by primitive savages could also be witnessed in 'our own time and towns', where men without wives 'just do as they can, and are neither over-nice nor over-scrupulous as to the manner'.[26] Faced with the disconcerting evidence of man's habitual promiscuity offered by amateur observers like Innes as well as the foremost authorities on anthropology, Darwin seems to have felt the need to strengthen the *Descent's* implicit argument that patriarchal sexual respectability was both natural and one of the main prerequisites for evolutionary progress.

Brazenly redeploying exactly the same anthropomorphic assumptions and romanticized images that he had previously projected onto the natural world, Darwin avowed that, judging 'from the analogy of the lower animals', most early humans would, like the connubial canaries as well as 'existing Quadrumana' who are 'strictly monogamous, and associate all the year round with their wives', be instinctually monogamous, or, at worst, polygamous (2:361). In addition to the apparent evidence against primeval promiscuity provided by this factitious analogy between animal and human behaviour, Darwin also briefly suggested that sexual 'jealousy' was universal amongst 'all male quadrupeds', which, by compelling such males to retain the exclusive possession of particular females, ensured that 'promiscuous intercourse in a state of nature is extremely improbable' (2:362). Significantly, this highly conjectural assumption afforded a reason for such unions to last for longer than the merely provisional pairings required by sexual selection, and, as will be discussed later, it would be given a much more prominent role in the *Descent's* second edition.

The *Descent's* incessant focus on sexuality obliged Darwin to be scrupulously careful in the language he used. Murray, reading through Darwin's manuscript in the autumn of 1870, was particularly alert to the need for discretion, and even counselled that the word 'Sexual' ought not to appear in the book's title. When Darwin proposed 'The Descent of Man & Selection according to Sex' as a compromise, Murray expressed himself 'glad' to be 'rid of an objectionable adjective'.[27] In the final title the specific connection between selection and sex was further diluted to merely '*in Relation to*', although Darwin and Murray's careful concessions were still not sufficient to spare the blushes of many American periodicals, which, in reviewing the *Descent*, deliberately misprinted the contentious final word of its title as either 'Sex*es*' (*Harper's New Monthly Magazine*) or, still more misleadingly, '*Sea*' (*Galaxy*). Others, such as *Scribner's Monthly*, simply ignored the full title and never referred to the book as anything other than merely *The Descent of Man*.[28]

The issues of language and tone were particularly problematic in relation to the delicate subject of female sexual response. Candid descriptions
of the means by which the male of a particular species 'allures or excites'
the female might be acceptable in natural historical accounts of animal
behaviour, but they would quickly become objectionable when human
sexual conduct was also included, especially in the light of long-established
cultural assumptions, articulated in medical treatises no less than in evangelical sermons and enshrined in the various social purity movements of
the late nineteenth century, regarding the natural modesty and sexual hesitancy of women (1:300).[29] Not surprisingly, Murray took exception to the
tone of a section of Darwin's manuscript dealing with the role of females
in courtship:

It is with a view to removing any impediments to its general perusal that I wd. call
your attention to the passage respecting the proportion of advances made by the
two sexes in animals and I wd. suggest that it might be toned down – as well as
any other sentence liable to the imputation of indecency if there be any.[30]

The passage Murray seems to have had in mind, though he was later unable
to locate it, described how, throughout the animal world, the 'coy' female
was, almost without exception, 'less eager than the male' and 'requires to be
courted to give her desires'. The final phrase, touching upon female sexual
desire, was taken from an observation made 'long ago' by the 'illustrious'
surgeon-anatomist John Hunter, and Darwin, as he informed Murray, had
assumed that a quotation, especially one from a respected eighteenth-
century source, would render the difficult subject matter 'less coarse'.[31]
Darwin had already carefully sidestepped Hunter's original reference to the
'female' being 'not so desirous for copulation', but he promised to alter
the sentence, and, in the published version of the *Descent*, the quotation
from Hunter appeared in a truncated form – 'she generally "requires to
be courted"; . . .' – which scrupulously avoided any mention of female
desires (1:273).[32] While it involved only a relatively minor textual amendment to the *Descent*, Murray's prudish intervention actually made the
book's implicit argument concerning female passivity in sexual pairings
much more pronounced, although Darwin's use of the overdetermined
term 'coy' to characterize female behaviour in such encounters also suggested, as will be examined later, the existence of other, less comforting,
possibilities.

Another of Darwin's methods of making the *Descent* less coarse did find
favour with Murray, who commended him for 'the note which you have very
properly veiled in Latin'.[33] In the 1840s, as Lynda Nead has noted, M. L.

Barré's vast catalogue of the archaeological discoveries made at Pompeii over the previous century had restricted access to information regarding the various licentious and pornographic artefacts that had been unearthed by simply 'leav[ing] all the quotations from classical writers untranslated', and similar strategies were employed in numerous literary, medical and philosophical works throughout the nineteenth century. For the Victorians, as Nead observes, 'Latin thus becomes the written equivalent of the sculpted fig leaf.'[34] Murray evidently had a similar objective in mind, and, although it is unclear exactly which of the *Descent*'s multitudinous footnotes he wished to veil rhetorically, there are at least two separate occasions when Darwin's footnoted commentary on particular points appeared, without any notice or explanation, entirely in Latin. Instead of merely leaving classical passages in their original form, moreover, Darwin actively translated the often rather earthy vernacular English of some his correspondents into the more demure idiom of an ancient language.

The first Latin footnote, near the beginning of the *Descent*'s opening chapter, referred to the role of smell ('odoratu') in the courtship behaviour of both humans and other quadruped mammals ('hominbus et Quadrumanis'), a topic that Darwin conceded was potentially unseemly ('turpius') and which he might have preferred to avoid discussing candidly at such an early stage in the book (1:13n.). It was, after all, precisely these initial pages that the general public – or possibly even indolent reviewers – were most likely to peruse casually in bookshops and libraries, perhaps even forming an impression of the *Descent* as a whole from merely such a cursory encounter with its opening section.

The *Descent*'s other footnote in Latin appeared much later in the book, in the second volume's chapter on secondary sexual characteristics in man, although the need to shield general readers from a similarly taboo and doubtless highly distasteful subject was, in this case, even more urgent. Drawing on his correspondence with Andrew Smith, a retired army surgeon who had been stationed in South Africa, Darwin described how the large 'posterior part' of 'Hottentot women . . . projects in a wonderful manner' and is 'greatly admired by the men' (2:345). This discussion of the local aesthetic preferences which, Darwin argued, were responsible for the different racial characteristics of humans was augmented by Smith's eye-witness account of a Hottentot female who was 'so immensely developed behind' that she was 'considered a beauty' although she was actually unable to stand and had instead to 'push herself along' (2:345–6). Appended to this grotesquely comic narrative of the curious consequences of sexual selection (which retained the same anecdotal tone in which Smith had originally related it to Darwin) was a more sedate footnote in Latin which referred once more to the same letter, from March 1867, in which Smith had apprised Darwin of the ideals of female beauty peculiar to the Hottentots:

Idem illustrissimus viator dixit mihi praecinctorium vel tabulam foeminae, quod nobis teterrimum est, quondam permagno aestimari ab hominibus in hâc gente. Nunc – res mutata est, et censent talem conformationem minime optandam est. (2:345n.)

The famous explorer told me that the very girdle or protuberance on women which we see as repulsive is thought to be of considerable value by the men of this tribe. Now, though, the case has changed and they think that such a shape is by no means desirable.[35]

Darwin distrusted his own rusty Latin and requested that his son Francis, who had recently graduated from Trinity College, Cambridge, cast a more practised eye over such passages.[36]

Even when veiled in an antique language that was generally the exclusive preserve of university-educated gentlemen, however, Darwin's footnote remained self-consciously vague and evasive about the precise nature of this 'praecinctorium vel tabulam [girdle or protuberance]' that was so repellent to Western tastes. And especially when compared with what Smith had actually told him in his letter, which had stated frankly:

so far as the Hottentot is concerned I can with certainty say . . . he some time ago used to value highly such of the females as had lengthened nymphae [i.e. the labia minora of the vulva] but now he rather views these ugly developments as undesirable if not as deformities. I have been told of some who had them as elongated as that they were able during sexual intercourse to encircle the man's loins and fix him by them until the appetite of both was thoroughly satisfied.[37]

The disparity between the *Descent*'s demure footnote and the rather earthy letter from a retired military man on which it was based suggests not merely Darwin's reluctance to refer candidly to certain areas of the female body. More significantly, it also indicates his unwillingness to countenance the voracious sexual dominance, and apparently proactive role in sexual selection, of Hottentot women suggested by Smith's anecdotal account, which contrasted markedly with the diffident coyness that was attributed to females of all species throughout the *Descent*, even while it conformed to traditional stereotypes of the primitive lasciviousness and concupiscence of black women.[38]

The anatomical peculiarity to which Smith referred had actually been noted regularly by travellers and explorers since the late seventeenth century, and, according to Londa Schiebinger, 'by the early nineteenth century

European interest in this aspect of Hottentot genitalia had grown into a grotesque voyeurism, to which naturalists were not immune.'[39] In 1815 Georges Cuvier had dissected the hypertrophied labia of the famous 'Hottentot Venus', Saartjie Baartman, who had been displayed to the curious gaze of paying audiences in both London and Paris, claiming that there was 'nothing more celebrated in natural history' than the mysterious form of her sexual parts.[40] More recently, the same genital features had been described explicitly – although again employing a sartorial euphemism and still partially in Latin – in J. Frederick Collingwood's translation of Theodor Waitz's *Introduction to Anthropology* (1863) as 'the much talked-of Hottentot apron, which . . . consists of a prolongation of the *praeputium clitoridis* and of the *nymphae*'.[41] Although sponsored by the anti-Darwinian and avowedly racist Anthropological Society, Collingwood's translation of Waitz's massive tome was one of Darwin's principal anthropological sources in the *Descent*, and the book's observation that in other regions of Africa 'the nymphae are artificially elongated' (presumably because they were attractive to men) suggested, along with the evidence presented in Smith's letter, that the development and subsequent disappearance of this racially specific female trait amongst Hottentot women could be accounted for by sexual selection.[42]

While it was just about acceptable to mention steatopygous females in the main text of the *Descent*, it was inevitably impossible for Darwin even to allude to anthropological accounts of such variations in women's genitalia, and especially to men's apparent preference for them. In the 1790s Elizabeth Helme's English translation of François Le Vaillant's account of his experiences amongst the natives of South Africa had expurgated all of the author's numerous references to the genitalia of Hottentot women, which, she claimed, 'would ill accord with the delicacy of a female translator, or indeed with the temper and genius of English readers'.[43] But Darwin, at pains to convince doubters such as Wallace of the effectiveness of his theory, could not afford to disregard entirely any evidence that apparently supported sexual selection, even if its potential to perturb the moral sensibilities of the *Descent*'s general readership meant that it had to be effectively smuggled into the book in an extremely circumspect footnote which, veiled in Latin, was intended never to be understood by the majority of the book's audience and to be meaningful only to the most erudite and specialist readers.

Even such carefully concealed intellectual contraband might nevertheless still be detected by wholly unsuitable readers, and the American humorist Richard Grant White warned ironically that to 'cloak' parts of the *Descent* in the 'obscurity of a learned language' was actually a 'doubtful expedient in these days – these practical days – when so many young women learn nothing of house-keeping but much of Latin'.[44] Rather than being genuinely concerned by the potentially invidious consequences of the advancement of female education, White's own response to the *Descent*, a comic lecture on *The Fall of Man: or, The Loves of the Gorillas* (1871) ostensibly delivered by an elderly simian naturalist, not only lampooned but also persistently drew attention to Darwin's strategic use of Latin. At one point, the human editor who claims to have witnessed and transcribed the gorilla's lecture in the interior of Central Africa appends to it a satirical footnote of his own which directs readers to 'See the passage in Latin in chapter i of "The Descent of Man."'[45] Similarly, at the end of the simian's discourse the editor unwittingly attracts the amorous attentions of an elderly female gorilla who has been part of the listening crowd, and observes, 'I thought of Darwin's book . . . and I remembered the dreadful words: "*et dignoscebat in turba, et advocat* [*sic*] *voce, gestuque* [and picked them out from the crowd, calling out to them with voice and gesture]"', which were part of the closing sentence of the same Latin footnote in the *Descent*'s initial chapter.[46] While, in this particular footnote, Darwin had endeavoured to veil a description of the incitement of a baboon's sexual frenzy ('furorem') by the sight of certain females ('aspectu feminarum') in decorous Latin that was intended to be intelligible only to a very restricted number of readers, White, in his satirical lecture, transformed the same passage into a drolly comic anecdote which, with its grotesque accompanying illustration, would, quite deliberately, be accessible to the broadest possible audience (1:13n.).

Perhaps because of these potential difficulties, another reference to the African fondness for steatopygous females made use of both of Darwin's favoured rhetorical means of ensuring the *Descent*'s moral rectitude. The observation that 'according to Burton, the Somal men "are said to choose their wives by ranging them in a line, and . . . picking her out who projects furthest *a tergo*"' not only veiled in Latin any potential indelicacy regarding the female behind, but was also part of a sentence quoted from an article in the *Anthropological Review* by the explorer and anthropologist Richard Burton. Nevertheless, Darwin, with Murray's previous advice regarding his earlier use of Hunter's words perhaps still in mind and no doubt well aware that, unlike the illustrious Hunter, Burton was a controversial figure whose notorious name conferred no tacit respectability on the statement, also removed a more direct reference to the female posterior in the remainder of the quotation, silently changing Burton's 'nothing can be more hateful to a Negro than a thin rumped woman' to the more circumspect 'Nothing can be more hateful to a negro than the opposite form' (2:346).[47] Despite his customary scrupulous attention to detail, Darwin was apparently willing secretly to modify passages extracted from some of his most authoritative anthropological sources merely in order to ensure the acceptability of his book to the majority of the Victorian reading public. Even the book's meticulous bowdlerization, however, could not prevent critics from complaining of an apparent obsession with sex which would make the *Descent* unsuitable reading material for all but the most worldly gentlemen.

NAMELESS SHAMELESS ABOMINATIONS

The strenuous endeavours of both Darwin and Murray to purge the *Descent* of any potential impropriety were, according to the *Dublin Review*, an unqualified success. While this organ of moderate Catholic opinion was already advocating Mivart's rival findings and considered sexual selection 'a subject that it is difficult to treat in any Review but a strictly scientific one', it was readily conceded that 'Mr. Darwin handles it in a way that entirely strips it of all offensiveness'.[48] The *Westminster Review* likewise agreed that Darwin 'with modesty and caution all his own . . . makes a temperate use of his discovery' of sexual selection.[49] Although the *Westminster*'s anonymous assurances regarding the *Descent*'s discretion were actually written by William Sweetland Dallas, who was hardly impartial having, amongst many other services to Darwin, compiled the book's index, historians have, for the most part, similarly assumed that Darwin's attempts to render his evolutionary account of human origins respectable were both relatively unproblematic and largely successful. The *Descent*, as Yeazell has suggested, resembled 'a respectable Victorian novel', while Desmond and Moore have likened Darwin's book to 'a tremendous family saga' which 'did not tax one's tolerance so much as entertain', and, more recently, have commented that 'the *Descent* had British gentlemanliness stamped all over it'.[50] But this was not necessarily the experience of much of the book's original audience; readers, after all, approach texts in a multiplicity of different ways and are notoriously resistant to authorially mandated meanings. Indeed, several reviewers of the *Descent*, both commendatory and adverse, drew attention to the explicitness and apparently unseemly tone of much that still remained even in its carefully expurgated pages.

For some of these reviewers the principal problem with Darwin's book was simply its timing. The *Descent* went on sale just as a bloody class war was breaking out on the streets of Paris, and, as *The Times* thundered: 'A man incurs a great responsibility who . . . advances at such a time the

disintegrating speculations of this book.' There was, moreover, a direct correlation between the *Descent*'s evolutionary account of morals and the brutal
insurrection now occurring in France, for, *The Times* insisted, if Darwin's
theories were accepted, 'conscience would cease to be a check upon the
wildest . . . most murderous revolutions', and such 'loose philosophy . . . is,
at all events, one potent element in the disorganization of French society.'[51]
Although Darwin dismissed the *Times* reviewer as a mere 'wind-bag', he
was not without concerns that such harmful insinuations might 'injure the
sale' of the book, and by this time some 4,500 copies of the *Descent* had
already been printed.[52]

The same revolutionary anxieties were also stoked by Mivart in an anonymous notice for the *Quarterly*, which endeavoured to reveal 'the entire and
naked truth as to the logical consequences of Darwinism', and warned
of 'the injurious effects which [Darwin's] work is likely to produce on too
many of our half-educated classes'.[53] In a subsequent article for the *Contemporary Review*, Mivart again insisted that Darwinian speculations 'cannot
but . . . produce results . . . [that] tend . . . in the political order to the
evolution of horrors worse than those of the Parisian Commune'.[54] The
revolutionary Paris Commune, a workers' government which briefly ruled
the French capital during the spring of 1871, was, according to reports in the
English press, led by, amongst others, the 'authors of licentious books', and
had given free rein not only to political anarchism, but also to sexual licence
and immoral depravity (including performances of the 'wildest *"cancan"*
that was ever danced in France', as *The Times* reported).[55] Certainly, the
Commune, amongst the many new laws that it hurriedly passed, liberalized
marriage and abolished the distinction between legitimate and illegitimate
children.[56] The *Descent*, Mivart's *Contemporary* article suggested, was implicated in the full range of these revolutionary horrors, and he added slyly
to his list of objections to Darwin's theories: 'I refrain from characterisiz-
ing their tendency in the moral order.'[57] With the alleged excesses of the
Paris Commune regularly filling the columns of English newspapers, concerns with the political dimensions of Darwin's recently published theories
regarding human evolution shifted readily to their relation to moral, and
even sexual, issues.

While Mivart coyly refrained from specifying the moral consequences
of Darwinism in the pages of the *Contemporary*, he had been far less circumspect a year earlier in his book *On the Genesis of Species*, which had
appeared in January 1871. Even before the *Descent* was actually published,
Mivart argued that Darwin's account of the evolution of moral feelings by
natural selection could never provide 'a higher degree of morality than was

useful' to the survival of any particular society, and, still more worryingly, this pragmatic, utilitarian and, worst of all, relativistic understanding of ethics could not ensure the permanent 'abhorrence of certain acts as impure and sinful'.[58] Mivart alleged that 'could the views of . . . Mr. Darwin on this subject . . . come to be generally accepted, the consequences would be disastrous indeed!', and he pictured a dystopian future of frightful 'moral disruption'.[59] Darwin's generally unfavourable opinion of primitive humans – and importantly Mivart ignored or was unaware of Darwin's opposition to primeval promiscuity – served likewise to 'degrade untruthfully our common humanity' and to give an undue prominence to man's bestial urges. According to Mivart, most native tribes actually displayed 'a strongly marked and widely diffused modesty, in sexual matters', as was epitomized by the 'decorum of . . . postures' and 'modesty exhibited by the naked females' of Tasmania.[60] Disputing the naturalistic continuity that Darwin discerned between man and the lower animals, Mivart insisted instead that all humans, including primitive races, were unique because of man's possession of a divinely endowed 'rationality' that was continually 'making use of and subsuming his animality'.[61] The rival account of human origins that Darwin was due to publish in the following month, Mivart's book forecast, would both dangerously undermine morality and exaggerate distastefully the more animalistic aspects of human nature, particularly in relation to sexuality.

Other reviewers similarly raised eyebrows at the *Descent*'s apparent preoccupation with sex, and at least part of the problem was the explicitness even of Darwin's overtly scientific language. The *Athenaeum*, long the *bête noire* of Darwinism, was simply lost for words, claiming: 'We scarcely know how to deal with Sexual Selection.' It was, the *Athenaeum* claimed, 'both a delicate and difficult subject', and, when a passage from the *Descent* dealing with the emergence of sexual dimorphism in early man was reprinted in the review, it was noted that 'we quote [it] with the omission of a few words that might displease the fastidious'. The potentially objectionable missing words were merely 'the excreta were voided through a cloaca', but the *Athenaeum*'s reprinted passage was also brought to an abrupt halt with the melodramatic aposiopesis, 'We decline to continue the extract', just as the particular section extracted from the *Descent* was about to move on to androgynous male mammals which 'possess . . . rudiments of a uterus with the adjacent passage' as well as 'rudiments of mammae' (1:207–8). Those readers willing to tolerate such explicit descriptions, the review advised, 'must have recourse to the book'.[62] Darwin's latest evolutionary monograph, it was clearly implied, transgressed the boundaries of acceptability even of a highbrow journal like the *Athenaeum*, and the widespread practice of general readers gaining a detailed knowledge of the latest scientific publications from periodical reviews and extracts was, in this case, considered inappropriate.[63]

The author of the *Athenaeum*'s censorious review was John R. Leifchild, the same 'wretched writer' who had earlier provoked Darwin's indignation by alleging, in a notice of *Man's Place in Nature*, that 'Prof. Huxley's aim is to degrade man'.[64] But even friends such as Wallace could not be relied upon to avoid such concerns entirely, and in his otherwise favourable review of the *Descent* in the *Academy* Wallace contrasted Darwin's frank discussion of sexual selection with the 'reticence with which the sexual relations of animals have been treated in popular works'.[65] In the revised second edition of the *Descent* published in November 1874 Darwin would respond to the anxieties of Wallace and others by exclaiming defiantly, in the preface to his discussion of courtship behaviour amongst humans, that 'no excuse is needed for treating this subject in some detail', and he gratefully appropriated a quotation from the 'German philosopher Schopenhauer' – whom Darwin appears not to have encountered before – carried in a recent article from the *Journal of Anthropology* which contended that such sexual relations were 'of more importance than all other ends in human life'.[66] This lay in the future, however, and in the meantime an even more forthright response to the *Descent*'s seemingly incessant focus on sex was to come in another of the old enemies of Darwinism, the *Edinburgh*.

The *Edinburgh*, the oldest of the heavyweight quarterly reviews, had carried Richard Owen's swingeing review of the *Origin* in 1859, and it now commissioned the geologist William Boyd Dawkins similarly to take on the *Descent*. Dawkins was in fact sympathetic to many aspects of evolution, and had, in 1869, been appointed as curator of the Manchester Museum at the behest of Huxley.[67] His anonymous review of the *Descent* seemed, at first, to warm to Darwin's new book, which, it observed, was 'on every side . . . raising a storm of mingled wrath, wonder, and admiration'.[68] It was only when he came to consider the *Descent*'s evolutionary account of morals that Dawkins reverted to the kind of abrasive rhetoric in which the *Edinburgh* had couched its previous discussions of Darwinism. In the view of Darwin's book, he contended, the 'sense of right and wrong . . . is no definite quality, but merely the result of the working together of a series of accidents controlled by natural selection', and, as Dawkins, with memories of the recent French insurrection no doubt still in mind, added: 'We need hardly point out that if this doctrine were to become popular, the constitution of society would be destroyed.'[69] Like Mivart (whose book he quoted regularly), Dawkins adhered to the conservative theological position that morality could be upheld only by divine authority, in the absence of which chaos and immoral depravity would inevitably ensue.

In his notice for the *Edinburgh* Dawkins drew more attention even than Mivart to the disconcertingly dominant role of sex in Darwin's thinking. After caustically dismissing the theory of sexual selection as 'altogether inconsistent with known fact', he observed:

Inferences might not unfairly be drawn from this portion of Mr. Darwin's work, to which we cannot in this place do more than advert. But we do him no injustice in ascribing to him the theory of Lucretius – that Venus is the creative power of the world, and that the mysterious law of reproduction, with the passions which belong to it, is the dominant force of life. He appears to see nothing beyond or above it. In a heathen poet such doctrines appear gross and degrading, if not vicious. We know not how to characterise them in an English naturalist, well known for the purity and elevation of his own life and character.[70]

The veritable obsession with sex and its attendant passions evinced by Darwin's latest book rendered Dawkins, like the *Athenaeum*'s reviewer, almost speechless. Even while acknowledging the exemplary nature of Darwin's own personal reputation, he insinuated that the overriding importance that the *Descent* placed on sexual selection in evolutionary development, and especially that of man, was as coarse and demeaning as the most lascivious philosophies of the corrupt pagan world. The *Descent*, it was implied, might even encourage the same kind of corrosive sexual abandon that had long been ascribed, as will be seen in the following chapter, to the Roman poet Lucretius.

But for readers of the number of the *Edinburgh* in which Dawkins's review appeared, the brief reference to a gross and degrading heathen poet would also have had other, and much more recent, associations. Less than a hundred pages before Dawkins's astringent notice of the *Descent*, the *Edinburgh* for July 1871 had also carried a similarly critical review of Swinburne's latest collection of verse, *Songs Before Sunrise*. Since the publication of the iconoclastic *Poems and Ballads* in 1866, which had transgressed gleefully almost every boundary of Victorian respectability, Swinburne had become infamous for his poetic treatment of pagan debauchery and vice. Amongst the contents of his notorious volume were frenetic dramatic monologues such as the Sapphic 'Anactoria' which explored the sado-masochistic cruelty and frustration of physical love – both heterosexual and homosexual – within various ornate classical settings, while in poems like the 'Hymn to Proserpine' the pagan deities of Greece and Rome were privileged over Christianity's 'ghastly glories of saints' and 'dead limbs of gibbeted Gods'.[71] *Poems and Ballads* was, of course, widely condemned for this apotheosis of what one reviewer called 'all the bestial delights that the subtleness of Greek depravity was able to contrive'.[72] Five years later, the *Edinburgh's* review of *Songs Before Sunrise* similarly noted Swinburne's dubious 'admiration for the ancients', and insisted that his moral perceptions were 'perverted . . . even from the Greek point of view'.[73] The close proximity of this literary notice in the *Edinburgh* provided a context in which Dawkins's passing allusion to an indecent heathen poet might signify not merely Lucretius, whose own reputation was hardly wholesome, but also perhaps the most infamously transgressive writer of verse of the entire nineteenth century. The adverse reviews of the latest books by Swinburne and Darwin that were published in the same number of the *Edinburgh* were also connected in several other ways.

Swinburne's *Songs Before Sunrise* championed atheism, republicanism and the revolutionary politics of Giuseppe Mazzini, though frequently employing the forms of religious prophecy and Christian hymns to convey its anti-theist message.[74] Some of the poems in the collection combined such democratic and heretical concerns with a mystical evolutionary pantheism. In 'Hertha', which experiments with conventional rhyme and metre while similarly reinterpreting the myth of Creation, the eponymous goddess of organic growth proclaims herself the source of an evolutionary power which ensures the continuity of all forms of life:

> First life on my sources
> First drifted and swam;
> Out of me are the forces
> That save it or damn;
> Out of me man and woman, and wild-beast and bird;
> Before God was, I am.[75]

As the transposition of tenses in the final line suggests, Hertha's own maternal, nurturing powers precede the false hierarchical dogmas of the orthodox Christian deity, and she now endeavours to reclaim the earth from the failed guardianship of a male divinity.

Inevitably, the *Edinburgh* considered that such verse was guilty of a wide variety of crimes, but, significantly, many of these alleged poetic transgressions closely resembled the charges that, later in the same number of the review, would be made against the *Descent*. The abnegation of morality and conscience seemingly exhibited in Swinburne's perverted poems threatened exactly the same destructive consequences as Darwin's evolutionary account of morality, for their logical inference was the 'abolition of all existing restraints, in the last resort the overthrow of all law and order, of all existing moral rules and established government'. In *Songs Before Sunrise*, it was observed, 'Mr. Swinburne and his friends seek . . . the aggregate of ungoverned impulse and passion known as the Red Republic', and, as with Darwin's similarly disintegrating speculations, the 'condition of France, and especially of Paris, during the last three months and at the present time' was the 'best possible commentary' on such profane and irreverent poetry.[76]

The *Edinburgh*'s review also harked back to the controversial sensuality and eroticism of *Poems and Ballads*, claiming that Swinburne perceived the 'glorification of sensual appetites and sensual indulgences as the highest exercises and elements of human nature'. Like Darwin in his presentation of the theory of sexual selection, Swinburne acknowledged nothing beyond the animalism and passions of physical love: 'He simply deals with the animal side of the passion – with lust instead of love – with the sensual appetite instead of the strong and pure spiritual feeling'.[77] The hostile notices of the two men's latest books carried in the July 1871 *Edinburgh* were both unsigned, and each quarterly number of the strictly anonymous review would have presented contemporary readers with a continuous single text with, as was usual with older periodicals, a particular party line that was adhered to in virtually every article. This juxtaposition of the two reviews, as well as their close verbal and thematic parallels, might have suggested to readers of the *Edinburgh* that the theories of Darwin, just as much as the dissolute verse of the more obviously transgressive Swinburne, threatened to replicate on the streets of British towns and cities the bloody revolutionary fervour and immoral depravity of the recent Paris Commune.

The obvious interconnections between the two reviews may actually have been deliberately intended by the *Edinburgh*'s bullish editor Henry Reeve, who oversaw the production of every article published in the journal and was notorious for constantly altering the work of his contributors.[78] Reeve, as will be seen in the following chapter, also expressed similar reservations about the moral consequences of modern science in his own articles for the *Edinburgh*, and it seems likely that, in the July 1871 number, he strategically positioned his contributors' notices, perhaps even making alterations which made the parallels between them still more conspicuous. Certainly, when, in the following year, Darwin published another book, *The Expression of the Emotions in Man and Animals*, which augmented many of the *Descent*'s main arguments, Reeve commissioned a review from Thomas Spencer Baynes, the reactionary polymath who had earlier penned the *Edinburgh*'s vitriolic notice of Swinburne's *Songs Before Sunrise*. As Reeve had perhaps antici-pated, Baynes's review of *The Expression of the Emotions* identified various shortcomings in Darwin's work which were almost identical to the moral and intellectual lapses in Swinburne's verse that he had already derided in the pages of the *Edinburgh*.

Whereas Swinburne, according to Baynes's review of *Songs Before Sunrise*, exhibited 'a feverish sensuality' and 'a passion . . . for reviling the higher powers and laws of the universe', Darwin likewise, as Baynes claimed in his notice of *The Expression of the Emotions*, 'engaged in the study of sensuous facts' until he had become 'relatively insensible to the phenomena and powers of the moral and spiritual universe'.[79] Similarly, Baynes's use of a scientific analogy to describe Swinburne's base poems as 'molluscs rather than vertebrate . . . fungoid growths rather than . . . strong well-proportioned trees' inevitably associated them with the preoccupations of Darwin, who, Baynes claimed, 'dwells . . . only on the lower and more animal aspects' of existence.[80] The aesthetic exploration of sensuality which, amongst other things, had made Swinburne's poetry so contentious could, in the adept hands of a critic such as Baynes, be made synonymous with scientific theories, like those of Darwin, that sought explanations in the material rather than the spiritual.

Even Baynes's criticism of the language used by Darwin and his followers, whose 'polemical writings . . . abound with the strained emphasis' and 'eager word-catching . . . which characterise the lower forms of religious controversy', resembled his earlier objections to the 'wild luxuriance of merely metrical diction' and 'monotony of . . . rhythmical effect' which Swinburne employed to 'revile in blasphemous language . . . the central religious doctrines'.[81] In fact, the overblown writings of the two, according to Baynes, appealed to an almost identical audience, with Swinburne's poetry having a 'disastrous fascination for excitable but weak and unbalanced natures', while the 'sect of the Darwinian evolutionists' was 'largely recruited from the crowd of facile minds ever ready to follow the newest fashion in art or science'.[82] Indeed, Baynes, in his review of *The Expression of the Emotions*, proclaimed that

in many circles, especially in certain sections of London, fluent conversational evolutionists are to be found whose literary culture hardly goes deeper than a slight knowledge of Mr. Swinburne's poetry, and whose scientific and philosophical training is restricted to a desultory acquaintance with some of Mr. Darwin's more popular works.[83]

After all the verbal and conceptual borrowings of the *Edinburgh*'s various reviews of their work, Baynes, for the first time, made the connection between Swinburne and Darwin explicit. Both, he contended, were equally guilty of denying the vital distinction between right and wrong, and of valorizing mere lustful desires as the highest form of love. Such trite and superficial teachings would, inevitably, seduce the shallow followers of metropolitan fashion, but their reckless acceptance of Darwin's dangerous doctrines, like the instant esteem which they bestowed upon Swinburne's sordid verse, might, if it went unchallenged, pose a very real threat to the rest of society.

Although Darwin was, by this stage of his career, widely revered as an almost saintly scientific sage, the *Edinburgh*'s explicit connection of his evolutionary theories with Swinburne's poetic iconoclasm was still potentially very damaging. In the early 1870s, as Rikky Rooksby has observed, Swinburne was an 'international figurehead for sexual, religious and political radicalism', and his 'very name' was 'charged with a satanic aura for the timid and conservative'.[84] He was regularly depicted in the press as a 'libidinous laureate of a pack of satyrs . . . grovelling down among . . . nameless shameless abominations', while his verse, much of which, it was claimed, 'could not be quoted out of Holywell Street', was considered little better than pornography.[85] Respectable publishers shunned any involvement with such incendiary poetry, and Murray's misgivings over the *Descent* were as nothing compared to his response, in early 1866, to the manuscript of *Poems and Ballads*, which he refused 'in terms which stung the poet to fury'.[86] It had even been rumoured that *Poems and Ballads* would actually be prosecuted under the recent Obscene Publications Act.[87]

Still more perturbingly, some of Swinburne's most notorious poems, including 'Laus Veneris' in which the insatiable goddess Venus 'laid hold upon' her lover with 'lips luxurious' and 'clove' to him 'clinging as a fire that clings', celebrated precisely the kind of sexually desirous and dangerously dominant women whose very existence Darwin, as has been seen, had been reluctant even to countenance.[88] Other elaborate panegyrics to the sensuous and cruel Roman goddess of love and beauty were voiced throughout *Poems and Ballads*, prompting reviewers to draw scornful attention to 'such lecherous priests of Venus as Algernon Swinburne'.[89] Significantly, in the light of Swinburne's admiring portrayal of Venus as a hypersexualized and devouring deity, Dawkins's barbed observation in the *Edinburgh*, quoted earlier, that Darwin was another acolyte for whom 'Venus is the creative power of the world' clearly assumes a disquieting new resonance.

Lingering fears over the possibility of such female dominance were evident throughout the *Descent*, and Darwin responded apprehensively to another naturalist's somewhat Swinburnean description of how a male spider 'was seized by the object of his attractions, enveloped by her in a web and then devoured' with the bizarrely incongruous observation that 'the female carries her coyness to a dangerous pitch' (1:339). Coyness generally signified a reserved shyness or modesty, especially with regard to sex, and this was the sense in which Darwin had used it earlier in the *Descent* when commenting on Hunter's observation that the female 'generally "requires to be courted"; she is coy' (1:273). At the same time, however, the term also carried the almost completely contrary connotations of self-consciously affecting such shyness or reserve in order to gain an advantage, and even of deliberately coaxing, enticing and alluring a potential partner. It was this sense of the word that was employed in Darwin's quotation of Lubbock's account of the 'coquetting' behaviour of the female of the insect species *Smynthurus luteus*, which 'pretends to run away' from the male and then 'turns coyly round' to ensure his attention (1:348). Richard A. Kaye has noted the prevalence of 'Darwin's depiction of a coyly calculating female' throughout the *Descent*, although even this knowing and manipulative version of coyness could, as Kaye contends, still be an adjunct of the lack of sexual desire that was intrinsic to the first sense of the word, and which Darwin attributed to females of all species, who might, after all, exploit the purportedly uncontrollable libidinous yearnings of males for their own particular non-sexual purposes.[90]

That the actions of the female arachnid whose devouring of her male partner was described with such evident unease in the *Descent* did not appear to exhibit this same sexual reticence threatened to undermine the view of female sexuality expressed elsewhere in the book. Darwin's rather odd locution asserting that she 'carries her coyness to a dangerous pitch' certainly acknowledged that the spider was potentially extremely cunning and thereby dominant over the male, but, in insisting specifically on her scheming coyness, it simultaneously implied that, in behaving with such calculating coldness, she was not necessarily motivated by sexual desires. While powerful females did occasionally appear in the *Descent*, which, as has been seen, depicted the females of the lower animals as the selectors in sexual selection, their apparently coy assertiveness was carefully detached from any hints of erotic desire. The curt avowal that the same spider's 'courtship is too tedious and prolonged an affair to be easily observed' or described, like the earlier eschewal of the account of sexually demanding Hottentot women in the 1867 letter from Smith which provided much of the *Descent*'s evidence for sexual selection amongst humans, similarly made evident Darwin's anxiety to expunge even the possibility of these dangerously desirous and carnal women from the pages of his respectable and overtly patriarchal monograph (1:339). To accept their existence would be to challenge the long-established double standard of sexual morality that acknowledged and tacitly condoned the allegedly irrepressible physical passions of men, while associating women only with maternal and asexual moral virtue.

The *Descent's* insistence on the immutability of male passion and female virtue actually contradicted an important aspect of its own argument for male choice in sexual selection amongst humans, which, as Angelique Richardson has shown, implicitly 'emphasized that men, in their superiority, are more closely associated with reason, women with intuition', and Darwin's paradoxical but ostensibly scientific support for the sexual double standard was enthusiastically exploited by many feminists and social purists in the late nineteenth century as a way of 'reinvesting women with the agency of selection on the grounds that only they were' capable of making 'responsible sexual choices'.[91] At the same time, it is important to recognize that, as Roy Porter and Lesley Hall have contended, 'support in Victorian Britain for a double standard of sexual morality . . . . was far from monolithic' with 'contrary beliefs . . . found in contemporary medical literature, and the existence of desire in individual Victorian females . . . well attested'.[92] Darwin's own apprehensive and contradictory repudiation of an active female sexuality became increasingly problematic, and less and less persuasive, when his book was read in relation to those aspects of nineteenth-century culture which challenged the customary sexual double standard.

The hyperbolically powerful, sadistic and sexually voracious *femmes fatales* who were a recurrent, and widely reviled, feature of the poems by Swinburne which Baynes and other reviewers in the *Edinburgh* connected with the *Descent* certainly diverged greatly from conventional constructions of feminine passivity. The eponymous pagan prostitute in 'Dolores' was once 'pure and a maiden', until, as the impassioned narrator observes, 'desire took thee by the throat', and she now inhabits a 'house not of gold but of gain' and entraps men with 'lips full of lust' and a 'cruel / Red mouth like a venomous flower'.[93] Indeed, this monstrous matriarch's

> . . . ravenous teeth . . . have smitten
> Through the kisses that blossom and bud,
> By the lips intertwisted and bitten
> Till the foam has a savour of blood.[94]

While Swinburne's poem evidently expresses a self-consciously perverse admiration for the devouring and blood-thirsty Dolores, nineteenth-century prostitutes had long been depicted in a more negative light as similarly aggressive, sexually predatory and destructive, especially during the passage of the various Contagious Diseases Acts in the 1860s.[95]

More recently, extremely similar representations of violent, antagonistic and sexually debauched women also appeared regularly in conservative reports of the revolutionary activities of the Paris Commune.[96] In its account of the bloody street battles fought in Paris in May 1871, *The Times* complained of 'women forgetting their sex and their gentleness to commit assassination, to poison soldiers, to burn and slay', while also lamenting how many of these unruly women were of 'decent and lady-like appearance' but, like Swinburne's Dolores, had had hidden violent, destructive and sexual impulses unleashed by the revolutionary tumult.[97] Akin to the other aspects of the French insurrection discussed earlier, such iniquitous associations with the dangerous, powerful and hypersexualized *femmes fatales* of both Swinburne's poetry and the Paris Commune might damage the *Descent*'s sales, and even alter how the book was read by its different audiences, negating all Darwin and Murray's careful attempts to remove any potentially indecent connotations from its pages.

In reality, the only nineteenth-century poet that Darwin even alluded to in the *Descent* was Alfred Tennyson, the eminently respectable Poet Laureate as well as a member of the Royal Society. In order to illustrate the 'highest stage in moral culture at which we can arrive', Darwin had used the stoical words of Queen Guinevere, in the first series of *Idylls of the King* (1859), renouncing even affectionate memories of her adulterous lover Lancelot:

> Not ev'n in inmost thought to think again
> The sins that made the past so pleasant to us.[98]

One of the dominant themes of Tennyson's Arthurian epic was the struggle to 'keep down the base in man', and the *Descent*'s allusion to the bestselling poem was perhaps intended to lend an air of epic grandeur to its own evolutionary narrative of how a highly developed species like humanity had become able to 'control our thoughts' (1:101).[99] Although Tennyson's early poetry had been condemned as overly sensual and was occasionally connected with the nascent axioms of aestheticism, he had since achieved a position of almost irreproachable respectability, and reassuring images of man's upward ascent now abounded in his verse. The famous lines from section CXVIII of *In Memoriam* (1850)

> . . . Arise and fly
> The reeling Faun, the sensual feast;
> Move upward, working out the beast,
> And let the ape and tiger die

had long been employed as a means of representing human evolution as a positive process involving the renunciation of man's erstwhile animalism, as they were, for example, in John Chapman's 1861 account of the simian inhabitants of Equatorial Africa in the *Westminster*.[100] Over three decades later, the same lines would be used again for an identical purpose in Huxley's celebrated Romanes Lecture *Evolution and Ethics* (1894).[101]

But Darwin himself, according to his wife Emma, did 'not read Tennyson' and apparently would not have understood even a playful reference, in a letter from Huxley, to *Idylls of the King*.[102] He clearly appears to have been oblivious to the lingering hints of the destructive power of female sexuality and desire inherent in the short passage from the poem that was quoted in the *Descent*. Huxley's own wife Henrietta also complained of Darwin's 'slyly disparaging remarks on my beloved Tennyson' and protested that he had quoted lines from the poem 'Sea Dreams' 'without the context shockingly Owenlike', and failed to appreciate the true merits of Tennyson's verse in a way that 'should have damaged your reputation for accuracy'.[103] In his auto-biographical recollections, Darwin famously claimed that 'for many years I cannot endure to read a line of poetry', and he admitted that his capacity for aesthetic appreciation extended only to 'moderately good' romantic novels which 'do not end unhappily' and featured beautiful heroines.[104] It seems probable therefore that it was actually the poetry-loving Emma, who is known to have copied the *Descent*'s manuscript and who occasionally read proofs for her husband, who suggested the inclusion of the lines from Tennyson's *Idylls*.[105]

Nevertheless, even the most superficial and contrived literary allusions, especially to the work of a poet who was the favourite of such redoubtable wives and mothers as Emma and Henrietta Huxley, could be used to denote the decency or respectability of particular scientific theories in relation to wider culture. As Helen Small has noted, in the writings of many nineteenth-century psychiatrists 'literary reference tended to be decorative: it was a mark of accomplishment, a guarantee of the doctor's credentials as a gentlemanly physician'.[106] Literary allusions suggested by the likes of Emma, meanwhile, would also be likely to resonate with the decorous values of the private, domestic sphere. So, while the *Edinburgh* sought to identify the doctrines of the *Descent* with the degrading and sexually explicit poetry of Swinburne, Darwin himself had meant them to be read as consistent with the more genteel values of Tennyson's highly regarded verse which regularly depicted humanity's transcendence of its sexual animalism. Tellingly, Swinburne himself later wrote a short skit alleging, in the style of contemporaneous claims that Francis Bacon had been responsible for the plays of Shakespeare, that Darwin had in fact been the author of Tennyson's poems.[107] With periodical reviewers like Baynes regularly contributing notices of both scientific and poetic publications, and frequently identifying almost identical transgressions in them, such competing literary associations could play an extremely significant role in the reception of a work like the *Descent* amongst non-specialist reading audiences.

It was, however, Mivart's criticisms, in both *On the Genesis of Species* and his reviews for various periodicals, which had most aggravated Darwin, and this Darwinian apostate now twisted the knife still further by similarly identifying his former mentor's theories with the scandalous poetry of Swinburne. Mivart's book, Darwin complained, had been 'savage or contemptuous about my "moral sense"', and he suspected that, 'stimulated by theological fervour', its Catholic author had played 'not . . . quite fair'.[108] Mivart's apparent unscrupulousness had only increased in the following years, and by 1873, in the first of a series of articles on 'Contemporary Evolution' for the *Contemporary Review*, he was linking evolutionary science to the 'licentious and sanguinary rites' of paganism.[109] Perhaps having read the review of *The Expression of the Emotions* published in the *Edinburgh* only five months earlier, Mivart also insisted that amongst Darwinian evolutionists:

the prevailing tone of sentiment has long been increasingly Pagan, until its most hideous features reveal themselves in a living English poet, by open revilings of Christianity, amidst loathsome and revoltingly filthy verses which seem to invoke a combined worship of the old deities of lust and cruelty.[110]

It was common practice to refrain from even naming Swinburne in the pages of more decorous periodicals – the *Cornhill Magazine*, for example, referred to him as merely 'a modern singer of no small power' – and readers of the *Contemporary*, where Swinburne had for many years been the subject of persistent vilification, would no doubt have understood the nature of Mivart's malevolent insinuations.[111] And even if they did not understand the first time, the charge was repeated in the article's peroration, with the suggestion that 'this system . . . has found in a contemporary poet its distinct lyrical expression'.[112] Such an allegation, of course, associated evolutionary theory with the taint of wantonness, blasphemy and, especially, sexual immorality that Swinburne's name unmistakably signified at this time, although few historians have acknowledged the persistent recourse to such sordid topics in Mivart's carping criticisms of Darwinism in the early 1870s. Less than a year after his *Contemporary* article, though, this aspect of Mivart's attacks would become unavoidable, and would even, for a short time, come to dominate the nineteenth-century debates over evolution.

FRIGHTFUL SATYR-LIKE FEATURES

Before moving on to examine the explosive denouement of Mivart's attacks on Darwin in the early 1870s, it is necessary to consider a further aspect of the response to the *Descent*'s apparent unseemliness which was particularly evident in Victorian visual culture. Since the early nineteenth century, as several historians have recently shown, popular perceptions of controversial scientific claims were importantly shaped by the visual experience of the reading public in a print culture that had been transformed by the burgeoning market for illustrated books and graphic journalism.[113] Certainly, Darwin's theories had, from at least the beginning of the 1860s, been portrayed extensively in visual form, often for satirical ends, and, as an American observer reflected, such 'humorists have done much to make Mr. Darwin's features familiar to the public'. The prominence given to certain aspects of Darwin's distinctive facial characteristics, and his protuberant, furrowed brow in particular, ensured that, as the same observer noted, such impertinent caricatures were 'not so likely to inspire respect for the author of *The Descent of Man* as they are to imply his very close relation to some slightly esteemed branches of the ancestry he claims', although it was avowed that 'probably no one has enjoyed their fun more than' Darwin himself.[114]

Historians have similarly noted Darwin's fondness for such satirical images of his own apelike features, many of which he obtained for a personal collection, and have generally emphasized the relative benignity and innocuousness of the numerous caricatures which appeared following the *Descent*'s publication. Browne, for instance, has observed that 'humorists gave Darwin's theory a relatively unthreatening place in Victorian homes – or at least depicted science as a folly ... about which respectable men and women need not overly concern themselves.'[115] However, when viewed in the light of the many contemporaneous reviews which drew remorseless attention to the explicit language and potential for immorality inherent in the *Descent*, such satirical depictions of Darwin and his evolutionary theories often assume more disquieting, and sometimes distinctly sexual, connotations. At the same time, the wider visual context of nineteenth-century representations of the apparently rapacious sexuality of gorillas and other simians, including pornographic etchings that explicitly identified themselves as responses to Darwinism, adds an illicit frisson even to the most seemingly innocuous portrayals of Darwin's famously hirsute and apelike countenance.

The notoriously whimsical and idiosyncratic brand of visual humour pioneered by the illustrated periodical *Punch* has long been assumed to have eschewed the vulgar excesses of earlier forms of comic journalism, especially once Shirley Brooks became editor in 1870. In the satirical weekly's response to the *Descent*, though, there were nevertheless numerous subtle hints regarding the more unseemly aspects of the book which had been identified in various reviews. A brief humorous poem published in early 1871 lamented the failure of nature to 'supply mankind with clothes' and contended that 'the Tailor's institution, / DARWIN, negatives your plan' and 'def[ies] all evolution', alluding implicitly to the *Descent*'s controversial argument that 'under sexual selection . . . man, or rather primarily women, became divested of hair for ornamental purposes'. Although principally a parody of a 'puff' for a certain tailor's 'celebrated Establishment', the satirical poem was in fact strikingly preoccupied with the prominence of human nudity, and especially that of women, in Darwin's potentially salacious account of how 'man became naked' (1:148). By emphasizing that 'Man and Women – him and her' were both members of 'the naked race', *Punch*'s lewd doggerel drew particular attention to exactly those aspects of the *Descent* that were most likely to affront the genteel sensibilities of its predominantly middle-class readers.[116]

Precisely these members of *Punch*'s audience were shown reading and responding to the *Descent* in George Du Maurier's comic engraving 'A Logical Refutation of Mr. Darwin's Theory', which depicted a middle-class father attempting to persuade his incredulous wife, who holds their young daughter tightly on her lap, that 'baby is descended from a hairy quadruped, with pointed ears and a tail. We *all* are!' (fig. 2.1). The couple face each other across a conspicuously tidy hearth, and the mother's indignant rejoinder, '*I'm* not descended from anything of the kind . . . and baby takes after me. So, there!', determinedly repels any potential Darwinian incursion into the well-ordered domestic realms of the home and nursery, even though an actual hairy quadruped with pointed ears and a tail – the family's pet cat – lurks just behind her. The flippant manner of the similarly hirsute and pointed-eared patriarch, who '*loves to tease*' his earnest spouse and lounges comfortably on a cushion in front of the fireplace holding an open copy of the *Descent* in one hand and a cigarette in the other, likewise associates the reading of Darwin's book with louche and distinctively masculine forms of pleasure.[117]

130   PUNCH, OR THE LONDON CHARIVARI.   [April 1, 1871.

A LOGICAL REFUTATION OF MR. DARWIN'S THEORY.

Jack (who has been reading passages from the "Descent of Man" to the Wife whom he adores, but loves to tease). "So you see, Mary,. Baby is Descended from a Hairy Quadruped, with Pointed Ears and a Tail. We are all are!"
Mary. "Speak for yourself, Jack! I'm not Descended from Anything of the Kind, I beg to say; and Baby takes after me. So, there!"

Fig. 2.1   G. M. [George Du Maurier], 'A Logical Refutation of Mr. Darwin's Theory', *Punch* 60 (1871), 130.

As with the reviews in the *Athenaeum* and elsewhere, Du Maurier's 'A Logical Refutation of Mr. Darwin's Theory' seems to imply that the *Descent* would be considered appropriate reading material only by worldly gentlemen with a penchant for such racy books, and this was precisely how it was interpreted by many contemporaries. The American geologist James D. Hague told Darwin: 'according to Mr. *Punch*, while the men seem to accept [the book] without dissent, the women are inclined to protest.'[118] In preparing the *Descent*, Darwin had enlisted his daughter Henrietta to comment on the manuscript and help correct the proofs, but *Punch* and other journals were soon presenting the published book as a distinctly gendered text that would inevitably offend the refined sensibilities of any female readers who dared even to peruse its pages. Still worse, on the page of *Punch* facing 'A Logical Refutation of Mr. Darwin's Theory' appeared the regular 'large cut' engraving, the visual centrepiece of each weekly number of the journal, which depicted two members of the Paris Commune's revolutionary National Guard ('(black) guards', according to the jingoistic *Punch*) who leeringly accost the vulnerable figure of Marianne, the female symbol of French liberty.[119] Significantly, both of these potential rapists are noticeably hirsute and, like the pet cat and bearded husband on the previous page, have pointed ears. The implicit dialogue between the two cartoons on adjacent pages of *Punch* once more connected Darwin's evolutionary theories with recent events across the Channel, as well as the undermining of sexual morality and rapacious attacks on feminine virtue.

Discussion of the *Descent* was again associated with the male pleasures of tobacco in another *Punch* cartoon, once more drawn by Du Maurier, which depicted two men, both holding cigarettes and seated in informal postures, who consider the implications of Darwin's book amidst the smoky atmosphere of what appears to be a gentlemen's club (fig. 2.2). The cartoon's ribald humour certainly corresponds to precisely such a patriarchal setting, for in reply to the first man's figurative contention 'what does it matther to me whether me *great-grandfather* was an anthropoid ape or not', the second man, who wears a top hat and speaks with an aristocratic lisp, remarks drolly, 'Haw! Wather disagweeable for your *gwate gwandmother*, wasn't it?'[120] The lewd inference of this overly literal response is the distinctly 'disagweeable' prospect that the first man's female ancestor – who is clearly assumed to have been human (although perhaps Irish) – shared her bed with a bestial anthropoid ape. There was, as Beer has noted, a certain 'sexual distaste . . . for many Victorians in the idea of kinship with other animal species', and this particular *Punch* cartoon, as Beer observes, is 'provocatively insistent that descent implies sexual congress'.[121] Far from transgressing the customarily genteel humour of Victorian comic journalism, however, such grotesque and disquieting insinuations that the shared genealogical lineage of humans and apes could even involve sexual relations between the two species had, in fact, already appeared in the pages of *Punch*.

A short skit entitled 'Most Natural Selection' had proclaimed that 'If Mr. Darwin's theory of the Descent of Man were true, we should . . . have to accept quite new views of marriage'. Insisting that it was preferable that married couples should not be near relations such as cousins, the skit claimed that 'if we are descended from Anthropoid Apes . . . we should conclude that there was no cause or just impediment whatever why we should not marry cousins so very many more degrees removed than any other as those arboreal and quadrumanous ones'.[122] Such droll and facetious observations regarding conjugal relations between cousins seem merely to

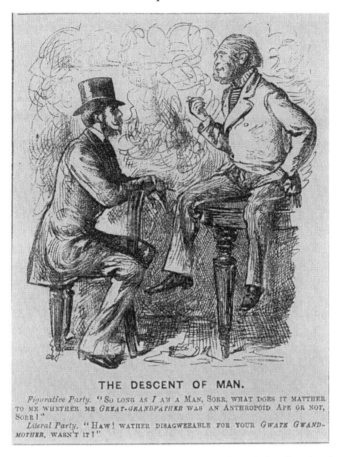

THE DESCENT OF MAN.

Figurative Party. "So long as *I* am a Man, Sorr, what does it matther to me whether me *Great-Grandfather* was an Anthropoid Ape or not, Sorr!"

Literal Party. "Haw! wather disagweeable for your *Gwate Gwandmother*, wasn't it?"

Fig. 2.2 G. M. [George Du Maurier], 'The Descent of Man', *Punch* 64 (1873), 217.

distort and politely satirize the Victorian concern with 'whether or not consanguineous marriages are injurious to man' that Darwin, who had himself married his Wedgwood cousin Emma, had addressed in the *Descent*'s conclusion (2:403). At the same time, though, they also had potentially much more troubling and disreputable connotations in the context of a culture in which marriage was widely assumed to be virtually synonymous with licit sexual activity, and was regularly employed, in the trope of the marriageable girl for example, as an acceptable means of representing sexuality in many novels of the period. Even the sanctity of the marriage bed would be desecrated by Darwin's incongruous insistence on man's intimate connection with simians, and in the pages of *Fun*, *Punch*'s main satirical rival, Darwin himself was shown accompanying an ape in the recent wedding procession of Queen Victoria's eldest daughter.[123] But such potentially bawdy insinuations were by no means confined to the bohemian coteries of *Punch* and *Fun*'s exclusively male contributors. Rather, concerns with the possibility of sexual relations between humans and other species, like the anxieties over miscegenation and the apparently more primitive sexuality of other races prompted by nineteenth-century imperial expansion, were surprisingly prevalent in broader areas of Victorian culture.[124]

While satirical images relating to Darwin's evolutionary theories featured gorillas far more commonly than any other simians, the species had in fact been almost entirely unknown to the Victorian public until 1861, when Paul Du Chaillu's *Explorations and Adventures in Equatorial Africa*, with its dramatic tales of hunting for aggressive gorillas and lurid accompanying illustrations, appeared in an English edition. Du Chaillu, whose sensational book was originally published in New York, soon crossed the Atlantic himself and began displaying stuffed gorillas at crowded public lectures in London during which he vividly recounted his first-hand experiences of this 'animal scarce known to the civilized world'.[125] Du Chaillu recalled how these simians looked so 'fearfully like hairy men' that after his first gorilla hunt he 'felt almost like a murderer', although he denied explicitly any potential evolutionary affinity between these creatures and humans, and his huge collection of gorilla skulls was put at the disposal of Owen in his bitter public dispute with Huxley over the existence of small cerebral distinctions between apes and man.[126] While considerable doubts were soon raised regarding the scientific credibility of many of Du Chaillu's findings, as well as the provenance of his specimens, it is nevertheless notable that, from its very first appearance in Victorian Britain, the gorilla was represented as a rapaciously sexual creature.[127]

The frontispiece of Du Chaillu's *Explorations and Adventures in Equatorial Africa* featured what seems, at least initially, an eminently Victorian representation of the male gorilla (fig. 2.3). The ferocious simian stands upright with fierce canine teeth projecting from its snarling, prognathous countenance, and its raised right arm grasping some overhanging foliage which, rather fortuitously, extends to cover its genital area. This full-length depiction of the gorilla had actually been purloined, without any acknowledgement, from the illustrations accompanying Isidore Geoffroy Saint-Hilaire's description of the collection of gorilla specimens held by the Muséum d'histoire naturelle in Paris, which had been published three years earlier in the *Archives du Muséum* (fig. 2.4). Indeed, the only substantive difference

Fig. 2.3 'The Gorilla'. Frontispiece of Paul B. Du Chaillu, *Explorations and Adventures in Equatorial Africa* (London: John Murray, 1861).

between the two engravings was the prudishly overhanging foliage of Du Chaillu's plagiarized image.

This ungainly amendment was noted implicitly in the pages of *Temple Bar*, which, in an article ostensibly contributed by an affronted gorilla, complained that Du Chaillu's illustrations were 'all copies, and very bad ones too. The full-length which forms the frontispiece to his "Adventures" is a mutilated copy from the coloured lithograph . . . which is in the paper by M. Geoffroy St. Hilaire.'[128] The eloquent indignation of this incensed simian, and especially its use of the emotive term 'mutilated', might also have been prompted by the literal removal of the sexual organs of the stuffed gorilla specimens which Du Chaillu displayed in London, although, paradoxically, this priggish taxidermic tableau actually elicited an exaggerated and

Fig. 2.4 'Gorille Gina'. Plate 1 of Isidore Geoffroy Saint-Hilaire, 'Description des mammifères nouveaux ou imparfaitement connus', *Archives du Muséum d'histoire naturelle*, 10 (1858–61).

prurient – as well as seemingly entirely unwarranted – interest in precisely this aspect of gorilla anatomy, and amongst women in particular. As Burton later observed with scholarly candour and condescension:

the private parts of the monkey . . . are not of the girth sufficient to produce that friction which is essential to a woman's pleasure. I may here allude to the general disappointment in England and America caused by the exhibition of my friend Paul de Chaillu's Gorillas: he had modestly removed penis and testicles . . . and his squeamishness caused not a little grumbling and sense of grievance – especially amongst the curious sex.[129]

The clumsily bowdlerized version of the illustration was, in a similar way, much more suggestive of the gorilla's sexual prowess than the more naturalistic French lithograph. Whereas in Geoffroy Saint-Hilaire's original the gorilla's genitals are shown, as in Burton's account, to be relatively diminutive and unremarkable, their self-conscious concealment in Du Chaillu's unauthorized copy actually draws attention to exactly this area of the gorilla's body, with the light shading of the foliage in sharp contrast to the darkness of the ape's hairy frame, as well as rendering its bestial sexual potency a matter for apprehensive conjecture.

The suggestive intimations of its apparently coy frontispiece were corroborated by the text of *Explorations and Adventures in Equatorial Africa*, in which Du Chaillu regaled readers with lurid tales of native women 'who have a lively fear of the terrible gorilla, in consequence of various stories current among the tribes of women having been carried off into the woods by the fierce animal'.[130] Such tribal legends of the animal's fearsome sexual potency had even given rise to the widespread 'superstition' that 'should the husband of a woman with child, or the woman herself, see a gorilla, even a dead one, she would give birth to a gorilla, and not to a man child'.[131] Although *Explorations and Adventures in Equatorial Africa* occasionally assumed a more staid and analytical tone, its ostensibly scientific narrative persistently foregrounded the more sensational aspects of its author's experiences. Elsewhere in the book, Du Chaillu reported how a female member of the Mbondemo tribe had been captured by an 'immense gorilla' and was generally assumed to have been killed. The woman nevertheless returned after a few days and 'related that the gorilla had misused her, but that she had eventually escaped from him'.[132] Du Chaillu's English publisher was Murray, and, as he would later with Darwin's *Descent*, he baulked at the explicitness of some of the book's descriptions of simian sexuality, insisting that, in the above sentence, Du Chaillu's original 'She related that the gorilla had forced her to submit to his desire' was toned down to the more chaste 'She related that the gorilla had misused her'.[133] Murray's intervention was perhaps motivated by rumors that a hack writer in New York had originally embellished Du Chaillu's shoddy prose to render the book more sensational. However, even in the expurgated form of Murray's English edition the preoccupation of Du Chaillu's narrative with the possibility of sexual intercourse between helpless female humans and rapacious male apes remained strikingly evident, a proto-King Kong scenario that was also depicted in a variety of nineteenth-century art works such as Emmanuel Frémiet's dramatic sculpture *Gorille enlevant une femme*, which was rejected by the Paris Salon in 1859, and Alfred Kubin's Expressionist painting of 1901 *Eine für alle*.[134]

Many of the details of Du Chaillu's contradictory account of his novel experiences in the interior of Central Africa were soon contested, not least by John Edward Gray in the *Athenaeum*, and Huxley, two years later, insisted that 'so long as his narrative remains in its present state of unexplained and apparently inexplicable confusion, it has no claim to original authority respecting any subject whatsoever.'[135] Perhaps most conspicuously, Du Chaillu's purportedly scientific account of gorilla behaviour appears to have drawn heavily on the longstanding 'reputation of the ape as the embodiment of male sexual rapacity', which, according to the art historian H. W. Janson, was already 'well established in the popular mind of sixteenth century England', and had originated as far back as the literature of classical antiquity.[136] Other nineteenth-century naturalists such as Spenser St John also alluded to native 'stories of the male orang-utans . . . carrying off their young girls' and inflicting 'injury beyond fright', while, as Donna Haraway has noted, a similar 'culturally overdetermined lust for sexualized violence' remained a distinctive feature of the work of many male primatologists even into the twentieth century.[137]

Perhaps in response to the habitually salacious descriptions of Du Chaillu and others, the historical survey of European accounts of the manlike apes with which Huxley's *Man's Place in Nature* began pointedly eschewed any reference to the sexual licentiousness that was widely attributed to male simians by earlier naturalists such as Buffon and Linnaeus.[138] Even Huxley's own more empirically rigorous book still contained occasional allusions to the alternate – and perhaps yet more disconcerting – possibility of human sexual desire for female apes. As Huxley noted, the orang-utan described by the seventeenth-century naturalist Jacob Bontius was actually 'nothing but a very hairy woman of rather comely aspect', and he also cited William Smith's eighteenth-century account of a captured female chimpanzee that was taunted by English sailors:

. . . one who hurt it, being checked by the negro that took care of it, told the slave he was very fond of his country-woman, and asked if he should not like her for a wife? To which the slave very readily replied, 'No this is no my wife; this is a white woman – this wife fit for you.'[139]

Although Smith's unruffled observation at the conclusion of the anecdote that 'the unlucky wit of the negro's, I fancy, hastened its death, for the next morning it was found dead under the windlass' makes clear just how provoking even humorous insinuations relating to such a taboo subject could be, the prospect of sexual relations between humans and simians was an issue that continued to fascinate, as much as to disgust, the nineteenth-century imagination.[140]

While obviously given new pertinence by the evolutionary affinity that Darwin and other nineteenth-century naturalists discerned between man and the lower animals, concerns with the sexual coupling of humans and other creatures extended at least as far back as classical antiquity. In particular, the satyr, a mythical amalgam of man and goat whose frenzied lust for wine and women associated it with the cult of Dionysus, was regularly represented copulating with both humans and animals in Greek and Roman art, and most notably in the notorious erotic artefacts that were discovered at Pompeii during the eighteenth century. In subsequent Christian depictions, this classical demigod was increasingly portrayed as a hairy and demonic creature which, significantly, came to closely resemble the imprecise descriptions of apes contained in ancient sources such as Pliny's *Historia Naturalis* as well as various medieval bestiaries. In fact, when living anthropoid apes were first brought to Europe in the seventeenth century, many naturalists, including the celebrated Dutch anatomist Nicolaas Tulp, considered that such manlike simians, with their hirsute appearance and purportedly licentious behaviour, must be actual examples of antiquity's fabled satyr, and the name was adopted regularly in early modern taxonomic classifications of primates.[141]

This long tradition of representing anthropoid apes as embodiments of the lecherous satyr of classical mythology persisted even in nineteenth-century natural-historical accounts of simians. Du Chaillu, at the melodramatic conclusion of a frantic gorilla hunt, observed that the 'hideous monster' which now confronted him had 'frightful satyr-like features' and wore a 'horrid look, enough to make one fancy him really a spirit of the damned'.[142] The gorilla's apparent resemblance to the half-goat satyr once again emphasized its rapacious sexual virility even as Du Chaillu was taking aim to shoot it, while the ancient convention of depicting the satyr in sexual congress with both humans and a variety of animals implicitly lent credence to tribal legends of gorillas capturing and molesting native women. Such a potentially salacious parallel, however, was not restricted to Du Chaillu's lurid and allegedly fictitious narrative of African exploration, with Huxley, in *Man's Place in Nature*, employing Linnaeus's original taxonomic categories of '*Satyrus indicus*' (orang-utan) and '*Satyrus Tulpii*' (chimpanzee) without further comment.[143]

Similarly, in *Punch's* much celebrated 'Monkeyana' cartoon (fig. 2.5), which responded satirically to the popular fascination with all things simian that Du Chaillu had helped to instigate, a gorilla eager to prove its kinship with humans and who wears a placard bearing the famous anti-slavery slogan 'AM I A MAN AND A BROTHER' (which also conveniently covers its groin *à la* Du Chaillu's frontispiece), inquires of the reader:

MONKEYANA.

Fig. 2.5 'Monkeyana', *Punch* 40 (1861), 206.

> Am I satyr or man?
> Pray tell me who can,
> And settle my place in the scale.[144]

This drolly anthropomorphic gorilla goes on to consider the dispute between Owen and Huxley over the anatomical divergence between the brains of humans and apes, but its perplexity regarding its precise taxonomical position would be no less even if it were shown definitively that it was, as Owen implied, satyr rather than man. The satyr was, after all, itself a mutable and hybrid creature, originally consisting of man and goat, and then appearing more and more frequently as a chaotic and unholy amalgam of human, simian and goat. Later in the nineteenth century, the eponymous vivisector in H. G. Wells's novel *The Island of Doctor Moreau* (1896) fashions a series of grotesque but incipiently human 'beast folk' by grafting together various animal forms, including 'a satyr-like creature of Ape and Goat' that represents 'a gleam of classical memory on the part of Moreau, his face ovine in expression – like the coarser Hebrew type . . . his nether extremities Satanic' and which, like Moreau's other experimental creatures, eventually reverts back to its original bestial condition.[145]

Although this satyr-like creature, as with the novel's numerous other hybrid beast folk, is the product of Moreau's innovative techniques in vivisection, its grotesque transgression of conventional taxonomic boundaries was nevertheless closely linked, for some readers at least, with the sexual coupling of humans and apes that had been inferred in the accounts of simian behaviour published earlier in the century. The campaigning journalist William Thomas Stead, in a brief review of Wells's novel, noted that while the 'law against sex intercourse with animals may be, and is, unduly severe . . . it is an offence against humanity to represent the result of the intermingling of man and beast', and he complained that the book's 'hybrid monsters are . . . exactly that which would follow as the result of the engendering of human and animal'.[146] The possibility of human couplings with simians producing such monstrous hybrid offspring had actually haunted the Western imagination for many centuries, from Peter Damian's eleventh-century compendium of ape lore to Gustave Flaubert's gothic story '*Quidquid volueris*' (1837).[147] More recently, the subject had been a recurrent concern of the esoteric footnotes which Burton appended to his translation of the *Arabian Nights* in the 1880s.[148] Stead himself was notoriously preoccupied with a variety of sexual matters, but his rather peculiar interest in the liminal offspring of such disturbingly chaotic sexual unions nonetheless resembled many earlier anxieties regarding the fracturing of human specificity that were prompted by Darwin's insistence on man's shared descent with simians.

The *Origin* had enumerated the advantages of cross-fertilization, as well as describing how various domestic animals were 'descended from two or more aboriginal species, since commingled by intercrossing', and the frightful prospect of a similar 'intercrossing of species' involving man and apes might have been suggested by Darwin's evolutionary account of human origins in the *Descent*.[149] The *Descent*'s discussion of how in the development of humans 'the crossing of races already distinct has led to the formation of new races' (even though the 'first result' of such crosses was invariably 'a heterogeneous mixture') might well have had such invidious connotations, especially when even Darwin, under pressure from the success of the polygenist doctrines of the Anthropological Society, acknowledged that 'a naturalist might feel himself fully justified in ranking the races of man as distinct species' (1:241 and 224).[150] Colonized races such as the Catholic Irish or black Africans were regularly depicted in Victorian Britain as atavistic throwbacks to a level of evolutionary development equivalent to that of simians, and Burton, the co-founder of the Anthropological Society, called for 'actual experiment' to 'ascertain . . . if human being and monkey can breed together'. Tellingly, Burton self-consciously employed the racially charged term 'miscegenation', which was coined in America during the febrile disputes of the 1860s over the rights of black slaves, to describe this potential intercrossing of ape and human, which, as with the famous 'missing link' whose absence currently helped to 'invalidate Darwinism', could not be considered scientifically impossible.[151] Scientific interest in human–simian hybridity actually intensified over the following decades, and in 1905 Ernst Haeckel, Germany's leading advocate of Darwinism since the 1860s, even gave encouragement to a speculative, and ultimately unsuccessful, scheme by the Dutch naturalist Herman Moens to artificially inseminate female apes with human sperm, advising that the two species were sufficiently closely related to permit such a radical hybridization.[152]

The coarse inferences of the long tradition of equating simians with the licentious satyr of classical mythology, as well as the bawdy insinuations of *Punch*'s various cartoons and skits, were made strikingly manifest in a little-known series of pornographic etchings produced on the Continent around 1879 which identified themselves explicitly as responses to Darwin's widely distributed monograph (several translations of the *Descent* had appeared soon after its English publication).[153] This trio of aquatint etchings, entitled *Transformismes* or *Darwiniques* and produced by the Belgian artist Félicien Rops, represented a variety of sexual encounters between human females and animals of various species. The initial two etchings featured strange, clearly imaginary creatures whose grotesque forms exhibited aspects of the primitive hermaphroditism discussed by Darwin in the *Descent* while also resembling the work of the thirteenth-century Flemish painter Hieronymus Bosch. The third, *Transformisme n°3 / Troisième darwinique. Le Prédécesseur* (fig. 2.6), which depicted an anthropoid ape performing cunnilingus on a reclining and entirely nude Caucasian woman, had more in common with other scurrilous prints of the period which graphically portrayed various simians engaged in sexual intercourse with

Fig. 2.6 Félicien Rops, *Transformisme n° 3 / Troisième darwinique. Le Prédécesseur,* drypoint/aquatint, 11 × 17.5cm, *c.* 1879, Collection Musée provincial Félicien Rops.

human females. The most prominent of these images were the numerous mid-nineteenth-century lithographs that illustrated the scene in the much reprinted French pornographic novel *Gamiani, ou Deux nuits d'excès* (1833) in which a 'lascivious' young girl named Sainte 'remembered having read that of all animals, that which the most closely resembles man, is the anthropoid ape' and then attempts to satiate her voracious lusts with a 'superb ourang-outang' (fig. 2.7).[154] Sainte perhaps recalls reading a work by a radical exponent of transmutation like Jean Baptiste Bory de Saint-Vincent, who, in the 1820s and 1830s, insisted on the close parallels between humans and apes, and, significantly, it is her putative encounter with such an evolutionary text that apparently impels her to perform the most transgressive acts of sexual depravity.[155]

While Du Chaillu's sensationalized account of simian sexuality had depicted the gorilla as a malignantly abhuman 'other' which compelled vulnerable and terrified native women to submit to its bestial desires, in Rops's etching, as in the other similar ribald prints that accompanied various editions of *Gamiani*, there existed an even more disconcerting possibility that nubile Caucasian females might actually welcome and even initiate such carnal encounters with creatures that, putatively at least,

Fig. 2.7   Sainte and the ourang-outang, illustration to Baron Alcide de M****** [Alfred de Musset], *Gamiani, ou Deux nuits d'excès* (Amsterdam [Paris]: n.p., 1840 [1864]), facing p. 92.

were so magnificently virile and sexually prepossessing. In *Troisième darwinique* the naked woman's face, turned provocatively towards the viewer, appears to be consumed with orgasmic pleasure, while her supine body is positioned to facilitate her simian partner's erotic attentions, the very nature of which are not generally indicative of male sexual aggression. The ape itself, a generalized Darwinian 'prédécesseur' rather than a specific simian species, has a muscular frame which, around the buttocks especially, closely resembles the human body, although its suggestively erect tail and prognathous countenance, which protrudes from between the woman's legs, denote its brutish animality. The close connection between this sex-ualized simian and the long tradition of representing apes as concupiscent satyrs was made particularly evident in the marginalia which Rops added to a collection of his etchings; on the page featuring *Troisième darwinique* he drew a small crayon sketch of a hoofed satyr copulating with a blonde woman which was presumably intended as an addendum to the themes addressed in the page's principal image.[156]

There are, of course, evident racial connotations in both Rops's engraving and other similar images, and Lisa Z. Sigel has proposed that the 'monkeys and apes that pop up in [nineteenth-century] pornography . . . seem to encode animals with racial taboos'.[157] Like the simians with which they were routinely equated, black Africans, of both sexes, were perceived to exhibit a primitive sexual appetite which was compounded by their apparently oversized genitals (as in Smith's 1867 letter to Darwin), and the chromati-cally contrasting figures depicted by Rops can be seen to conform to much European art, in which, as Sander Gilman has noted, the 'black' emerges as 'an icon for deviant sexuality' when 'paired with a white figure of the opposite sex'.[158] Such wider concerns, though, cannot be detached from the specific context of the response to particular aspects of the *Descent* in the 1870s. After all, the apparently consensual sexual coupling of human and simian represented in *Troisième darwinique* enacts a rupturing of the boundaries of conventional taxonomic classifications that is identified in its title as explicitly Darwinian. This transgressive sexual tableau not only emphasizes the mutability of species identity, but also draws out the impli-cations of Darwinism's refutation of human uniqueness in new and pro-vokingly taboo ways. Indeed, the artist's friend Eugène Rodrigues suggested that the 'vigorous animal . . . pleads, in an impassioned language, the cause of its race', which, intriguingly, implicitly aligns Rops's sexualized simian with the petitioning gorilla portrayed in *Punch*'s celebrated 'Monkeyana' cartoon.[159]

In particular, Rops's etching insists on the essentially animal nature of the sexual desires exhibited by human females, a persistent trope of much nineteenth-century pornography, which, in deliberate opposition to preva-lent cultural assumptions regarding the natural modesty and coyness of women, habitually represented them as beings who were regularly over-come with insatiable and unmanageable desires.[160] In the *Descent*, Darwin had anxiously repudiated any such suggestions, but, paradoxically, had at the same time actually made them more conceivable by rooting every aspect of human sexuality in animal behaviour. In his self-consciously Darwinian etching, Rops, by visually representing man's intimate affinity with the lower animals in the explicit idiom of pornography, inexorably drew attention, as had those reviewers who associated Darwinism with Swinburne's voracious *femmes fatales*, to precisely the same perturbing implications of human evolution that Darwin had refused to countenance even in the face of relevant evidence, and which Murray, in his proposed amendments to the *Descent*'s manuscript, had been particularly anxious to conceal. Most notably, Rops's pornographic representation of uncontrollable female lust powerfully contradicted Darwin's contentious insistence that, with humans, it was only males who played an active role in sexual selection. Paradoxically, moreover, this particular critique aligned scurrilous pornographers like Rops with many late nineteenth-century feminists and social purists who, for admittedly very different reasons, likewise endeavoured to restore the agency of selection to women.[161]

Like Sainte's putatively ruinous exposure to earlier transmutationist writings in *Gamiani*, *Troisième darwinique* also implied that the very act of reading evolutionary works such as the *Descent* might potentially stimulate aberrant sexual desires. Rops attributed the origins of the engraving itself to precisely such an affecting and imaginatively charged textual encounter, recalling, in a letter, that 'having found a volume . . . by one very savant clerk of the country of Great Britain called Darwin, it made a horrific dream'.[162] Similarly, Rodrigues identified the naked female in his friend's engraving as a 'young disciple of [Émile] Littré', the strident French Positivist whose materialist views were frequently elided with those of Darwin, and he proposed that she had engaged in such an intimate act with a 'large monkey' in order to 'prove' the arguments advanced in books by Littré, Darwin and others that 'he is really the ancestor of man'.[163] While *Punch* had already raised anxieties regarding the *Descent*'s potential to perturb the refined sensibilities of female readers, Rops's *Troisième darwinique* suggested that there were actually far more profound consequences for any women who might dare to peruse Darwin's dangerously arousing tome, the very reading of which might stimulate the same sexual animalism inferred in its own pages.

As with most of Rops's numerous erotic and ribald images, *Troisième darwinique* was most likely produced for a select audience of libertine collectors in Paris, and its existence would, inevitably, have been known only to a very small coterie of gentlemanly connoisseurs on the other side of the Channel (imported 'etchings could be . . . bought individually' on the British market, according to Sigel, but their high price generally restricted access to an 'exclusive audience').[164] Darwin himself, on the other hand,

FUN.—November 16, 1872.

THAT TROUBLES OUR MONKEY AGAIN.

Female Descendant of Marine Ascidian :—"REALLY, MR. DARWIN, SAY WHAT YOU LIKE ABOUT MAN; BUT I WISH YOU WOULD LEAVE MY EMOTIONS ALONE!"

Fig. 2.8   G. T. [Gordon Thomson], 'That Troubles Our Monkey Again', *Fun* 16 n.s. (1872), 203.

had by the early 1870s attained the status of a scientific celebrity and his iconic features were one of the most highly prized commodities in the burgeoning market for graphic journalism. Even such widely circulated visual images, though, were not devoid of insinuations regarding the potential implications of Darwin's insistence on the analogous nature of human and animal reproductive behaviour.

Fun's characteristically mordant response to *The Expression of the Emotions in Man and Animals* once more caricatured the book's author as an anthropoid ape (fig. 2.8). With a tail which is as conspicuously erect as that of the sexualized ape in Rops's erotic etching, this scientific simian gauges the capillary circulation of a fashionably dressed 'Female descendant of Marine Ascidian', who opines: 'Really, Mr. Darwin, say what you like about man; but I wish you would leave my emotions alone!'[165] *The Expression of the Emotions*, which appeared in November 1872, considered women's emotional responses at great length, claiming, amongst other things, that 'a pretty girl blushes when a man gazes intently at her' because the man's desirous stare alters the flow of blood to her skin. Additionally, the book also gave examples of a 'girl, who unwillingly consented to serve as a model' and at once 'reddened when she was first divested of her clothes', as well as another 'little girl, shocked by what she imagined to be an act of indelicacy' who also 'blushed all over'.[166] A lingering fear of similar acts of indelicacy perhaps induces the increased flow of blood in the young woman whose delicate wrist is clasped, apparently against her will, by Darwin's darkly simian hands in *Fun*'s cartoon.

Such insinuations become especially potent when the image is viewed, as it may have been by at least some of the comic periodical's original readers, in the light of other visual images, like those of Du Chaillu, Rops and the illustrations to *Gamiani*, which depicted anthropoid apes as highly sexualized creatures. Within the broader context of both the numerous reviews of the *Descent* which, as was seen earlier, bemoaned the book's apparent unseemliness and preoccupation with sex, as well as the widely prevalent representations of gorillas and other simians in Victorian visual culture examined in this section, a certain illicit frisson can be seen to attend even the most apparently innocent and charming portrayals of Darwin's famously hirsute and apelike features.

HIDEOUS SEXUAL CRIMINALITY

While Darwin seems never to have mentioned Swinburne in his voluminous correspondence, and famously kept a personal collection of the numerous caricatures of his apelike countenance that appeared in comic periodicals, there are nevertheless certain circumstances which make it clear that he did not always retain his customary diffidence and genial demeanour in the wake of critical imputations that, in the *Descent*, he was peddling a degrading and potentially corrupting view of human existence. In fact, in the years following the book's publication Darwin seems to have become increasingly perturbed by suggestions that his evolutionary theories might encourage immorality and licentiousness. Both Darwin and Murray, as has been seen, had endeavoured scrupulously to expunge any potentially indecent connotations from the *Descent*'s first edition, but even in such a bowdlerized form the book was still subjected to considerable criticism for its apparent indecency. Darwin's growing concern with this aspect of what he termed the 'fiery ordeal through which the book has passed' is suggested, in part, by the further alterations that he made to the revised and augmented second edition which appeared in November 1874.[167]

In opposition to the findings of leading anthropologists such as McLennan and Lubbock, the *Descent* had contended that patriarchal sexual respectability was both instinctual, and therefore entirely natural, and one of the main prerequisites for evolutionary progress. In the first edition of the *Descent* this argument had been based mainly on the evidence provided by the impact of sexual selection on human development, as well as the analogy of the apparently chaste behaviour exhibited by numerous other species. Sexual jealousy, which, Darwin assumed, prompted each male to desire to possess his own female partner, was mentioned only briefly (and was not included in the book's index) as a further reason why monogamy was innate to man and most other animals. By 1874, though, it was this sense of jealousy that had become the principal bulwark against the anthropological arguments of McLennan and Lubbock for the prevalence of promiscuity amongst early humans.

Whilst preparing the *Descent*'s new edition the role of sexual jealousy in human evolution seems to have become ever more important in Darwin's thinking, and, as he explained to McLennan, his view of the development of marriage systems now suggested not only that such 'jealousy . . . [had] determined the first stage' of primeval monogamy, which was supplanted once infanticide and a system of polyandry had 'undermin[ed] natural jealousy', but that 'a feeling of property in women growing up in aid of natural jealousy' had finally 're-established . . . monogamy' as the dominant mode of human marriage. With Darwin now attributing such a pivotal role to this apparently overwhelming sense of jealousy, McLennan cautioned that 'man [was] not only a creature with natural jealousy, but a combining, conspiring creature' too, and with 'criminal records' showing 'several men' regularly 'joining to secure a woman . . . for sexual purposes . . . even in this country in late times' he warned that, in view of the available evidence, monogamous exclusivity could only be regarded as relatively unusual.[168]

Darwin paid little heed to McLennan's reservations concerning such distastefully crowded sexual arrangements, and the *Descent*'s second edition made no acknowledgement of any doubts regarding the role of sexual jealousy. Instead, the revised text actually gave it a far more prominent position in the book's argument against primitive promiscuity than it had had in

1871. While, for instance, the first edition had claimed that 'nevertheless from the analogy of the lower animals . . . I cannot believe that this habit [i.e. promiscuous intercourse] prevailed at an extremely remote period', in 1874 this had become: 'Nevertheless from the strength of the feeling of jealousy all through the animal kingdom, as well as from the analogy of the lower animals . . . I cannot believe that absolutely promiscuous intercourse prevailed in times past' (2:361).[169] The dubious analogy of animal behaviour, which merely reflected back the same anthropomorphic assumptions that Darwin had already projected onto the natural world, was not discounted entirely in the amended version, although it was clearly downgraded to merely a secondary function in comparison with what was termed, in another addition to the 1874 text, the 'natural and widely prevalent feeling of jealousy, and the desire of each male to possess a female for himself'.[170] Unlike sexual selection, which required only temporarily monogamous sexual couplings, the assumption that sexual jealousy was a virtually universal instinct amongst males of all species afforded a clear reason why permanent monogamous unions should be more prevalent in the natural world than promiscuous or merely provisional pairings, and its greater prominence in the *Descent*'s second edition can be seen as a clear attempt to reinforce the book's implicit naturalization of nineteenth-century standards of marriage and sexual respectability.

More particularly, masculine sexual jealousy, as Darwin had suggested in the original version of the *Descent*, would, as an inevitable consequence of the male's own desire for an exclusive sexual relationship, also 'lead to the inculcation of female virtue', which would eventually even 'spread to unmarried females' and form the basis of the civilized 'self-regarding virtues' of feminine 'chastity' and 'celibacy'. Although its slowness in extending the same chastity to unmarried members of the 'male sex' was still evident 'at the present day', as Darwin noted once again upholding the conventional double standard of sexual morality, the instinctual sexual jealousy exhibited by men with spouses was integral to the *Descent*'s naturalistic explanation of the emergence of modesty and coyness in women as an evolutionary response to the needs of dominant male partners (1:96). With critics regularly calling attention, as has been seen, to the *Descent*'s apparent potential to undermine such feminine virtues, as well as associating Darwin's theories with Swinburne's voracious *femmes fatales* and other similarly disconcerting representations of female sexual behaviour, the textual revisions made to the book's 1874 second edition implicitly strengthened Darwin's insistence that an evolutionary account which rooted human sexuality in animal behaviour did nothing to imperil long-standing assumptions regarding the female's absence of overt sexual desires, and could even offer a scientific rationale for why this diffident coyness had actually evolved, and subsequently become innate, in women.

Darwin was assisted in the preparation of the *Descent*'s second edition by his son George, who had lately begun to contribute scientific articles of his own to various periodicals. Soon after his father's revised manuscript was submitted to Murray in April 1874, George's most recent article, an orthodoxly Darwinian account of human breeding entitled 'On Beneficial Restrictions to Liberty of Marriage', was the subject of a violent and melodramatic critical attack that was launched anonymously by Mivart in Murray's *Quarterly*. Having read George's essay, which had been published in the *Contemporary* in the previous summer, in haste and with a predisposition to view anything written by a member of the Darwin clan as morally suspect, Mivart mistakenly claimed that its author 'speaks in an approving strain of . . . the encouragement of vice in order to check population'.[171] George had in fact merely noted, in a historical survey of various marriage customs, that amongst early Teutonic tribes 'prostitution was not merely tolerated, but was secretly promoted as a check to over-population, as in Japan at the present day', a point which, significantly, had also been made by his father, and with the same accompanying example, in the *Descent*, which stated: 'Licentiousness may also be added to the foregoing checks [to overpopulation] . . . there is reason to believe that in some cases (as in Japan) it has been intentionally encouraged as a means of keeping down the population' (1:134).[172] Female prostitution inevitably carried awkward connotations of precisely the kind of promiscuous and sexually desirous women whose very existence Darwin had been at pains to deny in the *Descent*, and, like his son, he was extremely careful not to suggest any espousal of a custom which he implicitly equated with infanticide.

Mivart nevertheless interpreted George's sentence – and by implication that of his father – as an explicit endorsement of such immoral practices, and, on this rather flimsy evidence, he declared:

There is no hideous sexual criminality of Pagan days that might not be defended on the principles advocated by the school to which this writer belongs. This repulsive phenomenon affords a fresh demonstration of what France of the Regency and Pagan Rome long ago demonstrated; namely, how easily the most profound moral corruption can co-exist with the most varied appliances of a complex civilisation.[173]

This vitriolic and potentially libellous allegation, which even its author later conceded contained 'an incautious expression . . . which I much regret having used', reverted to exactly the same lurid rhetoric that Mivart had employed, as has already been seen, in his own contribution to the *Contemporary* a year earlier to condemn those Darwinian evolutionists who articulated an 'increasingly Pagan' naturalistic worldview which was essentially the same as that expressed in the 'loathsome and revoltingly filthy verses' of Swinburne.[174] Still worse, such imputations were now being made against not only unspecified supporters of a Darwinian school, but individual members of Darwin's own family.

In Darwin's private autobiographical recollections, which were published posthumously in 1887, it was claimed that, throughout his scientific career, he had 'almost always been treated honestly by my reviewers' and that he 'rejoice[d] that I have avoided controversies' which 'rarely did any good and caused a miserable loss of time and temper'.[175] Significantly, though, Darwin's original manuscript, which was never intended for publication and was expurgated by his eldest son Francis, had included a single exception to this general absence of controversy and rancour: 'I must, however, except Mr Mivart.'[176] In fact, Mivart's lurid and hyperbolic attack on George so enraged Darwin *père* that, in a peculiarly vicious and personal confrontation, he orchestrated his former follower's ostracism from polite society, ensuring that Mivart would continue to be blackballed from the Athenaeum Club and deliberately 'tak[ing] every opportunity', as he told Edward Burnett Tylor, 'of saying how false a man I consider him to be'.[177] From this point on, as Mivart later recalled, all 'manifestations of friendly feeling ceased' between himself and Darwin's influential circle of colleagues and supporters.[178] Darwin was even ready similarly to 'cut' Murray, and requested that his publisher print a clarification in the very next number of the *Quarterly* which, in terms that Darwin helped his son to draft, denied that 'any thought or word' in George's original article could possibly 'lend itself to the support of the nameless crimes . . . referred to'.[179] Never before had Darwin become so embroiled in such a personal and spiteful controversy, and what Browne has termed the 'Mivart episode' has long been recognized by historians as revealing much about the underlying tensions and concerns of the evolutionary debates of the late nineteenth century.[180]

Darwin's unusually vehement reaction to Mivart's own characteristically sordid insinuations certainly gives perhaps the clearest indication of just how exasperated he had become, three years after the *Descent*'s publication, with the innumerable accusations, made against the book, himself and even his own family, of impropriety, indecency and sexual immorality. Historians have suggested that the ferocity of the confrontation reflected Darwin's sense of personal betrayal at Mivart's earlier defection from his circle of supporters, but for Darwin the fundamental issue at stake was simply Mivart's 'infamous & explicit accusation' regarding George's apparent endorsement of vice and prostitution.[181] There was actually, as Darwin advised his son, only one 'accusation which it seems necessary for you to rebut, i.e. about licentiousness'.[182] Darwin was particularly concerned at reports that at least 'one person has been disgusted and horrified at George, from believing in the *Quarterly*', and, having himself endured similarly damaging insinuations for the last three years, he seems to have felt compelled to adopt an especially hard line against this particular aspect of Mivart's long-running campaign to undermine both natural selection and the Darwinian understanding of evolution more generally.[183]

Huxley, Darwin's most vociferous supporter in this and many other controversies, likewise identified Mivart's imputation of encouraging sexual immorality as the specific accusation which necessitated such an urgent and resolute response. Huxley's rhetorical strategy, though, was simply to turn the tables and suggest that, beneath a thin veneer of priggish respectability, it was actually Mivart himself who transgressed public standards of taste and decency. While George Darwin was known to his friends for his 'somewhat ascetic habits', Huxley maintained in the *Academy*, his deceitful accuser adopted a 'high moral tone' but nevertheless 'outrages decency by insinuations' which merely betray his 'blind animosity against all things Darwinian'.[184] Huxley was already confirmed in his opinion of Mivart's priggish moral hypocrisy long before the controversy over George's article, insisting, in 1871, that if men were to act upon Mivart's anti-evolutionary axiom that moral actions are never instinctive and are always directed by a conscious act of will 'they will simply become a set of most unendurable prigs'.[185] In private, Huxley and others in the Darwinian inner circle regularly articulated even more damning opinions of their former colleague's duplicity, with Darwin noting how Mivart had once been 'flattering, almost fawning' and Huxley observing, with evident distaste, that he 'sticks to me like a leech and thanks me all over – having no doubt ends in view'.[186] Mivart's subsequent betrayal and scandalous attack on George, as John Tyndall remarked, was simply the 'natural outflow of his character'.[187] While Mivart himself insisted that he '*never dreamed* of implying anything whatever *against Mr. Darwin personally*', and instead maintained that George was no doubt a man 'of the highest character' who had 'advocate[d] principles without in the least degree realizing their consequences', his Darwinian opponents were clearly determined to make his own apparently defective personal character and morality a defining feature of the ostensibly scientific controversy.[188]

Unlike Darwin, Huxley had an excellent and wide-ranging knowledge of literary culture, and another aspect of his rhetorical strategy against

Mivart was to associate his adversary with particular literary archetypes of hypocrisy and duplicity. In the *Academy*, he noted disdainfully of the 'high moral tone' adopted by Mivart in his impertinent *Quarterly* article that even 'Joseph Surface could not have done better', thereby identifying both Mivart's motives and actions with the treacherous and hypocritical gentleman whose falsely moral sentiments are finally exposed at the conclusion of Richard Brinsley Sheridan's *A School for Scandal* (1777).[189] Similarly, when Mivart wrote to Huxley in December 1874, in a letter marked 'Private & Confidential', attempting to justify his regrettable lapse of judgement, Huxley angrily scrawled '*Tartuffe redivivus*' in purple ink across the top of the first page. Tartuffe, the eponymous impostor in Molière's 1664 dramatic comedy, was, of course, an odious religious hypocrite whose apparent piety merely masked his lust and obsession with the pleasures of the flesh, and Huxley's outraged addendum to Mivart's missive implied that it was in fact Mivart himself, rather than any of the proponents of Darwinism, who, like a latter-day Tartuffe, was secretly preoccupied with sex.

What perhaps provoked Huxley's particular indignation was Mivart's insistence, in the same apparently contrite letter, that even if he had been mistaken about George Darwin's views:

With respect to 'hideous sexual criminality' I may say that I know a most highly cultured and intellectual man, of the school I intend to oppose, who deliberately maintains that the propagation of the criminality referred to [i.e. prostitution] would be most useful and beneficial to society as tending to limit population without requiring what he calls the 'immorality' of ascetic self-denial.[190]

Even in a rueful letter of apology written on Christmas Eve, Mivart was unable to refrain from making still more sordid insinuations regarding the apparent sexual depravity of the supporters of evolutionary theory, and Huxley, as chapter five will suggest, was probably well aware of the particular member of the Darwinian circle whose radical opinions on prostitution Mivart seems to have had in mind.

The uncharacteristic vitriol of Darwin's response to Mivart's attack on his son's apparent advocacy of immoral forms of checking overpopulation has generally been interpreted as revealing his powerful sense of personal betrayal – as well as sheer anxiety – at his former follower's defection and subsequent incarnation as perhaps the most effectual scientific critic of Darwinian evolution. However, by locating the so-called 'Mivart episode' within the wider context of the persistent attacks made on the *Descent*'s moral propriety that have been examined in this chapter we can also understand Darwin's exceptionally agitated response as an indication of just how deeply perturbed he had become by his entanglement throughout the early 1870s with the issues of immorality, indecency and sexual licentiousness. Mivart's notorious allegations against George, which drew on exactly the same lurid rhetoric he had already employed in tainting Darwinian evolution by association with Swinburne's scandalous verse, were not in any way unusual, and, as this chapter has suggested, can instead be seen as the culmination of the similarly sordid criticisms which began with the *Descent's* publication over three years earlier.

Such accusations of encouraging sexual immorality had become increasingly integral to the opposition to Darwinism in the early 1870s, and Darwin may have viewed Mivart's fallacious and misjudged jibes as the perfect opportunity to put an end to this irksome vein of criticism. Others amongst his supporters, though, seem not always to have taken the matter quite so seriously, with Huxley mocking Mivart's contention that Darwinian 'speculations are to bring back among us the gross profligacy of Imperial Rome', and considering, with ironic anxiety, whether his own evolutionary views 'should land me in the cruelties of Caligula, and lead me to . . . indulg[e] in Heliogabalian gluttony'.[191] Darwin had earlier warned Huxley that 'great is the power of misrepresentation', and, despite the tone of contemptuous ridicule which Huxley adopted towards any suggestion that the worldview of scientific naturalism was intrinsically pagan and therefore necessarily immoral, precisely this allegation, as the following chapter will show, was starting to become both extremely prevalent and highly problematic for other members of Darwin's circle of friends and supporters.[192]

CHAPTER 3

John Tyndall, Walter Pater and the
nineteenth-century revival of paganism

In September 1874, a month after delivering the Presidential Address to the British Association for the Advancement of Science in Belfast, John Tyndall sat in the Athenaeum Club reflecting on the 'numberless strictures and accusations, some of them exceeding fierce' to which he was now, almost every day, subjected. The Address, and most notably its radical assertion that the 'promise and potency of all terrestrial Life' is inherent in matter and does not require a distinct creative act, had, Tyndall conceded, 'provoked an unexpected amount of criticism'.[1] The apparent materialism of Tyndall's Address, as Ruth Barton and Stephen S. Kim have both pointed out, was carefully qualified by his insistence that all phenomena have their roots in a vaguely understood cosmic life.[2] But this concession was to be virtually ignored by what Tyndall later termed the 'roaring lions of Belfast'.[3] Instead, a torrent of furious indignation had quickly erupted from pulpits of various denominations, as well as from across much of the print media, accusing Tyndall of peddling irresponsible and dangerously anti-Christian doctrines. As Tyndall told his close friend Thomas Archer Hirst: 'you can form no notion of the religious agitation. Every pulpit in Belfast thundered of me.'[4] One complainant even urged Tyndall's prosecution for blasphemy and inferred that his denial of divine authority would only be punished adequately by his being shot.[5] With the Belfast Address, as Frank M. Turner has claimed, Tyndall 'succeeded in sparking perhaps the most intense debate of the Victorian conflict of science and religion', and for a period his notoriety as a controversialist eclipsed even that of his friend and colleague Thomas Henry Huxley.[6]

The controversy surrounding the Address that Tyndall delivered in Belfast's Ulster Hall, and its relation to the larger context of nineteenth-century scientific and theological disputes, has, unsurprisingly, attracted considerable historiographic attention. Historians have examined not only the precise philosophical underpinnings of Tyndall's alleged materialism, but also the role of the press in determining the reception of the Address, as well as how differing responses to it were shaped by specific cultural geographies.[7] One important element of the Address and its reception, however, has rarely figured in these accounts: the explicit connection that Tyndall made between the conclusions of modern science and the atomism advanced by ancient authorities such as the Greek philosopher Epicurus and the Roman poet Lucretius. This contentious parallel, as will be explored in this chapter, was a recurrent concern of many of the most hostile criticisms of the Belfast Address, and the exposure of its apparent absurdity afforded an expedient opportunity for discrediting Tyndall's wider scientific naturalist programme, especially for those among his adversaries whose educational training had largely consisted of classical literature rather than modern physical sciences.

In the wake of his controversial Address, Tyndall was widely pilloried for presenting an intellectual anachronism as a manifestation of mental progress at a meeting supposedly dedicated to the advancement of science. The doctrines of atomism had been discarded amidst the decay of the Roman Empire, and would not now, so it was claimed, satisfy the vastly more complex intellectual requirements of the nineteenth century. The resemblance between aspects of classical and contemporary science celebrated by Tyndall in fact merely undermined the pretensions of modern thought. This censure of the scientific revival of an ancient understanding of the natural world, as Turner has pointed out, had several polemical advantages:

The scientific publicists would lose the benefit of novelty, and their modernity would stand discredited. Liberal Christians could make themselves appear more intellectually advanced and even modern than men of science . . . the defenders of religion would achieve a new, much needed self-assurance and self-confidence from knowledge that they opposed a philosophy that Christianity had overcome in the past and by implication could overcome again.[8]

The extensive deprecation of Tyndall's rediscovery of classical atomism, though, had a further, and extremely significant, polemical advantage that Turner has overlooked, and which will be the main focus of this chapter.

The classical world served principally, of course, as an exemplar of the political, educational, and artistic values, amongst many others, which the Victorian age most revered.[9] But many aspects of the period, and especially that of the late Roman Empire, were far less acceptable to the nineteenth century, as had been revealed most shockingly by the archaeological excavations at Pompeii and Herculaneum since the middle of the previous century. The debauchery of Roman life and thought was also confirmed by evangelical historians tracing the emergence of the early Church, who depicted 'an epoch of which the horror and the degeneration have rarely been equalled, and perhaps never exceeded, in the annals of mankind'.[10] In such partisan historical accounts, as Matthew Arnold remarked ironically, 'what a sink of iniquity was the whole pagan world', and he noted how the colours of their picture are 'laid on very thick', with incessant examples of 'how one Roman fed his oysters on his slaves, how another put a slave to death that a curious friend might see what dying was like', but no mention of instances of 'virtue in individuals' like Marcus Aurelius's mother.[11] Even Arnold nevertheless acknowledged the 'manifest failure' of the 'carnal and pagan sense', with its blithe 'religion of pleasure', in affording the same 'general, popular, religious sentiment' which would later be provided by the Christian emphasis on sorrow, and he conceded that 'Pompeii was a sign that . . . the measure of sensualism had been over-passed' and Roman civilization had fallen into extremes of corruption.[12]

Nor was the earlier Hellenistic era entirely exempt from similar disparagement, for 'Rome', according to the same evangelical historian of early Christianity quoted above, had 'learnt from Greece her voluptuous corruption'.[13] Evolutionary accounts of the development and decline of various nations also identified the later Greeks as a race for whom, as William Rathbone Greg observed, 'luxury and success had nearly extinguished' their 'hard energy', and Charles Darwin, in *The Descent of Man* (1871), concurred that the 'Greeks may have retrograded . . . from extreme sensuality'.[14] Classical Greece and Rome, as both Church historians and the proponents of evolution agreed, had exhibited symptoms of moral corruption and degeneracy alongside their many cultural and political achievements. This dark side of the ancient world, the 'little puzzle' which confronts the 'reverend tutors' who offer a moral training in the classics in Byron's *Don Juan* (1819), had a variety of potential uses.[15] It could, for instance, be used to undermine any attempt, like that of Tyndall, to arrogate the conventional cultural authority of ancient authors, long the exclusive preserve of the Anglican establishment schooled in the classics at Oxford and Cambridge, on behalf of modern scientific thought. With only those possessing the appropriate literary training able to distinguish ancient writers who were spiritually uplifting from those that were depraved and dissolute, it would become clear that the growing cultural and moral authority of narrowly educated men of science might pose considerable dangers to the future prospects of Victorian Britain.

More significantly, the Victorian exponents of Epicurean *physics* could also be portrayed by their opponents as implicitly advocating the disreputable hedonist *ethics* long ascribed to that school. Epicurus had actually promoted merely the avoidance of pain and the pursuit of an abstemious happiness, although the prominence given to pleasure in his ethical maxims had allowed adversaries – first Stoics, and then Christians – to interpret the Epicurean philosophy as a dangerous inducement to sensual excess. Even Alfred Tennyson's sombre dramatic monologue 'Lucretius', which was first published in 1868, implied that the 'sober majesties / Of settled, sweet, Epicurean life' would always ultimately descend into a corrosive sexual abandon.[16] The alleged unwholesomeness of the classical authorities whom Tyndall had chosen to endorse so publicly could only confirm lingering suspicions regarding the moral tendency of materialism and unbelief, as well as allowing opponents to cast damaging aspersions on Tyndall's own personal reputation. Indeed, Tyndall's advocacy of the atomistic understanding of the natural world was readily equated with support for the immoral sensualism that had, it was claimed, precipitated the downfall of classical antiquity and might now similarly endanger Britain's own imperial destiny.

Similar associations with the moral corruption of the classical world had, as was noted in the opening chapter, already been exploited by Richard Owen in his attacks on Huxley and other rival palaeontologists in the 1850s, while accusations of reawakening the immoral lusts of the pagan world were, as was seen in the previous chapter, made against Darwin as well as members of his family. However, the particular correlation of Tyndall with ancient immorality that began in 1874 was much more prevalent and would prove to be even more enduring. In only the previous year, moreover, the aesthetic philosophy adumbrated in Walter Pater's *Studies in the History of the Renaissance* (1873), which urged that maximizing the intensity of experience was the only valid aspiration of this brief existence and advocated the sensual enjoyment of art above all else, had been widely reviled for offering nothing more than a modern revival of the insidious hedonism of Epicurus. As this chapter will argue, exactly the same insinuations of pagan sensualism that were levelled at Pater were later used to admonish Tyndall and his Belfast Address, and the widespread connection of Epicurus with the scandalous doctrines of late nineteenth-century aestheticism provided a context in which attacks on Tyndall's identification of the Greek philosopher as a forerunner of scientific naturalism might prove even more damaging. In fact, the controversies over the pagan precursors of modern science and aestheticism were often linked explicitly, with an article in the *Cornhill Magazine* in 1878 observing that

Just as we have had the atomic theory . . . of Democritus and Epicurus . . . reha-
bilitated in nineteenth-century English, as the newest thing in science . . . so, in
literature and art, more than half of the disputations . . . are neither more nor
less than revivals of old discussions with new names. One of the most fashionable
fallacies that have recently cropped up . . . has been discussed under the attractive
and, to some extent misleading title of: 'Art for Art's Sake'.[17]

Despite such clear connections being made between the Belfast Address
and the amoral aesthetic creed made famous by Pater in only the previous
year, Tyndall would nevertheless go on to defend his reputation, and that
of his scientific position, against imputations of paganism in a remarkably
similar way to that later employed by Pater in his novel *Marius the Epicurean*
(1885).

EXPLODED DELUSIONS OF PRIMITIVE HEATHENISM

A profound distaste for anything pertaining to pagan beliefs had characterized the evangelical movement of the early nineteenth century, and the
imminent revival of a debauched paganism remained a surprisingly pervasive concern in late Victorian Britain. This was not only the case with regard
to art and literature, where pagan themes and motifs had competed with
Christian ones since at least the Renaissance, but also in relation to science
and naturalistic thought more generally. As an article on 'The Survival of
Paganism' in the November 1875 number of *Fraser's Magazine* warned, the
'old Paganism was never exploded, never overcome and slain in single combat by Christianity', and had instead merely 'retired into the background to
await under altered conditions new developments and find new alliances'.[18]
Revived amidst the 'bright and cultured' atmosphere of Renaissance Italy,
pagan beliefs, according to the *Fraser's* article, had attracted fervent disci-
ples throughout the following three centuries, although it was only in the
more scientific climate of the nineteenth century that this re-emergence
had become really conspicuous:

The old mythology stripped of its imagery (it may be said), unidealized and resolved
into its pristine elements, is a system of natural philosophy; and modern science in
its latest phase is little more than a return to the old opinions under a new nomen-
clature. It would be strange indeed if the rumour of Pan's death, promulgated so
long ago, should prove unfounded after all![19]

This scientific paganism would inevitably have deleterious social and moral
consequences that were already starting to become obvious. The disdain that was increasingly felt towards the ideals of Christian marriage,
complained one pamphlet on the subject, was but another of the 'evil

fruits of that popular "Nature"-worship, which is nothing but paganism according to nineteenth century notions'.[20] With the decline of Christian standards of morality, it was implied, humanity might cast off all restraint, including conjugal monogamy, and descend once more into the debauchery of the old pagan world.

Even prior to the Belfast Address, the main proponents of Darwinism and scientific naturalism, and Tyndall especially, were already being represented as enthusiastic adherents of this disquieting revival of paganism. As St George Mivart observed in the *Contemporary Review* in 1873, 'there is little doubt that the prevailing tone of sentiment has long been increasingly Pagan', and he urged that this was an inevitable consequence of the naturalistic tendency of modern science:

the whole modern movement from the humanists of the Renaissance to the present day has been and is a Pagan revival; the reappearance of a passionate love for and a desire to rest in and thoroughly sympathize with mere nature, accompanied by a more or less complete and systematic rejection of the supernatural, its aspirations, its consolations, and its terrors.[21]

This exclusive concern with the natural world also entailed an implicit revival of ancient pagan idolatry which, tellingly, could be readily accommodated with the specific theories and language of scientific naturalism. In the absence of traditional Christian Revelation, Mivart proposed, 'a new Pagan cultus may, should its need be felt, be . . . evolved in connexion with the Philosophy of Mr. [Herbert] Spencer', while

what more worthy symbol of beneficent modes of the Unknowable could be selected for an object of worship than the Sun? . . . For its worship some revival of antique rites might be gradually engrafted on existing forms – for the principle of continuity must be recognized and acted on – while glowing passages from the works of Professor Tyndall may well supply antiphons and suggest hymns for its ritual.[22]

Tyndall, with his well-known penchant for effusive and quasi-religious rhetoric, was portrayed by Mivart as a high priest of the pagan sun-deity whose cult had been briefly established as the supreme religion of Rome by the notoriously depraved emperor Heliogabalus (the subject of a languorous 1866 painting by the aesthetic artist Simeon Solomon). Tyndall's lengthy panegyric on the supreme importance of the sun in *Heat Considered as a Mode of Motion* (1863), in which he drew on Greek mythology in eulogizing the remarkable 'mechanical force' by which this 'Proteus works his spells', might even constitute a new heathen prayer book for what Mivart termed the 'naturalistic Pagan revival' of the nineteenth century.[23]

Mivart, as has already been seen in the previous chapter, had discerned the 'most hideous features' of the licentious modern culture allegedly inaugurated by Darwinian science amidst the 'loathsome and revoltingly filthy verses' of Swinburne. He similarly represented Pater, widely regarded as a leading member of Swinburne's dissolute aesthetic clique, as a 'sympathetic historian' of the recovery of pagan beliefs which reached its apotheosis in Tyndall's heliocentric eulogy.[24] Such a revival of ancient attitudes would, according to Mivart, inevitably 'approach little by little towards the worst phases of Paganism, as the corruption of morals gradually increase[d]' and dangerous ideas like 'Free-love' and the 'hatred of marriage' gained wider acceptance.[25] Remarkably, it was against this fraught background of widespread concern with paganism that Tyndall, occupying, as President of the British Association, a public platform of enormous prestige and visibility, chose to draw attention to, and even celebrate, the apparent parallels between the understanding of the natural world in pagan antiquity and the most advanced conclusions of contemporary science.

It was not actually until the autumn of 1868 that Tyndall had first encountered the 'old Sage' Lucretius, 'a translation of whose work "de rerum natura"', as he explained in a letter to Hirst, 'fell into my hands a few days ago'. This poetic exposition of Epicurean principles, Tyndall reported, was 'to me . . . *intensely* interesting', with 'wonderfully interesting thoughts flash[ing] out . . . here and there'. The most noteworthy aspect of the book, which Tyndall read in H. A. J. Munro's 1864 translation, was that Lucretius had 'deduced the world and all that therein is . . . from the "fortuitous concourse of atoms"', and, as Tyndall added, 'of course I am at home among these.'[26] In fact, earlier in 1868 the *Spectator* had remarked that the 'poetry of Lucretius reads as if it might almost have been published by some imaginative devotee of modern science, – say, some poetic Tyndall of our own days'.[27] At precisely the same time, however, Fleeming Jenkin, a leading member of the 'North British' group of Presbyterian physicists and engineers who consistently challenged the intellectual credibility of the largely metropolitan advocates of scientific naturalism, attempted to appropriate Lucretius as an ancient antecedent of the rival physical theories of James Clerk Maxwell and William Thomson.[28] In 'The Atomic Theory of Lucretius', published in the *North British Review* for March 1868, Jenkin contended that the description of unaccountably swerving atoms in the opening book of *De Rerum Natura* showed that the Roman poet 'desire[d] to devise an explanation of Free-will' that was fundamentally at odds with Tyndall's own materialist and deterministic outlook.[29]

Now, six years later, Tyndall used the opening section of his Presidential Address in Belfast to reclaim Lucretius as a precursor of his own particular views, and to map out a highly tendentious narrative of heroic scientific triumph from Lucretius, and his Greek predecessors Democritus and Epicurus, to such celebrated nineteenth-century thinkers as Darwin. Tyndall was a loyal member of Darwin's inner circle of supporters, and, whilst preparing his script for Belfast, had asked that Darwin himself might 'glance over that portion of the address which relates to you', receiving fervent thanks for his eulogistic account of how the 'discernment of new truth . . . colours and warms the pages of Mr. Darwin' (44).[30] Charles Lyell would later write to congratulate Darwin on Tyndall's 'manly and fearless' Address at the Belfast meeting, which, he insisted, gave 'an ovation' to 'you and your theory of evolution'.[31] But nor was the Belfast Address's appraisal of apparently like-minded ancient philosophers any less laudatory. Commencing in fifth-century BC Athens, Tyndall maintained that certain 'free-thinking and courageous men' became dissatisfied with the 'anthropomorphic form' of current ideas concerning the universe. There 'grew with the growth of scientific notions', he went on, 'a desire and determination to sweep from the field of theory this mob of gods and demons, and to place natural phenomena on a basis more congruent with themselves'. In 'the depths of history', Tyndall discerned the beginnings of a rigorously naturalistic explanation of the universe which eschewed any form of supernatural intervention (1–2).

Democritus, Epicurus and Lucretius were the chief exponents of this epistemology in the ancient world. Between them, they developed an 'atomic philosophy' which asserted that atoms in empty space, combining in accordance with mechanical laws, were the materials from which all things are constructed (4). Both organic and inorganic bodies were compounds of these everlasting atoms which continually disperse and enter into new combinations. Epicurus considered that this philosophy, which teaches that 'Nature pursues her course in accordance with everlasting laws, the gods never interfering', could 'free the world from superstition and the fear of death' (6). These brave and heroic thinkers, according to Tyndall's account, established a scientific agenda which expunged the primitive idea of capricious divinities operating in the natural world for several centuries.

Tyndall explicitly connected these prophetic ancient physical doctrines with some of the leading developments of nineteenth-century science. Democritus's propositions, he observed, 'are a fair general statement of the atomic philosophy, as now held' (4). Likewise, Empedocles's proposition that combinations of atoms which are suited to their environment adhere for longer than unsuited compounds was equated by Tyndall with modern theories of evolution: 'more than 2,000 years ago the doctrine of the

"survival of the fittest", which in our day, not on the basis of vague conjecture, but of positive knowledge, has been raised to such extraordinary
significance, had received at all events partial enunciation' (5). One of Tyndall's most important sources for the Belfast Address had been particularly
insistent on this parallel between ancient and modern science. The German
historian Friedrich Albert Lange's *History of Materialism* ('to the spirit and
to the letter of which', Tyndall acknowledged, 'I am equally indebted' (3))
stated:

> *Out of nothing arises nothing; nothing that is can be destroyed. All change is only*
> *combination and separation of atoms* [Democritus]. This proposition . . . contains
> in principle the two great doctrines of modern physics – the theory of the inde-
> structibility of matter, and that of the persistence of force (the conservation of
> energy).[32]

In his Address, Tyndall used this historical connection to identify Victorian
scientific naturalists not as radical innovators, but rather as part of a lengthy
tradition of naturalistic thought which predated the Christian beliefs of
their parvenu clerical adversaries.

Tyndall's highly partial narrative of intellectual history privileged the
exponents of classical atomism and denigrated the ancient founders of
metaphysics and psychological dualism. Plato and Aristotle, according to
Tyndall, had initiated an abstract anti-scientific approach to the fundamental questions of existence, which gained influence only after the more
solid atomic philosophy had been devastated by Attila and the barbarian hordes. Their pernicious metaphysical 'yoke', he observed, 'remains to
some extent unbroken to the present hour' and could still be discerned
in the 'degrading . . . spiritualism' that had prompted such widespread
interest in Victorian Britain (10–12). However, the darkness into which the
mind of Western man had been cast since the barbarian destruction of
Greek scientific reasoning was periodically dispersed by the true light of
science. Properly scientific ways of thinking, Tyndall insisted, re-emerged
in the Renaissance with the 'epoch making work' of Copernicus, Bruno,
Descartes and others, while the old atomic theory was revived in the work
of Pierre Gassendi (19).

It was, above all, Gassendi's recovery of the atomic philosophy that
had underwritten the development of the physical sciences in the nineteenth century, and Tyndall contended: 'In our day there are secessions
from the [atomic] theory, but it still stands firm . . . In fact, it may be
doubted whether, wanting this fundamental conception, a theory of the
material universe is capable of scientific statement' (26–7). Later in the

Belfast Address, Tyndall expressed reservations concerning the simplistic ontological materialism advanced by ancient philosophers, especially in an imaginary dialogue between Bishop Butler and a disciple of Lucretius on the issue of consciousness. He nevertheless made it clear that most of what he styled the 'grand generalizations' of 'our day' were, in essence, experimentally verified developments of the old pagan conception of atoms combining in empty space (45). The immense advances made by modern science, which Tyndall commemorated so imperiously in the final sections of the Address, had their origin, it was claimed proudly, in a philosophy of matter that was over two thousand years old.

When Tyndall eventually sat down in the Ulster Hall after delivering the stirring peroration to his Presidential Address – in which he insisted that 'religious theories . . . which embrace notions of cosmogony . . . must . . . submit to the control of science' – his bellicose words prompted an unstoppable storm of controversy that would last for several years (61). Amidst the relentless accusations of materialism, blasphemy and unbelief (as well as occasional calls for ecumenical conciliation), Tyndall was also assailed for intellectual hubris and even plain ignorance, particularly in heralding the failed theories of an archaic past as the very latest manifestations of scientific progress. Indeed, while Jenkin's article on Lucretius in the *North British Review* had cautiously insisted that, despite the many apparent similarities, there remained a 'vast difference between the old hazy speculations and the endeavours of modern science', Tyndall was perceived to have brazenly disregarded such evident historical distinctions.[33] The Scottish theologian John Tulloch, writing in *Blackwood's Edinburgh Magazine*, contended that Tyndall merely 'hang[s] out . . . old rags of Democritism as if they were new flags of scientific triumph'.[34] It was 'curious to trace the revival of the Atomic Philosophy and the rejuvenescence of its great leaders, Democritus and Epicurus', Tulloch observed, 'but it is surely absurd for our modern Positive philosophers, with their advanced ideas, to make so much of these ancient names.'[35] The editor of the *Edinburgh Review*, Henry Reeve, similarly expressed surprise that the most recent manifestations of so-called intellectual advancement merely reproduced 'the exploded delusions of primitive heathenism'.[36] This curiously anachronistic reliance on the obsolete philosophies of ancient Greece and Rome, agreed commentators like Tulloch and Reeve, made clear just how little the modern scientific thought represented by Tyndall had actually advanced in the intervening millennia.

Reeve's opinions of the ethics of modern science have already been noted in the previous chapter, and his article in the *Edinburgh* also discerned an implicit, but nonetheless highly significant, association between Tyndall's endorsement of ancient atomism and the notoriously dissipated ethics of the pagan world. In a discussion of the 'Lucretian doctrines of Professor Tyndall', Reeve complained: 'Are we to return to Paganism or something behind Paganism – to the flux of Heraclitus, the *voûs* of Anaxagoras, or the atoms of Democritus – are we to take our morals from Epicurus and our gods from Lucretius?'[37] Atomism, Reeve implied, was only one component of the ancient world's larger intellectual outlook and could not be detached from the period's other beliefs and principles. These, of course, included the moral teachings of Epicurus, which, so it had long been claimed, encouraged a bestial emphasis on earthly pleasure. Atomism and Epicurean ethics were inextricably linked together in the general pagan mindset, and could not, as Tyndall had misguidedly attempted, be considered in isolation from each other.

Tyndall, perhaps anticipating such cavils regarding the respectability of the ancient authorities he had chosen to endorse, had assured his auditors at Belfast (amongst whom, as *The Times* noted, there were '600 ladies') that 'Democritus looked to the soul as the ennobling part of man; even beauty without understanding partook of animalism.'[38] He similarly contradicted the allegations of innumerable Christian polemics against Epicurus, and insisted that the Greek philosopher 'rated the spirit above the body; the pleasure of the body was that of the moment, while the spirit could draw upon the future and the past' (5–6). But critics like Reeve, whose *Edinburgh* article derided Tyndall's reliance on 'meagre compilations on the history of philosophy' and other 'inadequate materials . . . to sound the depths of Greek philosophy', could easily maintain that Tyndall – who, after all, had read Lucretius's *De Rerum Natura* only in Munro's standard translation – was in no position to arbitrate on the finer points of classical ethics.[39] Reeve, moreover, was to be by no means the only critic of the Belfast Address who inferred that the ancient physical doctrines to which Tyndall had paid such an effusive tribute might, even inadvertently, help uproot nineteenth-century standards of morality. In fact, many other detractors of the Belfast Address were to be far less oblique in making the same damaging connection between Tyndall's scientific doctrines and the iniquities of the pagan world.

EAT, DRINK, AND BE MERRY

Tyndall's antagonistic Address had been delivered in a city that was famous as a hotbed of both Catholicism and Calvinism, and the pulpits of Belfast soon reverberated with sermons imprecating Tyndall and his apparently materialist conclusions. It was, as even the supportive Lyell acknowledged, no 'wonder that the Belfast clergy of the Calvinistic school . . . preached against such opinions'.[40] Many of these sermons, both Calvinist and Catholic, also drew parallels between classical atomism and the infamous sensualism long regarded as one of the principal reasons for the decline and fall of pagan antiquity. The Catholic Bishops of Ireland, led by Cardinal Paul Cullen, issued a Pastoral which claimed that Tyndall's scientific doctrines were 'born of a corrupt paganism' that had the potential to 'ruin . . . society' and incite 'a universal unchaining of all the worst passions, ravenous for satisfaction', and Cullen himself fasted for three days to ward off such pernicious influences of the Address.[41] Similarly, while Tyndall had extolled the rejection of the primitive notion of anthropomorphic deities operating in the natural world as evidence of human progress, Calvinist theologians, with their emphasis on man's fallen condition, contended that it would leave him bereft of any sense of moral responsibility. Without a metaphysical criterion for morality, they warned, civic society would soon collapse under the intolerable burden of man's unconstrained sinfulness.

In a sermon preached at Belfast's Fisherwick Place Church, Robert Watts, Professor of systematic theology at Belfast Presbyterian College, made an explicit connection between Tyndall and Epicurus:

Epicureanism, as interpreted and expounded by the poet Lucretius, constitutes the warp and the woof of Professor Tyndall's philosophy. His mission, like that of Epicurus, is to rid the world of the gods. Epicurus aimed at the extirpation of the gods of Greece; Dr. Tyndall aims at the extirpation of the Jehovah of the Bible.

As part of this wider Epicurean agenda, Watts argued, Tyndall's apotheosis of a pre-Christian conception of the universe, as well as his own more recent materialist doctrines, would inevitably entail a revival of the debauched ethics of the ancient world. Indeed, Tyndall's perfidious Address had, according to Watts, the potential to lead the inhabitants of nineteenth-century Belfast astray and even to cast them into a sordid pit of pagan depravity. He declared:

The very name of Epicure has become a synonym for sensualist. The system has wrought the ruin of the communities and individuals who have acted out its principles in the past; and if the people of Belfast substitute it for the holy religion of the Son of God, and practice its degrading dogmas, the moral destiny of the metropolis of Ulster may be easily forecast.[42]

Despite his lurid rhetoric and gloomy prognostications, Watts was in no way a marginal or eccentric participant in the disputes surrounding Tyndall's Address. Instead, he was widely regarded as Belfast's principal defender of orthodox Calvinism, as well as having earlier advocated more irenical relations between science and theology, and he challenged Tyndall to confront him in a local public debate and considered his subsequent refusal a tacit admission of defeat.[43]

Even expatriate members of the Irish Presbyterian Church soon became embroiled in the controversy fomented by Tyndall at Belfast. James McCosh, who had left Ulster in 1868 to become the President of Princeton College in New Jersey, issued a resolute response to Tyndall after having 'procured a copy' of his now notorious Address while 'about to set sail from Great Britain . . . on my return to America'.[44] Like his former colleague Watts, McCosh warned that, under the guise of scientific naturalism, the irreligious hedonism which had precipitated the degeneration of the Roman Empire might re-emerge to similar effect in the foremost imperial power of the nineteenth century. He claimed:

the Epicurean philosophy exercised an influence in deteriorating the character of the Romans, in hastening their ripeness into rottenness, and determining their fall; we can understand this when we look into these fragments of obscene Epicurean verses which have come out of the fires of Pompeii to testify against the inhabitants. We confess that we have fears of the results when the new physics come to crystallize into the creed of the rising generation, and to lead the literature and inspire the prevailing sentiment of the age.[45]

The modern physical sciences earnestly propounded by Tyndall and others were aligned with the miscellaneous obscenities which had shocked and bewildered archaeologists at Pompeii since the 1740s. By the 1860s these discomfiting artefacts had begun to be catalogued systematically, although precise knowledge of them was still generally confined to gentlemanly connoisseurs who had received a university education in the classics.[46] McCosh, however, strategically exploited the lurid myths and general notoriety concerning Pompeii's secret erotic relics that had developed amongst the wider population (cleverly implicating Epicurus in the depravity of first-century Rome) to insinuate that disgusting, although largely unspecified, forms of moral corruption were the inexorable consequences of the unbelief predicated by Tyndall's scientific doctrines. The same obscene 'drawings on the walls of Pompeii' had been used by Darwin, in *The Descent of Man*, as an example of the 'indecency' and 'licentiousness' of insufficiently evolved primitive societies, but to McCosh they instead provided a monitory instance from history of the degeneration that inevitably accompanied the general acceptance of a naturalistic and secular worldview.[47]

Nor were such insinuations concerning the Belfast Address confined to the older quarterly periodicals, Catholic edicts or fervid Calvinist sermons.

George Sexton, a leading London spiritualist and editor of the *Spiritual Magazine*, similarly lamented Tyndall's endorsement of 'the old Athenians', and maintained that their heretical doctrines, whether in ancient Greece or Victorian Britain, could lead only to sensual indulgence:

Epicurianism to-day means indulgence in the animal appetites to their utmost bounds . . . his philosophy was the search for pleasure, not for truth, and as such is calculated to mislead all who adopt it . . . Happiness he held to be the chief end and aim of man, and happiness with him was synonymous with pleasure, a doctrine both false and dangerous in the extreme.[48]

These similar denunciations of Tyndall's scientific creed from a wide variety of denominational perspectives can be located in a long tradition of Christian enmity towards Epicureanism, which dated back to the last centuries of the Roman Empire. In the closing years of the pagan world, the Epicurean conception of an empirically explainable natural world unaffected by impassive gods had been a rival epistemology to the emergent Christian doctrine of a divinely ordered universe. In particular, the Epicurean repudiation of any form of resurrection was wholly antagonistic to the early Church's insistence on the promise of an eternal hereafter. Paradoxically, the Victorian conflict between science and religion, which, as Turner and many others have pointed out, was largely a contest between theological and scientific publicists over which group of intellectuals should steer the increasingly urbanized and industrial nation through the vicissitudes of modernity, was fought out in precisely the same terms as this archaic dispute.[49]

Several critics of the Belfast Address also invoked specific passages from the New Testament in their rebuttals of Tyndall's implicit Epicureanism, and especially the warning of Saint Paul, in his first epistle to the Corinthians, that, lacking firm belief in the Resurrection, men would inevitably revert to the licentious pagan maxim: 'let us eat and drink; for to morrow we die' (I Corinthians 15:32).[50] This infamous hedonist slogan was ascribed to Tyndall's scientific principles with exasperating regularity. In a sermon preached at Wellington parish church in Somerset, Edwin Marriner employed it in exhorting his Anglican congregation to eschew the insidious unbelief recently propounded with so much publicity in far-away Belfast:

if there is no Hereafter . . . then, of what use are gifts, attainments, memories, studies, if they are all to be, as if they had never been, in a few short years? Why, then, we had better enjoy ourselves as mere animals, to the fullest possible extent, saying with the worn-out voluptuary, 'Vanity of Vanities!' . . . 'Let us eat and drink, for to morrow we die!'[51]

Like the fractious Corinthians of the first century, the parishioners of Wellington were admonished against embracing a debauched pagan belief system which denied the possibility of an eternal hereafter.

It was not merely in sermons, though, that this Pauline rhetoric was used to advance the pessimistic conjecture that, without the metaphysical buttress to morality afforded by the prospect of divine judgement in a spiritual afterlife, society would inevitably collapse under the burden of man's unfettered natural selfishness. A humorous 'Epistle in Verse' by James Casey also imputed such pagan depravity to Tyndall and other prominent representatives of modern science:

> . . . the folly and pride of those arrogant men
> Would fain make the world turn pagan again;
> Would unchain every vice, every passion release,
> And drive from the world all order and peace –

Casey's jaunty and irreverent doggerel went on to invoke precisely the same hedonist slogan used by the conservative clergyman Edwin Marriner. He maintained:

> If you preach to mankind there's no heaven nor hell,
> Will they cease to do evil or care to do well?
> And will they not rather repeat the old cry,
> 'Eat, drink, and be merry, to-morrow we die'?
> Does not reason then tell us how sad is the fate
> Of those who seek wisdom from Tyndall the great?[52]

Despite their self-conscious joviality, Casey's barbed couplets lampooned Tyndall's scientific position from the same eminently orthodox theological perspective that had been endorsed in numerous sermons and religious pamphlets. While the damaging association between the scientific naturalist agenda set out in the Belfast Address and the ruinous immorality of the ancient world had initially been made by classically educated critics who were alert to the varying reputations of different ancient authorities, it had now begun to permeate even popular culture and its proliferation would not be halted for several years to come.

When James Knowles, three years after the Belfast meeting of the British Association, solicited the opinions of a variety of experts on the vexed question of 'The Influence upon Morality of a Decline in Religious Belief' for his new monthly periodical the *Nineteenth Century*, many of the contributors reiterated exactly the same points that had been made against Tyndall's now infamous Presidential Address. Although not directly naming Tyndall, the High Church Liberal Lord Selborne voiced the familiar complaint that modern science could not provide a steadfast criterion for morality: 'If man were merely a higher order of the organisation of matter . . . what reality would there be in the conception of a moral law of obligation?' Significantly, Selborne also identified these naturalistic doctrines with the specifically Epicurean hedonism with which Tyndall had earlier been associated, and observed:

'Live while we may' – 'Let us eat and drink, for to-morrow we die' – are natural corollaries from the doctrine of Epicurus; whatever more refined conceptions that philosopher, or any of his followers, may have propounded. Such will ever be the effect, in the world generally, of a popular disbelief in the doctrines of immortality and retribution.[53]

Once again, scientific naturalism and its best-known proponents were tainted by their implicit association with the disreputable pagan shibboleths long ascribed to Epicurus, and Tyndall's valorization of classical physics in the Belfast Address was clearly still, even as late as 1877, being equated with support for such licentious hedonism.

THE FASCINATION OF CORRUPTION

Only a year before the Belfast Address, exactly the same accusations that would be made against Tyndall were used, with considerable effectiveness, to tarnish the reputation of a small volume of essays concerning the art and culture of sixteenth-century Italy: Walter Pater's *Studies in the History of the Renaissance*. Although Pater himself was a notoriously reclusive and self-effacing Oxford don, the essays in his book, many of which had originally appeared in liberal periodicals like the *Fortnightly Review*, contested John Ruskin's influential portrayal of the Renaissance in *The Stones of Venice* (1851–3) as a calamitous fall from the grace of the Gothic Middle Ages and instead boldly celebrated its apparent return to the liberty and unashamed sensuality – including homoeroticism – of the pagan world. Defying historiographic conventions, Pater's evocative and impressionistic essays traced the rebellious sensualism which purportedly characterized the Renaissance from Peter Abelard in medieval France to Johann Winckelmann in Enlightenment Germany, often dwelling on grotesque or recherché details that appealed to his own particular aesthetic predilections. This overtly subjective approach was justified in the 'Preface' to the book which insisted on the primacy of individual responses to art over the ostensibly shared aesthetic values enjoined by critics like Arnold.

Still more controversially, the volume's notorious 'Conclusion', which had initially been published in the *Westminster Review* as the concluding section of an unsigned review of William Morris's poetry, switched to the present day and apotheosized a life of refined connoisseurship brimming with aesthetic experience as the most astute response to the stark version of human existence predicated by recent scientific and philosophical discoveries. In it, Pater famously asserted:

. . . we are all *condamnés*, as Victor Hugo says: *les hommes sont tous condamnés à morte avec des sursis indéfinis*: we have an interval, and then our place knows us no more. Some spend this interval in listlessness, some in high passions, the wisest in art and song. For our one chance is in expanding that interval, in getting as many pulsations as possible into the given time.[54]

While such sentiments, self-indulgent of course but also ruthlessly cold-blooded in their terse acceptance of mortality and articulated in the sharp and trenchant tones of a homiletic sermon, had attracted little attention when they first appeared in the radical and anonymous *Westminster*, they were almost immediately denounced as a dangerous revival of the insidious doctrines of Epicurus once they were reprinted in a book whose title page not only named Pater but also identified him as a Fellow of Brasenose College.

Margaret Oliphant, reviewing Pater's volume for *Blackwood's*, reviled its 'new version of that coarse old refrain of the Epicureans' gay despair, "Let us eat and drink, for to-morrow we die"'.[55] Similarly, the *Examiner* likened Pater's ethical position to that of another ancient proponent of transitory pleasures, Aristippus of Cyrene, and designated his aesthetic creed 'Modern Cyrenaicism'.[56] Even the editor of the *Fortnightly*, John Morley, identified his regular contributor as an unabashed 'Hedonist', although this time in a relatively positive review of Pater's book.[57] While the blithely agnostic Morley seemed oblivious to the difficulties that this particular label might entail, Pater himself was only too aware of the insidious connotations attached to such ancient epithets, and he wished that critics 'wouldn't call me "a hedonist"; it produces such a bad effect on the minds of people who don't know Greek.'[58] Like Tyndall's scientific position in the following year, Pater's aesthetic philosophy was rebuked for attempting to overthrow the moral standards of Christianity and replace them with the debauched, and always ultimately unfulfilling, ethics of paganism.

In the 'Preface' to *Studies in the History of the Renaissance*, Pater self-consciously articulated his impressionistic approach to art in the language of empiricist science, insisting that the 'aesthetic critic' must 'distinguish, analyse and separate from its adjuncts' the particular sensation produced by a painting or book in the same way that a 'chemist notes some natural element'.[59] By continually scrutinizing and refining the subjective impressions which an art work evokes, Pater implied, the critic might actually approach a paradoxically disinterested, or even objective, mode of aesthetic knowledge. George Levine has argued that Pater's formulation drew strongly on a tradition of 'ascesis' within nineteenth-century scientific epistemology that urged 'an austere, rigorous restraint of the self that, from the basis of an inevitable subjectivity, issued in an impersonality that opened both to art and to truth'.[60] This fastidiously ascetic discipline, according to Levine, was fundamental to Pater's aesthetic approach to art. Richard A. Kaye, on the other hand, has instead suggested that 'Pater's sensualism is expressed in the terms of a detached scientist' only in order 'to protect himself against charges of emotionally charged hedonism' and Pater's insistence on an ascetic objectivity, Kaye implies, was merely a superficial and strategic affectation.[61]

Regardless of the sincerity or otherwise of Pater's engagement with scientific epistemology, the allegedly hedonistic tenets enunciated in his book were, for many reviewers, actually made worse by their implication with various aspects of contemporary science. As the *London Quarterly Review* observed, 'it would be hard to find a book so completely uninfluenced by the moral side of our nature', and it insisted that the impact of the 'most advanced modern science' was at the heart of Pater's flagrant amorality.[62] In *Blackwood's*, meanwhile, Oliphant characterized Pater's creed as 'elegant materialism', an aesthetic equivalent of precisely the same pejorative designation which Tyndall and other scientific naturalists had for many years, as was discussed in the first chapter, been most concerned to dissociate themselves from.[63] Even before the Belfast Address, then, the teachings of secular modern science were being widely associated with the immoral paganism that was allegedly to be found in Pater's recent collection of essays.

This was especially the case at the two ancient universities, where Pater's influence was most pervasive, and, of course, where the study of classical authors formed an integral element of the curriculum. Frederick William Farrar, the University Preacher at Cambridge, delivered three sermons in the spring of 1873 in which he lamented the advent of modern unbelief, and alluded more than once to Pater's recently published volume. It was, primarily, recent advances in science that Farrar saw at the root of 'the ever-widening scepticism of this generation', which was evident even amongst Cambridge's own undergraduates.[64] Naturalistic science, Farrar maintained, could not affirm the idealist truth which was necessary to morality in the Christian tradition, and could instead offer only a return to the ruinous pagan ethics advanced by Epicurus and his followers:

If we sin, what does it matter to blind infinite Forces which may crush us, but cannot love? . . . Are we any better than what the Greek atheist said we were, 'dumb animals, driven through the midnight upon a rudderless vessel, over a stormy sea'? 'Let us eat and drink, for to-morrow we die.'[65]

Alongside such familiar quotations from scripture and classical literature, Farrar's sermons, as Paul White has shown, were also seeded with 'large amounts of English verse recited from memory' and were 'noteworthy for their effect of sealing moral truths . . . with colourful illustrations from poetry' and other forms of contemporary literature.[66]

Perhaps once more quoting from memory, Farrar, in the very next paragraph of his 1873 sermon at Cambridge, implicitly connected Pater's aestheticism with the corrupt moral values of the Epicureans, as well as with nineteenth-century scientific naturalism. He admonished his undergraduate auditors:

And though these opinions, and such as these, have for the young all the 'fascination of corruption', – though they have all that destroying and agonising beauty which the great painter infused into the horror of the Gorgon's countenance, on which men must gaze though it turned them into stone, – yet God forbid that there should be many of you, my younger hearers, who should have subtly slidden into such treacherous unbeliefs.[67]

This passage, in which Farrar exhorted his youthful audience to eschew the siren voices of science and unbelief, contains an unattributed quotation from 'Lionardo Da Vinci', one of the essays that had recently been included in *Studies in the History of the Renaissance*. In it, Pater had remarked, apropos of Leonardo's painting *Medusa* in the Uffizi Gallery (now attributed to an unknown painter of the Flemish School): 'What may be called the fascination of corruption penetrates in every touch its exquisitely finished beauty.'[68] This characteristically Paterian expression, with its ambiguous affirmation of vice and degeneration and knowing escalation of the 'tempestuous loveliness of terror' which Percy Shelley had earlier discerned in the same painting, was used by Farrar to exemplify the insidious allure that unbelief, and its ensuing self-indulgence, might have for the impressionable young.[69] Despite its putative attribution to Leonardo and Shelley's 1819 poem 'On the Medusa of Leonardo da Vinci, in the Florentine Gallery', the actual painting discussed in Pater's essay was little known in Victorian Britain, with no engraved reproductions appearing to have been published during the nineteenth century. Pater's highly-wrought description of the

Leonardoesque rendering of the Greek gorgon nevertheless provided Farrar with an apposite symbol of the moral petrifaction that awaited those unfortunates who were seduced by the dogmas of contemporary science.

Yet Farrar was by no means a narrowly conservative evangelical, and his philological research on the origin of language had enabled him, like fellow liberal Anglicans such as Charles Kingsley, to develop a close friendship with Darwin – he would later deliver the sermon at Darwin's funeral – and other leading men of science.[70] In the same sermons at Cambridge, he even commended the 'great thinker who originated the theory [of evolution], and whose name it is impossible to mention without admiration and respect'. Darwin, according to Farrar, had 'distinctly declared himself against an atheistic materialism', although his scientific imprimatur had been deceitfully arrogated by 'violent and reckless followers' who claimed that 'Man sprang up from a single primordial moneres . . . and that therefore the belief in a Creator is unscientific and exploded'.[71] Significantly, Farrar later suggested that the inescapable outcome of such extreme beliefs, falsely attributed to Darwin, was revealed by the recent emergence of 'an ideal so wretched and so base as that it is best to crowd life with the greatest number of pleasurable sensations'. While, once again, Farrar refrained from directly naming Pater, he went on to condemn his disgusting 'theories of an artistic effeminacy, which . . . would have made even Antisthenes and Epicurus blush', an oblique allusion – though one which Farrar's Cambridge audience could hardly have failed to comprehend – to the languorous homoeroticism of much of *Studies in the History of the Renaissance*.[72] Farrar, despite his friendship with Darwin, insinuated that there was an inevitable correlation between what were commonly, although in the main erroneously, characterized as Darwinian views and unspeakable forms of debauchery that would surpass even those of the pagan world.

During the controversy prompted by Tyndall's Belfast Address in the following year, the damaging association between modern science and Pater's scandalous aesthetic philosophy, with its apparent endorsement of hedonism, was revived, intensifying the potential danger of Tyndall's identification of Epicurus and Lucretius as forerunners of scientific naturalism. The connection was made particularly explicit by William Hurrell Mallock, a self-styled guardian of High Church conservativism who first came to prominence soon after Tyndall's Address. By 1877 Mallock had made his name with *The New Republic*, a satirical *roman-à-clef* lampooning Victorian Britain's leading liberal intellectuals, Tyndall and Pater included, which became the literary sensation of the season. Still in his twenties, Mallock soon emerged as one of the most prolific contributors to the principal monthly and quarterly reviews, and Knowles solicited his opinion on the question of 'The Influence upon Morality of a Decline in Religious Belief' for the *Nineteenth Century*. Mallock's uncompromising response insisted on 'the intimate connection of morality and religion, or rather their essential identity . . . what destroys one will destroy both'.[73] Human nature, in Mallock's view, was inevitably corrupt and sinful, and required the supernatural sanction of religion to curb the base sensual instincts to which men – and sometimes even women – were constantly subject.

The lofty assurances of man's natural altruism given by scientific naturalists, as well as by rationalist philosophers and Broad Church liberals, were unsupported, Mallock claimed, by the distressing testimony of the real world. While 'Professor Tyndall tells us that, though he has now rejected the religion of his earlier years, yet . . . there is . . . no act of self-renouncement . . . that would not still be his' (also the 'implicit teaching of all George Eliot's novels' according to Mallock), such 'modern moralists' could do nothing to halt the increase of immorality and vice that, in the absence of religious belief, was rendered inevitable by human nature. There were, after all, other, less principled, proponents of unbelief who would 'call nothing common or unclean' and 'would make us free to eat any fruit in the garden'. In fact, as Mallock observed:

at least one of this school, in our day, has been clear enough on the matter; and he explicitly bases his teaching on the teachings of modern science. 'Each moment', says Mr. Pater, 'some form grows perfect in hand or face; some tone on the hills or sea is choicer than the rest; some mood or passion, or insight, or intellectual excitement, is irresistibly real and attractive for us.' And thus, 'while all melts under our feet', he goes on, 'we may well catch at any exquisite passion, or any contribution to knowledge, that seems by a lifted horizon to set the spirit free for a moment, or any stirring of the senses, strange dyes, strange flowers, and curious odours, or the work of the artist's hand, or the face of one's friend.'[74]

This lengthy quotation was, inevitably, taken from the infamous 'Conclusion' to *Studies in the History of the Renaissance*, and Mallock insisted that Pater's amoral creed of aesthetic hedonism was based explicitly on the doctrines of contemporary science and was an inevitable consequence of the disavowal of supernatural religion implicit in the naturalistic views advanced by Tyndall and others.

Tyndall's close connections with Victorian literary culture were already well known at the time that Mallock made this accusation. He wrote effusive verse that recorded his response to the grandeur of Alpine scenery, as well as famously expounding the necessity of using the imagination in scientific hypothesizing at the British Association meeting of 1870.[75] Tyndall also later commented that 'writings apparently far apart from science have often spurred me on in the pursuit of science'.[76] The literary works which offered him such inspiration, however, were emphatically not those of Pater and his aesthetic cohorts. Rather, Tyndall found particular expression of his own values in the stately, meditative poems of Tennyson (whose strategic use by Darwin has already been examined in the previous chapter), and, most notably, in Thomas Carlyle's evocation, in books such as *Sartor Resartus* (1834), of the sublime grandeur of the naturalistic, although still spiritually and morally uplifting, universe. Such 'Natural Supernaturalism', as Carlyle paradoxically termed it, formed the basis of a personal spirituality that was detached entirely from theological cant, and gave a new sense of vocation to those, like Tyndall, who endeavoured to understand and interpret the higher meaning of the natural world for the benefit of society.[77]

By the 1860s, Tyndall's growing scientific renown had enabled him to forge close personal friendships with both the revered Poet Laureate and the conservative Sage of Chelsea, although each of them continued to espouse distinctly anti-materialist opinions, with Tennyson, in 'Lucretius', even implying a causal connection between the ancient atomism that Tyndall would champion at Belfast and the degrading erotic fantasies which, in the poem, inveigle the mind of the Roman poet once he has imbibed his wife's love philtre. Unlike Darwin and Huxley, Tyndall also sided with Carlyle's authoritarian position (as did Tennyson) over the notorious Governor Eyre controversy in 1866, defending the governor of Jamaica's right to employ brutal force in suppressing a rebellion on the island. Despite Carlyle's growing insularity and political intransigence, Tyndall eulogized his elderly friend in the conclusion to the Belfast Address as 'one amongst us, hoary, but still strong, whose prophet-voice some thirty years ago, far more than any other of this age, unlocked whatever of life and nobleness lay latent in its most gifted minds' (62). Confronted with Tyndall's conservative literary tastes and eminently respectable, if somewhat illiberal, network of connections, Mallock was forced to acknowledge that the principal proponents of scientific naturalism were, on the whole, earnest and virtuous men, but he continued to insist that their teachings were nevertheless directly responsible for the scandalous vices now being encouraged by the new forms of aesthetic art and literature.

In his book *Is Life Worth Living?* (1879), Mallock contended that the 'modern Parisian school' of artists and writers 'start[ed] from the same pre-misses as do the positive moralists' but had 'come to a practical teaching that [was] singularly different'. Most notably, Théophile Gautier's disreputable novel *Mademoiselle de Maupin* (1835), with its veneration of impurity and apparent endorsement of every form of sensual experience, made the horrible reality of 'love when dereligionized' shockingly evident.[78] Worryingly, Mallock also discerned similar consequences in the aesthetic art now produced on the other side of the Channel, and he urged that, in order to see how the irreligious 'teaching' that the 'one thing to live for, is happiness in this life . . . is gradually changing the world', one need only 'go to Burne Jones, and he will show you the direction where men, of themselves, are sure to look for happiness'. In paintings such as *Laus Veneris* and *Chant d'Amour*, Mallock observed, Edward Burne-Jones depicted men and women

evidently . . . in command of all life's resources, and . . . choosing, presumably, what they think the best of them. What they choose is love . . . a love that could not be wronged, for nothing could make it worse than it is . . . The only sorrow they know is the languor of exhausted animalism.[79]

While Burne-Jones was a close associate of Swinburne and other prominent members of the aesthetic movement, and in *Laus Veneris* borrowed several elements from Swinburne's languorous poem of the same name, his deliberately ethereal and otherworldly paintings were actually meant to indicate his own antipathy towards the materialism of the age. Indeed, he avowed that the 'more materialistic science becomes, the more angels shall I paint'.[80] Mallock's misjudged criticism of Burne-Jones infuriated the artist's many friends, and Ruskin especially. Since his emergence into public life, Mallock had assiduously cultivated Ruskin as a mentor, gushingly dedicating *Is Life Worth Living?* to him, and he was greatly embarrassed at having caused such offence.[81]

But Burne-Jones was not in reality the principal target of Mallock's impertinent censure. Instead, it was the scientific naturalists who, along with the philosopher John Stuart Mill, had done their utmost to obliterate the religious criterion for morality whom he held responsible for the perversion of spiritual love into mere sensual indulgence. It 'makes me smile', Mallock wrote, 'to think of [Mill] with his logic turning the handle, and grinding out the "Laus Veneris"' and the 'Chant d'Amour'.[82] However much Mill, Tyndall and their Positivist associates (and Mallock deliberately conflated the differences between secular thinkers) might insist upon humanity's natural dignity, they could not regulate the base physicality that their irresponsible theories had unleashed, and which was now valorized in numerous recent works of art and literature. In *Is Life Worth Living?* Mallock also linked such allegations to the specific charges made against Tyndall in the aftermath of his Belfast Address, castigating modern science for 'rocking the moral ground under us, overturning and engulfing the former landmarks, and re-opening the graves of the buried lusts of paganism'.[83] The moral corruption of the ancient world, as Tyndall's many critics had already made abundantly clear, provided a cautionary warning of the inevitable outcome of the unbelief predicated by scientific naturalism. These frightful consequences, as Mallock now proposed, could in fact already be perceived in the unashamed sensuality of aesthetic literature and art.

The problematic association with both ancient immorality and the sensualism of contemporary aesthetic art was potentially much more damaging to Tyndall's personal reputation than to that of his closest scientific colleagues. Already sensitive about his Irish ancestry and the low social class of his parents, Tyndall, unlike such stalwart family men as Darwin and Huxley, was still unmarried at the time of his Presidency of the British Association. Most of Tyndall's scientific career had been spent at the Royal Institution in London, where he had served as Professor of Natural Philosophy since 1853 and was made Superintendent in 1867, and the regular Friday Evening Lectures that he gave there were notorious for attracting a rapt audience of fashionable young women. Indeed, those who attended Tyndall's Royal Institution lectures were, according to Jill Howard, 'predominantly female', and he was 'well known for his flattery and flirtatious remarks to ladies in the audience'.[84] At the same time, women looking for husbands at Royal Institution lectures, as well as having their metal-framed crinolines drawn involuntarily towards the lecturer's podium during demonstrations of magnetism, had become a running joke in many satirical periodicals. *Punch* regularly carried items such as the fictional memoirs of a 'young wife' who, after acknowledging that 'One thing . . . I *do* owe to the Royal Institution – I met my husband there', relates how she and her future spouse had attended 'Friday night lectures' together and fell in love while they 'inhaled the same gases, [and] started at the same explosions'.[85] With such temptations apparently surrounding him, Tyndall's prolonged period as a bachelor occasioned wry comments amongst his friends and colleagues.

Juliet Pollock, with whom Tyndall shared an extremely intimate correspondence for over twenty years, reflected in 1874 that he was 'a single (still) but not a solitary man', and, at her home theatricals, she insisted that he perform the parts of various Shakespearean lovers, telling him: 'soften your heart as much as your laboratory will let you'.[86] Huxley likewise joked about bringing his friend 'under the yoke of a "rare and radiant", – whenever I discover one competent to undertake the ticklish business of governing you. I hope she will be "radiant", – uncommonly "rare" she certainly will be.'[87] Tyndall himself, although he readily conceded that he would make 'a poor hand at looking after the small needs & comforts of . . . ladies', evidently longed for female company, and, as far back as the mid-1850s, had confessed to Hirst, 'I covet my neighbour's wife when she is handsome.'[88] He had in fact already been refused by Mary Adair in 1869, and since 1872, as he admitted in a letter to Hirst, an aristocratic young woman twenty-five years his junior, Louisa Hamilton, had become 'an object of great, if only of theoretic, interest to me'.[89] Even if ostensibly only theoretic, however, this gauche and perhaps rather desperate fondness for the opposite sex was not just perceptible to Tyndall's close friends. Many of his adversaries took advantage of it to cast damaging aspersions on his moral authority, even after his eventual marriage to Louisa in 1876, and especially in the wake of the charges of encouraging pagan licentiousness which followed the Belfast Address.

Notably, it was the 'North British' group of Presbyterian physicists and engineers, whose antagonism towards metropolitan scientific naturalists and rival appropriation of Lucretius as an ancient forerunner of their own physical theories were noted earlier in this chapter, who most regularly articulated such disreputable insinuations. At the beginning of the 1870s Maxwell alluded to precisely this aspect of Tyndall's personal life, as well as his proclivity for breaking out into an excitably effusive and ardent scientific language, in his parodic poem 'To the Chief Musician Upon Nabla: *A Tyndallic Ode*' (1871).[90] The atomistic doctrine that Tyndall would later expound in Belfast was depicted by Maxwell in unmistakably sexual terms, with coalescing 'molecules with fierce desires' that come together and 'shiver in hot embraces', which perhaps also reflected their scientific champion's own putatively libidinous yearnings.[91]

One of Maxwell's staunchest followers certainly witnessed, at close quarters, what he perceived to be Tyndall's unseemly hankering for the opposite sex. As well as delivering the Presidential Address at the Belfast meeting of the British Association, Tyndall had also introduced the Evening Lectures given by Huxley and Sir John Lubbock, commending the latter, on 'Common Wild Flowers Considered in Relation to Insects', for, amongst other things, its 'beautiful diagrams'. These illustrations of assorted carpels and stamens were, Tyndall observed, the 'production of one of whom he was compelled to speak with a certain degree of reserve and respect, Miss [Amy] Lubbock', a young woman he had known since she had 'scarcely attained the age of five or six years, and who had now grown up and become all that those who loved her could desire her to become'.[92] For some members of the audience in Belfast, this profuse praise for a friend's seventeen-year-old daughter – and her botanical illustrations of the reproductive organs of wild flowers – aroused certain suspicions regarding Tyndall's apparent penchant for young women. Oliver Lodge, who attended Lubbock's Evening Lecture as a young physicist increasingly opposed to Tyndall's naturalistic emphasis and instead adopting Maxwell's more numinous theories of electromagnetism, later recalled the 'illustrations by his daughter, over which (or whom) Tyndall in returning thanks waxed enthusiastic and emotional'.[93] As Lodge's furtive parenthetical aside insinuated, such effusive praise for an attractive young woman, especially from a middle-aged bachelor, could be interpreted in ways that might be damaging to Tyndall, particularly at a time when several sermons, both in Belfast and elsewhere, were connecting his scientific position with the sensual indulgence of the ancient world.

Neither Maxwell's nor Lodge's lewd intimations were actually published during the 1870s, however, and once again it was Mallock who made the clearest public connection between the controversy over the Belfast Address and such insinuations regarding Tyndall's personal life. In his famous satirical novel *The New Republic*, Tyndall was caricatured as the loquacious Mr Stockton, whose dreary conversation invariably involved 'explaining that the Alps looked grander, and the sky bluer than ever, to those who truly realised the atomic theory'.[94] Such 'teachings' of Stockton's 'irreligious science' had, as one character in the novel observes, been condemned as 'simply reproductions of . . . Epicurus and Democritus – which had been long ago refuted'.[95] Despite his proud advocacy of such ancient authorities, Stockton himself, Mallock's narrator insists, was in fact a 'Philistine – a mere man of science, who was without even a smattering of Greek or Hebrew'.[96] As *The New Republic* made clear, scientific naturalists such as Tyndall, unlike Mallock with his Oxford education and experience as a translator of Lucretius, could not be trusted as interpreters of the classics or, indeed, as moral arbiters in the present day.

While Mallock's *roman-à-clef* received several adulatory notices in the conservative press (it was a 'brilliant book' and 'capital squib' according to the *Contemporary*), many reviewers remained uneasy with the book's indiscreet ridicule of the private foibles of public figures.[97] The *Saturday Review* complained that it took advantage of 'close observation of the daily habits and conversation of the subjects', often exhibiting a marked 'want of taste' in its portrayal of their behaviour, and other critics similarly noted the 'glib and sinister insinuations' present in Mallock's work for those readers who could 'listen beneath his sentences'.[98] Like Mivart, whom, as was seen in the previous chapter, Huxley likened to a latter-day Tartuffe, Mallock was also condemned for a similarly hypocritical 'preoccupation about sexual

sins', and an anonymous American critic proposed that his various attacks
on modern science were spawned by an 'imagination [that] is not quite
clean' and which rendered them 'unpleasantly suggestive of the famous
Tartuffe scene, where Dorinda is requested to draw closer her kerchief'.[99]
Certainly, throughout *The New Republic*, Stockton, who never mentions
a wife and speaks of love 'in a melancholy voice', takes a conspicuous
interest in the attractive young women who join in the novel's main debate
on the aims of existence, which must, presumably, have been informed
by salacious rumours concerning Tyndall's personal life.[100] Stockton, for
instance, observes of the 'dear Duchess of – ' that 'there's a fascination
even in the way in which she says good morning', and he later feels his
'spirits suddenly rise' when he meets Lady Violet, whom he declares to be
'a charming girl'.[101] Stockton seems most attracted to the glamorous Miss
Merton, whom 'his eyes rest on . . . with an appealing melancholy' following
a speech on life's emergence from 'a brainless, senseless, lifeless gas' (a parody,
of course, of the Belfast Address), but his amorous attentions arouse in her
only 'an unfortunate sense of absurdity' and 'a most inappropriate desire
to laugh' at her potential suitor.[102]

Even worse, though, in *The New Paul and Virginia, or Positivism on
an Island* (1878), Mallock's limp follow-up to *The New Republic*, a ship-
wrecked positivist, based, as Mallock later acknowledged, on 'an atheistic
professor, such as Tyndal [*sic*]', is inadvertently successful in seducing a
glamorous society beauty – who has only recently married a Bishop –
with his message that 'we have nothing to strive and live for except to be
unspeakably happy'.[103] Although the professor 'had dissected many dead
women, he knew very little of the hearts of live ones', and he is 'over-
powered' by a 'sense of shyness' when his beautiful companion, released
from the constraints of morality by his own positivist teachings, declares:
'let us kiss each other all day long. Let us enjoy the charming license
which exact thought shows us we shall never be punished for.'[104] By 1876,
Tyndall had married Louisa Hamilton in a ceremony shorn of religious
references at Westminster Abbey, receiving an 'exquisite' teapot as a gift
from an overjoyed Darwin, although the disparity in their ages may only
have augmented long-standing suspicions about Tyndall's alleged fondness
for younger women.[105] In Mallock's spiteful and malicious satires, both of
which came out subsequent to Tyndall's nuptials, the earlier rumours concerning his ostensible predilections, as well as underhand jibes about his
lack of proper experience of women during his long period as a bachelor,
were linked explicitly – although under the convenient cover of fiction –
with the charges of encouraging immorality and vice that had dogged him

since 1874. Such aspersions on Tyndall's personal reputation, as well as on the intellectual and moral authority of scientific naturalism more generally, could clearly not go unanswered.

GRAND OLD PAGANS

In the Belfast Address, as an editorial in *The Times* concluded, Tyndall had made 'unfortunate' rhetorical errors which had 'afford[ed] an opportunity' to his opponents, 'of which they ha[d] not failed to take advantage', of 'exhibiting to their followers in a concrete and visible form the . . . real tendency and ultimate result of [the] insidious inventions' of nineteenth-century science. His biggest mistake, according to *The Times* leader, was to align his scientific position with 'the doctrine of a school of heathen philosophers who flourished 600 years before CHRIST' and who had long been 'reprobated by Divine authority' for promoting 'flagrant materialism, atheism, [and] animalism'.[106] Turner too has judged Tyndall's comparison of classical and modern physical sciences a 'rhetorical blunder', although, as was noted earlier, for reasons other than allowing the principles of scientific naturalism to be connected with ancient immorality.[107] The Belfast Address did, undeniably, allow unscrupulous opponents to add substance to long-standing suspicions regarding the ethical tendency of materialism and unbelief, as well as giving new life to the similar vein of criticism that had been directed at Darwin's *The Descent of Man* for much of the previous three years. Tyndall nevertheless insisted that his discourse had been long 'thought over' with 'a sense of the gravest responsibility' during a summer spent in Switzerland, and was not, as one critic suggested, rashly thrown together on 'the spur of the moment' (although the opening section dealing with ancient atomism was one of the last parts of the Address to be composed) (vi).[108] Tyndall's response to the 'strange calumnies' and 'coarser attacks' that his Address had subsequently provoked was, at least initially, similarly robust (vii–viii).

Just two months after his bruising experience at Belfast, Tyndall delivered a public lecture in Manchester Town Hall on 'Crystalline and Molecular Forces' in which he alluded wryly to the accusations of paganism that had so recently been made against him. He remarked: 'You have probably heard of late of certain disturbers of the public peace named Democritus, Epicurus, and Lucretius. These men adopted, developed, and diffused the dangerous doctrine of atoms and molecules.' This supposedly seditious creed, Tyndall told his proudly Mancunian auditors, had actually 'found its consummation in this city of Manchester at the hands of the immortal John Dalton' in his experimental work on magnetism and molecular force.[109] Throughout his life, Tyndall had been proud to identify himself with various aspects of the ancient world, apparently describing himself as a 'Stoic' during his early career as a surveyor for the Irish Ordnance, and, following his marriage several decades later, telling friends that his wife 'rejoices in being as much a pagan as I am'.[110] By linking ancient atomism to the civic pride of his popular audience in Manchester, he now sought to forge an incongruous alliance between the respectable middle classes of Victorian Britain's industrial cities and what he termed – in a strategic paraphrase of Carlyle's affectionate epithet for the much-respected Romantic writer Walter Savage Landor – the 'grand old pagans' whose controversial reputation was, according to Tyndall, entirely undeserved.[111]

Some of Tyndall's scientific colleagues also added their voices to this defence of pagan antiquity, with William Kingdon Clifford complaining in an 1875 article for the *Fortnightly* of Christianity's 'vulgar vituperation of the older culture' and constant 'dwell[ing] on the dark side of Pagan Society'. Like Arnold in the *Cornhill Magazine* ten years earlier, Clifford protested that while 'we hear enough of the luxurious feasting of the Roman capital' and its 'bad and mad emperors', 'we are not told of the many thousands of honourable men who . . . administered a mighty empire so that it was loved and worshipped' and whose 'common action' exhibited a true morality.[112] In another *Fortnightly* article in the same year, Clifford also defended the integrity of the 'parallelism' between ancient and modern physical theories 'recently brought before the public by Professor Tyndall in his excellent address at Belfast', and he lambasted those unscientific critics of Tyndall's Address who, being 'acquainted with classic literature . . . have thought that a knowledge of the views of Democritus and Lucretius would enable them to understand and criticize the modern theory of matter'.[113] It was, perhaps, the confidence imbued by his own training in the classics at Cambridge that allowed Clifford to challenge the erudition of Tyndall's similarly educated adversaries, and to emerge as the most strident defender of the self-taught account of ancient thought given in the Belfast Address.

Tyndall himself was more assured in responding to allegations of uprooting nineteenth-century standards of morality, even if he joked uneasily, when sending a copy of the 'iniquitous Address' to Mary Adair: 'If it seems the proper fate for it pray put the book in the fire.'[114] Tyndall evidently felt no need for the assistance of an Irish correspondent who warned that his 'opinions have been denounced as immoral' and offered to conduct a vigorous defence on his behalf, remarking to Huxley that his would-be protector was probably 'slightly mad' (although Huxley himself considered there to be 'method in our Irish friend's madness').[115] Tyndall's own vindication of his moral position came in another Presidential Address, this time to the Birmingham and Midland Institute in 1877, in which he explicitly rejected the Presbyterian sentiments of Robert Burns's 'Epistle to a Young Friend': 'The fear of hell's a hangman's whip, / To keep the wretch in order.'[116] He contended instead that nature had 'endowed us with moral constitutions which take pleasure in the noble, the beautiful, and the true' regardless of the existence of a spiritual hereafter.[117] It was, in fact, often those who had abjured the false comforts of religious orthodoxy who, despite the contemptible insinuations of their opponents, upheld the strongest sense of personal morality. There were, Tyndall declared, 'many whom the gladiators of the pulpit would call "atheists" and "materialists", whose lives, nevertheless, as tested by any accessible standard of morality, would contrast more than favourably with the lives of those who seek to stamp them with this offensive brand', and he proposed Darwin and George Jacob Holyoake as exemplars of such 'moral elevation' amongst unbelievers.[118]

In 1873, Tyndall had urged, in a series of lectures on the properties of light delivered in North America, that science itself, when 'cultivated for its own sake, for the pure love of truth', was 'wholesome . . . as a means of discipline' in which 'high intellect and upright character are combined'.[119] This was a familiar claim of scientific naturalists, as was noted in chapter one, and had been regularly articulated by Tyndall since his private journals of the 1840s, although never did he insist on it with more urgency than in the difficult years following the Belfast meeting of the British Association. At the same time, as James E. Strick has argued, in Tyndall's experimental work on the possibility of spontaneous generation during 1876 and 1877 overdetermined terms such as 'purity' became 'just as much moral descriptions of his . . . motives as they were descriptions of the state of microbial growth in tubes of boiled infusion'.[120] The numerous accusations of encouraging immorality that Tyndall encountered following the Belfast Address can be seen to have had a significant impact upon not only his rhetoric in various lectures and periodical articles, but perhaps even on the actual practice and content of his scientific endeavours for at least the remainder of the 1870s.

In his Address to the Birmingham and Midland Institute, Tyndall also responded to the many charges of hedonism made against him that had employed the rhetoric of Saint Paul. Judging from 'much that has been written of late', he observed, the 'astounding inference' that without 'theologic sanctions . . . we shall all . . . become robbers, and ravishers' had apparently found 'house-room in many minds'. In reply, Tyndall averred: '"Let us eat and drink, for to-morrow we die" is by no means the ethical consequence of a rejection of dogma.'[121] This staunch position reflected Mill's celebrated defence of Epicurean ethics in *Utilitarianism* (1861), in which it was claimed that such an 'accusation [as Saint Paul's] supposes human beings to be capable of no pleasures except those of which swine are capable', when in reality humans 'have faculties more elevated than the animal appetites, and . . . do not regard anything as happiness which does not include their gratification'.[122] Tyndall, like Mill, insisted that it was actually his theological opponents who held a truly degraded and immoral view of human life.

The hedonist slogan which Saint Paul ascribed to the followers of Epicurus had already provoked the ire of one of Tyndall's closest scientific friends even before the publication of Mill's main contribution to ethical theory in 1861. Huxley disputed exactly the same scriptural passage in a remarkable letter to Kingsley following the death of his baby son Noel in 1860:

As I stood behind the coffin of my little son . . . the officiating minister read, as part of his duty, the words, "If the dead rise not again, let us eat and drink, for to-morrow we die". I cannot tell you how inexpressibly they shocked me. Paul had neither wife nor child, or he must have known that his alternative involved a blasphemy against all that was best and noblest in human nature. I could have laughed with scorn. What! because I am face to face with irreparable loss . . . I am to renounce my manhood, and, howling, grovel in bestiality?[123]

Over three decades later, in his celebrated Romanes Lecture *Evolution and Ethics* (1894), Huxley would even amend this same Pauline aphorism and suggest that it was actually religious theodicies which led men to ask themselves: 'Why strive to improve the best of all possible worlds? Let us eat and drink, for as to-day all is right, so to-morrow all will be.' Such complacent justifications of the present iniquitous state of the universe, Huxley went on, could themselves provide 'an inscription in letters of mud over the portal of some "stye of Epicurus"', although he declined responsibility for this particular 'libel upon Epicurus'. When comprehended properly, Huxley insisted, the doctrines of Epicurus were not necessarily 'compatible with existence in a stye', and he expressed a wish that 'fewer illusions about Epicureanism would pass muster for truth' amongst those who had either never read, or had misinterpreted, the Greek philosopher's ascetic teachings.[124]

Such a principled defence of humanity's natural dignity against the pessimistic theological assumptions of Saint Paul, however, was not the exclusive preserve of reputable philosophers and men of science, and was also adopted by Pater in his 1885 novel *Marius the Epicurean*. As the narrator of this philosophical *bildungsroman* set in second-century Rome observes:

Let us eat and drink, for to-morrow we die! – is a principle, the real import of which differs immensely according to the natural taste and the acquired judgement, of the guests who sit at the table . . . [and] since on no hypothesis does man 'live by bread alone', it may come to be identical with – 'My meat is to do what is just and kind'; while the soul, which cannot pretend to the apprehension of anything beyond the veil of immediate experience, yet never loses a feeling of happiness in conforming to the highest moral idea it can sincerely define for itself; and actually, though but with so faint hope, does the 'Father's business'.[125]

The infamous Epicurean creed, Pater's narrator proposes, could easily become interchangeable with more orthodox ethical positions, and, as the novel's daring incorporation of various scriptural passages implies, might even become synonymous with Christian doctrines. Pater, by the 1880s, had done much to shed his earlier scandalous notoriety, and *Marius the Epicurean* was avowedly intended to redirect 'those young men' who, as Pater conceded in 1888, he 'might possibly mislead' in the 'Conclusion' to *Studies in the History of the Renaissance*.[126] Pater's still rather audacious attempt to justify, at least implicitly, the refined aesthetic hedonism eulogized in his earlier book might nevertheless continue to tarnish by association the similar arguments of Huxley, Mill and Tyndall that even those who could not believe in anything beyond the existence of the material world would continue to behave with moral rectitude.

Tyndall certainly remained extremely sensitive to any suggestions that he endorsed pagan sensualism even until the very end of his life. A year before his death in December 1893 he reflected on the unbeliever born a 'thousand summers ere the time of Christ' in Tennyson's 1885 poem 'The Ancient Sage', who espouses the recognizably Epicurean sentiments

'Yet wine and laughter friends! and set
The lamps alight, and call
For golden music, and forget
The darkness of the pall.'[127]

This pagan sceptic and hedonist, Tyndall acknowledged, was clearly 'what we should call a materialist', with his 'moral and religious fibre . . . gone', whose heretical views the 'nineteenth-century poet' evidently endeavoured to 'combat'. Having himself long endured similar aspersions, however, Tyndall radically inverted the ostensible meaning of his friend's poem and avowed that the words uttered by the ancient materialist were 'far from being the language of a libertine' and were actually 'more surpassingly beautiful' than anything else 'even in Tennyson's own pages'. There was, the elderly Tyndall insisted, a 'celestial melody' inherent in the pseudo-Epicurean creeds that Tennyson's poem articulated only in order to condemn, and this ineluctable dignity confuted even the most 'foul' accusations of hostile commentators.[128]

Despite the robustness of his response to his numerous critics, Tyndall also remained extremely wary about anything that might impugn his respectability. In the fifth edition of *Fragments of Science*, published in 1876 and the first to include the text of the Belfast Address, he explained that, in the revisions he had made to the previous edition of this collection of his miscellaneous writings, his principal 'desire has been that they should utter nothing base'.[129] Such scrupulous concern to reform and control the potential range of meanings contained in his writing shows that Tyndall was well aware of the undesirable connotations that many readers, swayed by ruthless critics who paraded their expert knowledge of the classics, might draw from the Belfast Address's endorsement of ancient materialism. As Tyndall told Louis Pasteur later in the same year regarding the question of spontaneous generation, the 'mass of men are so unenlightened and stupid . . . that any differences between you and me will be sure to be misinterpreted', which also echoed Darwin's anxious warning to Huxley, noted in the previous chapter, that 'great is the power of misrepresentation'.[130] Certainly, Tyndall's admiring discussion of the physical theories of Democritus, Epicurus and Lucretius in the opening section of the Belfast Address was widely misinterpreted (at least in Tyndall's terms) as either a covert or an unwitting espousal of a pagan theory of ethics which had always, when put into practice, led to unrestrained vice and immorality.

Many of these misinterpretations were, of course, malicious, and such deliberately partial construals of Tyndall's meaning were part of what Bernard Lightman has identified as 'a concerted effort . . . to transform Tyndall's image in the public eye' following the Belfast Address.[131] They also, however, marked a more general escalation in the attacks made on scientific naturalists during the 1870s as their position amongst the cultural elite of Victorian Britain, often at the expense of members of the Anglican clergy, became more entrenched. As Tyndall and his associates gained ever greater institutional power and prestige, it became even more necessary to dissociate themselves, as well as their wider scientific programme, from any dangerous associations or connotations – and particularly those involving issues of sexual respectability – that might potentially be exploited by opponents. The necessity of doing this, as is examined in the following chapter, would bring the proponents of Darwinism into bitter conflict with various freethinkers who espoused greater sexual freedoms but who were otherwise largely supportive of an evolutionary and naturalistic agenda.

CHAPTER 4

Darwinism, Victorian freethought and the Obscene Publications Act

While travelling through Italy in the spring of 1870, St George Mivart, the Catholic comparative anatomist who was now recanting his erstwhile support for Darwinism, encountered an unexpected and somewhat disconcerting reminder of home. He was, as he later recounted in a letter to Charles Darwin, both 'amused and saddened to see our friend Huxley's "Man's Place in Nature" for sale at most of the railway stations amongst a crowd of *obscenities*'. Although he did not specify the exact nature of the other publications that were displayed alongside Thomas Henry Huxley's evolutionary account of human ancestry at such disreputable station bookstalls, Mivart nevertheless implied that *Evidence as to Man's Place in Nature* (1863) was itself of a similarly questionable character. Indeed, 'it was evident', as he informed Darwin, 'that the vendors counted on what we may term a "tendency to reversion" and I fear not a few of the purchasers would *prefer* to find that Man "diverged" *above* the *Cynocephali*.'[1] Huxley's book, as was noted in chapter two, had deliberately eschewed any reference to the licentiousness that was traditionally attributed to the manlike apes, but Mivart insinuated that the recently published cheap Italian edition was being purchased primarily by those who welcomed any evidence that might justify their own base animalism. The dog-headed Cynocephali with whom such debauched readers apparently identified were, like other mythological hybrids such as the satyr, part of a long tradition which, since classical antiquity, had conflated these legendarily concupiscent creatures with the purported licentiousness of baboons and other simians.[2] Scientific descriptions of man's close affinity with such dissipated forebears, as unscrupulous Italian booksellers appeared to have recognized, might prove as remunerative as even the most salacious and titillating 'railway novel'.

Although Darwin himself had been 'struck with admiration' for *Man's Place in Nature*, he was accustomed to hearing his friends complain of the distastefulness of both the format and contents of Huxley's six-shilling monograph. Joseph Dalton Hooker had described it as a 'coarse looking

116

little book. – not fit as somebody said to me, for a gentleman's table', while Hugh Falconer was reportedly 'disgusted' with the book's lurid woodcut of a cannibal butcher's shop '& would let no young Lady look at it'.[3] However, the ostensibly humorous allusion to *Man's Place in Nature* in the letter which Darwin received from Mivart, whose skilful deployment of similarly furtive intimations concerning Darwin's own writing has already been discussed in chapter two, was actually considerably more invidious and calculating than either Hooker or Falconer's insistence that Huxley's book was unacceptable, from the perspectives of both class and gender, to respectable readers. In fact, Mivart's apparently jocular reminiscences of the various insalubrious publications that he encountered on his Italian sojourn had very specific and deleterious connotations in relation to a recent clarification in Victorian legislation on obscenity.

In April 1868, the Lord Chief Justice, Sir Alexander Cockburn, had provided the first legal definition of obscenity in the celebrated case of *Regina v. Hicklin*, proclaiming that the 'test of obscenity is this, whether the tendency of the matter charged . . . is to deprave and corrupt those whose minds are open to such immoral influences and into whose hands a publication of this sort might fall'.[4] Before studying anatomy with Richard Owen at the Royal College of Surgeons, Mivart had initially been trained as a lawyer at the neighbouring Inns of Court, and he retained, as Huxley later complained, a tendency to cross-examine Darwin and his evolutionary theories 'as an Old Bailey barrister deals with a man against whom he wishes to obtain a conviction, *per fas aut nefas*'.[5] The disingenuously genial comments regarding the potentially obscene character of *Man's Place in Nature* contained in Mivart's letter to Darwin from April 1870 certainly evinced an acutely legalistic awareness of the implications of the new judicial precedent on obscenity established exactly two years earlier. In correcting the proofs of his book, Huxley had heeded the circumspect advice of Charles Lyell to excise certain 'naughty' passages which chastised his opponents as 'uncircumcised' and 'emasculate', but Mivart, in accordance with Cockburn's ruling, did not mention the actual contents of *Man's Place in Nature*.[6] Instead, he drew attention to the potential response of its audience, and in particular to the book's capacity, even if wholly unintended by its author, to degrade and corrupt its more susceptible readers. At the same time, Mivart's allusion to the grubby railway station bookstalls at which cheap reprints of Huxley's monograph were apparently being openly displayed corresponded exactly with Cockburn's judicial anxieties over the promiscuous availability of such dangerous publications in the emergent mass urban culture of Victorian Britain.[7]

The initial attempt to legislate against the more pernicious aspects of the nineteenth-century publishing trade, Lord Campbell's Obscene Publications Act, had been passed in August 1857, although a precise legal definition of obscenity was not established until Cockburn's judicial clarification eleven years later.[8] By focusing on the susceptibilities of vulnerable readers rather than the actual contents or intentions of a particular publication, Cockburn's notorious 'test' – which would continue to be invoked throughout the following century – ensured that *Man's Place in Nature* was not the only explicitly scientific, or even specifically Darwinian, work that would become implicated with the nascent forms of legislation on obscenity in nineteenth-century Britain. While the Victorian concern with the legal regulation of obscenity has recently attracted considerable attention from a wide variety of historians, there has been hardly any consideration of the contentious and highly significant role of scientific publications, many of which inevitably dealt with otherwise unmentionable sexual matters, in what Lynda Nead has described as the 'attempt . . . to redraw the boundaries between the permissible and the forbidden' in nineteenth-century culture.[9] Several purportedly scientific works were, as this chapter will show, threatened with prosecution under the 1857 Obscene Publications Act, and the very possibility that the avowedly disinterested discourse of science might, at least for some readers, be corrupting or even sexually arousing was central to widespread concerns about the actual viability of legally defining obscenity.

Mivart's wily letter to Darwin notwithstanding, however, the avowed opponents of Darwinism, whose habitual allegations of immoral sensualism and indecency have been examined at length in previous chapters, only rarely alluded to the problematic relation between science and the new legal understandings of obscenity established by Campbell and Cockburn. It was instead freethinkers, such as Charles Bradlaugh and Annie Besant, who were largely sympathetic towards evolutionary and naturalistic doctrines, and even attempted to appropriate them for their own radical political aims, who most regularly insisted on the illicit potential, at least in the view of the law, of many of the scientific works produced by Darwin and his circle of supporters. Moreover, while Mivart's insidious intimations concerning *Man's Place in Nature* were made in a private letter to Darwin, the proclamations of such radicals concerning the potentially obscene nature of elite scientific publications were made in some of the most prominent forums of Victorian society, including the High Court of Justice, and were widely reported in both organs of the establishment like *The Times* as well as in the radical gutter press.

As with other freethinkers, Bradlaugh, who loudly declaimed his conviction that 'between the cabbage and the man I know no break', did not
consider that Darwinism was in any way immoral or obscene.[10] Such radicals were instead merely attempting to defend their own publications, generally cheap tracts on reproductive physiology although occasionally more
expensive scientific works on sexuality, from the same charge of obscenity
by establishing that, within current legal definitions, even highly respected
scientific and medical works such as William Benjamin Carpenter's *Principles of Human Physiology* or Darwin's *The Descent of Man* could be likewise
accused of corrupting vulnerable readers whose minds might be affected
by their explicit discussions of human physiology and reproduction.

Many of the cheap freethought publications which radicals like
Bradlaugh and Besant claimed were only as potentially licentious as the
more expensive writings of Darwin and Carpenter espoused the necessity of artificial checks to fertility to prevent working-class families falling
into poverty. Birth control, as is well known, was an explosive and highly
taboo subject in the nineteenth century, largely because it was feared that
separating sex from procreation would inevitably remove the traditional
constraints on promiscuity, for women especially. Despite its apparent similarity to the more familiar Malthusian checks to overpopulation, like disease, conflict and famine, on which natural selection was famously predicated, Darwin, as well as Huxley and others, vehemently opposed any
attempts by radicals to appropriate evolutionary theory to justify their support for contraception. While the proponents of birth control declared
themselves 'Neo-Malthusians', Darwin himself continued to adhere to the
more abstemious remedies for overpopulation, most notably chastity and
late marriage, which Thomas Malthus had originally proposed in the early
nineteenth century. Nevertheless, the rancorous controversy in 1874 over
George Darwin's apparent endorsement of prostitution as a means of checking population that was examined in chapter two made it evident just how
easily his father's own scientific theories could be misconstrued, wilfully or
otherwise, as an endorsement of even the most disreputable and libertine
antidotes to overpopulation, and radicals like Besant would, as will be seen,
readily exploit such ambiguities for their own particular purposes.

Although most radical secularists agreed on the necessity of some form
of artificial check to population, attitudes to birth control, and sexual policy more generally, were by far the most divisive issue within the British
freethought movement in the nineteenth century. The movement was split
between those, like George Jacob Holyoake, who insisted that contraception should only ever be practiced by married couples, and others, such

as George Drysdale, whose commitment to birth control was merely one element in a wider programme of sexual emancipation for both sexes. Darwin's deliberate, and often rather haughty, eschewal of any connection with those on what Michael Mason has termed the 'pro-sensual' wing of Victorian freethought has been noted regularly by historians, although the simultaneous endeavours of some of his principal supporters, including Huxley and John Tyndall, to forge closer connections with those free-thinkers and radicals who espoused what Mason describes as a 'progressive anti-sensualism' are less well known.[11] Such complex negotiations with the various strands of the Victorian freethought movement, and especially their divergent attitudes towards sexuality, were crucial to the endeavour to establish Darwinism, which freethinkers of both wings regularly claimed allegiance to, as a moral and eminently respectable social theodicy. Even into the 1890s, though, Darwin's own work would continue to carry the taint of a potentially criminal obscenity.

NO PHYSICAL FACT IS AN INDECENT FACT

In December 1864 the works of Darwin, Huxley and other prominent advocates of scientific naturalism were denounced in the 'Syllabus erro-rum' issued by Pope Pius IX. While the Vatican, soon also to proclaim the Pope's infallibility, was resolved to prohibit the reading of such heretical books amongst Catholics, the prospect of these and other renowned and bestselling scientific publications being similarly proscribed by the Protes-tant legal establishment in Victorian Britain seemed utterly remote. Yet during the decades following the passage of the Obscene Publications Act in August 1857 the precise legal status of many of the most celebrated works of Victorian science was brought into question at various levels of the legal system. Prominent men of science, as well as leading publishers of scien-tific books, were regularly subpoenaed to appear as witnesses in some of the most notable obscenity trials of the period. There were even concerns that such legislative interference, including seizure by the police of offend-ing material, might seriously impair the international standing of British science, and at the close of the nineteenth century the *Kölnische Zeitung* lamented that the

Hypocrites and prudes in Old England are on the war-path again. Not against music halls and theatres but against scientific, medical, and anthropological works is their zeal directed this time . . . We will next hear . . . that Darwin's great works will be brought before an Old Bailey jury . . . [and] the tinker, the tailor, the candle-maker, presided over by the Recorder of London, will sit in judgement over the *Origin of Species* and the *Descent of Man*.[12]

Darwin was deliberately invoked in this German newspaper report from 1898 as not merely an icon of British science, but also as an exemplar of the disinterested and almost saintly scientific sage, the potential prosecution of whose internationally renowned works could be considered only as incongruous and absurd. Nevertheless, two decades earlier, Darwin, as well as some of his closest friends and colleagues, had in fact been directly implicated in previous judicial attempts to establish certain forms of scientific discourse as obscene.

Although, as Nead has noted, 'claims to scientific accuracy and objectivity, bolstered by pages of footnotes' had, since at least the eighteenth century, been used to distinguish the discerning appreciation of the erotic aspects of high culture by connoisseurs and worldly gentlemen from the brutalizing consumption of the mere quotidian smut that was peddled in London's infamous Holywell Street, there remained long-standing concerns that, in certain circumstances, even science itself might transgress existing legal standards of decency and tastefulness.[13] At the beginning of the 1840s, when groups such as the Society for the Suppression of Vice relied on launching private prosecutions under the ill-defined law of obscene libel that had been on the statute books since 1727, the author and barrister Sir Thomas Noon Talfourd, in his celebrated defence of an unexpurgated edition of the poetry of Percy Shelley against the charge of blasphemy, warned that, as with parts of challenging literary works when read out of context, even

details and pictures in works of anatomy and surgery are either innocent or criminal, according to the accompaniments which surround them, and the class to whom they are addressed. If really intended for the eye of the scientific student, they are most innocent; but if so published as to manifest another intention, they will not be protected from legal censure by the flimsy guise of science.[14]

The obscenity and indecency commonly detected in a variety of publications by the zealous vigilance of the Vice Society were not, as Talfourd implied, absolute or unchanging categories; rather, their presence or absence depended entirely upon the context in which particular passages from a larger work might appear and the specific audiences to which they were addressed. While descriptions and illustrations of the intimate details of human anatomy or physiology were obviously necessary to the advancement of science and the practice of medicine, early nineteenth-century obscenity legislation, like that covering blasphemy, meant that even they, when excerpted and taken out of their customary context, could not be exempted entirely from potential criminality.

Despite this perturbing possibility, Lord Campbell's endeavours in the mid-1850s to both modernize and strengthen the law on obscenity, which were assisted by evidence provided by the Vice Society, were actually commended by several medical and scientific commentators, who expressed concern at the debilitating physiological effects of an addiction to pornography.[15] In June 1857, moreover, the *Daily Telegraph* reported that one additional benefit of the prospective Obscene Publications Act was that 'young medical students anxious to pick up cheap copies of QUAIN's Anatomy or the "London Pharmacopoeia"' would be able to search for them at the numerous second-hand bookstalls in the grubby purlieus of Holywell Street without inciting a 'volley of ribald jokes' from the 'dissolute and the brutal, who intentionally misconstrue the purpose of their visit'.[16] The new legislation was aimed principally at cheap and mass-produced publications, which, Campbell claimed, were proliferating in modern urban culture and 'corrupting the morals of youth' as well as 'shock[ing] the common feelings of decency' held by the majority of the populace, and it was considered that its implementation could only benefit more legitimate forms of publishing like science and medicine.[17]

While Campbell assured his aristocratic opponents in the House of Lords that the Act would have no implications for depictions of sexuality in classical or high art, there was in fact no certain means of preventing the more general application of the law. Lord Cockburn's judicial clarification in 1868, as has been seen, actually increased the remit of the Act by defining obscenity according to a publication's capacity to deprave and corrupt those readers most susceptible to immoral influences. A legal defence of putatively obscene material as being for the 'public good' was not formulated until 1877, when James Fitzjames Stephen, in his *Digest of Common Law*, insisted that a 'person is justified in exhibiting disgusting objects, or publishing obscene books, papers, writings, prints, pictures, drawings, or other representations, if their exhibition or publication is . . . necessary or advantageous to', amongst many other things, the 'pursuit of science'.[18] By this time, however, the distribution of a cheap but avowedly scientific publication had already provoked one of the most notorious obscenity trials of the entire nineteenth century, at which the names of Darwin, Huxley and Carpenter were frequently, and often impertinently, invoked.

In the early nineteenth century, obscenity and sexual libertinism were important aspects of the activities of many radicals and freethinkers, while the Society for the Suppression of Vice, formed during the turbulent period of the Napoleonic wars, generally operated on behalf of the political and religious establishment.[19] After mid-century, the freethought movement largely eschewed the deliberate indecency of the Regency's radical counterculture, although vigilance groups such as the Vice Society and the evangelical Christian Evidence Society continued to goad the authorities into using obscenity legislation to prosecute radicals and secularists. The two groups were certainly suspected of initiating proceedings against Bradlaugh and Besant in April 1877, when the pair, both prominent members of the National Secular Society as well as the co-editors of the leading freethought journal the *National Reformer*, were arrested and charged with printing and publishing an 'indecent, lewd, filthy, bawdy, and obscene book'.[20] The offending book was *Fruits of Philosophy*, a forty-five year-old treatise on reproductive physiology by the American physician Charles Knowlton, which, after decades of being sold inconspicuously in radical bookshops, had been reissued in a provocative new edition, costing just sixpence, under the imprint of the recently founded Freethought Publishing Company. Bradlaugh and Besant in fact deliberately invited prosecution under the Obscene Publications Act, and published advertisements stating that they would 'sell personally the first hundred copies' of the revised version of Knowlton's explicit medical treatise at the offices of the Freethought Publishing Company in East London.[21] At their eventual trial in June 1877, which was heard in the Court of Queen's Bench and, significantly, presided over by Lord Cockburn, the pair even insisted on conducting their own defence, as well as personally issuing subpoenas to their chosen witnesses.

A peculiarity of Campbell's original legislation against obscenity, as Beverly Brown has pointed out, was that, in a reversal of customary legal practice where the prosecution must demonstrate the guilt of the accused, the defendants had instead to prove their own innocence.[22] In the months before the trial which they, as the accused, had had to initiate, Bradlaugh and Besant sought to enlist several high-profile witnesses whose expert testimony might help to establish their innocence of the charge of disseminating, under the cover of science, a depraved work that could corrupt those most vulnerable to its apparently immoral influence. However, most of the potential witnesses whom Bradlaugh and Besant approached, including Samuel Butler and the blind political economist Henry Fawcett, refused to have any involvement with such a distasteful and controversial subject.[23] Darwin was similarly aghast when Bradlaugh wrote to him expressing his intention to subpoena him in the impending trial, and remonstrated that after 'many years much out of health . . . it would be great suffering to me to be a witness in a court. It is indeed not improbable that I might be unable to attend.' Even the mere prospect of such an ordeal, Darwin implied, might seriously impair his famously fragile constitution, and he warned that 'apprehension of the coming exertion would prevent the rest which I require doing me much good'.[24] Darwin's resolute refusal to testify on behalf of Bradlaugh and Besant, as well as his intense anxiety at the prospect of appearing at an obscenity trial, has been discussed frequently by historians, and will be examined in more detail later in this chapter.[25] It has not, however, previously been noted that another highly eminent man of science, who was a long-standing friend of Darwin and many of his inner circle of supporters, actually did appear as a witness, albeit very briefly and disobligingly, at an early session of the legal proceedings against Bradlaugh and Besant's allegedly obscene medical treatise.

For the initial hearing of their case at the Guildhall Magistrate's Court on 19 April 1877, Bradlaugh and Besant, as they reported in the following week's *National Reformer*, summoned certain 'medical and publishing witnesses', including Charles Drysdale and Edward Trübner. Whilst such physicians and scientific publishers had, for the most part, accepted the inconvenience of being subpoenaed with courteous forbearance, the irritable and haughty disposition of perhaps the most eminent of the medical witnesses was a conspicuous exception. As Besant recorded: 'Dr. W. B. Carpenter was a strange contrast to these; he was rough and discourteous in manner, and . . . was the only one of those summoned who forgot either his duty as a citizen or his courtesy as a gentleman'. Carpenter, according to Besant's account of the proceedings carried in the *National Reformer*, 'remarked loftily: "I am a public man, Mr. Bradlaugh"', with the accused quickly retorting, 'And I am a public prisoner, Dr. Carpenter', after which the reluctant witness refused to answer any questions in open court.[26]

Bradlaugh wanted, in particular, to cross-examine Carpenter over the more explicit passages concerning reproduction in his own widely used textbook, *Principles of Human Physiology*, which had first been published over thirty years earlier in 1842. In response to such enquiries, Carpenter 'rudely said that he was not responsible for "Human Physiology by Dr. Carpenter", as his responsibility had ceased with the 5th edition' of 1855, after which, in 1863, Henry Power had begun editing and updating all subsequent editions of the book. Now in its eighth edition, *Principles of Human Physiology* nevertheless still traded on the prestige of Carpenter's imprimatur, and Besant remarked wryly that

It seems a strange thing that a man of eminence, presumably a man of honour, should disavow all responsibility for a book which bears his name as author on the title-page. Clearly, if the "Human Physiology" is not Dr. Carpenter's, the public is grossly deceived by the pretence that it is.[27]

Carpenter gladly took no further part in the proceedings. Even in such a brief cross-examination, however, Bradlaugh, already a notorious atheist who was now charged with disseminating wantonly obscene material, had turned the tables on his renowned and distinguished witness and impugned not only Carpenter's conduct as a gentleman but even his probity as a commercial author. In fact, most of the passages from *Principles of Human Physiology* over which Bradlaugh wished to cross-examine Carpenter, and which, as will be seen, he would later read aloud in the Court of Queen's Bench, had initially appeared in those earlier editions of the book for which its putative author was indeed personally responsible.

Carpenter, who was sixty-three at the time of his fractious appearance at the Guildhall Magistrate's Court, had long been one of the most renowned and highly respected men of science in Victorian Britain, and, since 1856, had also served as the Registrar of the University of London. After initially training in medicine at the University of Edinburgh, he had opted instead to pursue a more precarious career as a lecturer and author of accessible textbooks on a diverse range of scientific and medical subjects, spanning from microscopy to physiological psychology. Having assiduously solicited the support of elite colleagues such as Sir John Herschel, Carpenter, as Alison Winter has shown, was able to evade early imputations of materialism, and, by the mid-1840s, establish himself as an 'exemplary scientific figure' whose 'works became the standard medical textbooks of his time'.[28] He was the son of a Unitarian minister, and his staunch faith informed his wide-ranging scientific views, which envisaged the material world as the product of a beneficent Creator who operated in accordance with natural laws. While he would later contend that, anterior to the physiological nervous structure, there existed a non-material causal agency, the Will or Ego, which acted upon the intellectual faculties, Carpenter's deterministic understanding of the natural world otherwise largely corresponded with that of many younger men of science, and he became a close ally of Huxley and other metropolitan scientific naturalists, as well as a consistent opponent of the rival idealist science advanced by Richard Owen.[29]

Carpenter's endorsement since the 1840s of progressive development, based initially on Ernst von Baer's embryology, also established him as an important, if somewhat equivocal, early advocate of Darwinism, and, although he continued to express doubts over natural selection, he controversially proposed Darwin for the Royal Society's Copley Medal in 1864.[30] Owen, in an anonymous review of Carpenter's *Introduction to the Study of Foraminifera* in the *Athenaeum* in March 1863, discerned the 'influence of Mr. Darwin's volume, "On the Origin of Species", on the mind of the writer', and proposed that Darwin and Carpenter were actually 'master' and 'disciple' who likewise advocated flawed and degrading views of the origin of life.[31] Although Carpenter angrily denied the validity of such a comparison (and even implied that his position might be considered '*anti-Darwinian*'), he continued to be regularly identified as a leading supporter of Darwinism, and upon Darwin's death in April 1882 was at once solicited by importunate editors of periodicals to contribute a 'notice of Darwin's Life and Work, based on my own relations with him'.[32] Carpenter and Darwin, who was his senior by only four years, had remained close friends and continued to correspond with each other into the 1880s.[33] The two men had much in common, not least their overriding concern with maintaining an exemplary personal reputation.

After Darwin's death, Carpenter told his friend Thomas Sadler, minister of the Rosslyn Hill Unitarian Chapel, that 'great as Mr. Darwin was as a scientific discoverer, he was still greater as a man', and, as Sadler later recalled:

he spoke as if he felt this testimony to character to be not only true, but also more to be desired than any testimony to intellectual ability could be. I think what was said is no less true of himself than it was of Mr. Darwin. The work of his life was great for its quality and for its extent; but pervading all one sees the man of highest moral principles.[34]

Although it was Darwin who, following his death, emerged as an icon of the saintly scientific sage, such concerns with moral probity were actually far more integral to Carpenter's scientific career than to that of Darwin. Indeed, Carpenter, as his son Estlin claimed in a posthumous memoir of his father, had initially 'embraced the study of science with a vivid moral ardour', and, even into old age, he continued to articulate many of his scientific views in explicitly moralistic terms.[35] Carpenter's frugal and puritanical personal life, as enumerated in his son's respectful memoir, merely reflected the stern morality of his distinctive understanding of the natural world.

As a Dissenter endeavouring to establish a remunerative scientific career whist promulgating a naturalistic worldview, however, Carpenter had often struggled to maintain such an elevated personal reputation. At the very beginning of his career, as Adrian Desmond has shown, he had had to 'manoeuver adroitly to . . . prevent civic propriety from taking fright' at his Unitarian naturalism.[36] By the mid-1840s, when Carpenter had established himself as a rising man of science, he supplemented his income by giving private tuition to the children of Lord Lovelace, but the arrangement was soon terminated after his aristocratic employer, who was already exasperated by Carpenter's refusal to consider himself a mere servant, implied that his relationship with the children's mother, Lord Byron's daughter Ada,

Countess of Lovelace, had become improperly intimate. Carpenter's anxious repudiation of such suggestions, and especially his prim avowal that the 'lesson I have just learned is too bitter a one for me easily to forget all that the most rigid prudence can require' and rather priggish insistence on the 'unsullied character of Dr. W. B. C.', reveal his acute sensitivity to any insinuations regarding sexual impropriety.[37] Intriguingly, despite Carpenter's vaunted assertion of his own moral probity, Lord Lovelace was soon reporting that 'some very disagreeable things' were once more being said regarding Carpenter's relations with another young woman in an unspecified new position, and his erstwhile employer reflected with malicious delight: 'his old folly – the sex will ruin him . . . He certainly exhibits himself in a contemptible light. If I meet him I shall remark upon it.'[38] Even now, almost forty years later, Carpenter's mere involvement in Bradlaugh and Besant's notorious obscenity trial, and especially his subjection to such an impertinent cross-examination, must have been extremely perturbing for the sexagenarian physiologist, as well as for those amongst the scientific naturalists with whom he had long been closely identified.

Carpenter, as his son's memoir readily conceded, could appear austere and humourless, and even friends like Huxley had encountered what Carpenter himself acknowledged was 'a rough and sometime prickly exterior'.[39] His peevish obstinacy at the Guildhall Magistrate's Court in April 1877 helped ensure that Carpenter was not called as a witness again when the proceedings against Bradlaugh and Besant recommenced at the Court of Queen's Bench two months later. In Carpenter's absence, though, Bradlaugh and Besant would exact a humiliating, and potentially extremely damaging, revenge for the renowned physiologist's haughtiness towards them at the case's initial hearing.

The principal argument advanced by Bradlaugh and Besant in defence of their revised edition of *Fruits of Philosophy* was that the allegedly obscene pamphlet was not actually different, in any significant way, from numerous other medical and scientific works that were sold openly in bookshops, and were even distributed to children, at the behest of the government, as school prizes. In fact, the only tangible difference between the medical treatise for which they had been impeached and such highly regarded scientific publications, Bradlaugh and Besant contended, was the price at which each was sold. Scientific books which sold for 10s. 6d. were, they alleged, often much more explicit and candid, and therefore potentially corrupting and obscene, than Knowlton's sixpenny pamphlet. Bradlaugh, an experienced demagogue as well as a former solicitor's clerk, knew how to exploit the melodramatic potential of a High Court trial, and much of the case for the defence was taken up with his, and Besant's, deliberately provocative exegetical examinations of passages from renowned scientific works that might be considered arousing, and thus, under the terms of Lord Campbell's legislation, obscene. Significantly, it was Carpenter's *Principles of Human Physiology*, more than any other similarly high-priced scientific publication, which, throughout the trial, was portrayed as potentially indecent in its graphic descriptions of human sexuality and reproduction.

Scientific and medical knowledge, Bradlaugh claimed in the Court of Queen's Bench, was generally agreed to be exempt from charges of obscenity and immorality, for 'in itself no physical fact is an indecent fact'.[40] Medical tropes were nevertheless a recurrent feature of Victorian pornography, and especially in novels such as James Campbell's anonymous *The Amatory Experiences of a Surgeon* (1881), in which a concupiscent physician exploits the pursuit of physical knowledge to seduce his nubile young patients. The physician's various sexual encounters are frequently narrated in the same vein as medical examinations ('I made her lie backwards on the couch, and open her legs as wide as possible . . . then proceeding with my examination . . . '), while an explicit paean to the sexual pleasures of the 'beautiful bottom of a fair woman' assumes the objective tone and particularized language of a scientific description: 'it must be owned that these parts themselves are wonderfully well adapted to the purpose. The natural construction of the entrance, the soft interior, and the length with which they are capable of receiving the longest male member . . . '[41] That the novel's 'narrator is a physician', Steven Marcus has argued in his classic study of nineteenth-century pornography *The Other Victorians* (1966), is merely a 'gimmick' which allows the 'sexualization of all reality' and in 'other novels, the same thing is done through making the narrator an attorney, a hotel manager, a travelling salesman – almost anything will do'.[42] This, however, is to ignore the sexual ambiguities peculiar to certain medical and scientific practices and forms of discourse.

In the eighteenth century the boundary between quasi-medical works and erotica was particularly indistinct, and even into the Victorian period many publishers deliberately traded on the implicitly erotic potential of emergent disciplines like anthropology, where detailed empirical descriptions of the sexual behaviour of colonized races could, according to Lisa Z. Sigel, 'simultaneously function as science and pornography'.[43] The English translation of *Untrodden Fields of Anthropology* (1896) affords a particularly striking example of this synthesis of the ostensibly scientific and the overtly erotic. In a preface to the book's first volume, its anonymous French author avowed that it was 'not an obscene work, but a psychological sketch of the history of the sexual passions of the human race' that made 'careful use of medical terms' to avoid 'overstepping the bounds of decency', while, at the beginning of the second volume, its English publisher, the notorious pornographer Charles Carrington, hinted knowingly that the book's 'anthropology . . . is never dull' and has a 'triple value, being the work of an acute physician, an experienced traveller, and a broad-minded man-of-the-world'.[44] Tellingly, the book was available to discerning gentlemanly collectors in a variety of expensive luxury editions. Feminists and campaigners against vivisection, meanwhile, also discerned disturbing parallels between the practices of nineteenth-century obstetric medicine, with its straps and stirrups, and pornographic representations of bondage.[45]

In George Eliot's *Middlemarch* (1871–2), the reform-minded physician Tertius Lydgate's youthful reading of the 'indecent passages in school classics' had left him with a 'general sense of secrecy and obscenity in connection with his internal structure'. It was perhaps this sense of potential illicitness which led him, when looking listlessly for 'freshness' and 'novelty' in his 'small home library' on a rainy day, to examine an 'old Cyclopaedia . . . under the heading of anatomy'; the precise moment, ironically, at which he realized his particular vocation for medicine.[46] There were, as Lydgate's uncertain motivations for his initial encounter with an anatomical text suggest, certain circumstances in which wholly legitimate physical facts, whether conveyed in expensive medical textbooks or cheap treatises sold on street corners, could be used improperly for indecent purposes. Medical and scientific texts on sexuality, as Roy Porter and Lesley Hall have suggested, could themselves have a 'pornographic function', and even 'works condemning masturbation may in fact lead to it'.[47] The dual purpose of such ostensibly educational works might also have contributed to the general reputation for dissoluteness which medical students had for much of the nineteenth century.[48]

Anxious at such an invidious possibility, the *British Medical Journal* warned in 1866 that no 'serious medical work' on sexuality 'should bear . . . those characters', even including gilt lettering on the spine, 'which belong to the class of works which lie upon drawing-room tables' and are perused indiscriminately by general readers.[49] Such difficult subjects, a later number of the journal insisted, must only 'be handled with an absolute purity of speech, thought, and expression, and, as far as possible, in strictly technical language'.[50] But it is inevitably impossible, as Susan Stewart has argued, to produce an objective metadiscourse on desire and sexual excitement, either in medical and scientific writings on sexuality or government reports on pornography, that may not itself potentially engender precisely such desire and erotic stimulation.[51] Bradlaugh, in his defence of *Fruits of Philosophy*, even proposed that some forms of scientific and technical language were much more likely to convey indecent and suggestive connotations, at least to those with sufficiently susceptible minds, than others.

At the pre-trial hearing of their case in April 1877, Bradlaugh and Besant directed the magistrates' attention 'to the style of the Knowlton pamphlet when compared with Carpenter', and contended that in *Principles of Human Physiology* they would 'find the same ideas conveyed, almost in the same words'.[52] While it was bad enough that Carpenter's physiological textbook was compared with a publication that had already been indicted for obscenity, the defendants then went on to claim that the respective passages in both works dealing with reproduction were actually 'worded in Carpenter with greater fullness, or, rather, were worded in the Knowlton pamphlet with greater delicacy, of expression', and that 'if either is tainted with any kind of suggestiveness, certainly Knowlton's pamphlet is free from that suggestiveness'.[53] Even worse, Bradlaugh then 'went, page by page, through . . . the volume of Carpenter's "Human Physiology"', reading aloud particular passages from the book which seemed to demonstrate that 'Dr. Knowlton's pamphlet . . . contains nothing arousing the kind of feelings which might be awakened in some minds by such a description as that given by Dr. Carpenter . . . of the attractive outward changes in the girlish form at the age of puberty' as well as of other aspects of female sexuality.[54]

Since the 1840s, as Huxley later observed, 'Dr. Carpenter's "Human Physiology"' had been the 'standard work on the subject in this country', and it 'retained its high and well-deserved reputation' into the 1870s. Of all the many praiseworthy aspects of this 'compendium of great excellence', Huxley particularly commended the 'admirably lucid style' in which it was written, which had allowed the academic textbook to be 'widely read by the public at large'.[55] For Bradlaugh and Besant it was precisely this eloquent and attractive style of writing that was actually the book's most problematic feature, especially in its descriptions of intimate sexual matters. After all, in the lengthy section dealing with the 'Female Generative system', Carpenter depicted the 'changes in which puberty consists' with an extremely sensual rhetorical flourish:

The external and internal organs of generation undergo a considerable increase of size; the mammary glands enlarge; and a deposition of fat takes place in the mammae and on the pubes, as well as over the whole surface of the body, giving to the person that roundness and fullness, which are so attractive to the opposite sex at the period of commencing womanhood.[56]

While Carpenter's description begins with a general, and depersonalized, itemization of particular physical changes, the specific effects of these changes are then portrayed with a discursive richness ('roundness and fullness') which emphasizes their sensual qualities. The descriptions in Carpenter's medical writing, as Gillian Beer has pointed out, generally assumed a normatively masculine perspective, and, in the above passage, the newly sensuous bodily shape is situated in a specific individual ('the person') whose attractiveness to the male gaze – seemingly including that of the narrator – the reader is encouraged to imagine vividly.[57]

An editorial in the *British Medical Journal* later acknowledged that a 'study of the pages' of various works on sexuality by medical authors 'shows us how difficult it is to avoid an exuberance of detail, and a certain unsavoury suggestiveness of style, which places their books outside the pale of ordinary readers, and even gravely diminishes their scientific value', and it warned prospective authors of such texts against including any 'suggestive detail'.[58] In an accompanying footnote to the above passage from *Principles of Human Physiology*, however, Carpenter even resorted to a conventionally erotic, and again highly sensuous, metaphor to explain geographical differences in the rate of female sexual maturation, observing that 'women (like fruits) reach maturity . . . much earlier in hot climates'.[59] The specific connection between women and fruit, of course, extended at least as far back as the garden of Eden, and, as with Eve's temptation by the alluring serpent, it traditionally had distinctly erotic connotations. In Byron's *Don Juan* (1819), for instance, the city of Seville is 'Famous for oranges and women', and within its precincts the philandering 'Don José, like a lineal son of Eve, / Went plucking various fruit'.[60] Incongruously, Carpenter's academic footnote detailing recent scientific studies of environmental influences on the age at which women begin menstruating invoked exactly the same metaphor, as well as a similar concern with sultry hotter climes, as Byron's scandalous epic of seduction and sexual adventure.

The principal problem with such descriptions, according to Bradlaugh, was that, perhaps in order to render the textbook more appealing to general readers, Carpenter's language – and both of the above passages had initially appeared in editions of the book for which he alone was responsible – had departed from the unadorned style of strictly technical and scientific discourse.[61] As Bradlaugh observed:

The plain, dry statement of physiological facts does not tend to produce lustful desires, and the perusal of a medical treatise does not throw a seductive charm over the sex opposite to that of the reader. It is necessary to throw over those details some veil of story, or of poetry, or of luscious description before they can exercise any attraction over the senses.[62]

With pornographic novels such as *The Amatory Experiences of a Surgeon* similarly dwelling on those 'usual indications of approaching puberty' exhibited by attractive young women, Bradlaugh implied that the overly figurative, and sometimes even lyrical language, employed in Carpenter's physiological monograph elided the necessary boundaries between the utilitarian discourse of science and the most calculatingly lurid pornographic writing.[63]

Yet, although Carpenter's sensuous descriptions of female sexual maturation were, in the opinion of the defendants, likely to generate licentious desires, and especially amongst younger readers, *Principles of Human Physiology* had been 'fixed by Her Majesty's Committee of Privy Council on Education as a prize-book for boys and girls'.[64] Scientific works, as Kate Flint has shown, were frequently recommended by educationalists and advice manuals as appropriate reading for girls, which, it was proposed, might correct their natural propensity for irregular thought and making deductions unsupported by evidence.[65] However, the suitability of specifically physiological texts for female readers had long been a highly contentious issue. At University College London, women were debarred from the study of physiology long after classes on botany and other scientific subjects were opened to them, and, as one physician complained in the *Medical Press and Circular*, an 'elementary knowledge of anatomy and physiology' was 'not only . . . non-existent' amongst 'women' of the upper and middle classes, 'but the demand for it, or the possession of it, would seem to be accounted barely modest and respectable. It is not, according to the refined notions of society, a proper thing that a lady should be tainted with such vulgar knowledge as that she is an item in the animal creation at all.'[66] While Bradlaugh and Besant were both committed to furthering the dissemination of such forms of knowledge amongst women and girls, they still exploited widespread concerns over the suitability of physiological textbooks for a female audience to assist their case for the defence.

As Lord Chief Justice, Cockburn was the presiding judge at Bradlaugh and Besant's trial at the Court of Queen's Bench, and they told him directly that if, under his own nine-year old legal definition, 'physiology is obscene', then Carpenter's widely used textbook was, without doubt, 'immeasurably more obscene' than their own more circumspect physiological publication.[67] Writing in the *National Reformer* soon after the trial's conclusion, Besant even envisaged a masturbatory scenario in which 'a person of prurient mind buys Dr. Carpenter's "Human Physiology", and reads the long chapter, containing over 100 pages, wholly devoted to a minute description of generation'. The 'effect' of such a lurid encounter with the book, she insisted, would inevitably 'be "to excite and create thoughts of" the "demoralising character"' originally described in Cockburn's 1868 test of obscenity, and therefore in the terms of the 'Lord Chief Justice's ruling, Dr. Carpenter's would then become an obscene book'.[68] Such an incongruous example of obscenity, Besant proposed, revealed the inadequacy and absurdity of a law which determined that 'books whose intention is to convey physiological knowledge . . . are obscene, if the reader's passions chance to be aroused by them'. The legal definition of obscenity, she claimed, had been deliberately 'narrowed in order to enmesh Freethought', but its 'net' would inevitably also 'catch other fishes' that the original legislation was never intended to include 'or else break under the strain and let all go free'.[69] With *Fruits of Philosophy* having been found guilty of being 'calculated to deprave public morals' (although the jury exonerated the defendants from 'any corrupt motive in publishing it'), Besant contended that it was preposterous that any scientific text, whether Knowlton's proscribed pamphlet or Carpenter's more expensive *Principles of Human Physiology*, should be regarded as obscene merely because of its potential misuse by onanistically minded readers.[70]

During their High Court trial, though, both she and Bradlaugh had continually questioned Carpenter's own motives, as well as those of his publisher, in couching his physiological descriptions in what the defendants considered was an unnecessarily sensuous and potentially arousing language. Bradlaugh even implied that commercial imperatives might have compelled Carpenter to deliberately devote large sections of his book to salacious subjects and to veer towards potentially obscene language in describing them. After comparing various passages from Knowlton's pamphlet and Carpenter's textbook, Bradlaugh concluded that

the female, her functions and organs . . . is . . . over and over again covered by this volume of Carpenter's, and covered in such a way as to show that the latter writer wanted to make his book interesting. It is amply clear that Knowlton had no such object. He had no interest in making his pamphlet even approach indecency.[71]

One of the last clauses appended to the Obscene Publications Bill during its passage through the House of Lords in August 1857 was a requirement that the prosecution must show that any indicted material was published principally for financial gain. This Parliamentary amendment was obviously intended to exempt high art and other forms of elite culture, including science, from the new legislation and the philistine police and magistrates who would most likely administer it.[72] Carpenter, as the author of several successful introductory textbooks on a variety of scientific subjects, had long been sensitive to charges that he was 'no better than a "trader in knowledge"'.[73] Still worse, Bradlaugh now implied that while the *Principles of Human Physiology* masqueraded as a disinterested and purely pedagogic work, it was in fact a shrewd and vulgarly commercial publishing venture, and, as such, was not deserving of any legal protection against the law on obscenity.

Even the long-standing publisher of *Principles of Human Physiology*, the reputable and established firm of J. & A. Churchill, was charged with cynically cashing in on the book's tawdry notoriety. Churchill's was a specialist medical and scientific publisher whose renowned founder, John Churchill, had died only four years earlier in 1873. Carpenter had, since the 1840s, been the firm's most prolific and prestigious author, but its most profitable venture had been the still anonymous evolutionary blockbuster *Vestiges of the Natural History of Creation*, which had been published in successive editions since 1844.[74] Although Churchill's were still making money from *Vestiges* into the 1870s, Bradlaugh alleged that the firm had nevertheless resorted to disreputable and underhand methods of boosting their profits. After taking the Court of Queen's Bench through the explicit contents of *Principles of Human Physiology* as well as various other of the firm's medical textbooks, he noted that 'since this prosecution has been pending, Messrs. Churchill have issued special circulars drawing attention to these works'. Bradlaugh did not 'blame the publishers for utilising the notoriety', and asked merely that the court acknowledged that 'since these proceedings began, the publishers are issuing advertisements, and that there has been an increased sale' of such physiological works outside the 'medical profession'.[75] While medical textbooks, as the *Daily Telegraph* had noted in 1857, had long been part of the legitimate trade in cheap books in London's Holywell Street, Bradlaugh insinuated that, in the production and marketing of *Principles of Human Physiology*, the motives of both Carpenter and Churchill's had been more in keeping with the nefarious pornographers who famously plied their illicit wares in the same street.

These outrageously impertinent accusations against Carpenter and his long-standing publisher were, it is important to remember, articulated in one of the most highly visible forums of Victorian Britain, and, while Bradlaugh and Besant had long been vilified as moral pariahs and were largely debarred from respectable society, their invidious imputations in the High Court were reported in *The Times* and other leading newspapers. With Carpenter, as well as all other prominent men of science, refusing to appear at the trial, such contentious testimony generally appeared without any contradiction or even qualification.[76] At the other end of the newspaper scale, every lurid detail of the trial was also chronicled by the defendants themselves in their tuppenny weekly the *National Reformer*, which devoted almost all its pages to the case, as well as in numerous propagandistic pamphlets issued by the Freethought Publishing Company.

As such radical publications revealed, moreover, even some of Carpenter's purported friends and allies seemed to concur with Bradlaugh and Besant's opinion of the potentially indecent tendencies of his work. Henry George Bohn, who in 1859 had published an edition of Carpenter's *Animal Physiology* as part of his 'Bohn's Scientific Library' series, actually volunteered to give evidence at the Court of Queen's Bench on behalf of the defendants, and he agreed with Bradlaugh that his former author's *Principles of Human Physiology* was 'substantially' the same as the pamphlet that had been indicted for obscenity.[77] Bohn's testimony, Bradlaugh's daughter Hypatia later recalled, was 'invaluable' in helping her father establish his case that *Fruits of Philosophy* was no more guilty of obscenity than numerous other scientific publications, although, in so doing, it also implied that Carpenter's own works might themselves, at least under existing legislation, be justifiably indicted for the same crime.[78]

Obscenity remained, throughout the Victorian period, an extremely ambiguous legal category, which consistently resisted any categorical definition, and, even following Lord Cockburn's attempt at judicial clarification in 1868, allowed those charged with the offence – radical freethinkers as well as commercial pornographers – to contend that many legitimate and well-known works (even including the Bible) were, in the ambivalent terms of the existing legislation, equally as obscene as their own proscribed publications, if not actually far more so. These persistent debates over the legal regulation of obscenity in Victorian Britain, as Nead has observed, reveal the 'perplexing problem . . . of cultural definition' inherent in any attempt to distinguish between different forms of representation of sexuality.[79] Despite the explicit intentions of the Obscene Publications Act's original sponsors, it was inevitably impossible to clearly demarcate elite science, like high art and serious literature, from other, less respectable and more readily available modes of discourse concerning human sexuality and reproduction.

Its ambivalent legal status notwithstanding, the mere imputation of obscenity, as the satirist Sydney Smith had reflected in the *Edinburgh Review* as far back as 1809, was enough to make a respectable man 'consider the very fact of being accused . . . almost sufficient to ruin him'.[80] In 1875 a correspondent to the *Athenaeum* still agreed that 'so timid are Englishmen where there is a question of being charged with encouraging vice, that I can fancy the effect . . . is like that which would once have been produced by the call of a functionary of the Inquisition upon a Spanish Jew.'[81] Those scientific authors who were accused, both implicitly and more overtly, of deliberately including salacious and potentially obscene material between the covers of their purportedly demure physiology textbooks would presumably have found such contemptible charges extremely perturbing.

The experience must have been particularly agonizing for Carpenter, whose son later reflected that 'anything that seemed like moral wrong caused him the most stinging pain; and to the imputations which he had occasionally to meet in controversy he was acutely susceptible.'[82] To make matters worse, in the two months following his humiliating cross-examination at Guildhall Magistrate's Court in April 1877 Carpenter also endured the deaths of both his younger brother Philip (24 May) and elder sister Mary (14 June), and, not unnaturally, sank into what he described as a 'depressed state of health' during the summer.[83] He may actually have suffered a mild form of nervous breakdown, as he later told Alfred Russel Wallace that during this time he had 'found myself so *completely prostrated* as to be utterly unfit for work of any kind'.[84] While Carpenter seems never to have commented directly, either in public or private, on the personal impact of his bruising experience at the hands of Bradlaugh and Besant, he conceded that his state of depression was only 'partly' attributable to the 'severe bereavements I have sustained'.[85] His extant correspondence from May and June 1877 suggests that he was particularly prickly about his scientific reputation, especially regarding the originality of certain claims made in 'my "Human Physiology"', and alarmed at any imputations of 'moral obliquity'.[86] It is perhaps also significant that, soon after the conclusion of Bradlaugh and Besant's High Court trial, he decided not to attend, for the first time in many years, the annual meeting of the British Association for the Advancement of Science, and, as he explained in a glum letter of apology to the organizing committee, intended to instead stay out of public view and 'devote' his entire 'vacation to [the] bodily and mental refreshment' which his travails earlier in the year had rendered necessary.[87]

Although the ninth and final edition of *Principles of Human Physiology* was published in 1881, Carpenter himself was not involved in its preparation, and in his own writing at this time he veered away conspicuously from anything that might be considered improper. In an article on the medical profession for the *Modern Review* in July 1881, he noted tersely that 'in regard to the Contagious Diseases Act, it is impossible in these pages to enter into any discussion.'[88] Carpenter made it clear that, whatever his actual views on the enforced medical examination of prostitutes in garrison towns, he would 'maintain a sober dignity of tone' and not say any more than was 'editorially thought fitting' for the 'pages of a respectable Review'.[89] The case for the defence in the trial of Knowlton's *Fruits of Philosophy* had exploited a certain generic indeterminacy in Carpenter's scientific language, and he now endeavoured to expunge any potential ambiguities from his writing, especially when it would be read by the non-specialist audience of a general periodical.

Bradlaugh and Besant's invidious insinuations against even such an eminent man of science as Carpenter might still be dismissed as merely the brazen hyperbole of desperate defendants, and historians have not hitherto discerned any significant implications for nineteenth-century science in the Victorian endeavour to regulate obscenity. But the concerns about the legal status of scientific and medical representations of sexuality raised at the Court of Queen's Bench continue to resonate in contemporary debates over science's relation to wider culture as well as the indeterminacy, both in terms of genre and meaning, of even apparently objective texts. As Ludmilla Jordanova has observed:

It may appear unreasonable to set so-called 'pornography' next to medical texts, since the former intentionally sets out to shock, provoke, titillate and excite while, at a conscious level at least, the latter set out to edify. There are, indeed, major generic differences here, but they do not invalidate comparisons. All texts work at many different levels, and beyond the expressed intentions of their creators. We are as entitled to find a form of violent eroticism in medicine as we are to note the philosophical dimensions of 'pornography'; neither case need involve the attribution of conscious motives to authors.[90]

Against the background of the relentless allegations concerning scientific naturalism's apparent endorsement of sensualism and immorality examined in previous chapters, moreover, the possibility of scientific works being used for indecent purposes assumes an even greater significance.

While exponents of radical freethought such as Bradlaugh and Besant were, of course, very different from more conservative critics of naturalistic science like Mivart and Mallock, their imputations might prove no less damaging to Carpenter's much-prized scientific standing, as well as, significantly, the public reputation of Darwinism. Indeed, Darwin himself, only a year after his old friend's mortifying exposure to the depredations of a court of law, seems to have become extremely anxious at the prospect that scientific publications might be charged with obscenity. Despite his habitual tendency to eschew controversy, Darwin told the son of Edward Truelove, a radical publisher of cheap physiological tracts gaoled under the Obscene Publications Act in 1878, that he considered his father's prosecution 'very harsh, as the publication of works of this nature can hardly be considered as obscene in the ordinary sense of the word' (although he still refused to sign a memorial in support of Truelove).[91] The ramifications of the notorious trial of Knowlton's *Fruits of Philosophy*, however, did not end in June 1877 and would continue to be highly problematic for Darwin and his inner circle of supporters for several years to come.

GREAT DANGER OF EXTREME PROFLIGACY

In February 1878, the Court of Error quashed the High Court's original judgement against Bradlaugh and Besant on a legal technicality, allowing the pair to continue selling their revised edition of *Fruits of Philosophy*, the demand for which had, inevitably, increased following the publicity of the trial. Within a few months, though, Knowlton's now notorious pamphlet – which had, after all, occasioned one of the most notable trials in Victorian legal history – was quietly withdrawn from sale by the Freethought Publishing Company. The principal reason for the pamphlet's prosecution under the Obscene Publications Act had been the practical advice that it offered regarding artificial checks to fertility, which, according to the prosecution, was deliberately intended to facilitate promiscuous intercourse amongst the unmarried (although even Lord Cockburn considered the accusation unfair). But *Fruits of Philosophy* had been written over forty years earlier, and much of its contraceptive advice, as Besant in particular recognized, was not only outdated but also involved practices, especially vaginal douching, that had subsequently become associated with prostitution.[92] Soon after the trial's conclusion in June 1877, Besant had determined to both modernize and enhance the physiological information available in Knowlton's rather old-fashioned treatise, and it was her pamphlet *The Law of Population* that took the place of *Fruits of Philosophy* in the Freethought Publishing Company's lists at the beginning of the following year. Although Besant's own manual of reproductive physiology was principally concerned with providing clear and reliable advice on family limitation to the hard-pressed working classes, she also used it to continue the strategic criticism of leading men of science which she and Bradlaugh had begun at the High Court in the previous summer. This time, moreover, even Darwin himself would be unable to avoid becoming implicated.

Birth control was a highly contentious and taboo issue throughout the nineteenth century. Since the 1820s, the campaigning handbills of Francis Place had ensured that concerns with reducing poverty through family limitation were invariably tainted by their association with a wider programme of radical political and social reform, even though many radicals were extremely reluctant to accept any practice which appeared to endorse the conservative social doctrines of Malthus. In reality, Malthus had explicitly denounced artificial checks to fertility in the 1817 edition of his *Essay on Population* and instead urged individuals to exercise self-restraint in regard to sex and marriage, while the most vocal support for birth control during the early nineteenth century came from Jeremy Bentham and his rationalist acolytes, who insisted on its practical utility.[93]

Malthusian forebodings concerning the urgent need to restrain the inexorable sexual instinct continued, as is well known, to cast a huge shadow over Victorian discussions of sex.[94] The vast majority of the medical profession agreed that contraception, by detaching intercourse from the responsibilities of procreation, would inevitably promote sexual promiscuity, amongst unmarried women in particular. Such an invidious possibility would also endanger the conventional nineteenth-century sexual double standard which acknowledged, and tacitly condoned, the existence of erotic desires only in men. By the 1870s, the military defeat and civic unrest of France, where artificial means of family limitation had been practised for several decades, was seen to provide a monitory example of the ruinous results of such unnatural practices.[95] Nevertheless, a number of works detailing various methods of contraception, including Robert Dale Owen's *Moral Physiology* (1831) and George Drysdale's anonymous *The Elements of Social Science* (1855) as well as Knowlton's *Fruits of Philosophy*, continued to sell in large numbers throughout the Victorian period, and it is likely that a large proportion of women from all social classes employed the advice of such publications (which generally proposed techniques for which the female was responsible), as well as private discussions with family and friends, to regulate their fertility by artificial means.[96]

Despite its widespread practical use, however, the issue of birth control remained beyond the acceptable boundaries of public discussion, and hints concerning the apparently sympathetic views of Lord Amberley and John Stuart Mill had scandalized polite society during the late 1860s and early 1870s. Even in scientific and medical textbooks the controversial subject was either condemned outright, as in Thomas Low Nichols's *Human Physiology* (1872) which berated those 'ignorant or unprincipled members of the medical profession' who prescribed such demoralizing checks, or else it was simply ignored altogether.[97] This was precisely the approach adopted by Carpenter in successive editions of *Principles of Human Physiology*, which, while carefully explaining every aspect of conception and gestation in explicit detail, circumspectly avoided providing any information as to how they might be averted.

Having already censured the apparent obscenity of Carpenter's physiological descriptions in the High Court, Besant, in *The Law of Population*, now utilized exactly the same details to provide advice to her readers on preventing pregnancy. Bradlaugh and Besant's case for the defence had insisted on the generic indeterminacy of *Principles of Human Physiology*, which, they had claimed, elided the boundaries between the unadorned style of scientific writing and the more figurative language of pornography. By shrewdly extracting particular passages from the same work, and, most importantly, by denuding them of their original context, Besant, in the following year, also transformed Carpenter's physiological textbook into a further type of scandalous and prohibited publication: a birth control manual.

In a section dealing with menstruation, Besant's *The Law of Population* deferred to the authoritative account provided in *Principles of Human Physiology*, and quoted the book's opinion that "'It is quite certain that there is a greater aptitude for conception immediately before and after that epoch than there is at any intermediate period" (Carpenter)'.[98] In Carpenter's textbook this statement had originally appeared as merely one of many physiological facts of relevance only to students and physicians, the authority of which, in accordance with the conventions of academic writing, was confirmed by the testimony of several other experts in the field.[99] In the following sentence the professional readers of *Principles of Human Physiology* were also alerted to the fact that 'coitus immediately after menstruation appears to have been frequently recommended as a cure for sterility, and to have proved successful', and were then informed, via a technical footnote, of the 'latest work on the subject' by the Polish physiologist Adam Raciborski.[100] When it appeared in *The Law of Population*, however, Carpenter's physiological fact was divested of such an academic framework, and, whilst retaining a clear parenthetical attribution to Carpenter himself, was transformed into a practical injunction to the pamphlet's plebeian readers that 'the avoidance of sexual intercourse during the few days before and after menstruation' might be used as a simple form of contraceptive check.[101]

While apparently paying due deference to the scientific authority of *Principles of Human Physiology*, Besant was actually utilizing its information to promote practices that had been deliberately eschewed in its own pages, and which, she must surely have known, would have been anathema to the book's author. Carpenter's own personal life seems to have been conducted upon strictly Malthusian principles, and, as he once told Ada, Countess of Lovelace, he had 'kept the passions of his manhood under control until his marriage at twenty-seven years old', after which he and his wife had raised five children.[102] Even the merest suggestion that he was in any way sympathetic to artificial means of family limitation might still have proved both socially and professionally disastrous. Besant nevertheless transformed Carpenter's physiological facts into explicit contraceptive advice which her readers might well have assumed was actually advocated by this eminent man of science.

Despite the urgency of the issue which she addressed, Besant used her birth control pamphlet to exact a further revenge for Carpenter's haughtiness in the witness stand that would have been equally as humiliating, and potentially just as damaging, as her and Bradlaugh's earlier insinuations that he was deliberately peddling pornography under the cover of physiological science. But Carpenter was not the only prominent man of science to be strategically upbraided in *The Law of Population*. He had, after all, at least appeared as a witness during the legal proceedings against *Fruits of Philosophy*, albeit only very briefly and without disguising his irritation at being subpoenaed in such a case. Darwin, on the other hand, had refused to take the witness stand altogether, and the tone of the letter in which he declined Bradlaugh's request that he appear at the Court of Queen's Bench had shifted from the meek enumeration of his many ailments to a resolute and rather terse avowal that, while he had 'not seen the book in question, but for notices in the newspaper', he would 'be forced to express in court a very decided opinion in opposition to you & Mrs Besant'. Darwin, as he went on to explain, was opposed to the use of any 'means to prevent conception', for he was convinced that 'such practices would in time lead to unsound women & would destroy chastity, on which the family bond depends'.[103] While Darwin's patriarchal reasoning concurred with the views of most other medical and scientific writers, in the specific context of a private letter to Bradlaugh shortly before the commencement of his and Besant's trial such comments might imply that the defendants were – whether unwittingly or deliberately – facilitating immorality and promiscuity, and especially amongst unmarried women.

In response, Besant turned the tables on Darwin in *The Law of Population* and implicitly impugned his own respectability in exactly the same way that she and Bradlaugh had denigrated Carpenter's reputation in the previous year. It was, she proposed, the outwardly respectable men who promulgated such wary and distrustful views of female sexual responsibility who did most to degrade the nation's women. Castigating patriarchal assumptions that women were deterred from wanton promiscuity only by the fear of conceiving a child out of wedlock, Besant maintained that

'English women are not yet sunk so low that they preserve their loyalty to one, only from fear of the possible consequences of disloyalty; their purity, their pride, their honour, their womanhood, these are guardians of their virtue.'[104] Darwin, soon after the publication of Besant's pamphlet, reiterated his fears to another advocate of birth control, George Arthur Gaskell, asking rhetorically: 'If it were universally known that the birth of children could be prevented . . . would there not be great danger of extreme profligacy amongst unmarried women, and might we not become like the "arreoi" societies in the Pacific?'[105] This apprehension that, without the threat of pregnancy, women might revert to a primitive and apparently instinctual sexual dissipation contrasted markedly with the natural coyness and passivity in sexual selection that, as was seen in chapter two, Darwin had attributed to females in *The Descent of Man* (even while it confirmed the fear of sexually voracious women that was also evident in the same book). But Besant discerned in such concerns evidence of an unnatural preoccupation with sex and immorality, and proclaimed: 'Shame on those who slander England's wives and maidens with the foul thoughts that can only spring from the mind and the lips of the profligate.'[106] While Darwin was not mentioned directly in this particular section of *The Law of Population*, his opposition to contraception on the grounds of maintaining the struggle for survival was revealed only three pages later, and Besant, who would undoubtedly have seen Darwin's curt letter of reply to Bradlaugh in June 1877, implied unmistakably that those, like him, who also justified a rejection of artificial checks with base and cynical views of female sexuality merely revealed their own shamelessness and depravity.

Despite his refusal to give testimony at the Court of Queen's Bench, Darwin's scientific views were invoked regularly during the trial of Knowlton's *Fruits of Philosophy*, and, as with Carpenter's physiological information, often for ends with which Darwin himself had no sympathy at all. Besant, for instance, assured the Lord Chief Justice that evidence 'from Mr. Darwin' showing that 'marriage has a distinctly lengthening effect on human life' would substantiate 'what Knowlton says about health' and the necessity of regular indulgence of the sexual instincts in his proscribed pamphlet.[107] The particular passage in the *Descent* to which she referred did not, of course, actually mention the alleged dangers of thwarting the natural impulse for sex, and, after merely noting that 'marriage in itself is a main cause of prolonged life', instead concurred with James Stark's conclusion that those who were married probably benefited from 'more regular domestic habits'.[108] There was, however, a suggestive ambivalence in Darwin's reference to 'regular domestic habits', and the expression was

clearly interpreted by Besant in overtly sexual terms. After all, in the conclusion to the *Descent* Darwin contended that 'all ought to refrain from
marriage who cannot avoid abject poverty for their children', an injunction
which makes sense only if it was presumed, as Darwin evidently did, that
marriage was virtually synonymous with sexual activity.[109]

As Besant acknowledged in the High Court, Darwin had written to the
defendants drawing their attention to this particular passage in the *Descent*'s
conclusion and its advocacy of precisely those abstemious remedies for
overpopulation, chastity and late marriage, which Malthus had originally
proposed.[110] But such self-restraint, as Besant insisted, was neither healthy
nor even actually possible, and, rather than having the beneficial social consequences which those such as Darwin naively anticipated, its enforcement
would instead lead to a far more invidious state of affairs. Shortly before
reciting the passage from the *Descent* to which Darwin had alerted her,
Besant told the High Court that

as a simple matter of fact, I must put it to you that men and women, but more
especially men, will not lead a celibate life, whether they are married or unmarried,
and that what you have got to deal with is, that which we advocate – early marriage
with restraint upon the numbers of the family – or else a simple mass of unlicensed
prostitution, which is the ruin both of men and women when once they fall into
it.[111]

Darwin, in the *Descent*, had already acknowledged the existence of societies
in which 'licentiousness' was used 'as a means of keeping down the population', while, in April 1874, Mivart, as was seen in chapter two, had provoked a rancorous controversy by alleging that Darwin's son George actually
approved of such 'encouragement of vice in order to check population'.[112]
Although Besant did not share Mivart's theological concerns with the moral
consequences of Darwinism, and instead considered that Darwin's remedies
for overpopulation were unrealistically abstemious, she still implied that his
scientific views would lead – inadvertently but inevitably – to exactly the
same iniquitous social consequences that Mivart had envisaged only three
years earlier.

Following the trial of Knowlton's *Fruits of Philosophy*, Darwin had, as he
explained to Gaskell, 'been led to reflect a little . . . on the artificial checks',
although he still continued to 'doubt greatly whether such would be advantageous to the world at present'.[113] In *The Law of Population*, however, Besant
appropriated an explicitly Darwinian rationale – as well as rhetoric – in her
advocacy of artificial means of restricting fertility, which, she proposed,
would fulfil exactly the same function in advanced human societies that

Darwin had attributed to the more conventionally Malthusian checks of conflict, disease and starvation in the natural world. As she declared in the Court of Queen's Bench: 'Nature balances herself, but if we remove her checks by civilization, and cure those whom she would kill, we must put some others in their place.' The artificial 'checks' which Darwin, in thrall to an irrational fear of female sexuality, opposed with such misplaced vehemence would simply 'eliminate the sickly, just as does the struggle for existence' in nature.[114]

Contraceptive techniques, Besant went on to suggest, might actually allow humans to gain control over the process of evolution, and to supplant the randomness of natural selection with a scientifically directed form of rational selection that would ensure the continued progress of the race. As Besant prophesized:

Scientific checks to population would just do for man what the struggle for existence does for the brutes: they enable man to control the production of new human beings . . . The whole British race would gain in vigour, in health, in longevity, in beauty, if only healthy parents gave birth to children.[115]

Whereas Darwin had envisaged birth control as a destructive and degenerative force which might render Victorian Britain little better than the primitive '"arreoi" societies in the Pacific', Besant strategically identified it (and especially in the shift in her language from the abstract 'man' to the more narrow 'British race') with the nation's future social and political advancement. Besant's view of the social benefits of such 'scientific checks' was not dissimilar to the proposals for human breeding which Darwin's cousin Francis Galton would soon term 'Eugenics', although Galton himself, as Karl Pearson later observed, strongly objected to 'unrestricted' or 'unthinking birth control' which was not legislatively enforced by the state, for the 'imprudent, the feckless and the feebleminded by their very nature will not control their births, and the higher intelligences will and do'.[116] Similarly, Besant's emphasis on contraception instead of feminine virtue and responsibility also distanced her from the strain of 'eugenic feminism' advanced by Ellice Hopkins and Sarah Grand.[117] By combining her quasi-Darwinian rhetoric with practical advice on the use of different contraceptive checks in a cheap and readily accessible pamphlet, Besant, in *The Law of Population*, implied that it was individual users of family limitation, especially amongst the urban proletariat, who would ensure the nation's future evolutionary progress.

Soon after the conclusion of the trial of Knowlton's *Fruits of Philosophy*, Besant and Bradlaugh, along with Charles Drysdale, founded a political organization whose principal aim was the removal of all legal restrictions to the public discussion of birth control. In calling the new organization the Malthusian League and in advocating 'preventive checks' and 'marital prudence' they self-consciously deployed, as Lucy Bland has argued, exactly the same language that Malthus had used in his jeremiads on overpopulation, while at time same time overtly rejecting the actual methods that Malthus himself had proposed for its alleviation.[118] Later, Besant would also appropriate and radically invert the Darwinian concept of sexual selection and give to women the active role in evolutionary progress which Darwin had explicitly denied them.[119] In her passionate advocacy of birth control at the Court of Queen's Bench, Besant similarly turned Darwin's vehement opposition to all forms of contraception on its head by employing his own evolutionary arguments, as she had with Carpenter's physiological facts, to demonstrate the urgent necessity of artificial checks to fertility, and even the presiding judge acknowledged that her argument was 'very well worthy [of] the serious consideration of Mr. Darwin'.[120] The *Law of Population* continued the Darwinian vein of Besant's demands for the widespread adoption of contraceptive techniques, and, as Desmond has observed, her '*6d* worth of sexual advice and adverts for intimate appliances . . . made the *Origin of Species* an argument for birth control'.[121] Besant would also later publish a pamphlet by her radical colleague Edward Bibbens Aveling entitled *Darwinism and Small Families* (1882), which likewise insisted that the 'principle of Natural Selection, a part of Darwinism, is in favour of small families'.[122] With their scientific views being regularly appropriated by Besant and other radical freethinkers, and often for political and social ends with which they had no sympathy whatsoever, it was imperative for Darwin and his friends and colleagues clearly to demarcate themselves and their intellectual positions from such disreputable associations.

FREETHINKING DOES NOT MEAN FREE LOVE

Darwin's aversion to the contraceptive remedies to poverty advanced by so-called 'Neo-Malthusians', and his continued adherence to an older and more abstemious version of Malthusianism, have been much discussed by historians, while his often terse and anxious replies to letters from advocates of artificial checks such as Bradlaugh and Gaskell makes Darwin's antipathy towards birth control and its supporters unmistakeable. A letter to Herbert Spencer from February 1860 nevertheless contains a tantalizing, but previously unnoticed, hint that Darwin may actually have been acquainted with one of the most important, and certainly most scandalous, proponents of contraception of the entire nineteenth century. In response to Spencer's request for suggestions regarding who he might send the subscription list for his mammoth 'System of Synthetic Philosophy', Darwin could think of only one recipient to whom the ten-volume, and mostly still to be written, series might be of interest:

> I know so few people, that I can really think of only one person, to whom it would be any good to send your gigantic programme. This one is
>   Dr Drysdale
>   care of Dr Lane
>   Moor Park
>   Farnham
>   Surrey.[123]

This 'Dr Drysdale', who is not mentioned anywhere else in Darwin's voluminous correspondence, was almost certainly a relation of Lady Elizabeth Drysdale, the mother-in-law of Edward Wickstead Lane, whose exclusive hydropathic clinic at Moor Park was used regularly by Darwin during the late 1850s.

The widowed Lady Drysdale was also Moor Park's lively hostess, and Darwin enthusiastically told Hooker that 'Dr Lane & wife & mother-in-law Lady Drysdale are some of the nicest people, I have ever met.'[124] Lane's embarrassing involvement in a scandalous divorce case in 1857 following allegations of improper relations between himself and a married female patient is well known to historians, as is Darwin's continued loyalty to his now infamous but still much trusted doctor (although, as Janet Browne has observed, he was 'nonetheless transfixed by the newspaper details').[125] What has not previously been noted is Lane's lifelong friendship with Lady Drysdale's eldest son George, who may well have been the 'Dr Drysdale' referred to in Darwin's letter to Spencer. Significantly, following their parallel medical educations in Edinburgh, where they resided in the same house, Lane shared many of Drysdale's more heterodox medical beliefs, and not only on the effectiveness of the water-cure.[126]

In particular, Drysdale advocated the use of birth control to enable the healthy indulgence of the sexual instinct without ensnaring poor families in intolerable poverty, and Lane may have agreed with his brother-in-law even on this. Although Lane's lawyers in the 1857 divorce case contended that the woman who claimed to be his lover, Isabella Robinson, was deluded by an erotomania brought on by 'taking measures to prevent conception', Mason has maintained that the evidence suggests that 'Lane did have intercourse with Mrs Robinson, and . . . the allegations about the latter's "uterine" delusions . . . were dishonest.'[127] The insinuations regarding Robinson's injurious use of contraception may therefore perhaps have been similarly malicious and used merely in a desperate attempt to discredit her moral character in the eyes of the divorce court. Certainly, Lane's later proposal in the *Medical Press and Circular* that only by providing the 'lower orders' with 'an elementary knowledge of anatomy and physiology' could the medical profession help overcome the 'fundamental' problem of an 'excess of population' hinted at a certain sympathy for artificial checks to fertility.[128] The patients at Lane's hydropathic clinic, meanwhile, often included known supporters of contraception such as James Stuart Laurie, whose controversial views were later publicly avowed at the London Dialectical Society, and, as J. Miriam Benn has suggested, it is likely that the 'conversation at Moor Park' included 'talk of Secularism, science and population control'.[129] Drysdale was, according to Tomo Sato, a 'frequent visitor [to Moor Park], if not having made his brother-in-law's home his own', and, along with his younger brother Charles who took up medicine in the mid-1850s and held similar views on birth control, would doubtless have been a regular participant in such discussions at Lane's hydropathic establishment.[130]

While Darwin seems to have spent most of this time at Moor Park in the company of genteel ladies like the novelist Georgina Craik, he also became 'much attached' to 'Dr L. & all his family'.[131] Indeed, as Darwin's letter to Spencer implies, he was not only acquainted with the 'Dr Drysdale' in question, but knew his views on various scientific and social subjects well enough to be able to recommend him to Spencer as a potential subscriber to the 'System of Synthetic Philosophy'. Amidst the apparently serene natural surroundings of Moor Park, Darwin's mind, as he explained in a letter to Hooker, was still never far from the 'truly wonderful' questions of population pressure and the inevitable struggle for survival between various plant and animal species, which would also have corresponded with many of Drysdale's own concerns at this time and perhaps prompted conversations between them.[132]

It is, of course, impossible to be certain from the cursory reference in his letter to Spencer that Darwin was alluding to this particular 'Dr Drysdale', and, as well as George's younger brother Charles, he could also have meant the Liverpool-based homeopathic doctor John James Drysdale, whose articles with William Henry Dallinger on monads and the origin of life Darwin later expressed admiration for.[133] In Darwin's brief correspondence with Dallinger between 1876 and 1878, however, there seems to be no suggestion of any prior acquaintance with the co-author of these important articles refuting spontaneous generation.[134] It is also unclear whether John James Drysdale was actually Lady Drysdale's son or merely one of her numerous stepchildren, the late Lord Drysdale having already had five children by two previous wives before he married her.[135] As such, John James Drysdale may well have been less involved with Moor Park, although he is known to have made occasional visits, and he certainly knew Lane, into whose care Spencer was instructed by Darwin to forward his subscription list, much less well than George Drysdale did (who, as Mason has noted, was a recluse and cagey about who knew his address).[136] Nevertheless, even without such certainty, the possibility that, at some point during the 1850s, Darwin had met George Drysdale, and that the two had at least briefly discussed scientific and social issues similar to those considered in Spencer's philosophical work, remains an intriguing prospect.

Whether or not they discussed population and fertility, which Spencer was writing on for the *Westminster Review* in the early 1850s, Darwin would doubtless have been aghast had he realized that Drysdale was in fact the anonymous author of a vast work which not only contested Spencer's *laissez-faire* assumption that the 'constant increase of people beyond the means of subsistence . . . involves . . . an increasing demand for . . . self-control – involves, therefore, a . . . gradual growth of . . . a higher form of humanity', but also reverenced the regular indulgence of the sexual instincts, in both men and women, as a quasi-religious act.[137] *Physical, Sexual and Natural Religion*, later retitled *The Elements of Social Science*, was first published by Truelove in 1855, and, alongside many arguments concerning wider issues of overpopulation, advocated that the sexual organs must be exercised in intercourse at least twice a week in order to maintain their healthful functioning. The 'complete sexual abstinence' prescribed by Malthus and his followers, it was contended, was 'in every case an evil' and the principal cause of the 'most miserable physical diseases' as well as 'unhappiness and discontent', especially amongst the young.[138]

Many mid-Victorian accounts of male sexuality, as Sally Shuttleworth has shown, similarly warned against the 'dangers of long betrothals which lead to sexually exciting ideas', and urged the necessity of 'the calming possibility of controlled emission' for regulating the energies of the male sexual economy.[139] Unlike other medical writers on sex such as William Acton, though, Drysdale insisted that this medical imperative for regular sexual activity applied to both sexes (although his rhetoric invariably assumed a male perspective) and actually overrode all moral concerns regarding marriage and monogamy. As his book asserted: 'Every individual should make it his conscientious aim, that he or she should have sufficiency of love to satisfy the sexual demands of his nature, and that others around him should have the same.'[140] In fact, *The Elements of Social Science* insisted on the 'insufficiency of marriage' to satisfy the normal sexual needs of both men and women, and warned that the 'complete *exclusiveness* of marriage, gives rise to very great evils' that could be alleviated only by 'freer sexual connections'.[141] Such permissive couplings, Drysdale proposed, should not be conducted in hypocritical secrecy and ought instead to be publicly avowed. While prostitution would be made unnecessary by this new and candid approach to sexual relations, prostitutes themselves, it was urged, should be regarded with 'reverence' and 'deep gratitude' for the beneficial role which they played in helping satisfy the 'great primary necessity of sexual intercourse' during society's current ill-advised adherence to an overly rigid code of sexual morality.[142]

In order that the hedonistic sensualism necessary to individual and social health did not swell the population to unmanageable levels, Drysdale's book also proposed the widespread use of contraceptive methods, and provided readers with practical tips on how they could be administered. *The Elements of Social Science* was, according to Mason, the 'most comprehensively subversive treatise on sexuality in the English nineteenth century', and for the sake of his family, and especially his mother, Drysdale maintained his anonymity – the book's title page merely declaring that its author was 'A Student of Medicine' – until after his death in 1904.[143] Darwin's potential involvement with the author of such an infamous work would, had he only known it, have been highly disconcerting, and, in the light of his own later problems with the *Descent*'s suitability for a general audience, extremely hazardous for his own public reputation.

During the 1860s, *The Elements of Social Science* precipitated perhaps the most profound schism in the nineteenth-century British freethought movement, with George Jacob Holyoake becoming increasingly concerned with Bradlaugh's apparent endorsement of Drysdale's medical justification of freer sexual couplings. Like most other radical secularists, Holyoake agreed on the urgent necessity of some form of artificial check to the rapidly expanding population, although he insisted that birth control should only ever be practised by married couples and must be separated entirely from any hint of sexual liberalism. Bradlaugh, on the other hand, refused to condemn the emancipatory agenda of Drysdale's tome, even its encouragement of merely temporary sexual liaisons, and recruited the book's anonymous author to write for the *National Reformer* under the pseudonym 'G. R.' These tensions between the leading figures of what Mason has termed 'progressive anti-sensualism' and 'pro-sensual' freethought became still more pronounced in the following decade, when Bradlaugh, and his new protégé Besant, disregarded the wishes of the radical publisher Charles Watts and brought out their own version of Knowlton's *Fruits of Philosophy*.[144] Significantly, appended to the Freethought Press's edition of the antiquated pamphlet were new medical notes by 'G. R.', who, the publishers proudly declared in the preface, was 'widely known in all parts of the world as the author of the "Elements of Social Science"'.[145] At the ensuing trial, Drysdale's younger brother Charles, who was himself often assumed to be the book's author, appeared as the principal medical witness on behalf of the defence, and, as was noted earlier, assisted Bradlaugh and Besant in founding the Malthusian League, being elected its first president in July 1877.

In the wake of the controversy over *Fruits of Philosophy*, Holyoake, Watts and several other radicals concerned with maintaining the respectability and moral probity of freethought seceded from the National Secular Society, of which Bradlaugh was president. In August 1877 they founded the rival British Secular Union, adopting the *Secular Review*, with Holyoake as its editor, as their mouthpiece and competitor to Bradlaugh and Besant's more profane *National Reformer*.[146] The subsequent trial and imprisonment of *The Elements of Social Science*'s original publisher Truelove for distributing another contraceptive manual seemed to confirm the wisdom of splitting from what was later dubbed the 'Erotic School of Freethought', although Bradlaugh's deliberately unrespectable brand of radical secularism remained considerably more popular amongst rank-and-file activists.[147]

The possibility that Darwin had once been acquainted with Drysdale notwithstanding, prominent men of science generally eschewed even the slightest connection with those radicals who were in any way associated with the sexual liberalism of *The Elements of Social Science* or the coarseness of the National Secular Society. Darwin himself had declined to assist Bradlaugh and Besant in the trial of Knowlton's *Fruits of Philosophy*, while Carpenter appeared in the witness stand but did nothing to disguise his irritable disdain for the pair. Even as late as 1890, the Cambridge physiologist Michael Foster returned the tickets which Bradlaugh had sent him to one of his public lectures, stating brusquely: 'I am sorry to say that I find I can't have the pleasure of hearing you.'[148] While at least one leading member of Darwin's circle of friends and supporters, as will be examined in the following chapter, enjoyed considerably more friendly relations with both Bradlaugh and Besant, and may even have endorsed certain aspects of Drysdale's subversive attitude towards sex, the National Secular Society's leaders were, for the most part, consistently cold-shouldered by proponents of evolutionary science anxious to maintain their respectability.

The founders of the rival British Secular Union, on the other hand, were received with considerably more sympathy. As Bernard Lightman has noted: 'elite agnostics generally held aloof from members of the NSS, disclaiming any sympathy with their coarse atheistic philosophy. The followers of the Holyoake tradition were better suited to their tastes.'[149] In fact, within two months of the British Secular Union's secession from the increasingly disreputable National Secular Society, the moral authority of its new leader was publicly endorsed by Tyndall, who, in his Presidential Address to the Birmingham and Midland Institute in October 1877, commended the 'name of George Jacob Holyoake' to his predominantly middle-class audience, and avowed that 'no Christian . . . need be ashamed' of the 'moral doctrine taught by this "Atheistic" leader', for whom 'moral shiftiness of any kind is subjectively unknown'.[150] Tyndall also took out a subscription to Holyoake's new *Secular Review* because he admired its eschewal of the scurrilous tone of the radical gutter press, and his warmly sympathetic words in Birmingham, which were soon reprinted in the *Fortnightly Review*, can be understood as a deliberate intervention on behalf of the British Secular Union in its bitter internecine rivalry with Bradlaugh's more popular but less respectable wing of the freethought movement.[151]

Like Tyndall, Huxley too expressed sympathy and admiration for the leader of respectable radicalism, who, as he acknowledged, had 'so long & so faithfully served the cause of Free thought', and Holyoake returned the compliment, later telling Huxley's son Leonard that he had so much 'affection for your father' that he would 'do anything I can to increase his fame'.[152] Those freethinkers who opposed the sexual policy of Bradlaugh's National Secular Society would continue repaying the favour of Huxley and Tyndall's support for many years to come. In 1895 William Stewart Ross, whose antipathy towards Bradlaugh's apparent endorsement of the emancipatory doctrines of *The Elements of Social Science* was even more uncompromising than Holyoake's, commemorated the death of Huxley in the pages of the *Agnostic Journal* in almost exactly the same moralistic terms that Tyndall had used in his earlier eulogy of Holyoake:

Huxley's reputation was pure and unsullied, and he was a living proof of the unscrupulousness of those Corybantic Christians who . . . tell us how wicked, how immoral, how utterly diabolical are the lives and ways of those whom they are pleased to call 'infidels'. No scandal ever had the name of our late champion for its butt; whatsoever things were true, honest, and pure, Huxley did with all his might.[153]

Tensions continued to exist between leading scientific naturalists and the moderates of the British Secular Union, not least over the radical appropriation of the term 'agnosticism' – which Huxley had coined in 1869 to define his position in the gentlemanly debates of the Metaphysical Society – as a more respectable alternative to Bradlaugh's dogmatic atheism.[154] There was, though, clearly a degree of mutual support and strategic assistance between the two networks that seems to have been aimed at ensuring their continued respectability, and, above all, at distancing them from the opprobrious sexual policy which had emerged as the overriding concern of Bradlaugh's rival brand of freethought.

Relations between prominent scientific naturalists and the leaders of the National Secular Society, however, were not always characterized solely by antagonism, even in the aftermath of the trial of Knowlton's *Fruits of Philosophy*. In particular, the emergence of Edward Bibbens Aveling, a lecturer in anatomy at the London Hospital as well as a prolific popularizer of Darwinism, as a close associate of Bradlaugh and Besant (with whom he began an affair) complicated the connection between the two groups. In October 1880, Darwin responded with ambivalent civility to Aveling's request for permission to dedicate *The Student's Darwin*, a collection of his *National Reformer* articles that was being published as part of Bradlaugh and Besant's 'International Library of Science and Freethought', to the book's eponymous subject, stating that he would 'prefer the . . . Volume not to be dedicated to me (though I thank you for the intended honour)'.[155] Nor was this the only occasion on which Aveling, who was elected vice-president of the National Secular Society earlier in the same year, sought to solicit Darwin's much coveted support for his freethinking views on both science and politics, and his direct appropriation of Darwinian arguments in support of birth control has already been noted.[156]

Darwin treated his self-appointed disciple with unstinting politeness and insisted that he was a 'strong advocate for free thought on all subjects', although in practice he remained extremely wary of becoming publicly associated with any of Aveling's numerous radical publications.[157] While Darwin's ambiguous attitude towards Aveling is extremely well known, largely because one of his tortuously polite letters to him was initially assumed to be addressed to Karl Marx, Huxley's similarly convoluted and complicated relations with Aveling have not previously been considered in detail by historians.[158] They are, nevertheless, extremely revealing of the particular anxieties of the proponents of Darwinism in relation to freethought in sexual matters.

Following Aveling's emergence as a leading figure in the National Secular Society during the late 1870s, science, and especially scientific education, began to assume a new importance in the Bradlaughite wing of the freethought movement. In particular, Besant, who was given private tuition by Aveling, excelled in her scientific studies, and, by 1880, she was assisting Aveling with the teaching at the movement's Hall of Science schools. However, in May 1883, after completing the preliminary stages of her B.Sc. degree at the University of London, Besant, along with Bradlaugh's daughter Alice, was refused admission to the Practical Botany Class at University College, because, as the College's Lady Superintendent Rosa Morrison announced haughtily, 'there was a prejudice against' them. Although in public Morrison refused to specify the precise nature of this 'prejudice', she conceded in a private letter to the College's Secretary that it related to 'a trial in which Mrs Besant had been engaged', a reference, of course, to the infamous prosecution of Knowlton's *Fruits of Philosophy* six years earlier.[159] Despite its liberal and expressly non-denominational origins, the Council of University College saw no reason to revoke the decision taken by its zealous Lady Superintendent.

As a Fellow of University College, Aveling at once drew up a memorial remonstrating against the gratuitous exclusion of the two women and demanding that the College's Council summon an extraordinary general meeting. As he had with Darwin over the previous few years, Aveling endeavoured to gain the support of the leading scientific luminaries in Victorian Britain, although most, including Tyndall, were clearly unwilling to risk being tarnished by the continuing repercussions of Bradlaugh and Besant's notorious obscenity trial. Huxley similarly declined Aveling's request, noting dryly that he returned the 'memorial unsigned'.[160] Huxley penned his laconic letter of refusal on 31 May 1883, but, curiously, his signature appeared on a copy of the memorial, written in Aveling's hand, that was submitted to the Council of University College at the beginning of June.[161] Aveling, at least according to his adversaries, was both utterly unscrupulous and an adept forger (it has been suggested that he forged Darwin's letters to him), and it might be presumed that he had simply fabricated Huxley's distinctive autograph and falsely claimed the support of one of the nation's foremost public intellectuals.[162] In a letter to Michael Foster written on 18 July, however, Huxley conceded that he had indeed 'signed the memorial requesting the Council of University College to reconsider their decision about Mrs. Besant and Miss Bradlaugh', although he insisted that it was 'very unlucky for me' especially now that he had been elected to the prestigious post of President of the Royal Society.[163] Having found Besant a 'hard-working student' who had 'conducted herself very well' in his own summer course on physiology at the Normal School of Science, and concerned that he ought to 'stand up for the principle of religious and philosophical freedom', Huxley, it would seem, was persuaded by Aveling to change his mind and, at the very last moment, give his approval to the memorial.[164]

With Huxley's tentative support, Aveling's incessant lobbying soon paid off, and the Council convened an extraordinary general meeting for 18 July, although by that time many of its members had already gone away for the summer. Huxley remained in London and agreed to attend the meeting in the Botanical Theatre of University College. Once there, though, he declined, to Aveling's evident chagrin, to actually contribute to the Council's heated discussions. Still worse, in the final division over whether Besant should be permitted to enter the College's science classes Huxley abstained from voting, an apparent abnegation of moral responsibility to which Aveling drew scornful attention in the next number of the *National Reformer*.[165]

On the very morning of the meeting, Huxley had expressed a concern that, following his endorsement of the original memorial, any further support for Aveling's campaign might prove dangerous by 'giving other people a hold for saying that I have identified myself with Bradlaugh', and he acknowledged that he would 'need all the dexterity I possess' to resist such a damaging accusation.[166] The meeting itself was dominated by the question of Besant's involvement with Bradlaugh and especially the edition of Knowlton's *Fruits of Philosophy* which they had published. 'Everyone present', as Aveling later reported, 'was thinking of a book as to which people talked generally far more than they thought.'[167] To publicly side with Besant in such an incendiary atmosphere might have made Huxley appear to be defending her and Bradlaugh's right to publish this infamously pernicious work, as well as endorsing the allegedly libertarian sexual policy of the wing of the freethought movement to which they both belonged. Other members of the Council clearly shared this concern, and it is notable that only nine out of the hundred or so who attended the meeting actually voted in favour of revoking Besant's exclusion from the College.[168]

Although he had not read the book, Huxley, as he insisted repeatedly in the days leading up to the Council's meeting, was repulsed by the depraved doctrines apparently advanced in the *Fruits of Philosophy*. He instead adhered to a strict code of sexual morality which was entirely different from that of Besant and her colleagues in the National Secular Society. As he told the philosopher George Croom Robertson:

I have never read this 'Fruits of Philosophy' and cannot get it − ; but, from what I have heard of its contents I fancy it must be particularly objectionable to people who, like myself, believe that the advance or retrogression of civilisation depends very much on the maintenance of a decent standard of sexual morality.[169]

In particular, Huxley was concerned that Knowlton's notorious contraceptive manual not only facilitated but even encouraged 'sexual intercourse among unmarried people', and he proclaimed that 'if Mrs Besant has made herself responsible for that doctrine . . . I have no objection to her exclusion'.[170] Besant and her fellow female students at University College would, after all, 'meet not merely in class but elsewhere', and the Council, in Huxley's view, would be acting entirely properly in 'declining to associate her with the other women students' if she had 'specially associated herself with the book' and its immoral attitude towards sex and marriage.[171]

While initially agreeing with Aveling's campaign against Besant's exclusion on the grounds of upholding religious and philosophical freedom, Huxley insisted that such speculative freedom did not extend to any considerations which challenged conventional attitudes towards sexuality and reproduction. Huxley, as he told the trade union lawyer Henry Crompton, had a 'strong feeling that freedom of thought should be carefully distinguished from laxity in morals'.[172] Maintaining precisely this distinction had long been one of the principal concerns of radicals and secularists eager to gain a respectable audience for their ideas, and John Chapman had reflected in his diary in 1851 that 'as I am the publisher of works notable for the[ir] intellectual freedom it behoves me to be exceedingly careful of the *moral* tendency of all I issue.'[173] Although Chapman's own personal life did not adhere to such elevated moral standards, in the mid-1850s he had helped establish Huxley's career by commissioning him to write for the *Westminster Review*, and, three decades later, Huxley now restated his former editor's injunction with a characteristically incisive turn of phrase: 'Freethinking does not mean Free love.'[174] With the success of the National Secular Society's deliberately unrespectable brand of freethought, as well as Bradlaugh's apparent endorsement of the sexual hedonism advocated in *The Elements of Social Science*, the separation of freethought from any hint of free love had never been more necessary, and, in Huxley's view at least, it was more important than the principles of religious and philosophical freedom which were threatened by Besant's exclusion from University College. In fact, Huxley's anxiety to maintain an irreproachable standard of sexual respectability was so great that it compelled him to deliberately eschew any consideration of contraceptive methods as a means of resolving the

pressing problem of overpopulation in his political writings of the 1880s
and 1890s, even while he prophesied that the 'hordes of vice and pauperism
will destroy modern civilization' by their relentless rate of reproduction.[175]

Huxley's abstention from voting at the Council's extraordinary general
meeting did not, of course, necessarily imply that he supported Besant's
exclusion, and, as was seen earlier, he willingly expressed his admiration for
her work and conduct when she was a student in his physiology classes during the summer of 1882. His opinion of Bradlaugh, though, was much less
ambivalent. Huxley, as he told Robertson, 'share[d], not without reason,
the Council opinion of Bradlaugh as a man', and he avowed that he 'should
refuse to associate with him'.[176] This personal distaste perhaps motivated
his adamant refusal to support Bradlaugh in his struggle to be allowed to
enter Parliament as the elected MP for Northampton without first affirming his belief in Christianity, even when friends such as Leslie Stephen and
Moncure Conway expressed a strong sympathy with the cause.[177] Anxious
at both politically motivated atheism and any suggestion of sexual liberalism, Huxley admitted to having a 'peculiar abhorrence' for 'Bradlaugh &
Co . . . & all their ways & works' which overrode his usual liberal and
rationalist instincts.[178]

Nor was this strength of feeling unreciprocated by those who were closest to Bradlaugh. In her biography of her late father, Bradlaugh's daughter Hypatia remarked angrily that Huxley had 'wearied Freethinkers by
tediously strategic combats' and 'reinforced reaction by contemptuous language towards men whose teaching is identical with his own'.[179] Huxley had
already been the subject of similarly barbed comments from Bradlaugh's
principal supporters, even in the immediate aftermath of his endorsement
of the memorial concerning Besant's exclusion from University College.
Aveling, despite having actually obtained Huxley's much coveted signature, seems to have felt let down by his subsequent conduct, and, just five
months later, publicly condemned Huxley for his mean-spirited annoyance
with Charles Watts for reprinting a private letter as if it were an official contribution to his new *Agnostic Annual*. While Besant apologized to Huxley
for her freethinking colleague's disrespectful behaviour and insisted that 'I
utterly disagree with him', Aveling, in the following year's *Agnostic Annual*,
repeated his accusation that 'Huxley writes boldly against Theism, and then
is moved to an almost tearful anger when his views are made public.'[180]
Aveling's satirical depiction of Huxley as a modern incarnation of 'Mr.
Facing-Both-Ways' in John Bunyan's *Pilgrim's Progress* clearly also hinted
at his own frustration with Huxley's persistent vacillation over whether or
not he agreed with Besant's exclusion.[181]

Such equivocation – or 'dexterity' as Huxley termed it – was entirely necessary, though, in order to avoid becoming identified with the more controversial aspects of Bradlaugh's political and sexual agenda. Indeed, notwithstanding the evident animosity which existed between him and Bradlaugh and his followers, Huxley was dogged by precisely this damaging association until the very end of his life. Even after retiring to the genteel seaside town of Eastbourne in the early 1890s, Huxley was still being told by members of the Salvation Army that he had a 'local reputation as a Bradlaughite'.[182] Although Bradlaugh himself had died in 1891, the pejorative label to which he gave his name continued to signify not only atheism, freethought and political radicalism (though, importantly, not socialism), but also carried the same connotations of sexual hedonism and the advocacy of birth control which it had accrued during the 1860s and 1870s. Following the infamous trial of Knowlton's *Fruits of Philosophy* in 1877, moreover, the imputation that Huxley was a Bradlaughite, however unfounded it might be, inevitably connected his overtly respectable scientific naturalism with the widespread concerns with obscenity which existed in late Victorian Britain.

DARWIN ON TRIAL

The natural sciences had been condemned as potentially indecent and obscene long before Lord Campbell's attempt to legislate against such pernicious publications in the mid-1850s. The first edition of the *Encyclopaedia Britannica* (1771) contended that the method for classifying plants devised by the Swedish naturalist Carl Linnaeus consisted of 'disgusting strokes of obscenity' that were articulated with 'such a degree of indelicacy in the expression as cannot be exceeded by the most obscene romance-writer'.[183] While Linnaeus's celebrated 'sexual system' of botanical classification employed provocative human analogies to explicate vegetable sexuality and reproduction, the prospect of issuing legal proceedings against such explicit scientific works remained virtually unthinkable until the final decades of the nineteenth century. As Bohn stated at the trial of Knowlton's *Fruits of Philosophy* in 1877, 'during his whole publishing life of sixty years he had never known one case where a prosecution was brought against a physiological treatise on the ground that it was obscene'.[184] Despite the eventual quashing of Bradlaugh and Besant's prosecution on a legal technicality, legislative action against avowedly medical and scientific works became much more frequent following their notorious trial. Truelove was gaoled in 1878 for publishing Robert Dale Owen's *Moral Physiology*, while, in the following decade, several booksellers were prosecuted for distributing copies of *The Wife's Handbook* (1886), the author of which was the prominent Yorkshire physician Henry Allbutt.[185]

Shortly before Bradlaugh and Besant's landmark trial, the anti-vivisection movement led by Francis Power Cobbe had demanded legal restrictions on physiological experimentation involving live animals. Although the subsequent Cruelty to Animals Act of 1876 left the autonomy of licensed experimenters largely intact, Carpenter, not long after his humiliating exposure to the potential implications of recent obscenity legislation for physiology textbooks, reflected scornfully that the 'original form' of the bill, which was drafted by his erstwhile friend Cobbe, would have

made it penal to prick the web of a Frog's foot with a pin, for the purpose of extending it for the observation of its blood-circulation under the microscope; and that, strictly interpreted, it might have been held to interdict a Teacher from pricking his own finger (as I was myself accustomed to do) to draw a drop of human blood for class-demonstration.[186]

For eminent men of science like Carpenter, Darwin and Huxley, as Desmond has noted, such restrictive 'laws were for publicans and prostitutes, not the professional elite of the nation', and they had used their contacts in the political establishment, including the Foreign Secretary Lord Derby, to forestall the prohibitions of Cobbe's proposed legislation.[187] By the close of the nineteenth century, however, several observers, most notably in Germany, expressed concerns that legislative interference was nevertheless seriously impairing the international standing of British science.[188] Licensed physiologists now had a legal right to experiment on live animals, but expressly scientific publications were still liable to prosecution under the Obscene Publications Act and even to seizure by the police. Despite his death almost two decades earlier, it was Darwin who, once again, was at the centre of the renewed debates over science and obscenity in the late 1890s.

In May 1898, more than twenty years after the unsuccessful prosecution of Bradlaugh and Besant, the radical bookseller George Bedborough was similarly arrested for selling a copy of Havelock Ellis's pioneering scientific analysis of homosexuality, *Studies in the Psychology of Sex: Sexual Inversion* (1897), to an undercover police officer posing as a customer. In Bow Street Magistrate's Court, Ellis's weighty sexological tome was subsequently charged with being a 'lewd wicked bawdy scandalous and obscene' book.[189] This avowedly scientific work fell foul, once again, of the judicial definition of obscenity established by Lord Cockburn in 1868, even though it was priced at a prohibitive ten shillings and every copy of the book, which was published by the freethinking University Press in Watford, carried an explicit warning that 'this book is a scientific work, intended for medical men, lawyers, and teachers. It should not be placed in the hands of the general public.'[190] While the charges against Bedborough were finally dropped after he paid a fine of £100 and assured the judge that he would cut all his connections with the proprietors of the University Press, the bookseller's entire stock, containing many other scientific works alongside various radical publications, was seized and impounded by the police, and it was made clear that he would be rearrested and gaoled if he ever attempted to sell such pernicious books again.[191]

Bedborough's arrest inevitably provoked a storm of radical protest, with the *University Magazine*, another venture of the freethinking University Press, condemning 'such a serious and wanton attack on the liberty of the press' and expressing concern that whilst 'Bradlaugh was a match for his prosecutors', the more reticent Bedborough might be made to 'suffer' by the courts.[192] Unlike Bradlaugh two decades earlier, however, Bedborough received the support of many members of the scientific and medical professions. There was, according to the *University Magazine*, particular 'indignation' at his prosecution amongst the 'scientific world', while the *Review of Reviews* reported that the

general contention of the medical profession . . . is that, if the sale of such a book as Dr. Ellis' justifies the wholesale seizure of every book on the premises of any bookseller, the sale of medical works will be very much restricted, and no one will be able to sell any medical literature without running the risk of a criminal prosecution.[193]

The strongest opposition to the prosecution of Bedborough came from Europe, where sexology was more established as a legitimate field of scientific study, and Ellis's German translator assured him that the 'whole of scientific psychology and medicine on the Continent is on your side'.[194] In the nascent era of intensive global competition at the close of the nineteenth century, there were even concerns that such prudish and narrow-minded legal restrictions to scientific publishing might seriously damage the international reputation of all areas of British science.

Despite these differences, there were certain aspects of the campaign against Bedborough's prosecution in the 1890s which closely resembled the strategies employed by Bradlaugh and Besant to forestall the charges of obscenity which they faced in the 1870s. Once more, radicals and freethinkers argued that if Ellis's *Sexual Inversion* was to be considered obscene, then exactly the same charge would have to brought against numerous other medical and scientific works, including such highly regarded and iconic texts as Darwin's *The Descent of Man*. In fact, a remarkable radical parody of the judicial process against Ellis's sexological work, once again published by the University Press, actually re-imagined Bedborough's trial as a prosecution of the *Descent* and other evolutionary works.

In *Darwin on Trial at the Old Bailey* (1899), written by the German émigré freethinker and petty criminal Georg von Weissenfeld under his habitual pseudonym 'Democritus', the prosecuting barrister Sir Richard Bully insists that Darwin's theory of '*Sexual Selection* is . . . highly suggestive and obscene, and . . . may create lustful desires in the liege subjects of our gracious Queen'.[195] He then reads aloud various passages from the *Descent*, proclaiming, amongst other things, 'what shall we say to this description of a nude Hottentot woman', and remarking that the 'author enters into the minutest details of generation, which should never be mentioned, and certainly never be printed to corrupt the pure mind of our children'. Darwin's celebrated book, the hectoring barrister concludes, is 'veiled by scientific terms, but deal[s] with an immoral subject' and is therefore deserving of prosecution under the Obscene Publications Act.[196] Significantly, this radical squib vindicating Ellis's *Sexual Inversion* once more drew attention to precisely those aspects of the *Descent* about which Darwin and his publisher John Murray, as was examined in chapter two, were most sensitive, and which had been frequently emphasized by hostile critics of the book in the early 1870s.

Various witnesses in this fictional Old Bailey trial protest that the 'prosecution really amounts to an indictment of our greatest men, the apostles of evolution' and insist that 'Darwin's . . . works do not contain one single indecent sentence, not one particle of obscenity'.[197] Sir Richard Bully, however, remains adamant that

it would have been best if Darwin's works had been suppressed from the beginning. Two years of hard labour would have kept him from his pernicious work. Now it is too late, and we must put up with the evil resulting from his teachings, but the police will have a sharp eye on all publications dealing with questions of 'Sex'.[198]

Finally, the spirit of Darwin descends on the court to denounce this 'vile hypocrisy, the nation's bane' in which 'no mind is pure, no body sane'.[199] As with Bradlaugh and Besant's earlier arguments in the Court of Queen's Bench, *Darwin on Trial at the Old Bailey* did not set out to reproach any aspect of Darwin's own evolutionary theories. Rather, Darwin himself, despite his death almost two decades before, was enlisted as a spectral advocate of Ellis's right to publish *Sexual Inversion*, and the aim of the radical parody was to expose the incongruity and absurdity of prosecuting any scientific work, whether Ellis's innovative exploration of modern sexual dysfunction or Darwin's highly renowned monograph on human descent, for corrupting its readers with obscene thoughts. But, like Carpenter's *Principles of Human Physiology* twenty years earlier, Darwin's *Descent* was still presented as a work of elite science that, in view of existing obscenity legislation, might potentially be prosecuted and its eminent author sentenced to gaol. Even at the very end of the nineteenth century, Darwinism remained in danger of becoming tainted by its appropriation by freethinkers in their own campaign to undermine judicial attempts to establish certain forms of scientific discourse as criminally transgressive.

Despite the vociferously proclaimed support for evolution of freethinkers like Bradlaugh, Besant, Aveling and Weissenfeld, it was just as imperative for Darwin's theories to be sequestered from radical protests against the arbitrariness of current obscenity legislation as from the more deliberately damaging accusations of their clerical and scientific adversaries examined in previous chapters. The growing legal concern with regulating a perceived proliferation of apparently obscene publications provided a new range of awkward and invidious associations which might be used to tarnish the reputation of Darwin, as well as those of his closest friends and colleagues, in the Victorian debates over evolution. That Darwinism's avowed opponents would have exploited any such involvement with freethinking attitudes towards sex will become clear in the following chapter, which examines the battle over the posthumous reputation of the only prominent member of Darwin's circle of supporters who expressed any sort of sympathy with the deliberate unrespectability of Bradlaugh and, significantly, perhaps even with aspects of Drysdale's outspoken advocacy of a more liberal code of sexual morality.

CHAPTER 5

The refashioning of William Kingdon Clifford's posthumous reputation

By September 1878, William Kingdon Clifford, the thirty-three-year-old Professor of Applied Mathematics at University College London, knew that he was almost certainly dying. Recuperative visits to Europe and North Africa had failed to stay the pulmonary disease that had been progressively destroying his lungs since the spring of 1876, and his trusted physician, Dr Andrew Clarke, could offer no further hope of a medical remedy. Before embarking on one last journey to Madeira in the new year, Clifford, with the assistance of his devoted wife Lucy, began to put his affairs into some sort of order, specifying exactly who should edit his unfinished mathematical papers, and also stipulating that he wanted to be buried in England on high ground and not under a tree.[1] One final thing Clifford conspicuously did not do, however, was to make his peace with the Christian deity whom he had forsaken whilst an undergraduate at Trinity College, Cambridge. Rather, during his painful last days in England, Clifford, as his friend Leslie Stephen remembered, 'enjoyed nothing so much as talk of a kind not calculated to edify believers'.[2] Despite having teasingly told Henrietta Huxley that to 'escape the torture I would say I believed in the Father, the Son, the Winking Virgin, the Devil, the Holy Ghost, and the Flying Dutchman', Clifford boarded the steamship to Madeira in January 1879 without having made any conscious effort to modify his popular reputation as a strident and refractory atheist.[3]

By the time of his death on the island at the beginning of March, Clifford, as the *Examiner* reported, was 'regarded by the timid orthodox with more fear and dislike than any other writer of the day', and, according to *The Times*, had gained the 'reputation in some quarters of being an extreme or violent writer'.[4] Clifford's refusal to separate clearly this popular notoriety from his international reputation as a brilliant and innovative mathematician had long exasperated more circumspect members of the British mathematical community, with James Joseph Sylvester observing: 'Clifford is a very great genius; I only wish he would stick to mathematics instead of talking atheism.'[5] Clifford's heterodox religious opinions, as Stephen concurred, had certainly 'drawn public attention from his merits as a mathematician'.[6] Even in death, though, Clifford continued to goad the orthodox; his parting shot was the heretical epitaph that adorned his gravestone:

> I was not and was conceived
> I loved and did a little work
> I am not and grieve not.

Until the very end of his short life, Clifford self-consciously cultivated his notoriety as a stoically implacable unbeliever and an incendiary freethinker, and while obituaries in the radical press acclaimed him as the 'greatest of English thinkers and . . . noblest of English men' he was at the same time condemned as a 'contemptuous and obtrusive denier of God' in more conservative publications.[7] Once his mortal remains were interred in the unconsecrated ground of Highgate Cemetery, however, the future fate of Clifford's reputation was entirely in the hands of others. His standing as both a leading mathematical specialist and an iconoclastic scientific publicist could now be reshaped in accordance with the various agendas of both his friends and allies as well as the numerous enemies he had made during his brief life.

Clifford was known principally as the leading British exponent of the non-Euclidean forms of geometry that had been developed on the Continent since the beginning of the nineteenth century, but he was also a highly skilful popularizer of science, with *The Times* praising his 'singular capacity for bringing the most advanced scientific ideas within the range of ordinary knowledge'.[8] In particular, throughout the 1870s Clifford proselytized on behalf of Charles Darwin's evolutionary theories as well as a more general naturalistic worldview, and as a frequent contributor to liberal periodicals like the *Fortnightly Review*, as well as a member of the Metaphysical Society and founder of the Congress of Liberal Thinkers, he developed close connections with the leading proponents of scientific naturalism. Even in his specialist mathematical research, which demonstrated that geometrical conceptions of space could only be drawn from our actual experience of the world instead of the untested assumptions about the eternal homogeneity of space upon which traditional Euclidean geometry rested, Clifford accorded with the central tenet of scientific naturalism that the transcendental was fundamentally unknowable. Refusing the possibility of geometrical truths, as well as any other kinds of truth, that were independent of experience, Clifford, like other scientific naturalists, denied the validity of reasoning that went beyond empirical facts, in religion as well as science.[9]

But Clifford, as several historians have noted, often held very different opinions from most of his scientific naturalist colleagues on a variety of epistemological matters, refusing to accept that the uniformity of nature was a universal truth and insisting that rationalist modes of enquiry were applicable to all aspects of ethics and moral psychology.[10] Born in 1845 as the eldest son of a prosperous bookseller and magistrate in Exeter, Clifford was also of a different generation and social background to self-made men like Thomas Henry Huxley and John Tyndall, and, already assured of the tacit respectability bestowed by a Cambridge degree, he was considerably less discreet in his public pronouncements. In fact, while Huxley and Tyndall both contributed regularly to genteel middlebrow periodicals like *Macmillan's Magazine* and *Longman's Magazine*, the strident iconoclasm that characterized Clifford's own scientific journalism was often not suitable for much of the Victorian print media. In 1877, Stephen, then the editor of the *Cornhill Magazine*, canvassed the opinion of his old university friend on scientists who might be willing to write for the family-orientated magazine, although he considered that Clifford himself would not be appropriate, telling him: 'when you do write ad populum [you] are apt to touch upon their religious prejudices.'[11] Even with the *Cornhill*'s circulation plummeting amidst a dearth of high-profile contributors, Stephen still could not countenance publishing the work of perhaps the most infamous scientific firebrand in Victorian Britain.

Stephen's editorial misgivings about Clifford's suitability for the respectable pages of the *Cornhill* were fully justified, for over the previous decade he had gained a certain notoriety as a libertarian, republican and even an anarchist, while his membership of radical groups like the Republican Club only added fuel to this invidious reputation.[12] Clifford also exhibited a cautious sympathy with Charles Bradlaugh and Annie Besant's deliberately unrespectable wing of the British freethought movement, which, as was discussed in the previous chapter, was consistently cold-shouldered by almost all other prominent men of science. Even worse, while Darwin, as was seen in chapter two, had unwittingly been tarnished by association with the scandalous verse of Algernon Charles Swinburne, Clifford actively embraced precisely those poems of Swinburne's which hostile critics had strategically identified with *The Descent of Man*, frequently quoting them in his essays and lectures as poetic expositions of Darwinian principles. It was, of course, imperative for Darwinism to be urgently protected from any such hostile associations, and, following Clifford's untimely death in 1879, it suited the purposes of earnest scientific professionals like Huxley that their late friend and colleague should be memorialized in ways that largely excluded his awkward connections with political radicalism, extremist atheism and Swinburne's controversial aesthetic poetry. This process involved both the scrupulous editorial supervision of numerous posthumous publications (and the decade following his death saw the publication of some seven monographs claiming to be authored, at least in part, by Clifford), as well as the discreet suppression of a variety of unpublished manuscript material. Such a strenuous recasting and chastening of Clifford's posthumous reputation was particularly necessary because the detractors of Darwinian science were equally determined to draw critical attention to Clifford's association with precisely these problematic issues.

At the same time, Clifford's disconsolate widow and two young daughters had been left totally unprovided for, and, notwithstanding a subsequent Testimonial Fund and Civil List pension, it was necessary for Lucy, who now owned the copyright of her late husband's works, to maximize the potential sales of his posthumous publications by not only keeping Clifford in the public eye, but also by ensuring that it was a generally positive – and thus marketable – portrayal of him that was presented.[13] Mrs W. K. Clifford, as she now styled herself, soon became both a best-selling novelist and a prolific literary journalist, and, as she gradually recovered from what she termed the great 'tragedy of my . . . life', she used her extensive literary contacts, as well as some extremely sharp journalistic practices, to help shape aspects of Clifford's reputation in accordance with her own views, which, significantly, did not always concur with those of her dead husband or his scientific naturalist colleagues.[14] In fact, Lucy was, over the next fifty years, the most active participant in the refashioning of her husband's posthumous reputation, and her vital role in shaping the way that Clifford would be viewed by posterity deserves the same scholarly attention already given to other Victorian scientific wives such as Henrietta Huxley.[15]

In 1886, however, both Lucy and her late husband's erstwhile friends and colleagues faced the greatest challenge to their efforts to reshape Clifford's posthumous reputation, with the re-emergence of potentially awkward details of his early engagement with radical freethought, especially in regard to the explosively provocative topics of sex, prostitution and birth control. Even several years after his death, the actual views and opinions which Clifford had articulated in various forums during his life were still too incendiary even to be acknowledged by his supporters, while at the same time becoming the subject of malicious rumours spread by his adversaries. In the late 1870s Darwin himself had joined the committee that organized the Testimonial Fund for Lucy and her children, as well as donating a generous £50, and Clifford's brief career and the subsequent battle to determine how he would be viewed by posterity were, as this chapter will examine, central to the incessant arguments concerning sexual respectability that were such an integral aspect of the Victorian debates over Darwinian evolution and scientific naturalism more generally.[16]

IT IS NOT RIGHT TO BE PROPER

In March 1868, Clifford, then a twenty-two-year-old mathematics Fellow at Trinity, concluded his first address to the Royal Institution by pointing to the urgent need for 'checking the growth of conventionalities' which might retard the nation's evolutionary progress. 'In the face of such a danger', he boldly insisted, '*it is not right to be proper.*'[17] This impudent peroration announced the arrival of an audacious and sensational new talent on the London scientific scene; Clifford, as Thomas Archer Hirst noted in his private journal, was the 'lion of the season'.[18] In Cambridge, Clifford was already renowned for his enthusiastic and eloquent advocacy of Darwinism and unbelief in the various debating clubs to which he belonged, as well as for his wickedly irreverent lampoons of Christian beliefs and practices. However, the formal requirement that Fellows of Cambridge colleges make an annual affirmation of their allegiance to the Church of England, which Clifford had refused to do since 1866, made his position at Trinity increasingly difficult, and strengthened the appeal of the greater intellectual freedom of the metropolis. By 1871, Clifford, with the support of a glowing testimonial from James Clerk Maxwell, had been appointed to the Goldsmid Chair of Applied Mathematics and Mechanics at University College London. In the more convivial surroundings of the non-denominational University College (often nicknamed the 'Godless Institution of Gower Street'), Clifford not only continued his researches on a wide variety of mathematical topics, but also became increasingly notorious for his frequent transgressions of the boundaries of Victorian middle-class acceptability. His lectures and journalism declared, amongst other things, the need for strong trade unions to represent the working classes, alleged that belief without sufficient evidence was a terrible sin against mankind, and, as was noted in chapter three, defended the ethical standards of pagan antiquity against the slurs of Christian historians.[19] As he had in his first, daring address to the Royal Institution in 1868, Clifford also continued to demand the abandonment of all fixity of opinion in favour of a perpetual flexibility of mind.

Clifford's move to London in 1871 was, according to the American Unitarian Moncure Conway, considered 'a great event' by metropolitan free-thinkers, and the youthful professor soon became an active member of the circle of radicals, republicans and bohemians who gathered at Conway's South Place Chapel in Finsbury.[20] The group, which included the political émigré Karl Blind and his step-daughter Mathilde, had been brought together by their enthusiasm for the elderly Italian revolutionary Giuseppe Mazzini, and Clifford too shared this passion. He also developed a fondness for the work of the self-proclaimed anarchist Pierre-Joseph Proudhon, who in the 1860s had coined the famous revolutionary slogan '*La propriété, c'est le vol*', although Clifford, as he told Henrietta Huxley, was disappointed to discover that Proudhon only 'puts on the air of a revolutionist' and was in reality the 'mildest of radicals'.[21] His own more daringly seditious views inevitably brought Clifford into close contact with many of the most prominent home-grown radicals and freethinkers. He personally sent Bradlaugh press reports of his public lectures, and swapped recommendations of the latest irreligious books with Besant, as well as inviting her to the weekly soirées held at his Bayswater home.[22] These leaders of popular freethought would, for decades to come, frequently invoke Clifford as one of their movement's principal heretical heroes.

Even before Besant's infamous involvement in the controversial obscenity trial examined in the previous chapter, though, Clifford was evidently wary of becoming too closely identified with such a high-profile exponent of plebeian radicalism and militant freethought. In the autumn of 1876 he replied cagily to Besant's request for a contribution to the freethought weekly the *National Reformer*, which she co-edited with Bradlaugh, claiming to have 'far too much on my hands now . . . to write anything which seems to me suited for the Nat. Ref.'[23] Besant clearly took Clifford's evasive excuse as a personal rebuff, and in the following year she prefaced an abstract of his latest heretical article in the highbrow *Fortnightly Review* by expressing the 'regret . . . that its publication at 2s. 6d. puts it utterly out of the reach of the majority of the people. It is impossible not to regret that some of these leading scientific men speak heresy only to the richer part of the community.'[24] Clifford had earlier refused a Fellowship of the Royal Society because, as he observed wryly, he did not want to be respectable yet, but, for all his impudent bravado about not being proper or respectable, his scrupulous eschewal of any connection with the radical gutter press (and in contrast to the *Fortnightly*, the *National Reformer* cost just two pence and was not stocked by W. H. Smith's) reveals the carefully defined limits of his essentially elitist iconoclasm. As the surgeon and radical journalist

John Munro later complained, if a passage from one of Clifford's *Fortnightly* essays had 'occurred in the pages of the *National Reformer* and in connexion with a signature *not* that of W. K. Clifford, we can very well imagine the Bishop of Manchester denouncing it as "flippant Atheism"'.[25] Nevertheless, Clifford's ambivalent involvement with metropolitan freethought and radicalism during the 1870s would, after his death, re-emerge as one of the most contentious issues in the battle over his posthumous reputation.

Although they were enthusiastically reprinted in the radical press, Clifford's heretical views were principally articulated in articles for middle-class periodicals such as the *Fortnightly* and the *Contemporary Review*, as well as in lectures addressed to the fashionable audiences of the Royal Institution and the British Association for the Advancement of Science. These essays and lectures on a variety of scientific topics informed, entertained and not infrequently outraged their predominantly bourgeois audiences, and by the mid-1870s Clifford had established himself as a kind of celebrity iconoclast who could always be relied upon flamboyantly to stick the boot into orthodoxy in all its forms. On occasion, however, Clifford transgressed the limits of personal freedom of opinion tolerated even by these liberal forums, and, in 1876, the *Fortnightly*'s editor John Morley revealed to Huxley that he had been made 'to suffer a storm of abuse and remonstrance for printing Clifford's paper on the Unseen Universe, in which he delivered some over direct thrusts'.[26] Similarly, Clifford's acerbic essay on 'The Ethics of Belief' in the January 1877 *Contemporary* was an instrumental factor in the decision of the review's new owners to terminate the contract of its editor James Knowles, and Clifford became an object of persistent vilification in the new more doctrinally conservative *Contemporary* that began to appear subsequently.[27]

What was perhaps most disconcerting about 'The Ethics of Belief', as with much of Clifford's other writing, was that he constantly disrupted the conventional assumptions of his readers while also reversing the traditional meanings attached to particular forms of language. He insisted with an almost parodic earnestness, for instance, that by accepting the 'prophetic authority' of a saint or other religious leader 'as an excuse for believing what he cannot have known, we make of his goodness an occasion to sin'.[28] In 'The Unseen Universe', Clifford's paradoxically dogmatic denunciation of religious dogmatism, he likewise contended that maintaining a courageous scepticism even in the face of death was not merely a 'healthy' but actually a 'holy thing', explaining that the two terms were originally 'one word whose meanings have become unduly severed'.[29] Such 'abrupt reversals' in Clifford's writing, as George Levine has argued, 'seem to anticipate, at least run parallel to, the Wildean pleasures of paradox', and Levine proposes that 'Clifford was the Oscar Wilde of the naturalists'.[30] Wilde himself certainly read Clifford's work extensively whilst an undergraduate at Oxford in the late 1870s, and he recorded his interest in the scientific and philosophical ideas expressed there, especially in regard to the development of individual conscience, in his commonplace notebooks.[31] Later, in his 1890 dialogue 'The True Function and Value of Criticism' (later renamed 'The Critic as Artist'), Wilde contended:

What is termed Sin is an essential element of progress. Without it the world would stagnate, or grow old, or become colourless. By its curiosity, it increases the experience of the race. Through its intensified assertion of individualism, it saves us from the commonplace. In its rejection of the current notions about morality, it is one with the higher ethics.[32]

This bold declaration appears to draw on, and extend into still more dangerous aesthetic territory, Clifford's 1868 address to the Royal Institution, in which he had insisted that 'propriety' represented a deleterious 'crystallization of the race', and that, paradoxically, the urgent necessity for society's continued evolutionary progress was the refusal of each individual to be proper.[33]

　But Clifford himself actually had a much closer affinity with another aesthetic writer whose scandalous notoriety for amoral sensual indulgence surpassed even that of Wilde. In May 1873, Clifford addressed the Sunday Lecture Society on 'The Relations between Science and Some Modern Poetry', showing how the best recent poetry gave expression to '*Cosmic emotion*', the feeling of veneration engendered by the 'universe of known things' and the 'universe of human action', which could serve as a stimulus to the fight for political freedom.[34] The modern poets who, for Clifford, best represented this new sense of sublime wonderment at the harmonious order of both the wider universe and the microcosm of man were the American Walt Whitman and, most notably, Swinburne. Clifford's lecture was delivered in the heart of the fashionable West End, and, according to the *Academy*, elicited 'hearty and general applause' from the 'crowded scientific and aristocratic *élite*'.[35] William Michael Rossetti reported to Whitman that the impressive young lecturer was 'a shining light among our younger men of science, very bold in his tone of thought'.[36] Most of Clifford's public lectures were swiftly reprinted in the liberal press; the *Fortnightly*, for example, published another of his addresses to the Sunday Lecture Society ('Body and Mind' from November 1874) within a month of its initial delivery. It was not, however, until over four years later that a substantially revised version of Clifford's lecture on the relations between science and modern poetry finally appeared in print.

Clifford's original lecture had venerated the verse of Swinburne, who, as was noted in chapter two, was a hugely controversial figure during the 1870s and was rarely commended in the press except by his small clique of aesthetic friends. While Clifford had previously quoted an unattributed passage from Swinburne's melancholy poem 'The Garden of Proserpine' to illustrate the principle of entropy in an 1875 article for the *Fortnightly*, it was only in the newly founded and overtly tolerant *Nineteenth Century*, which Knowles had begun after being ousted from the more conservative *Contemporary*, that he was able to publish his four-year-old lecture that actually named the still highly notorious poet.[37] In fact, 'Cosmic Emotion', which appeared in the October 1877 number of the *Nineteenth Century* and was Clifford's first full-length contribution to the new monthly review, contained extensive quotations from both *Songs Before Sunrise* (1871) and *Poems and Ballads* (1866), as well as smaller passages from Whitman's *Leaves of Grass* (1855). In it, Clifford declared that to the organic forces which constantly engender new life 'it seems to me that we may fitly address a splendid hymn of Mr. Swinburne's . . . into whose work it is impossible to read more or more fruitful meaning than he meant in the writing of it'.[38] The particular poem to which Clifford referred, and quoted at considerable length, was 'Mater Triumphalis' from *Songs Before Sunrise*, which brazenly appropriated ecclesiastical rhetoric to celebrate both the evolutionary forces of the natural world and the political liberty of *Risorgimento* Italy. In a section of the poem quoted in Clifford's article, Swinburne proclaims of the originating mother of organic growth and political emancipation who predates the orthodox Christian deity:

> Thine hands, without election or exemption,
> Feed all men fainting from false peace or strife,
> O thou, the resurrection and redemption,
> The godhead and the manhood and the life.[39]

Amongst the other poems from *Songs Before Sunrise* quoted by Clifford in 'Cosmic Emotion' was 'The Litany of Nations', in which Swinburne draws a similarly contentious parallel between the oppressed condition of the masses in contemporary Europe and Christ's agony in the garden of Gethsemane.

Swinburne's principal aim in such boldly anti-theistic verse was to venerate the prophetic role of the republican revolutionary Mazzini, to whom *Songs Before Sunrise* was dedicated, and Clifford, who shared these radical sympathies, may actually have met Swinburne through their mutual friend and fellow Mazzini enthusiast Moncure Conway, who recalled that he 'used to see a good deal of Swinburne in the time of his controversy with Philistines'.[40] Although no such meeting is mentioned in the correspondence of either man, Swinburne and Clifford certainly shared a number of mutual acquaintances amongst the radicals who met at Conway's South Place Chapel, and, as will be seen later, they seem to have both attracted the romantic attentions of Karl Blind's lovelorn step-daughter Mathilde. Clifford's potential involvement with Swinburne and his circle, as well as his public advocacy of the poet's controversial verse at a time when Swinburne was often not referred to by name in more decorous periodicals like the *Cornhill* ('a modern singer') and *Contemporary* ('a living English poet'), seem to have provoked little attention at the time, but would soon become a central issue in the portrayal of Clifford immediately after his untimely death.[41]

ANYTHING SERVES THE OTHER SIDE FOR THE THIN END OF A WEDGE

Before his death, Clifford's enemies in the conservative press had portrayed him as a vulgar and profane neophyte whose fatuously controversial statements, as the *Quarterly Review* proclaimed, would 'sully our pages and shock our readers', and this charily dismissive tone characterized many of the remarkably unsympathetic obituaries that appeared in 1879.[42] These anti-panegyrics blubbed crocodile tears, but nevertheless cast subtle aspersions on Clifford's moral judgement, and, significantly, drew attention to his recent endorsement of Swinburne. Richard Holt Hutton, the editor of the *Spectator*, suggested that the late Professor 'showed signs of a curious nakedness of the finer moral sensibilities', and added that the

indulgence in cosmic emotion seems to us very like pitching ourselves down the backstairs of a universe which has backstairs – the backstairs of gradual dissolution and decay, – which backstairs, however, we need not descend quite so rapidly, if we refused to indulge in such cosmic emotions as Mr. Swinburne's.[43]

Even worse, William Hurrell Mallock, writing anonymously in the *Edinburgh Review*, identified the damaging influence of Swinburne at the very centre of Clifford's scientific thought, sneering that

Like most other young men . . . he read and quoted the poetry of Mr. Swinburne, and thought 'Songs before Sunrise' some of the wisest and most precious poems ever written. All this was bound up closely with his scientific theories; and . . . he regarded . . . Mr. Swinburne as the prophet of evolution.[44]

Meanwhile, *Fraser's Magazine* weighed in with the wholly inaccurate assertion that 'Clifford quotes no poet except Mr. Swinburne and Walt Whitman', which it took as another of the 'curious indications of fanaticism' in his thought.[45] In truth, Clifford's unvarnished and forthright prose style, as Gillian Beer has shown, drew upon the work of the Dorset dialect poet William Barnes, while his essays regularly quoted verse such as Augustus De Morgan's reworking of Jonathan Swift's 'Poetry, a Rhapsody'.[46] This, however, was deliberately disregarded in hostile obituaries that were determined to identify him solely with the hugely controversial work of Swinburne.

The tarnishing of a prominent scientific naturalist by association with Swinburne was, of course, nothing new. During the early 1870s, Darwin's *The Descent of Man* had been widely connected by hostile reviewers with Swinburne's political radicalism, as well as with the infamous poet's notoriety for amoral aesthetic sensualism and flagrant sexual depravity. Clifford's scientific writing, and especially his own conception of the evolution of morality as a form of cosmic emotion, was now similarly identified with precisely the same transgressive aesthetic poetry. But while Darwin had strategically allied his evolutionary account of man's ascent to civilization with the epic grandeur of Alfred Tennyson's more respectable verse, Clifford had actually made the controversial association with Swinburne himself. By the early 1880s, moreover, precisely the same terminology that Clifford had employed to describe Swinburne's relation to contemporary science had been adopted by Wilde on his flamboyant lecture tour of North America, during which he remarked on the 'great cosmical emotion . . . of science to which Shelley has given its first and Swinburne its latest glory of song'.[47] Wilde's appropriation of the language of cosmic emotion only served to reaffirm the controversial nature of Clifford's literary tastes, although now that he was dead his friends and colleagues could begin to extricate his reputation from the taint of wantonness, blasphemy, and immorality that Swinburne's name emphatically signified. This retrospective chastening of Clifford's heretical reputation would become a crucial endeavour for some of the main proponents of Darwinian science over the next few years.

The effort to present a more innocuous portrayal of Clifford began in the friendly pages of the *Fortnightly*, where Frederick Pollock acknowledged his late friend's 'preference for modern poetry', but pointedly avoided identifying the particular poets to whom he had been drawn.[48] He also conceded that it was 'possible to take offence at certain passages in his writings', while at the same time insisting that it was 'impossible not to like the man'.[49] Pollock then addressed Clifford's moralizing critics directly, declaring that 'being always frank, he was at times indiscreet; but consummate discretion has never yet been recognized as a necessary or even a very appropriate element of moral heroism.' This, he advised the potential readers of Clifford's work, 'must be borne in mind in estimating such passages of his writings as, judged by the ordinary rules of literary etiquette, may seem harsh and violent'.[50] Those readers who had not previously encountered Clifford's work in the liberal press, though, were not to be given the chance of forming an estimate of such passages.

Pollock's generous elegy for his dead friend was reprinted later in 1879 as the introduction to the collection of Clifford's non-mathematical writings, *Lectures and Essays*, which he co-edited with Leslie Stephen. Appended to the end of this introduction was an inconspicuous admission, removed in all subsequent editions of the book, that 'certain passages have been omitted which we believe that Clifford himself would have willingly cancelled, if he had known the impression they would make on many sincere and liberal-minded persons whose feelings he had no thought of offending.'[51] These circumspect editorial interventions included excising almost four pages from the original *Fortnightly* version of 'The Unseen Universe', dealing with, amongst other things, the intimate connection between orthodox Christianity and the 'vile and detestable . . . fraud' of spiritualism (although a reviewer in *The Times* did not notice even this omission, stating blithely that 'all the papers are preserved in their original form').[52] Significantly, Pollock's private correspondence with Macmillan & Co. seems to reveal that it was not just he and Stephen who were involved in the initial consultations over the form that *Lectures and Essays* should take. Rather, the brooding shadow of Huxley looms over the book's partially bowdlerized pages, with Pollock telling the publisher Alexander Macmillan in April 1879 that 'your letter of the 1st has been seen by Huxley & L. Stephen. We think your offer in the main acceptable, and have only one or two points to remark on.'[53] Pollock's letter to Macmillan then discusses photographs of Clifford that might be used, which suggests that *Lectures and Essays* was the book referred to as it was the only one of his posthumous publications to have a photograph of Clifford on the frontispiece. Although it was confidently insisted that Clifford would have 'willingly' assented to them, the significant editorial modifications made to *Lectures and Essays* can instead be seen as a clear attempt to reshape his posthumous reputation in accordance with the different scientific and political agendas of his powerful friends and allies, and in particular scientific naturalists like Huxley.

The attempt to disengage Clifford's reputation from the Swinburnean connotations of prurience and recklessness with which it had been tarnished in the conservative press is also evident in the circumstances of the much delayed publication of his more specialist mathematical writings. Perhaps surprisingly, however, it was Clifford's widow Lucy rather than his more obviously scientific colleagues who seems to have been most sedulous in ensuring that Clifford's standing as a mathematician was not damaged by the underhand tactics of his enemies. In early 1885, Karl Pearson, Clifford's successor at University College, completed the laborious revision of one of his predecessor's unfinished manuscripts, now titled *The Common Sense of the Exact Sciences*. Before it was published as part of Kegan Paul's 'International Scientific Series', Pearson asked Mrs Clifford to look over the brief preface he had written for the book. She commended him on his 'excellent taste', and suggested that it 'could not be improved upon' except in one incidental but highly significant detail. The 'only point I have rather an idea might be altered', she wrote,

is 'Clifford was wildly excited over his theory' &c. It is quite correct. Only all things considered it might be as well to say 'entirely taken up' or something like that. This is merely because I never like – considering many things he wrote – that the other side shd. think any of his statements may [be] put down to mere excitement.

She closed the letter by warning: 'Anything serves the other side for the thin end of a wedge you know.'[54] Pearson seems to have sympathized with these anxieties, and the amended line appeared as 'Clifford was much occupied with his theory of "Graphs", and found it impossible to concentrate his mind on anything else', even though, as Lucy readily conceded, the original description of Clifford's state of mind had in fact been entirely accurate.[55]

The particular problem with using an otherwise innocuous expression like 'wildly excited' to describe Clifford's attitude towards his mathematical deliberations was that it might further intensify his association with the sort of unrestrained fervency for which Swinburne's verse had for many years been notorious. The *Edinburgh* had, after all, censured Swinburne for his 'unpruned exuberance of language and imagery', 'wild luxuriance' and 'feverish sensuality', all of which made his poetry so dangerously alluring to 'the ill-governed hey-day of youthful blood' and 'excitable but weak and unbalanced natures'.[56] Similar insinuations of incontinent impetuosity might easily be made against the late mathematician who had publicly commended Swinburne's unruly verse, and whose own writing had condemned orthodox beliefs and practices with such unrestrained vehemence.

In *Lectures and Essays*, Pollock and Stephen had attempted to forestall such accusations by insisting, in an editorial footnote appended to the end of the notorious 'The Unseen Universe', that it was instead Clifford's critics who exhibited extremes of 'grotesqueness . . . recklessness or impudence.'[57] Such potential allegations, though, were clearly perceived by Clifford's defenders to be no less detrimental to his status as a scientific specialist than to his standing as an iconoclastic popularizer. Indeed, one reviewer of his highly abstract *Mathematical Papers* (1882) had remarked that the 'exuberant philosophy of his popular works . . . must have harmed his reputation for solidity of thought'.[58] Allusions to Clifford's cerebral exuberance and lack of restraint also had important implications for his wider reputation, for Victorian ideals of moral character, as Stefan Collini has pointed out, required a 'certain habit of restraining one's impulses', and, as Collini observes, the 'contrast was with behaviour which was random, impulsive, feckless; and where the impulses were identified . . . with the "lower self" . . . conceived as purely appetitive'.[59] The absence of restraint in Clifford's mathematical speculations implied by the original wording of Pearson's preface might therefore have had unfortunate connotations of a physical, or even sexual, impulsiveness. Such an imputation would, for reasons that will become clear later, be of particular concern to Lucy, and by 1885 she was no longer willing to take any more risks with Clifford's mathematical reputation or that of his moral character more generally. Her insistence on such an apparently minor amendment to the preface of *The Common Sense of the Exact Sciences* reveals the lengths she was prepared to go to defend her late husband against the disreputable aspersions cast by those on 'the other side'.

Lucy, however, could do nothing to protect the book against exactly such damaging insinuations when it came to be reviewed in the press, especially when prominent reviewers included long-standing adversaries of her husband. In June 1885 the scientific weekly *Nature* carried a closely argued notice of *The Common Sense of the Exact Sciences* which filled her with contemptuous animosity towards both the reviewer and the editor who had allowed it to appear. The signed review was by Peter Guthrie Tait, Professor of Natural Philosophy at Edinburgh University and the fiery bulldog of the 'North British' group of Presbyterian physicists and engineers who perpetually sought to undermine the intellectual credibility of the largely metropolitan advocates of scientific naturalism.[60] In it, Tait implied that Clifford's mathematical career had been characterized by an impulsive 'rapidity' and was confined to merely those subjects 'on which he could be persuaded to bestow sufficient attention'. Still worse, Tait then alleged that, as a result of this Swinburne-like exuberance and lack of self-discipline, Clifford had often 'dispense[d] with important steps which had been taken by his less agile concurrents' and then 'consequently gave them (of course in perfect good faith) without indicating that they were not his own'. As such, Clifford's 'statements were by no means satisfactory (from the historical point of view) to those who recognised, as their own, some of the best "nuggets" that shine here and there in his pages'.[61] Upon reading this implicit accusation of intellectual plagiarism, Lucy littered the margins of her copy of *Nature* with angrily indignant exclamation marks and strident refutations of particular points; at the top of the first page of Tait's review she scrawled: 'This is what I expected from P. G. T.!'[62] Tait, as Lucy knew, had particular reason to assail her late husband's reputation for intellectual accuracy, for his co-authored book, *The Unseen Universe, or Physical Speculations on a Future State* (1875), had been the subject of one of Clifford's most vociferous and outspoken attacks on science informed by religious orthodoxy.

Tait's review of *The Common Sense of the Exact Sciences*, Lucy subsequently told Pearson, was 'disgraceful' and 'simply shameful', and its captious tone merely exposed it as 'a bitter remembrance, of course, of my husband's attack on Tait and Balfour Stewart's "Unseen Universe"'.[63] In further letters, she called on Pearson (as well as Sylvester, who declined) to pen a resolute response in which he 'might resist the accusation of absolute dishonesty brought against my husband and remark that Prof. Tait is probably still sore about the "Unseen Universe". That will worry him.' Lucy was also just as concerned that *Nature*'s editor Norman Lockyer, who had earlier sided with Tait in a similar dispute with Herbert Spencer, had 'allowed Prof. Tait to review the book remembering his known attitude towards my husband. It was an unfair thing to do.'[64] Pearson's spirited rejoinder duly appeared in *Nature*'s next number, but Lucy, furious that Tait had, in his own words, 'grown cockier and cockier' under the patronage of Lockyer, and evidently determined to carry on fighting her husband's scientific battles long after his death, seems at this time to have decided to take a more hands-on approach to defending Clifford's posthumous reputation against the damaging insinuations of Swinburnean recklessness and impetuosity.[65]

Mrs W. K. Clifford, as Marysa Demoor has shown, was extremely adept at fashioning her own identity as a novelist and literary journalist, even altering her date of birth to appear younger, and substituting exotic Barbados for mundane London as the place of her birth.[66] Lucy was equally willing to use some extremely sharp journalistic practices to similarly refashion the posthumous identity of the late husband whom she so profoundly missed. Charles Kegan Paul had resisted her request to demand that Sylvester should write a favourable review of *The Common Sense of the Exact Sciences*, admonishing her that his publishing company had 'always made it a rule to interfere in no way whatever with reviews of any books we publish', but Lucy herself was nevertheless soon in a position to facilitate such literary 'puffing'.[67] Already the author of a bestselling novel, *Mrs Keith's Crime* (1885), and several short stories, in the mid-1880s she became one of the most prolific contributors to the 'Literary Gossip' column in the *Athenaeum*, a prominent weekly review now edited by her close friend Norman MacColl.[68] The journal's strict policy of anonymity allowed her surreptitiously to promote her own work in the column, and, in the wake of her recent bitter experience with *Nature*, also to publicize the posthumous publication of her husband's writings.

A number of the *Athenaeum* in June 1886, for instance, contained an anonymous announcement of the imminent publication of 'a new and cheaper edition, in one volume, of the late Prof. W. K. Clifford's lectures and essays'.[69] As the editor's 'marked file' of the *Athenaeum* reveals, this notice was written surreptitiously by Lucy, the book's chief financial beneficiary.[70] She also contributed occasional titbits of information to the 'Science Gossip' column, which allowed her to promote the work of her husband's allies, disclosing that 'Prof. Karl Pearson will contribute a volume to the "International Series" which will be to physics what Prof. Clifford's "Common Sense of the Exact Sciences" (which Prof. Pearson edited) is to mathematics.'[71] With the *Athenaeum*'s strict adherence to anonymous publication and the apparent complicity of an amenable editor, Pearson could repay the favour, and in July 1887 he contributed a highly laudatory review of the recently published second part of *Elements of Dynamic*, which, he averred, presented 'Clifford pure and simple' and could not fail to reawaken the 'oft-told regret that Clifford did not live to reshape the teaching of elementary dynamics in this country'.[72] Pearson's review also countered indirectly Tait's earlier insinuations regarding Clifford's apparent intellectual recklessness, insisting on the 'solid foundations' of his work on force and matter, as well as emphasizing the sturdy, forthright language – and the term 'stuff' in particular – in which Clifford had 'Saxonized Newton's . . . theologico-scientific concepts'. While it was, of course, somewhat unethical for Pearson furtively to review the work of his erstwhile friend, he nevertheless used the opportunity to deliver an even more direct riposte to Tait, remarking that Clifford 'had entirely shaken off the prejudices which some imbibe from the perusal in student days of a well-known disquisition on the laws of motion; or it may be that that disquisition had remained for him a mystery – it described for him an "unseen universe".'[73] Fulfilling the request that Lucy had made some two years earlier, Pearson pointedly alluded to Clifford's bitter war of words with Tait and Balfour

Stewart, over their doctrinally orthodox interpretation of the second law of thermodynamics; the title of their well-known book being used as a convenient synonym for abstruse and overly abstract scientific speculation.

Having been so perturbed by the negative portrayal of her husband in the signed pages of *Nature*, Lucy Clifford seems to have used her position and contacts at the anonymous *Athenaeum* to ensure favourable coverage of him, enrolling friends to write reviews of his work which she could guarantee would be complimentary. At precisely this time, however, Lucy and her friends among the scientific naturalists faced the greatest challenge to their efforts to reshape Clifford's posthumous reputation, with the re-emergence of potentially awkward details of his early involvement with radical freethought.

HE HAD SOME RATHER WILD IDEAS

Following the skirmish with Tait and *Nature*, Lucy's friendship with Pearson grew still closer (he was 'oddly akin' to her husband she told him), and they began discussing aspects of Clifford's early life and opinions.[74] In the summer of 1885, in the wake of William Thomas Stead's lurid journalistic exposé of child prostitution in the 'Modern Babylon' of London, Pearson had brought together a small group of radicals, feminists and socialists, both male and female, who were all eager to discuss the increasingly piquant subject of sex.[75] The Men and Women's Club also invited external contributions to its self-consciously 'advanced' discussions, and around this time Pearson seems to have quizzed Lucy concerning her famously unorthodox husband's views on such matters. Clifford, she confessed in a long and strictly confidential letter, had 'had some rather wild ideas . . . concerning those questions', although she cautiously insisted that this had been 'before we knew each other' and that he had afterwards 'modified them'. While the 'very strong views' on the proper relations between men and women which Clifford held before his marriage to Lucy in 1875 'would not do for the majority', he had articulated them in an early essay that was now in the possession of Mathilde Blind, a German émigré and bohemian poet who in the 1870s had been a member of the radical circle which met at Conway's South Place Chapel.[76]

This unpublished paper had the provocative title 'Mistress or Wife'.[77] It argued, Lucy told Pearson, that 'making divorce easier wd. make marriage more popular which was to be desired as the only real check on prostitution, & that it would put the relations of men and women on a realistic basis'. If 'the absolute constancy and confidence' necessary to a happy marriage began to fail '& if the desire for divorce arose', Clifford had apparently postulated, 'it shd. be discussed and reasoned in together, & if mutually desired shd. be obtainable' (although the 'difficulty of the children' in divorce cases had continued to 'perplex him'). In 'easy divorce', which would end the social obligation to protract sexually dysfunctional marriages, 'lay the only real solution of the prostitution question'. Clifford's audacious essay also disclosed, Lucy informed Pearson, that 'in purity for men he simply did not believe. Half of his hatred for priests arose from the fact that he thought they had unnatural or secretly immoral lives.' In fact, for Clifford 'men & women were meant to be together, & . . . love . . . was the great lever of passion & placed it among the highest feelings.'[78] While Lucy's account of her husband's unpublished paper did not refer to the related, and highly contentious, issue of population control, Clifford, by insisting with such vehemence on the unnaturalness of celibacy, effectively repudiated the remedies for overpopulation originally proposed by Thomas Malthus, namely chastity and late marriage, and instead allied himself with those radicals who controversially supported artificial checks to fertility.

Since 1868 the miscellaneous freethinkers of the newly founded London Dialectical Society, which extolled the 'principle of absolute liberty of thought & speech' and the 'unbiased consideration of all . . . important questions', had frequently debated precisely the same vexed subjects of marriage, prostitution and birth control.[79] The small debating society, as one member proudly claimed, did 'not find it necessary to exclude those explosive subjects of religion, politics, and sex, which are generally tabooed', and, as Michael Mason has argued, it soon became the most 'important forum for advanced ideas on sexuality' in Victorian Britain.[80] Controversially, the London Dialectical Society also welcomed women to its twice-monthly meetings, and included such notorious radicals as Bradlaugh and Besant amongst its members (the society even offered sureties for the bail of the pair during their obscenity trial in 1877).[81] On several occasions during the early and mid-1870s, this self-consciously radical society considered views extremely similar to those apparently expressed in Clifford's unpublished paper.

In 1871, for example, Conway read a paper to the society entitled 'On Marriage' which likewise proposed making divorce easier as a method of checking vice (as well as overpopulation in Conway's view), and in the ensuing debate the physician Charles Drysdale concurred that 'prostitution was often the result of unhappy marriage' and 'in all probability, facility of divorce would do a great deal for society'.[82] Conway later recalled how at precisely this time an acquaintance with Clifford 'made at Cambridge became friendship in London', and it seems likely that Clifford would have discussed such controversial subjects with his new Unitarian friend and may even have written 'Mistress or Wife' with a view to presenting it at another meeting of the London Dialectical Society.[83] In fact, although there is no record of his having ever spoken at a meeting of the group, Clifford served as the London Dialectical Society's president towards the end of his life, with Conway acting as his vice-president.[84] The society's vigorous meetings, moreover, were generally held at Langham Hall in Great Portland Street, a location which Clifford knew well as it was also where he gave his regular addresses to the Sunday Lecture Society. Now, over a decade later, the incendiary combination of radical freethought and the frank discussion of sexuality contained in Clifford's unpublished paper was exactly the kind of provocative 'advanced' material that Pearson wanted to present at the meetings of his own new discussion club.

Before giving the strict instructions that '*I don't want you to repeat all this as applied to us personally* but you can use the substance of it if it is useful', Lucy explained to Pearson that her late husband had attempted to conduct his own private life according to the same rational standards adumbrated in 'Mistress or Wife'. She told him that 'if during our married life he had been tempted with any sort of unfaithfulness he wd. at once have told me, as he wd. have told me of any other stray or lustful thoughts that overtook him.'[85] During a debate on the relations of the sexes at the London Dialectical Society in 1878, one member had similarly proclaimed that 'what is absolutely necessary in free unions [i.e. marriages where divorce was readily attainable] is, that there should be no deceit between the parties, and that each should understand the responsibilities of their position,' and Clifford's heterodox attitudes towards sex, even when applied to his own personal life, once again corresponded with many of the views expressed at this notorious forum of sexual radicalism.[86]

Even more significantly, aspects of Clifford's progressive views on sexuality might also have been influenced by George Drysdale's infamous *Physical, Sexual and Natural Religion* (1855; later retitled *The Elements of Social Science*), which, as was seen in the previous chapter, condemned sexual abstinence as not only unnatural but actually deleterious to physical and mental health. Like 'Mistress or Wife', Drysdale's anonymous monograph, which appeared in several new editions during Clifford's time in London, proposed that the 'irrevocability of the marriage contract, and the impossibility of procuring divorce, lead to the most fearful evils' and were the principal 'cause of *prostitution*'.[87] While Clifford departed from *The Elements of Social Science* on the value of marriage and monogamy, his conduct of his own marriage largely concurred with the book's earnest injunction that 'we should endeavour to act in an open and dignified manner towards those, with whom we have sexual relations . . . Neither man nor woman should ever pretend to be constant, when they are not so, nor feign a passion which they do not feel.'[88] Accordingly, Lucy herself had been made to promise 'that if I ever found myself loving him less, or thinking of anyone else I would go & tell him naturally as a matter of course', and she told Pearson that 'this was the key to his whole feeling in regard to marriage that there shd. be absolute constancy and confidence & that if the constancy failed the confidence shd. not.'[89] Despite certain misgivings regarding the highly personal nature of her late husband's essay, Lucy initially consented to Pearson's plan of 'getting the paper (if you can) from Miss Blind & reading it', although she demurred at the prospect of him then reading it aloud to the members of the Men and Women's Club.[90]

The problem, of course, was that if such candid details of Clifford's youthful 'wild' views, and especially his apparent endorsement of certain aspects of the subversive attitude towards sex expressed in *The Elements of Social Science*, leaked into the public realm they would inevitably be exploited by his numerous enemies to tarnish his posthumous reputation still further. In fact, there were more than enough hints during Clifford's lifetime to suggest that his adversaries were already well aware of the potential existence of a paper like 'Mistress or Wife' with its frank discussion of taboo subjects such as prostitution. In 1874, during the contretemps over George Darwin's apparent endorsement of vice as a means of checking population, the anti-Darwinian comparative anatomist St George Mivart had, as was noted in chapter two, insinuated to Huxley that he knew of

a most highly cultured and intellectual man, of the school I intend to oppose, who deliberately maintains that the propagation of the criminality referred to would be most useful and beneficial to society as tending to limit population without requiring what he calls the 'immorality' of ascetic self-denial.[91]

This highly partisan interpretation clearly does not accurately represent the opinions that were expressed in 'Mistress or Wife', which, at least in Lucy's summary of it a decade later, proposed methods of eradicating the social evil of prostitution rather than of propagating it.

Nevertheless, such deliberate distortion, as Huxley knew all too well, was Mivart's stock-in-trade, and there seems little doubt that the unnamed member of the Darwinian school who allegedly advocated such invidious criminality was actually Clifford. Mivart's disdainful reference to 'what he calls the "immorality" of ascetic self-denial' closely resembled several passages from Clifford's lectures and journalism during the 1870s, which frequently railed against the 'institutions of monasticism and a celibate clergy; which stunted the moral sense', and, as Lucy would later tell Pearson, he privately considered that celibate priests must perforce lead 'secretly immoral lives'.[92] As with George Darwin's innocuous allusion to prostitution in his historical survey of various marriage customs, it was easy for Mivart maliciously to misinterpret Clifford's radical views on the same subject as in some way a pernicious endorsement of vice and licentiousness.

Mivart's malevolent allegation that an anonymous member of the Darwinian school considered the propagation of prostitution to be beneficial to society was made in a personal letter to Huxley expressly marked 'Private & Confidential'. Exactly the same misapprehension of the views articulated in 'Mistress or Wife' would soon also appear in public, and in a form that made Clifford easily identifiable as the promoter of such dangerously immoral opinions. In Mallock's *The New Republic* (1877), the scientific atheist Mr Saunders is a cruelly transparent parody of Clifford's outspoken antagonism towards orthodox religion. Like Clifford, Saunders angrily denounces the 'degrading . . . fetish-worship of celibacy, of mortification, and so forth', and many of his other impertinent declarations in the novel are likewise thinly veiled lampoons of some of Clifford's more contentious statements in the liberal press.[93] There are also slight touches of Swinburne in Mallock's depiction of Saunders, most notably in his conspicuous 'red-headed' demeanour, as well as in an otherwise unaccountable fondness for aesthetic 'knickerbockers' and 'pink stockings', which, even before the publication of 'Cosmic Emotion', called attention implicitly to Clifford's veneration of the scandalous poet.[94]

In particular, *The New Republic*'s depiction of Saunders, as with the same novel's portrayal of Tyndall as the lovelorn Mr Stockton, seems to have drawn on prevalent rumours and innuendo, and hinted ominously at Saunders's amorality and flippant attitude towards sex and marriage. On one occasion, he insists that 'that preposterous idol of the marketplace, the sanctity of marriage' is 'already doomed', and earlier in the novel, in almost exactly the same terms that Mivart had putatively attributed to Clifford, Saunders proclaims:

We think it, for instance, . . . a very sad thing when a girl is as we call it ruined. But it is we really that make all the sadness. She is ruined only because we think she is so. And I have little doubt that that higher philosophy of the future that Mr. Storks speaks of will go far, some day, towards solving the great question of women's sphere of action, by its recognition of prostitution as an honourable and beneficent profession.[95]

Mr Storks, who represents the views of Huxley in *The New Republic*, has earlier insisted that 'science will establish an entirely new basis of morality,' although his evolutionary and relativist model of ethics can do nothing to preclude the kind of immoral interpretation of it advanced by Saunders, at whom Storks 'glar[es] with indignation'.[96] Significantly, the almost comically sanguine view of prostitution adumbrated by Saunders resembled Drysdale's insistence, in *The Elements of Social Science*, that prostitutes should receive the 'deep gratitude of mankind' and that 'instead of contempt, these poor neglected girls deserve the warmest thanks of society.'[97] It was also reminiscent of certain statements made at the London Dialectical Society, where, during a meeting in the late 1860s, it had been declared by various members that a 'woman should not be looked on as degraded by her unchastity' and that 'becoming a prostitute was not always a fall, sometimes it was a positive rise'.[98] Like Mivart, Mallock was clearly not only well aware of the views – or at least a maliciously distorted version of them – that Clifford had formulated in the unpublished paper which was perhaps written to be read at another meeting of the same society, but also of their potential to perturb and exasperate other, more morally conservative proponents of scientific naturalism such as Huxley.

During the early 1870s, Clifford's allegedly dissipated opinions on the prostitution question seem to have become the subject of conspiratorial gossip and innuendo amongst metropolitan intellectuals. Indeed, Mallock would later admit that many of the grubby details paraded in his unremittingly hostile obituary of Clifford for the *Edinburgh* had come from an undisclosed 'source . . . [who] seemed to us to be trustworthy'.[99] *The New Republic* brought such scandalous opinions into more general discussion, although under the convenient cover of fiction, and the views articulated by the ostensibly fictional Mr Saunders were, inevitably, almost at once identified with those of his real-life counterpart. The *Quarterly Review*, in a notice of Mallock's novel, hypocritically complained of the book's 'tendency to personal allusion drawn from sources which, being private, ought to remain sacred', and then immediately implied that, like his fictional incarnation, Clifford harboured 'peculiar tastes', which 'if carried into practice, would turn the world into a menagerie let loose'.[100] The perpetuation of such pernicious rumours concerning his contentious views was clearly of huge benefit to those, like Mallock and Mivart, who wished to impugn Clifford, and scientific naturalism more generally, with upholding a corrupt and essentially immoral attitude towards human existence.

It would only be counterproductive for the defenders of Clifford's posthumous reputation to now corroborate unnecessarily some of the malicious innuendo and gossip disseminated over many years by his sworn foes; a tight-lipped silence over 'Mistress or Wife' was the only realistic option. Lord Amberley's ignominious defeat at a parliamentary election in 1868 after certain comments on birth control that he had made at the London Dialectical Society appeared in the press had, after all, provided a monitory example of the perils of openly avowing the contentious views that were tolerated at meetings of this self-consciously radical society.[101] While editing *Lectures and Essays* in 1879, Pollock had looked over 'one or two early writings which Clifford must have deliberately not chosen to print' and was adamant that he could 'not find anything that would do to publish'.[102] Seven years later it would still be extremely dangerous to allow details of Clifford's early engagement with radical freethought, especially with regard to sex, to appear semi-publicly, even if only in the debates of an elitist intellectual discussion group like the Men and Women's Club.

After consulting Leslie Stephen about 'Mistress or Wife', who was aghast that her 'freethinking friends' might inadvertently provide a 'pretext for accusing her of supporting immoral opinions', Lucy came to 'the conclusion that I don't want it read at any meeting', telling Pearson that if her husband 'had wished to publish this paper or its substance – he would have done so'.[103] She nevertheless offered him a second chance, suggesting that Pearson himself should confer with Pollock and Stephen, and affirming that 'if *either* of these approve it shall be published, or if Prof. Huxley does', and then 'you shall read it at yr. club if you like'. Perhaps conscious of the dubious ethics of her own sharp practice at the *Athenaeum*, Lucy also insisted on a further condition:

> if it *is* published it must be in the most public place, in the XIXth with his name . . . seeing the bold subject it is on I shd. like it done in the light of day, not virtually in secret as if he was afraid to face those whom he knew wd. demur. There is something cowardly to my mind in that. It wd., and properly, be a slur on him, wd. give the enemy a title & wd. weaken all his previous work.

It was, she told Pearson apologetically, 'the *subject*' of the paper 'that makes it so necessary to be extra careful', and if it were decided that it should not be published then 'we are all bound in honour for ever to hold our peace concerning it'.[104] Given their circumspect editorial modifications of *Lectures and Essays*, it seems highly unlikely that the peremptory triumvirate of Pollock, Stephen and Huxley would have been willing to countenance Pearson's scheme to expose the 'wild' contents of 'Mistress or Wife' to public view. Nor would they have been any more sympathetic to Lucy's plan of publishing it in an overtly liberal and open-minded periodical like the *Nineteenth Century*. Meanwhile, the involvement of Mathilde Blind, who in the early 1870s told friends that she was romantically involved with Swinburne as well as sharing with Clifford what she claimed was 'an intimacy which I see more & more is very rare between men & women', would have made avowedly respectable scientific naturalists like Huxley and Stephen even less inclined to sanction the publication of Clifford's problematic early paper.[105]

'Mistress or Wife' was never published in the *Nineteenth Century* or any other periodical (and the manuscript seems no longer to exist), but subtle traces of Clifford's controversial opinions on marriage and prostitution did still appear in the pages of the radical press at this time. In February 1887, just a month after Lucy had prohibited the reading of her late husband's essay at the Men and Women's Club, Pearson published his own discussion paper, 'Socialism and Sex', in the Fabian Society journal *To-Day*. Towards the end of his eugenicist argument, Pearson contended that 'when the relations of men and women are perfectly free and they can meet on an equal footing, then so far from this free sexual-relationship leading to sensuality and loose living, we hold it would be the best safe-guard against it.' Every 'man and woman', he continued,

would probably ultimately choose a lover from their friends, but the man and woman who being absolutely free would choose more than one would probably be the exceptions; – exceptions, we believe, infinitely more rare than under our present legalised monogamy accompanied as it is by socially unrecognised polygamy and polyandry – the mistress and the prostitute.[106]

The close resemblance of this passage to Lucy's summary of the argument of Clifford's early essay in her recent letter to Pearson was not merely coincidental. Rather, as Pearson acknowledged in an appended footnote: 'Some of the above remarks we owe to the letter of a woman-friend; they express our own views in truer words than we have been able to find for ourselves.'[107] When Pearson's paper was reprinted, without the above footnote, in the following year as the concluding essay of *The Ethic of Freethought*, Lucy told him: 'It is a fine book . . . I am so proud to think you owe . . . some of it to my husband.'[108] Clifford's own hesitancy over contributing to the radical gutter press notwithstanding, and despite the apparent determination of Pollock, Stephen and Huxley effectively to suppress his early radical writing, the heterodox opinions on highly taboo subjects expressed in 'Mistress or Wife' were smuggled, under the cover of a threefold anonymity, into a cheap socialist periodical, which, in the very same number, also published an instalment of one of the first English translations of Karl Marx's *Capital*.

The absolute necessity of concealing Clifford's posthumous involvement with Pearson's freethinking writing was reinforced two years later when the Catholic critic William Samuel Lilly denounced, in his book *On Right and Wrong* (1890), the very passage from *The Ethic of Freethought* which drew upon Lucy's summary of 'Mistress or Wife' as a particularly repugnant example of the 'social forecast of one of the most accomplished and zealous of English "advanced thinkers" [i.e. Pearson]', who considers that 'marriage is . . . a source of stupidity and ugliness to the human race' and 'would summarily abolish it'.[109] Earlier in the same book, Lilly had identified Clifford, along with Huxley, Tyndall and Spencer, as one of those whose 'invalidation of the moral code' of Christianity and replacement of it with a new creed of 'ethical agnosticism' had been 'unspeakably disastrous, both in speculation and in practice', and had precipitated an 'actual crisis of morality' in Victorian Britain.[110] The *Academy*, in a scornful review of *On Right and Wrong*, observed mockingly that in all the voluminous 'writings of the school incriminated' in the book there was not 'a single passage that even the practised "manipulation" of Mr. Lilly could pervert into the sense required'.[111] If, however, it had been known that it was actually Clifford who was responsible, at least in part, for the more extreme views on marriage and prostitution now being promulgated by Pearson, it would clearly have afforded substantial corroboration to the argument of Lilly, and of many others as well, that such apparently corrosive and immoral beliefs were an inevitable consequence of the doctrines of Darwinian science.

CONVERTED FROM CLIFFORDISM

The dilemma over Clifford's early radical writings, and whether she should follow the promptings of freethinking friends like Pearson and Blind or the more circumspect advice of Pollock, Stephen and Huxley, led Lucy to ponder her role as the guardian of her late husband's scientific *oeuvre* and the principal defender of his posthumous reputation. The 'remit I am acting upon', she had told Pearson regarding the early unpublished paper, 'is simply my duty as past guardian of what he left,' and she insisted that

If he had left as the result of serious conclusion papers to the effect that Mormonism was the revealed religion or that murder & lying shd. be cultivated as fine arts I shd. have felt it a matter of conscience to publish them. My business is not to criticise his opinions but only to be quite certain that they were his.[112]

Lucy's role in maintaining her dead husband's public profile, however, had never involved simply the disinterested promulgation of his known opinions, no matter how repugnant they might be. Rather, she had, for several years, subtly refashioned aspects of Clifford's actual personality that might now play into the hands of his numerous adversaries. She had, after all, conceded that Pearson's original description of Clifford's 'wild excitement' over the theory of 'Graphs' in his preface to *The Common Sense of the Exact Sciences* was 'quite correct', but insisted on amending it all the same.[113]

Lucy, even as her own literary fame continued to grow, assiduously fashioned for herself the passive self-image of a meek and dutiful widow in interviews, photographs (in which she was invariably portrayed in black velvet widow's weeds) and eccentric personal conduct. In 1897 the journalist Sarah A. Tooley detected in her sombre manner 'the suggestion of a heart fraught with sadness, a mind looking forth in pity and sorrow upon human misery', while, less charitably, Virginia Woolf, in her diary for January 1920, remarked on Lucy's 'large codfish eyes' and penchant for 'black velvet', finding her manner 'morbid – intense . . . with a dash of the stage'.[114] But despite this vaunted fidelity to her late husband's memory, Lucy actually soon began to differ considerably from Clifford on some of his most important beliefs.

In her correspondence with Pearson over 'Mistress or Wife', for instance, Lucy explained that, in opposition to the optimistic view of free unions expressed by her husband, she herself considered that

divorce . . . shld. be much easier for the woman to attain than for the man, for the man . . . wd. often feel tempted to go on ruining one pretty woman after another . . . shocking her by mere intimate contact with his nature if he knew he could as easily get rid of her.[115]

Such mildly feminist sentiments, though, were as nothing compared to Lucy's divergence from her husband on questions of metaphysics and eschatology. While Clifford had asserted implacably that the world was 'made up of material molecules and of ether' and 'no room is here to be found for either ghosts of the dead, or "superior intelligences", or bogies of any kind whatever', his wife, just two years after his death, anonymously published 'Lost' in *Macmillan's Magazine*, a short story which details the anguish experienced by a spectral dead woman as she watches her living husband from beyond the grave.[116] The story's ghostly narrator is reassured by her unwavering conviction that 'as the clay-fetters fall, dear . . . we shall see each other once more face to face, and out of the darkness of human pain shall come everlasting light', and her experiences throughout the narrative appear to endorse the very spiritualist axioms which Clifford had found most repugnant.[117]

After reading 'Lost', Lucy's friend William James told his wife that 'obviously she cares much about immortality, but thinks it her duty to care nothing for it. Don't tell anyone she wrote it; she seems in a deadly fear lest Leslie Stephen should find it.'[118] When James later recounted a visit to Lucy's Bayswater home where her daughters had recited their nightly prayer to their late father, his friend Francis Child commented that 'Mrs. Clifford will be converted from Cliffordism if she goes on that way.'[119] Even as late as 1925 (just four years before her own death), Lucy confessed guiltily to Pearson that although 'none of us are orthodox . . . I can never bring myself to believe, or rather to *feel*, that genius is absolutely extinct (tho' he did) . . . I dread the least ghost of a chance being lost.'[120] By the mid-1880s, Lucy had also developed a distinct circle of new friends, including the 'ethical mystic' Victoria, Lady Welby, whose religious and spiritual views were strikingly different to those of her late husband, and whose influence over her had begun to perturb many of the older friends, like Pearson, whom she had met principally through Clifford.[121]

Despite her evident lack of sympathy with many of her husband's most deeply held and characteristic opinions, Lucy remained Clifford's most loyal defender and by far the most active participant in the refashioning of his posthumous reputation. This situation seems not to have concerned unduly his erstwhile friends and colleagues amongst the inner circle of scientific naturalists. While Lucy could be relied upon to memorialize her husband strategically in ways that largely excluded his awkward connections with political radicalism, Swinburne's controversial poetry, and, most importantly, freethinking immorality, they were apparently willing to turn a blind eye to her occasional eccentricity – including having her books inscribed 'W. K. & Lucy Clifford' long after her husband's death – and growing interest in mysticism and immortality.[122]

Occasionally, Lucy had required prompting from her more vigilant friends, as Stephen had done regarding the incendiary essay 'Mistress or Wife', but even into the twentieth century she remained willing to accept Frederick Macmillan's circumspect advice about the inadvisability of allowing the overtly radical Rationalist Press Association to publish a cheap edition of her husband's *Lectures and Essays*.[123] Clifford himself had been an adherent of the Comtean doctrine of 'subjective immortality' and believed that his survival was ensured by his words and deeds continuing to reverberate in the hearts and minds of the living.[124] His brief career and much lengthier afterlife nevertheless reveal that, for the proponents of Darwinism, the maintenance of a reputation for moral and sexual probity was considerably more important than the truthful acknowledgement of all aspects of their much lamented colleague's beliefs and principles.

CHAPTER 6

T. H. Huxley, Henry Maudsley and the pathologization of aestheticism

In the September 1877 number of the *Contemporary Review*, the Irish literary critic Edward Dowden proclaimed that 'scientific ideas of comparatively recent date', and especially the 'conception of evolution' and the related 'idea of human progress', had emerged as a 'great inspiring force with literature'.[1] Dowden's article, entitled 'The Scientific Movement and Literature', contended that both science and literature now taught that 'duty is social' and enjoined a 'doctrine of self-development' and 'moving upward' in which lower 'egotistic desires . . . must be sacrificed' as part of an evolutionary movement towards a higher state of 'self-surrender'.[2] Nor, in Dowden's view, did imaginative literature merely respond passively to prior scientific developments, for the 'statement, justified by science, of the nature of duty' was 'but a rendering into abstract formulae of the throbbings of the heart which lives at the centre of such creations as "Romola" . . . and "Middlemarch"'.[3] George Eliot's fiction, as well as Alfred Tennyson's poetry, were, according to Dowden, literary works that were not only 'nourished by . . . scientific doctrine' but which also gave expression to the deeper truths still to be revealed by contemporary science.[4]

Dowden's argument regarding the close correspondence between Victorian science and literature, however, was predicated upon the deliberate exclusion of a highly significant nineteenth-century literary movement, which, as has been seen throughout this book, had a much more complex and problematic relationship with contemporary science than did writers such as Eliot or Tennyson. When 'artists devote themselves, as they say, to art for art's sake', Dowden insisted at the beginning of 'The Scientific Movement and Literature', 'no great art is possible', and throughout the article he continued to revile all manifestations of aestheticism, denouncing the 'Parisian coterie of literary artists, whose art possessed no social feeling, and who took for their *drapeau* the words, "L'art pour l'art"'.[5] Only by dismissing entirely a form of literature that provided 'nothing save a supply to the senses of delicate colours and perfumes' could Dowden contend successfully that, like science, 'literature addresses itself . . . to the total nature of man' and conveyed vividly the primacy of social duty over the rights of the individual.[6]

Dowden's antipathy towards aestheticism had long preceded his interest in the unity of nineteenth-century science and literature, and in a previous article for the *Contemporary* published more than ten years earlier he had similarly condemned Victor Cousin's argument for the 'independence of art', which, Dowden claimed, had been 'popularized by the leaders of the Romantic movement in literature' with the notorious 'watchword of theirs now so well known, *"L'art pour l'art"*'.[7] Although Dowden's scorn in 'French Aesthetics', which was published in the *Contemporary*'s February 1866 number, was reserved principally for the practitioners of aesthetic art and literature on the other side of the Channel, his criticisms began to appear just as a distinctly English version of aestheticism was coming to prominence with the publication of Algernon Charles Swinburne's stridently amoral *Poems and Ballads* in the summer of 1866. In the following year, Swinburne appropriated Cousin's infamously circular slogan, which he rendered as 'Art for art's sake first of all', in his critical study of William Blake, while, a few months later, Walter Pater similarly enjoined the 'love of art for art's sake' in an anonymous article for the *Westminster Review*.[8] The phrase had first been introduced into English during the 1830s, but it was only with Swinburne and Pater's more provocative usage that it gained wider currency as a byword for sensuous artistic indulgence and the adjournment of all other responsibilities.[9] By the time of Dowden's 1877 article for the *Contemporary*, aestheticism had become a widespread, as well as a much reviled, aspect of cultural life in Victorian Britain, and it was necessary for him to continue his long-standing critical onslaught against the proponents of art's independence of extra-aesthetic moral or didactic concerns in order to establish a connection between science and literature which presented both as socially responsible and, above all, respectable modes of intellectual activity.

Dowden was not alone in reviling aesthetic writers and artists for exactly this same purpose, and, as this final chapter will show, many of the leading supporters of Charles Darwin's evolutionary theories, and Thomas Henry Huxley in particular, similarly adopted an overtly antagonistic attitude towards any form of literature or art which, because of its apparent disregard for quotidian concerns, was labelled with the disreputable soubriquet 'aesthetic'. It is well known that Victorian men of science frequently employed literary allusions and analogies in their own writing, drawing especially on the work of highly renowned and respectable writers such as Tennyson. Huxley also included references to both controversial older literature and recent avant-garde works in his own writings, and he even intervened on behalf of the cause of artistic freedom in cultural controversies over issues like the depiction of female nudity in the visual arts. But, despite this apparent cultural liberalism, aestheticism was consistently denounced by Huxley for what was considered its uniquely repulsive transgression of all conventional moral and artistic standards.

The condemnation and actual diagnosis of aestheticism as a pathological form of artistic activity even became a prevalent feature of certain aspects of evolutionary theorizing in the final decades of the nineteenth century. As Darwinian pessimists such as the psychiatrist Henry Maudsley proposed, an evolutionary regression or degeneration was both possible and an extremely potent threat to advanced societies like contemporary Britain. The alleged languidness, egotism and sensualism exhibited in various works of aesthetic art and literature, Maudsley implied, were particularly acute symptoms of this wider process of degeneration. While the wide-ranging and generally respectful literary allusions contained in Maudsley's psychiatric writings have been noted frequently by scholars, the actual analysis of recent literary movements in his treatment of both individual and societal degeneration, in which Maudsley employed a literary critical rhetoric very similar to that used in hostile reviews of Swinburne's poetry, is much less known. It nevertheless became an increasingly important element of his overtly scientific prognostications regarding the prevalent ills of modern civilization.

In Maudsley's discussions of evolutionary regression, it was the scientific expert rather than the literary critic who was now most able to uncover and condemn these potentially degenerative and enervating forms of artistic activity, an augmentation of scientific authority which became particularly evident with Max Nordau's notorious synthesis of medical diagnosis and conservative cultural criticism in the mid-1890s. Although Nordau himself was widely condemned as a charlatan whose work was riddled with examples of intellectual rashness and imprudence, aestheticism was increasingly depicted in the final years of the nineteenth century as the most conspicuous cultural symptom of the degeneration of British society, appearing as such even in novels like H. G. Wells's *The Time Machine* (1895), which, significantly, was written by one of Huxley's erstwhile students at the Normal School of Science. After decades in which numerous adversaries, from the technically accomplished anatomist St George Mivart to the vituperative novelist and critic William Hurrell Mallock, had regularly tarnished Darwin's theories by association with the alleged excesses of aestheticism, degeneration theory provided a means by which Darwinian scientists could not only detach their arguments from such pejorative associations, but could also present themselves – rather than periodical reviewers or nascent specialist literary critics – as the best equipped to diagnose and remedy such pathological forms of art and literature.

Both Dowden's rather haughty dismissal of the French-inspired aesthetic movement and Maudsley's pathologization of its leading figures as the purveyors of dangerous degenerative diseases enabled the construction of an expedient, although clearly very partial, version of the interaction of science and literature which accorded with their own particular interests. It is significant therefore that Dowden's strategic and highly contingent vision of the harmonious relations which apparently existed between science and literature in the nineteenth century provided a convenient model for twentieth-century scholars eager to overcome longstanding assumptions that scientific and literary discourses were the products of contrasting worldviews and value systems. Tess Cosslett, in a book that took its title, *The 'Scientific Movement' and Victorian Literature* (1982), directly from Dowden, proposed that her own examination of how 'scientific writers, novelists and poets can all be found putting forward similar views . . . often by means of similar language and imagery' would 'develop further some of [the] hints and signs' implicit in Dowden's original article.[10] Following Dowden, Cosslett's book, like much subsequent scholarship on the subject, took most of its examples of these conceptual and linguistic similarities from the morally unimpeachable works of Eliot and Tennyson.

More recent studies of Victorian science and literature have been dominated by what has come to be known as the 'One Culture' model, which similarly subsumes disciplinary differences within a unitary cultural context that facilitates the interconnection of the two modes of discourse.[11] Implicit in this model is the assumption that such discursive interchanges are, even when unintended, invariably creative and positive for both science and literature, providing fresh ways for writers and scientists to imagine the world as well as new modes of organizing their insights. As with Dowden's original argument, however, the 'One Culture' model likewise necessitates the exclusion of aesthetic art and literature, which, as has been seen throughout this book, frequently implicated scientific writers with more iniquitous kinds of literary association that were not in any way desirable. This final chapter, by examining how various proponents of Darwinism maintained an unwavering, and vociferously proclaimed, opposition to all manifestations of aestheticism, will offer a further confirmation of how literary interconnections were regarded as being dangerous and deleterious as much as creative and productive.

THE TRANSPORTS OF AESTHETICISM

Just six months before Dowden's 'The Scientific Movement and Literature', the *Contemporary* had published another article which articulated a very different view of the relation between science and contemporary literature. In 'The Greek Spirit in Modern Literature', Richard St John Tyrwhitt berated the so-called 'Hellenico-sensuous school' of art, whose members, including Pater and John Addington Symonds, not only enjoined that 'while you do what you like you can't do wrong', but actually encouraged the 'total denial of any moral restraint on any human impulses'.[12] The cultivated amorality of such practitioners of aestheticism, Tyrwhitt insinuated, might finally result in 'phallic ecstasy and palpitations at male beauty' and even 'unnatural practices between men'.[13] While the virulent homophobia of Tyrwhitt's article has been examined in great detail in recent scholarship on aesthetic literature, it has not previously been recognized that modern science was also implicated in his malevolent attack of the homoerotic writings of Pater and Symonds.[14] In fact, Tyrwhitt directly equated scientific naturalism's suspension of judgement with regard to the transcendental with aestheticism's rejection of shared moral knowledge and insistence on the private nature of all aesthetic experience, remarking upon the 'peculiar subjectiveness or egotism of the new agnostic style'.[15] Like agnosticism's refusal to countenance universal truths that were independent of experience, aestheticism similarly repudiated fixed axioms of aesthetic authority and instead made the individual perceiver the arbiter of artistic merit. In their validation of the individual against established authority, Tyrwhitt implied, the two doctrines were virtually indistinguishable, and therefore equally pernicious in their potential social consequences.

    The philosophical category 'agnosticism', which Huxley had coined less than a decade earlier, could, in any case, be differentiated from commonplace 'atheism' only by those with the 'natural or acquired ingenuity' necessary to maintain what was, for Tyrwhitt, an entirely groundless and mendacious distinction.[16] Writers such as Pater and Symonds were themselves representatives of 'the artistic wing' of this 'great army of atheism' which was then threatening to overrun the last bastions of orthodox belief, and their writings, as Tyrwhitt noted, made a 'curious appeal . . . to the mental discipline of physical science'. Such an appeal to the supposed disinterestedness and austerity of scientific method, though, was made only 'in the hope that natural science will . . . save [them] from any ideas about sin and forgiveness, or right and wrong' and underwrite their flagrant eroticism and iniquitous celebrations of male beauty.[17]

Tyrwhitt had spent much of his career as a clergyman, most recently as the rector of St Mary Magdalen in Oxford, but since the late 1860s he had been the *Contemporary*'s regular art critic as well as the devoted secretary of John Ruskin, then Slade Professor of Fine Art at Oxford.[18] Accordingly, his aesthetic views were informed by both an unfaltering conviction that true beauty and meaningful art were impossible in the absence of orthodox Christian faith and by Ruskin's own more idiosyncratic conception of the 'Theocratic' faculty of 'moral perception and appreciation of ideas of beauty'.[19] This ethical mode of artistic receptivity, as Ruskin adumbrated in the second volume of *Modern Painters*, was contrasted with the 'Aesthetic' faculty that 'properly signifies mere sensual perception of the outward qualities and necessary effects of bodies'. The same volume would later be reprinted in 1883 as an 'early and so decisive warning against the . . . folly' of the 'aesthetic cliques' whose inanities had 'in recent days . . . made art at once the corruption, and the jest, of the vulgar world'.[20] In an article for the *Nineteenth Century* in 1878, Ruskin opined that the latest works of even his own Pre-Raphaelite protégés had begun to manifest a similarly 'morbid and mischievous force', which, significantly, he inferred was the result of what were 'vulgarly called "scientific" modes of investigation' that taught that the 'knowledge of the difference between acids and alkalies is a more respectable one than that of the difference between vice and virtue'.[21] Although Ruskin had hardly been reticent in expressing his almost hysterical antipathy to John Tyndall and his allegedly materialist understanding of glaciers during the previous decade, he appears to have left it to his secretary Tyrwhitt to make the insinuations of his *Nineteenth Century* article more specific by proposing that it was the irreligious scientific agenda of Tyndall and others which, by contesting the efficacy of orthodox Christian beliefs as well as the cultural authority of their proponents, was largely responsible for many of the most insidious developments in recent art and literature.[22]

The intimate connection between scientific naturalism and aestheticism was certainly made even more explicit in another of Tyrwhitt's regular articles on art for the *Contemporary* published just over a year after Ruskin's contribution to the *Nineteenth Century*. Since James Knowles's defection to the *Nineteenth Century* in 1877, the *Contemporary* had become increasingly doctrinally conservative as well as overtly antagonistic towards the rival *Fortnightly Review*'s endorsement of both naturalistic science and aesthetic literature, and Tyrwhitt, who (with Ruskin's encouragement) had supported Alexander Strahan during his contretemps with Knowles, emphasized the new direction of the monthly review by warning readers that 'science, culture, and aesthetics, or their best advertised professors, are at present united by a joint cupidity, founded on a common atheism.'[23] But such an invidious coalition could never escape the precariousness of each of its individual components, nor expunge the religious element necessary to all successful art. As Tyrwhitt declaimed:

> The appeal so eagerly made by artistic immoralists to science, begging her, on the ground of a common atheism, to come down and deliver them from virtue, can never lead to a stable alliance. Science may be godless if men will have it so, and scientific men may be immoral, though we do not know any who are at all that way; but mere denial and plain wickedness will not produce any beauty, or disprove the fact that the traditions of art were preserved by religious persons.[24]

Significantly, in this passage Tyrwhitt paraphrased a line from Swinburne's notorious poem 'Dolores', which was first published in *Poems and Ballads* in 1866. In this hymn to a sadomasochistic pagan goddess of lust and cruelty, an inhabitant of early Christian Rome implores: 'Come down and redeem us from virtue, / Our Lady of Pain.'[25] In Tyrwhitt's rendering of the line, it was science which assumed the role of Swinburne's libidinous pagan deity, facilitating that 'highly undesirable insurrection against decency' which Tyrwhitt perceived as the defining characteristic of contemporary art and literature.[26]

Tyrwhitt, in the above passage, nevertheless acknowledged that while 'scientific men may be immoral' he himself did 'not know any who are at all that way'. The high standards of personal morality exhibited by the likes of Darwin and Huxley, as has been noted in previous chapters, was integral to their vindication of their scientific and ethical positions against various charges of encouraging vice and immorality. It evidently seems to have precluded antagonists like Tyrwhitt from extending their arguments to their most injurious and unwarranted conclusions, and, as Tyrwhitt conceded in a discussion of rival pedagogic schemes, in comparison with the erotic pitfalls entailed by the 'study of the dead languages . . . Professor Huxley's scientific grammar of primary education is at least not phallic or orgiastic'.[27] It was, though, 'at least interesting', as Tyrwhitt observed, 'to know what view is taken by physicists, professing high morality without creed, as to artistic rejection of creed and morality together', and he concluded that 'to do them justice, we believe they would prefer right with a faith, to wrong without one.' In fact, Tyrwhitt remarked, 'Professor Huxley, if we remember right, did something to moderate the transports of aestheticism a few years back, by a few severe words, pithily administered in one of his lectures', although the remainder of Tyrwhitt's article continued to insist that, despite Huxley's judicious warning, the sensuous and irreligious hedonism advanced by aesthetic artists and writers would inevitably corrupt all ethical systems which eschewed Christian dogma.[28]

While it is impossible to be certain which of Huxley's numerous lectures from the late 1860s and early 1870s Tyrwhitt actually had in mind, there are certain passages from his public talks of that period which might be interpreted as an implicit rebuke of aestheticism's insistence on the primacy of art, as well as its attendant amorality. In a talk on 'Scientific Education' given at the Liverpool Philomathic Society in April 1869, Huxley avowed that he would be 'profoundly sorry' to 'observe a tendency to starve or cripple literary or aesthetic culture for the sake of science', but he at the same time insisted that although 'education is almost entirely devoted to the cultivation . . . of the sense of literary beauty', the only true 'beauty will follow in the footsteps' of the 'wisdom and uprightness' taught by practical science.[29] Indeed, there was, Huxley complained,

no sight in the whole world more saddening and revolting than is offered by men sunk in ignorance of everything but what other men have written; seemingly devoid of moral belief or guidance, but with the sense of beauty so keen, and the power of expression so cultivated, that their sensual caterwauling may be almost mistaken for the music of the spheres.[30]

A similarly self-absorbed sensualism, as well as the daring apotheosis of beauty and expression over morality and ethics, were amongst the principal criticisms which reviewers had made against Swinburne's *Poems and Ballads* less than three years earlier. Robert Buchanan, writing anonymously in the *Athenaeum*, proclaimed that in Swinburne's verse 'sensuality [is] paraded as the end of life', and, like Huxley, he employed a celestial image to express the fundamental emptiness and futility of literature which eschewed moral concerns, depicting Swinburne as 'seated in the tub of Diogenes, conscious of the filth and whining at the stars'.[31] The music of the spheres was actually a favoured trope of aesthetic poets, appearing in Swinburne's 'Hymn of Man' and 'In the Bay' as well as in Dante Gabriel Rossetti's 'The Blessed Damozel', and it seems likely that Huxley was referring directly to such writers when making his criticism of the apparent excesses of 'aesthetic culture', which was contrasted with the discipline and moral guidance provided by practical scientific education.

In the peroration to another lecture, on 'Administrative Nihilism', delivered two years later, Huxley similarly berated those who spent their lives 'grovelling in the rank and steaming valleys of sense' instead of 'striving towards . . . morality and refinement', which, once again, might be interpreted as an implicit condemnation of the values of aestheticism. Huxley's stricture certainly drew on precisely the same abrasive rhetoric employed by many of the critics of Swinburne's sensuous verse, which Huxley's friend John Morley had accused of 'grovelling down among . . . nameless shameless abominations' and revelling in 'intoxicated sensuality' (although as editor of the *Fortnightly* Morley would later retract these charges).[32] Significantly, it was precisely the lectures on 'Scientific Education' and 'Administrative Nihilism' which marked, as James Paradis has argued, the important transition in Huxley's views 'sometime between 1869 and 1871' when he abandoned his earlier belief in a 'principle which would unify natural law with social law' and began the 'vigorous attack on what he identified as social "laissez-faire"' that he would continue to articulate until the end of his life.[33] Confronted with the utter amorality of the cosmic processes of nature, human societies, argued Huxley, depended upon individuals acting at variance with the natural world and instead substituting man's ethical sensibility for natural laws. Those, like aesthetic writers and artists, who self-consciously repudiated such moral precepts were potentially just as dangerous to the social polity as the *laissez-faire* doctrines of the unfettered pursuit of self-interest advanced by Herbert Spencer and his followers.

Such apparent denunciations of recent trends in contemporary literature also accorded with Huxley's wider endeavours, particularly during the mid-1870s, to assure the readers of middlebrow periodicals like *Macmillan's Magazine* that even if a 'man is a materialist' there was no necessary reason for 'respectable folk [to] look upon him . . . as an actual or potential sensualist'.[34] Sensualism was one of the chief accusations made against Swinburne (he 'worships sensuality', claimed the *Eclectic Review*, and it was for this that he had 'acquired his unenviable notoriety'), although even Darwin himself had been similarly censured for his debasing preoccupation with mere 'sensuous facts' in his evolutionary account of human origins.[35] In the dangerous figure of the sensualist, the scientific prioritization of the material over the spiritual and the poetic celebration of the earthly pleasures of the physical form became virtually synonymous, and Huxley, even while continuously resisting accusations that he was a materialist, acknowledged the urgent necessity of detaching such alleged materialism from the cognate but even worse charge of sensualism. Unlike the more taciturn response of Darwin to this overdetermined and opprobrious designation examined in chapter two, Huxley, in attempting to demonstrate its incongruity and inappropriateness, actually made clear his own abhorrence of those aesthetic writers and artists who, he implied, were the wholly legitimate targets of such abrasive rhetoric.

Huxley's famously bad-tempered response to an unexpected encounter with Oscar Wilde at his Marlborough Place home during the mid-1880s – the much-quoted though unsourced 'that man never enters my house again' – is merely the best-known manifestation of this distinctive and long-standing strategy to dissociate Darwinian science from the taint of aestheticism. Huxley's most explicit and forthright denunciation of such transgressive trends in contemporary literature occurred during a contretemps with the Catholic critic William Samuel Lilly in the winter of 1886.[36] Writing in the November number of the *Fortnightly*, Lilly had articulated the familiar argument that the growing dominance of the empirical and unspiritual doctrines advanced by modern science had precipitated a 'moral crisis' which now extended to virtually every aspect of contemporary life.[37] As he observed ruefully:

Everywhere I note the practical triumph of that earth-to-earth philosophy which will see nothing beyond experience, which shuts off the approach of science to all that cannot be weighed and measured. Everywhere literature and art are losing themselves in the most vulgar sensuousness. Look throughout Europe, and what, in every country, are the great majority of the educated classes, who give the tone to the rest? Sceptics in religion, doubters in ethics, given over to industrialism, and to the exact sciences which minister to it, respecting nothing but accomplished fact and palpable force, with nerves more sensitive than their hearts, seeking to season the platitude of existence by a more or less voluptuous aestheticism, a more or less prurient hedonism. Such are the men of this new age. The intellectual atmosphere is charged with Materialism.[38]

Like many other antagonists of scientific naturalism including Mivart, Mallock and Tyrwhitt, Lilly averred that the voluptuous hedonism and debauched sensualism now apotheosized in the work of modern writers was a direct and entirely inevitable consequence of the allegedly materialist epistemology adumbrated by the exact sciences, which had dangerously vitiated the popular belief in a transcendental intelligence that regulated the natural world and enforced ethical behaviour.

The *Fortnightly* was almost Huxley's own in-house journal, and in the very next number he was given the opportunity to respond to Lilly's censure of the ethical consequences of scientific naturalism, gleefully depicting himself and his Catholic adversary as 'dialectic gladiators, fighting in the arena of the Fortnightly, under the eye of an editorial lanista, for the delectation of the public'.[39] Despite this vaunted enthusiasm for such cerebral pugilism, in 'Science and Morals' Huxley actually found himself concurring with many of Lilly's more disconsolate conclusions regarding the excesses of modern civilization. As he affirmed at the very beginning of the article:

'I so much admire Mr. Lilly's outspokenness, I am so completely satisfied of the uprightness of his intentions, that it is repugnant to me to quarrel with anything he may say.' In particular, Huxley then went on to insist:

I sympathise so warmly with his manly scorn of the vileness of so much that passes under the name of literature in these times, that I would willingly be silent under his by no means unkindly exposition of his theory of my own tenets, if I thought that such personal abnegation would serve the interest of the cause we both have at heart. But I cannot think so.[40]

Lilly had specifically reproached the 'vulgar sensuousness' of a 'more or less voluptuous aestheticism', and Huxley, in the above passage, clearly intended to align both himself and his scientific position with this particular vein of cultural criticism. He and Lilly, Huxley insisted, had the same fundamental 'cause . . . at heart', and, notwithstanding certain epistemological disagreements, they were both equally repulsed by literature which flamboyantly avowed its own disinterest in matters of mere morality and ethics. There was, as Dennis Denisoff has observed, a frequent 'association of literary unconventionality with disturbing sexuality' in the response to aestheticism in Victorian Britain, and Huxley, in his loudly proclaimed approval of Lilly's 'manly scorn', deployed exactly the same gendered rhetoric as those literary critics, like Buchanan, Tyrwhitt and others, whose rancorous antipathy towards aesthetic writing was often prompted by its apparent connections with effeminacy and the disruption of conventional gender roles.[41]

Significantly, in the very next sentence of his article, Huxley also included a clear and readily-identifiable allusion to Shakespeare's *As You Like It*, observing that 'my creed may be an ill-favoured thing, but it is mine own, as Touchstone says of his lady-love.'[42] Such droll and pithy allusions to Shakespeare and other canonical authors had enlivened Huxley's prose from the very beginning of his career, and he had even made a point of visiting the Bard's tomb in Stratford whilst on honeymoon in the summer of 1855.[43] But this was not the limit of Huxley's engagement with the most revered writer in the language. Indeed, his identification with Touchstone, the unassuming and down-to-earth jester in Shakespeare's pastoral comedy, was deliberately self-depreciatory, and strategically aligned his still contentious scientific creed with the homely virtues of quotidian common sense.

Similarly, in a lecture on 'Science and Art in Relation to Education' delivered before the Liverpool Institution in February 1883 Huxley enlisted Shakespeare to exemplify his implicitly anti-aesthetic argument that, from an educational perspective, art's true aim was 'what is called "truth to nature"'. The 'literature we esteem', he contended, 'is valued, not merely because of having artistic form, but because of its intellectual content; and the value is the higher the more . . . true is that intellectual content.' After all, while a 'little song of Shakespeare . . . is pure' and 'exquisitely beautiful, although its intellectual content may be nothing', this exclusively aesthetic appreciation – like the 'mere sense of beauty in colour' in the visual arts – could not lead to a full comprehension of the essential truthfulness of Shakespeare's writing. As Huxley, then in his late fifties, insisted: 'No man ever understands Shakespeare until he is old . . . the reason being that he . . . harmonises with the ripest and richest experience of the oldest.'[44] The youthful appreciation of form alone, Huxley implied, could never be enough to realize the mature ethical teachings inherent in Shakespeare's writings, which were fully accessible only to those with sufficient experience of the world. Even Darwin, who, in his autobiographical recollections, famously recounted how he had lost his youthful 'intense delight in Shakespeare' and now found his writing 'so intolerably dull that it nauseated me', still acknowledged that this 'lamentable loss of the higher aesthetic tastes' had been a 'loss of happiness, and may possibly be injurious . . . to the moral character' by excluding his mature self from the ethical harvest to be garnered from such canonical works of literature.[45]

Precisely this conservative and 'uncritical admiration of . . . Shakespeare', Wilde would later complain in a defence of aestheticism in the *Fortnightly* at the beginning of the 1890s, was the most important instance of how the philistine establishment '*make use of the classics of a country as a means of checking the progress of Art.* They degrade the classics into authorities. They use them as bludgeons for preventing the free expression of Beauty in new forms.'[46] In the particular context of Huxley's own *Fortnightly* article in December 1886 endorsing Lilly's sneering contempt for the 'prurient hedonism' of recent aesthetic works of literature, the brief reference to the work of Shakespeare certainly served to confirm his attachment to a very different, and much more respectable and gentlemanly, literary tradition, which itself, at least in Huxley's account, was distinctly opposed to aestheticism's privileging of form over content. As with Darwin's strategic use of Tennyson in *The Descent of Man* discussed in chapter two, such competing literary associations were extremely significant in establishing the moral credibility, or otherwise, of different scientific positions.

In a rejoinder to Huxley's article, again published in the *Fortnightly*, Lilly reiterated his view that much of the 'literature of the day . . . is redolent of Materialism in its most putrid forms', and then reflected: 'here Professor Huxley warmly sympathises with me, as we might have felt sure he would'.[47] Huxley's approval of his adversary's censorious views of modern literature and culture, however, was not necessarily as inevitable as Lilly appeared to assume. Instead, Huxley, the range of whose literary knowledge was remarkable even amongst Victorian men of science, often exhibited a decidedly tolerant attitude towards controversial works of literature and art, whether historical or contemporary.

In a technical footnote to his article on 'Yeast' in the *Contemporary* for December 1872, Huxley observed mischievously that the 'most surprising paper that ever made its appearance in a grave scientific journal' had 'not unjustly ridiculed' a particularly far-fetched theory of the structure of microscopic organisms in a 'somewhat Rabelaisian imaginary description of the organization of the "yeast animals"'.[48] Although such a nonchalant and sardonic allusion to the work of a sixteenth-century French writer like François Rabelais was hardly unusual in Huxley's writing, by the early 1870s English translations of Rabelais's notoriously scatological work, and the bawdy *Gargantua et Pantagruel* in particular, were increasingly attracting the vigilant attentions of the Society for the Suppression of Vice, who contended that popular editions of such vulgar books were now prohibited under the Obscene Publications Act. The publisher Henry George Bohn was even compelled to withdraw Rabelais's works from sale when his firm was taken over by a more respectable company in the early 1870s, while the literary merits of the French author were defended against the Vice Society's philistinism by Swinburne – himself hardly an uncontroversial writer – in a contemptuous letter to the *Athenaeum* in 1875.[49] Against such a background, Huxley's allusion to the apparently Rabelaisian style of an anonymous contribution to the journal *Annalen der Pharmacie* would perhaps have carried a distinctly controversial frisson for respectable readers of the conservative *Contemporary*, which Huxley, with his habitual facetiousness and taste for scurrilous mordancy, might well have deliberately intended.

Nor did Huxley appear to have any qualms about entering public controversies on behalf of equally contentious works of contemporary art. When Philip Hermogenes Calderon's historical painting *The Renunciation of Saint Elizabeth of Hungary* was displayed at the Royal Academy's Summer Exhibition of 1891 it at once prompted a storm of disapproval on account of its depiction of the Catholic saint stripped entirely naked at the moment of her renunciation. It was, the Catholic Duke of Norfolk protested, an 'indecent travesty of the sacred incident' which attributed a 'sinful act of gross immodesty to a canonized saint'.[50] In *The Times* the Jesuit Father Richard Clarke added that the representation of Elizabeth as 'guilty of an act of indecency from which any woman of ordinary modesty would shrink in disgust' was also a 'cruel calumny' on the 'high virtue and spotless reputation' of her spiritual adviser Conrad of Marburg, who in Calderon's painting was shown fully clothed in a dark monk's cowl looming voyeuristically over his naked protégé.[51]

Calderon's earlier paintings of female nudes had been attacked as too 'modern and Parisian', and his treatment of Saint Elizabeth, as Philip McEvansoneya has noted, gestured to 'aspects of modernity and realism in contemporary French art' including the 'presence of discarded clothes and naked females and clothed male figures', and, in any case, such 'encounters with and between monks and nuns were an historical staple of pornographic literature'.[52] Huxley, though, could not resist the chance to goad his Catholic enemies, even if it entailed vindicating the historical accuracy of a highly controversial painting that was widely condemned as both indecent and dangerously sensuous. In response to Clarke's letter to *The Times*, Huxley fired off his own epistle, translating a passage of medieval Latin which implied that being 'stripped to their shifts' and 'well whipped' was the 'penance which that "man of high virtue and spotless reputation", Conrad of Marburg, thought fit to inflict on Elizabeth and her maids, thereby shocking the somewhat obtuse sense of decency of his contemporaries'. With such historical evidence of the sexually ambiguous atonements administered by this leading dignitary of the Catholic Church, Huxley closed his letter by advising that 'surely Mr. Calderon might plead that such a Habbakuk [i.e. Conrad] was "capable de tout"' and therefore very likely to have insisted on Elizabeth's stripping.[53] Far from baulking at the controversial eroticism of French-inspired modern art, Huxley's intervention in the bitter war of words over Calderon's painting actually endorsed, and indeed appeared to relish, the contentious interpretation of it which perceived a distinctly erotic tension between the clothed Conrad and the naked Elizabeth, even if his principal concern was the anti-Catholic element which such an interpretation identified in the painting.

While Huxley's appreciation of the scientific insight displayed in Tennyson's poetry is well known and was noted in chapter one, he was also equally enchanted by the formal qualities of Victorian verse, and, as his son Leonard later recalled, 'he had a keen sense for beauty, the artistic perfection of expression, whether in poetry, prose, or conversation'.[54] Robert Browning, Huxley had once enthused, 'really has music in him', and he declared of his friend Tennyson that he was the 'greatest English master of melody except Spenser and Keats'.[55] Pater had famously scorned the critical emphasis on the 'mere matter of a poem' in his essay on 'The School of

Giorgione' (1877), instead insisting that, in the 'constant effort . . . to obliterate' the 'distinction' of 'matter from . . . form', all valuable '*art constantly aspires towards the condition of music*'.[56] With his apparent enthusiasm for precisely this sensuous and non-referential musicality in the verse of poets like Browning and Tennyson, Huxley's attitude towards the aesthetic axioms promulgated by Pater and others was inevitably much more complex and nuanced than it often appeared.

In the 'ideal University', as Huxley proclaimed in a lecture on 'Universities: Actual and Ideal' delivered in February 1874, the 'very air . . . should be charged with that enthusiasm for truth, that fanaticism of veracity' which was the 'heart of morality'. Following his dispute with Matthew Arnold over the appropriate balance of the curriculum in the British education system, Huxley nevertheless acknowledged that

the man who is all morality and intellect, although he may be good and even great, is, after all, only half a man. There is beauty in the moral world and in the intellectual world; but there is also a beauty which is neither moral nor intellectual – the beauty of the world of Art.[57]

Huxley, as Paradis has suggested, seems to have had the blithe, spontaneous and implicitly ethical Hellenistic approach to art celebrated by Arnold's *Culture and Anarchy* (1869) in mind when writing this passage.[58] But Huxley, in also asserting that the 'Aesthetic faculty' needed to be 'roused, directed, and cultivated' only alongside the clearly separate 'moral sense' as part of a humane and civilizing education, actually went beyond the position of Arnold, who remained anxious at the tendency of Hellenism to lapse into 'moral indifference'.[59] In fact, Huxley's conception of an artistic beauty that was wholly independent of moral or intellectual concerns seems closer to the defiantly amoral sense of beauty apotheosized in only the previous year in Pater's *Studies in the History of the Renaissance* (1873), which had avowed that in fulfilling the 'desire for beauty . . . art comes to you professing frankly to give nothing but the highest quality to your moments as they pass, and simply for those moments' sake'.[60] While such Paterian overtones were presumably not intended by Huxley, they at least suggest a certain willingness to countenance the separation of aesthetics from ethics that was clearly lacking in the more dogmatic arguments of critics of modern literature such as Lilly or Tyrwhitt, and even in the more liberal views of Arnold.

In his own private reading, moreover, Huxley clearly took up, and even seemed to find pleasure and instruction in works by aesthetic writers. When, towards the end of his life, he was made a Privy Councillor, Huxley replied to the congratulations of Wilfrid Ward by observing drolly: 'Morris has a poem somewhere about the man who was born to be a king, and became one in spite of probability. It is evident to me now that I was born to be respectable. I have done my level best to avoid that honour, but behold me indelibly stamped.'[61] The poem by William Morris in which Huxley discerned an ironic foreshadowing of the unexpected respectability of his own later career, 'The Man Born to be King', had originally been published as part of the first series of *The Earthly Paradise* in 1868. Significantly, this collection of pseudo-medieval narrative poems began with an explicit avowal of its aesthetic credentials, with the languid narrator of all of the volume's verse declaring:

> Why should I strive to set the crooked straight?
> Let it suffice me that my murmuring rhyme
> Beats with light wing against the ivory gate,
> Telling a tale not too importunate
> To those who in the sleepy region stay,
> Lulled by the singer of an empty day.[62]

This, written before Morris's later and more familiar incarnation as a socialist, was precisely the kind of artistic abnegation of moral responsibility and encouragement of sensual self-indulgence which Huxley, along with Lilly, Tyrwhitt and many others, had appeared to find so repugnant.

The particular poem from *The Earthly Paradise* to which Huxley referred in his letter to Ward concluded by meditating upon the original hearers of its medieval legend 'grown weak and old' with 'old desires within their wasted eyes'.[63] It was precisely this sense of the 'desire of beauty quickened by the sense of death' that was not only celebrated by Pater in his review of Morris's verse for the *Westminster Review* in October 1868, but which also prompted that 'strange transition from the earthly paradise to the sad-coloured world of abstract philosophy' in which Pater, in the conclusion to his review, adumbrated his infamous aesthetic creed that the 'love of art for art's sake' was the most astute response to the inevitability of impending death.[64] While Huxley admittedly made only a very brief reference to Morris's 'The Man Born to be King', it is noticeable that in the context of a private letter to a younger friend, although one who was staunchly Catholic, he did not feel the same need to denigrate such a conspicuously aesthetic work that he seems to have felt in many of his public writings.

There was a clear disparity between Huxley's apparently tolerant attitude towards even controversial works of contemporary art and literature and his publicly avowed repulsion at aestheticism's amorality and alleged sensualism. Such vacillation, however, was not unusual in Huxley's career, and in the mid-1880s Edward Bibbens Aveling spitefully designated him the 'Mr. Facing-Both-Ways' of science.[65] Huxley did indeed proffer contrary opinions on contentious issues such as the moral and pedagogic value of the Bible which seemed to shift with the nature of the publications in which they appeared, proclaiming himself 'in favour of reading the Bible' in elementary schools in the respectable *Contemporary*, while lambasting the 'authoritative propagation of the preposterous fables by which the minds of children are dazed and their sense of truth and falsehood perverted' in the preface to a book by the radical German Darwinian Ernst Haeckel.[66] It was similarly necessary for Huxley, in articles such as 'Science and Morals', to strategically present himself as a staunch opponent of the excesses of disreputable modern literature, even while offering divergent views in other formats. Only by publicly participating in the conservative critique of aesthetic art and literature could he safeguard his own naturalistic worldview from exactly the same opprobrious accusations of uprooting traditional morality and codes of behaviour, which, as this book has examined, had been made since at least the beginning of the 1870s.

THE BRAIN-WORK OF WEAK DEGENERATIVE MINDS

Despite Huxley's endeavours since the late 1860s to make clear his abhorrence of many aspects of modern culture, in the closing years of the nineteenth century scientific naturalists continued to be condemned in precisely the same terms as aesthetic writers such as Swinburne and Pater. In September 1893 the *National Review* featured an article, pithily entitled 'The Immorality of Evolutionary Ethics', which depicted an imaginary 'exponent of Evolutionary Ethics' who considered himself a 'worthy man', but who was 'in reality . . . an egoist of the deepest dye; hedonistic to the last degree'.[67] The article's author was William Earl Hodgson, a protégé of Mallock whose feeble satirical novel *Unrest; or, The Newer Republic* (1887) unsubtly adumbrated the conservative beliefs of the 'striking . . . essayist . . . Mr. William Muriel Hallock' and disputed the moral consequences of the naturalistic views of the same scientific 'demigods' that Mallock had lampooned in his own *The New Republic* ten years earlier.[68] In Hodgson's article such habitual and long-standing allegations were also supplemented with additional accusations more appropriate to the particular concerns of the 1890s, and it concluded by contending that in making 'morality . . . self-conscious' rather than innate any evolutionary account of ethics 'proceeds in galloping consumption to the final degeneracy which supervenes when the "malady of thought" has made us distrust natural instincts'.[69] Concerns with degeneracy were widespread by the time of Hodgson's article, and with the term itself, as Daniel Pick has argued, constantly shifting between a multiplicity of different connotations, it could be expediently employed to signify, amongst many other things, the moral corruption and decline apparently instigated by the proponents of evolutionary ethics.[70] Nevertheless, theories of degeneration could, at the same time, also provide perhaps the most effective means by which the proponents of Darwinian science could sequester their arguments from the long tradition of pejorative associations with aestheticism.

Degeneration was initially defined by Bénédict Augustin Morel in *Traité des dégénérences* (1857) as the morbid deviation from an original type, and was later identified in Edwin Ray Lankester's *Degeneration: A Chapter in Darwinism* (1880) as a mode of evolutionary retrogression precipitated by an organism's adaptation to less complex environmental conditions. At no point in its existence, though, did degeneration constitute a single, coherent scientific theory, and the concept was instead applied indiscriminately to a variety of *fin de siècle* concerns with deviance, decline and decadence, which manifested themselves in everything from the most simple forms of organism to the fate of great imperial civilizations. It was, as Pick has noted, the late nineteenth century's 'ultimate signifier of pathology', and was employed as a procedural designation which both marginalized its ostensible victims, including criminals, hysterics and primitive races, and established them as the subjects of rigorous scientific scrutiny.[71]

Several theorists of degeneration, as historians have long recognized, viewed even literature in similarly diagnostic terms, interpreting certain forms of deviation from conventional artistic standards as evidence of the pathological condition of many modern authors. The last decades of the nineteenth century, Allon White has contended, witnessed a 'growth of "symptomatic reading"', an analysis of literature not so much for the accuracy or truth of its rendering of reality, but for the mental disposition of the writer'.[72] This was especially the case with aesthetic writers, whose unnatural emphasis on style and form was seen to indicate their falling away from the healthy standards of canonical literature as well as betraying the diseased state of their minds. Scientific arguments regarding degeneration, as Stephen Arata has observed, routinely became 'entangled in what have to be considered as forms of literary criticism', both in examining literary texts for signs of pathology and in subjecting the somatic symptoms exhibited by various victims of degeneration to critical modes of reading and interpretation.[73]

The opponents of various movements in literature and art had, of course, been invoking models of disease and insanity since at least classical antiquity, with Goethe famously declaring in the 1820s that 'Romanticism is disease, Classicism is health'.[74] By the second half of the nineteenth century, however, such tropes were founded, for the very first time, on specifically scientific and medical arguments.[75] As the Italian criminologist Cesare Lombroso proposed in his study of *The Man of Genius* (1891), his own medical writings on degeneration 'may, I hope (while remaining within the limits of psychological observation), afford an experimental starting-point for a criticism of artistic and literary . . . creations'.[76] Lombroso's self-appointed protégé, Max Nordau, whose massive tome *Degeneration* was first published in an English edition in 1895, has generally been regarded as the principal exponent of this diagnostic form of literary criticism, especially in his book's lengthy chapter on 'Decadents and Aesthetes'. Degenerates, Nordau observed, were 'not always criminals, prostitutes, anarchists, and pronounced lunatics; they are often authors and artists', and his endeavour to 'characterize aesthetic fashions as forms of mental decay' was an 'attempt at a really scientific criticism' which employed the 'psycho-physiological' categories developed by Lombroso – to whom *Degeneration* was dedicated – to read and analyse literary texts.[77] Swinburne, along with many other modern authors, painters and composers, was diagnosed by Nordau as a 'higher degenerate' whose poetry 'partakes . . . of the depraved and the criminal', while an analysis of the verse of Rossetti revealed that the particular 'peculiarities of the poet', and especially his propensity for rhythmic repetitions, 'characterize the brain-work of weak degenerative minds' and indicated an extreme and debilitating case of echolalia.[78]

While most historians of degeneration have concentrated on Nordau's infamous book, over a decade before its publication the psychiatrist Henry Maudsley had likewise emphasized the degenerative potential of certain forms of literature, and, once more, it was aestheticism in particular that was the target of his invective. Maudsley's antagonism towards aesthetic art and literature was extremely similar to that articulated by Huxley in a variety of public forums, and, like Huxley, he appropriated precisely the same gendered rhetoric that had earlier been used to censure aesthetic writing by conservative cultural critics such as Tyrwhitt and Lilly. Maudsley was the most prominent alienist in late Victorian Britain, although his arrogant and cynical manner, as well as an increasingly pessimistic outlook, isolated him from most other leading practitioners. His prolific contributions to the study of psychology, even when intended for a specialist audience, also evinced an unusually wide-ranging knowledge of European literature.

The works of Goethe and Shakespeare were particular favourites, and, according to Helen Small, such canonical literature provided Maudsley with a 'conceptual cohesion which contemporary medical science could not offer'. For Maudsley, Small argues, 'great literature . . . surpasses science in that it orders the disordered appearance of insanity . . . while "all that has been written in the guise of science" can speak only of devolution and degeneration.'[79] At the same time, however, Maudsley's astonishingly broad range of reading, initially encouraged by an unmarried aunt with a passion for poetry, inevitably meant that he encountered many other forms of literature that he would have considered neither great nor conducive to intellectual cohesion, and his marked preference for 'Goethe and German philosophy rather than for French authors and French style' has been noted by Elaine Showalter.[80] In fact, as with the case of Dowden considered at the beginning of this chapter, Maudsley could only maintain his view of literature's essential cohesiveness and order by the deliberate exclusion of any literary forms that did not conform to these exacting artistic standards.

As Maudsley's writings became increasingly preoccupied with degeneration and the gloomy fate awaiting human civilization, his attitude towards this wider literary culture became still more complex and fragmented. Imaginative literature, Maudsley had stipulated in *The Physiology and Pathology of the Mind* (1867), should represent 'nature developed through man', and this 'recreation of nature by human means' – which, importantly, was illustrated by a footnoted quotation from Shakespeare's *The Winter's Tale* – revealed that the 'well-grounded imagination of . . . the poet is the highest display of nature's organic evolution'.[81] While in his sanguine early works Maudsley referred only to literature that conformed to this precise axiom of correct aesthetic form (which closely resembled Huxley's own insistence that art's true aim was 'truth to nature'), in his more pessimistic later writings he also acknowledged the existence of literary works that instead flaunted their deliberate unnaturalness, and which, for Maudsley, became emblematic of the opposite end of the evolutionary scale of mental processes.

In the apocalyptic final chapter of his typically caustic diagnosis of modern psychological disorders *Body and Will* (1883), entitled grimly 'What Will Be the End Thereof?', Maudsley examined the evidence for the cessation of evolutionary progress presented by individual psychological disorders as well as more general features of modern life. After reiterating his earlier contention in *The Physiology and Pathology of the Mind* that the creative 'imagination' – along with the 'will' – was the 'highest becoming of things' in the universal 'evolutionary *nisus*', Maudsley then prophesied gloomily that this progress would soon 'come to an end, and in its stead will prevail a lower becoming of things, first manifest in the highest human feeling, imagination and will'.[82] Shakespeare's dramas, in Maudsley's earlier book, had represented the imagination as the apex of progressive evolution, and the 'forewarning indications' of the inverse 'disillusioned and degenerative end of mankind' considered in *Body and Will* were again provided by imaginative literature.[83] But in striking contrast with his reverent attitude towards writers such as Shakespeare and Goethe, Maudsley now articulated a contemptuous scorn for those modern authors whose 'emasculated sensualities in art masquerading as art for art's sake' afforded such a conspicuous presentiment of the world's coming degenerative dissolution.[84]

The prominent reference to 'art for art's sake', the infamous slogan which Swinburne and Pater had made fashionable only a decade earlier, would have left even Maudsley's more specialist readers in little doubt as to which contemporary writers were the objects of his extravagant disdain. Aestheticism, more than any other contemporary art form, came to exemplify Maudsley's conception of pathological literature. Such diseased literary works, he avowed, had infected wider society with 'exaggerated egoisms' and a 'luxury of incontinent feeling', and Maudsley contrasted this 'modern incontinence of emotion with the calm, chaste, and manly simplicity of Homer', before devoting over a page of his ostensibly scientific monograph to a lengthy quotation demonstrating the composed serenity of the *Iliad*'s restrained verse.[85] Homer was again contrasted with contemporary literature in Maudsley's own study of Shakespearean drama (and issues like the madness of Hamlet had long been *cause célèbres* of Victorian psychiatry), which contended that with Shakespeare himself being

Homer-like in his fresh and direct converse with realities and pure melody of natural utterance, his absolute return to nature, it is all the more wonder nowadays that our modern poets . . . should for the most part set themselves painfully to work to get as far as possible from living touch of real life and direct simplicity of diction; the more pleased with themselves, apparently . . . the more startling and obscure they can strain themselves to be.[86]

With Homer and Shakespeare providing an original or normative type for literature in the Western tradition, modern writers had deviated wilfully from these conventional artistic standards until their works, as Maudsley proposed in *Body and Will*, had become actively pathological and actually dangerous to their readers.

In similarly condemning Rossetti, Swinburne and other members of the so-called 'Fleshly School of Poetry' for their 'morbid deviation from healthy forms of life', Buchanan drew upon precisely the same terms with which Morel had originally defined degeneration in *Traité des dégénérences*.[87] Buchanan's notoriously captious and hyperbolic critique of recent works by Rossetti and Swinburne in the October 1871 number of the *Contemporary* also noted their 'hysteric tone' and accused them of 'diligently spreading the seeds of disease . . . wherever they are read and understood'.[88] Such verbal and conceptual borrowings between scientific works on degeneration and literary criticism of aestheticism, however, by no means operated in only one direction. Instead, Maudsley's diagnosis of the degenerative effects of the work of those writers associated with the slogan 'art for art's sake' invoked similar critical precepts, and exactly the same abrasive tropes and rhetoric, that were employed regularly in periodical reviews of aesthetic literature.

Most notably, Maudsley's argument relied upon the prevalent critical assumption that the improper use of literary language, and especially the privileging of sensuous sound over abstract writing, might entail a loss of individual bodily restraint which had potentially very deleterious consequences for the welfare of society.[89] His repeated expressions of contempt for the 'modern incontinence of emotion' and 'luxury of incontinent feeling' apparently encouraged by recent poetical works closely resembled the critical terminology used in a notice of Swinburne's verse in the July 1871 number of the *Edinburgh Review*, which proposed: 'If the main characteristics of his writings were to be summed up in a single word . . . incontinence would perhaps be the most appropriate word.'[90] The unrestrained language of such poetry, both Maudsley and the review of Swinburne in the *Edinburgh* insinuated, induced a loss of self-control that might prove extremely dangerous both to the individual reader and to the wider social polity, the regulation of which relied upon individual moral restraint especially with regard to the body.

In insisting that Swinburne's poems were 'incontinent in the use of strained and violent language', and in berating their 'wild luxuriance of merely metrical diction' and 'obscurity of thought and expression', the *Edinburgh*'s vituperative notice, which was written by Thomas Spencer Baynes, perhaps also gives an indication of exactly which contemporary writers Maudsley had in mind in the passage from his psychological study of Shakespeare quoted above, which condemned those 'modern poets' who departed from 'direct simplicity of diction' and instead sought to be as 'startling and obscure [as] they can strain themselves to be'. At the same time, the review in the *Edinburgh* also alleged that *Poems and Ballads* exhibited the symptoms of a 'feverish sensuality' and 'deadly moral leprosy', which were particularly manifest in its 'loathsome' preoccupation with 'morbid letches'.[91] While Maudsley invoked an extremely similar literary critical rhetoric, Baynes's notice of Swinburne's verse in the *Edinburgh*, like Buchanan's attack on 'The Fleshly School of Poetry' in the *Contemporary*, itself drew implicitly upon contemporary discourses of pathology, and revealed, once more, how the vocabularies of degeneration and conservative literary criticism became virtually interchangeable in the late nineteenth century.

Maudsley's flamboyant anti-feminism and misogynistic views of women's mental capacities have been much commented on by historians, and it is noticeable that his critique of aestheticism in *Body and Will* insinuated that the slogan 'art for art's sake' was used merely as a masquerade to divert attention from the 'emasculated sensualities' which were the real preoccupation of the depraved literary works of Swinburne and others, and which compared so pitifully with the 'manly simplicity of Homer'.[92] This marked apprehension at a loss of manliness, and even of male sexual potency, was integral to Maudsley's understanding of degeneration, which he depicted as an 'emasculation, physical, moral, and intellectual, of the race', that would inevitably result in an 'impotence to face life's struggles'.[93] In the following decade, Nordau would likewise describe the degenerative '*fin-de-siècle* mood' as the 'impotent despair of a sick man' who jealously 'sees a pair of young lovers making for a sequestered forest nook'.[94] Earlier in the century, the physical process of entropy had been depicted by the physicist William Thomson in similarly gendered terms, with the traditionally masculine sun anthropomorphically 'suffering dissipation' from the 'primitive store of heat in his body'.[95] Entropy was an important empirical buttress to the general sense of deterioration and decay prognosticated by theorists of degeneration, and Thomson, Nordau and Maudsley all envisaged the decline of both physical and mental energies as a painful loss of male virility.

As with Huxley's praise for Lilly's 'manly scorn' of the vileness of contemporary literature, Maudsley's concern with rooting out such degenerative unmanliness also corresponded with the distinctly gendered rhetoric of much literary criticism relating to aestheticism. Notably, Alfred Austin, writing in *Temple Bar* in 1869, had employed precisely the same terminology as Maudsley in berating 'Swinburne's emasculated poetical voice'.[96] Maudsley's insistence that this emasculation was perfidiously masked by meaningless artistic slogans like 'art for art's sake', meanwhile, closely resembled Buchanan's avowal that Swinburne was an 'intellectual hermaphrodite, to whom the very facts of day and night are lost in a whirl of aesthetic terminology'.[97] Victorian ideals of moral character, as Stefan Collini has noted, were predicated on a combination of 'candour and manliness', and it was precisely these attributes that were conspicuously absent, according to both Maudsley and Buchanan, from the deceptive and effeminate work of Swinburne and other aesthetic writers.[98] The 'main objection' of Baynes's review of Swinburne's poetry in the *Edinburgh*, moreover, was that 'much of it is not virile or even feminine, but epicene'.[99] By promiscuously collapsing conventional gender distinctions, and particularly by postulating a liminal position beyond sexual difference, Swinburne's transgressive verse both threatened to disrupt the existing socio-sexual order in late Victorian Britain, and portended the disturbingly enervating and epicene consequences of degeneration.

Despite Maudsley's evident appropriation of precisely the same gendered literary critical rhetoric that was a regular feature of reviews of aesthetic literature in general periodicals like the *Edinburgh* and *Contemporary*, his own antagonism towards aestheticism was afforded a scientific authority by his insistence on its direct relation to wider patterns of degeneration and mental pathology. Notably, soon after his intemperate condemnation of 'emasculated sensualities . . . masquerading as art for art's sake' Maudsley switched to a self-consciously technical vocabulary in diagnosing the 'exaggerated egoisms' induced by such noxious forms of literature as 'a true egoistic hyperaesthesia – and actually disintegrant in their effects'.[100] While 'hyperaesthesia' was, since the mid-nineteenth century, an established medical term for the excessive and morbid sensitiveness that regularly accompanied hysteria, its clear etymological relation to words like 'aesthesis', which Ruskin, in the 1883 revised edition of the second volume of *Modern Painters*, used interchangeably with 'aesthetic' to signify the 'mere animal consciousness of the . . . sensual pleasures' of art, suggests that for Maudsley it may also have carried connotations of the serious medical consequences of the solipsistic and overwrought physical sensitivity to art encouraged by the proponents of aestheticism.[101] After all, Lombroso later noted that amongst the 'characters which very frequently . . . accompany . . . fatal degenerations' was an 'excess of some faculty' such as 'aesthetic taste', while Buchanan had discerned a corresponding 'superfluity of extreme sensibility' in the verse of the 'Fleshly School of Poetry', which could offer 'nothing completely sane' to its unfortunate readers.[102] For Maudsley, the production of aesthetic literature became itself a manifest symptom of a specific form of hysterical hyperaesthesia, which was spread further by the widespread consumption of these contagious texts amongst reading audiences susceptible to degenerative diseases. Such explicitly scientific descriptions of the pathological effects which seemingly accompanied certain improper uses of literary language inevitably gave a new – and ostensibly objective – authority to the abrasive rhetoric of conservative literary criticism.

Discourses of pathology and degeneration, as Robert A. Nye has contended, 'gave to medicine and its ancillary sciences the right to mediate between the general public and deviance' and to 'pronounce on its causes' in a wide variety of areas including literature and art.[103] The 'hegemony of a medical model of deviance', Nye proposes, 'guaranteed that contemporaries would have regular doses of cultural pessimism administered by doctors and hygiene specialists'.[104] Theorists of degeneration such as Maudsley were certainly able to assume a new tone of medical authority in their analysis of modernity's deviation from conventional artistic standards, even while they replicated almost precisely the same range of allegations – and an exactly identical critical vocabulary – that were employed in the hostile reviews of works of aesthetic literature which had been appearing in various non-specialist periodicals since the mid-1860s. Significantly, this diagnostic model of literary criticism in the late nineteenth century implied that it was the man of science rather than the periodical reviewer or even the nascent professional literary critic who was now best placed to root out potentially degenerative and enervating forms of literary activity.

In *The Man of Genius*, Lombroso included Darwin himself amongst those 'madmen of genius' who exhibited the 'signs of degeneration . . . more frequently . . . than even . . . the insane', pointing to his 'cretin-like physiognomy', 'short snub nose' and apparent 'musical daltonism', before finally diagnosing Darwin as a 'neuropath' whose regular 'giddiness' and 'curious crotchets' suggested an unrecognized 'epilepsy' and even 'moral insanity'.[105] However, by giving scientific authority to the arguments of anti-aesthetic literary criticism such theories of degeneration also provided the proponents of Darwinism with perhaps the most effective means of detaching their arguments from the pejorative associations with aestheticism that their antagonists, as has been seen throughout this book, had been making for several decades. While Maudsley's earlier conception of the brain's evolutionary development through hereditary transmission was, as Gillian Beer has noted, more indebted to Spencer than Darwin, his understanding of degeneration was identifiably Darwinian.[106] Indeed, Maudsley had long served as an intermediary between Darwin and other members of the British psychological community, and having been praised in *The Descent of Man* for his 'good remarks' on numerous elements of human psychology, Maudsley returned the favour by insisting, in his Presidential Address to the Medico-Psychological Association in August 1871, that the 'evidence of evolution and degeneration of mind which the study of psychology, healthy and morbid, reveals' afforded 'weighty facts and arguments in support of . . . the well-known views of Mr. Darwin'.[107] Maudsley's conspicuous attack on aestheticism in *Body and Will* can therefore be interpreted as a continuation of Huxley's strategy of publicly participating in the conservative critique of such disconcerting forms of contemporary culture in order to neutralize its capacity to tarnish various aspects of Darwinian science.

In the mid-1890s this medico-scientific model of cultural pathology was made much more explicit, and brought to the attention of a considerably larger audience, with the publication of Nordau's *Degeneration*, the English translation of which ran through seven editions within six months and prompted what the *Review of Reviews* called a 'Nordau "boom"' in the publishing world. Nordau had turned his back on the specialist medical training he received in his native Germany to become a journalist in Paris writing on a huge variety of subjects, and while the self-consciously populist *Review of Reviews* applauded his bestselling volume's capacity to satisfy the 'most sensation-loving reader' it also acknowledged that *Degeneration* was 'generally wrong-headed' in its indictment of modern culture.[108] The sententious and overly literal cultural philistinism of Nordau's book – which, for example, attributed the distinctive visual style of Pre-Raphaelite painting to a retinal dysfunction – was soon widely denounced, or, worse still, merely mocked, and, as William Greenslade has remarked, 'in due course its fate was ironic dismissal.'[109] Despite Nordau's discredited use of the same pathologization of contemporary literature that Maudsley had employed a decade earlier, aestheticism continued to be widely identified as the most conspicuous cultural symptom of the broader processes of degeneration that appeared to be besetting late Victorian society, and especially in works of popular fiction.

Nordau's *Degeneration* appeared in Britain only months before Wilde's famous prosecution for gross indecency, and his diagnosis of the pathological 'ego-mania' of this 'chief . . . among the Aesthetes' was widely reported in newspaper accounts of the trials during the summer of 1895.[110] In Bram Stoker's novel *Dracula*, which was published two years later, the eponymous vampire, according to Talia Schaffer, 'represents the ghoulishly inflated version of Wilde' that was portrayed in the contemporary press, and, like Wilde, Dracula is designated a 'criminal, and of criminal type', with Mina Harker observing: 'Nordau and Lombroso would so classify him.'[111] This prominent allusion to the two most widely known degeneration theorists of the 1890s has been much discussed by critics of *Dracula* and is used by Schaffer to exemplify Stoker's ambivalent interest in the pathologization of homosexuality in the period.[112] What has not previously been noted is that the novel's enumeration of the Count's solipsistic 'selfishness' and propensity for 'multiplying the evils of the world' by infecting others with a noxious vampirism that disrupts conventional gender roles as well as rendering its victims both hypersensitive to physical contact and no longer in control of their bodies closely resembles many of the allegations made against aestheticism, both by scientific proponents of degeneration and conservative cultural critics.[113] The status of Dracula's principal adversary, Abraham Van Helsing, as the pre-eminent authority on the 'continuous evolution of brain matter' perhaps also hints at parallels with the earlier views of the similarly qualified Maudsley on the degenerative tendency of aesthetic writers.[114]

In H. G. Wells's *The Time Machine* (1895), which was published at the height of the storm of publicity surrounding Nordau's sensational tome, the childlike and epicene subspecies of Elois into which humans have degenerated by the year 802,701 are likewise depicted in similar terms to those that were used to attack the exponents of aestheticism. Their fragility and languid appearance remind the time traveller of the 'more beautiful kind of consumptive – that hectic beauty of which we used to hear so much', which once again associates concerns with beauty with tropes of disease and morbidity.[115] With their existence characterized by an indolent futility, Elois civilization is notable only for the beauty of its buildings, which are so different from the brutally utilitarian underground dwellings of their Morlock adversaries. Such highly decorative architecture, as the time traveller speculates, represents the 'last surgings of the now purposeless energy of mankind'. This superfluous energy, he continues, invariably 'takes to art and to eroticism, and then comes languor and decay', and his reflections evidently provide a satirical commentary on some of the cultural tendencies of the society which the time traveller has left behind.[116] Harry M. Geduld has noted 'Wells's hostility to the Aesthetes' and proposed that the languorous Elois are 'embodiments of his contempt for certain ideals of the late nineteenth-century Aesthetic Movement'.[117] Although located in the far future, the dissipated and effete condition of the Elois nevertheless affords a glimpse of the ultimate outcome of the degenerative potential which scientific writers such as Maudsley and Nordau had already identified in contemporary aesthetic art and literature.

Unlike Stoker's conspicuous reference to the views of Nordau and Lombroso in *Dracula*, however, it was Huxley's particular conception of degeneration that Wells drew upon most notably in *The Time Machine*, and which, in the novel's fictional futurity, had determined the Elois's languorous fate. In the 'Prolegomena' to *Evolution and Ethics*, his famous Romanes lecture of May 1893, Huxley noted how the meaning of the term 'evolution' had recently 'been widened to include the phenomena of retrogressive metamorphosis . . . from a condition of relative complexity to one of relative uniformity' which was occasioned by the 'elimination of that . . . intense and unceasing competition of the struggle for existence'.[118] For humans, Huxley proposed, the maintenance of a certain level of struggle – although not a state of complete *laissez-faire* – actually tended 'to the good of society' by ensuring that 'those who are endowed with the largest share of energy' were 'in possession of wealth and influence'.[119] Its complete removal, on the other hand, would inevitably precipitate a process of degeneration as individuals adapted to less complex and difficult conditions.

In the future society of *The Time Machine* there is no longer the 'grindstone of pain and necessity' which had previously honed mankind's competitive instincts, and, as was anticipated in Huxley's 'Prolegomena', because there was 'no danger of war or solitary violence, no danger from wild beasts, no wasting diseases to require strength of constitution, no need of toil', the Elois had gradually been denuded of every useful human capacity, retaining only an overdeveloped 'artistic impetus' which would itself 'at last die away'.[120] Wells's time traveller also observes of the degenerative future he encounters, 'my general impression of the world I saw . . . was of . . . a long-neglected and yet weedless garden', which directly parallels Huxley's comparison of the removal of struggle from human society to the process by which an area of uncultivated 'native vegetation . . . was made into a garden'.[121] Wells had studied under Huxley at the Normal School of Science in 1884, and his dystopian vision of the future a decade later was explicitly informed by his erstwhile teacher's own speculations on the darker possibilities of evolution during the early 1890s. Unlike Maudsley or Nordau, though, Huxley never alluded to any manifestations of contemporary culture in his discussion of degeneration. Instead, it was in Wells's *The Time Machine* that Huxley's earlier strategy of publicly condemning aesthetic art and literature and his subsequent concerns with the potential for retrogressive metamorphosis were finally brought together in the model of cultural pathology established by theorists of degeneration like Maudsley and Nordau, and exemplified by the atrophied aestheticism of the listless and ultimately doomed Elois.

CODA: ONE CULTURE?

The multivalent concept of degeneration implied that, far from being furtively implicated with aestheticism, exponents of the exact sciences like Huxley or Maudsley were actually those best placed to diagnose and remedy what were now viewed as dangerously pathological forms of art and literature. This pathologization of aestheticism affords a very different understanding of the relationship between science and literature in the Victorian period to that presented in much recent scholarship, which, as was noted earlier, has tended to emphasize only the positive and creative aspects of the interconnection. Even when entirely unintended, these discursive interchanges have been perceived, employing Harold Bloom's familiar tropes of 'poetic misprision' and 'creative revisionism' (which themselves draw on the scientific analogy of the '"swerve" of the atoms' described by Lucretius), as invariably productive for both scientific and literary modes of writing.[122] From Robert M. Young's seminal thesis, first adumbrated in the late 1960s, of the 'common intellectual context', which evoked the verbal and conceptual interconnectedness of science, politics, theology and literature in the 'rich interdisciplinary culture' of mid-Victorian Britain and bemoaned its eventual fragmentation at the hands of cloistered scientific specialists and 'pretentious hacks' who popularized natural knowledge for new audiences of a 'markedly lower intellectual standard', to more recent elaborations of the so-called 'One Culture' model which assert that 'literature and science are mutually shaped by their participation in the culture at large', there has been an implicit assumption that the interconnection of the two in the nineteenth century was almost always constructive and beneficial for all concerned.[123] In fact, the transition from such a unified intellectual culture to something resembling C. P. Snow's 'Two Cultures' has become, especially in Young's emotive account, a kind of secular fall from the purported organic wholeness of the mid-Victorian period, precluding modern science and literature from the kinds of fruitful interchange that were once apparently so prevalent. 'To talk of two cultures is almost always to regret it,' as Theodore M. Porter has recently commented.[124]

The widespread association of Darwinism with aesthetic writers such as Swinburne and Pater, however, suggests that the relationship between science and literature in the nineteenth century could be considerably more complex – and much less fruitful or productive – than has generally been assumed in more sanguine scholarly accounts. The connection with such disreputable literary figures was often highly embarrassing and extremely problematic for scientific naturalists attempting to maintain a reputation for respectability and moral probity in a culture that was allegedly being overwhelmed by an inexorable proliferation of sexual imagery, poetic sensualism and other manifestations of a pervasive indecency. Rather than celebrating or even acknowledging the intellectual and creative potential of these literary interchanges, exponents of evolutionary science instead collaborated with conservative literary critics in berating aestheticism's sexual and moral transgressiveness, and finally drew upon their own empirical expertise in diagnosing it as a dangerous agent of both cultural and mental degeneration which required an urgent remedy that could be administered only by scientific specialists.

In the light of the awkward interconnection of Darwinian science and aestheticism from the late 1860s to the mid-1890s examined in this book, it becomes difficult to maintain a view of the Victorian age as the exemplar of the organic, unified and invariably creative 'One Culture' implicitly celebrated in much modern scholarship. Rather, the findings of this book accord with those critiques of the prevalent 'One Culture' model that have begun to emerge over the last decade. Helen Small, for instance, has questioned the validity of scholarly presumptions that nineteenth-century 'medicine and fiction shared much the same language and the same assumptions' when the medical profession's increasing specialization and critique of the culture of sensibility meant that 'by the 1860s relations between them had become far more complex.'[125] More recently, Paul White has contended that the 'science and literature of the Victorian period' should be 'approached not as aspects of an interdisciplinary or predisciplinary "culture" . . . but as resources for the forging of identities and communities'. White proposes that the nineteenth-century's unified literary and scientific high culture was a 'polemical construct' that afforded men of science such as Huxley, as well as men of letters like Arnold, an opportunity of advancing their own status while negating the significance of other groups of intellectuals.[126] In adopting this more pragmatic and strategic understanding of how the relations between science and literature operated in Victorian Britain, however, it also becomes evident that the interconnections between the two could just as easily prove dangerous and deleterious as creative and constructive. They were, as has been seen, frequently exploited and manipulated by those seeking either to discredit the cultural authority of evolutionary science by linking it with aestheticism, or, alternatively, to establish it as a respectable secular theodicy by denying such a connection and instead emphasizing links with more reputable contemporary writers like Tennyson and revered figures from literary history such as Shakespeare.

Since the beginning of the twentieth century, aesthetic views of art and literature and the naturalistic sciences of the Victorian period have often been presumed to represent diametrically opposed secular understandings of the nature and value of human existence. There were, Linda Dowling has contended,

two moral horizons that came to serve late Victorians in Britain and America as alternatives to belief in God: the scientific ethic of unbelief adopted by such figures as Leslie Stephen, Thomas Huxley, and Samuel Butler and the Romantic ideal of self-contemplation through art followed by Morris, Walter Pater, and Oscar Wilde.[127]

But this absolute demarcation was much less evident to the Victorians themselves, and for many in the period, from critics of both naturalistic science and aestheticism like Mallock to supporters of the two such as John Morley, the language and assumptions of the apparently divergent positions were actually virtually interchangeable. Like so many other aspects of our contemporary understanding of the nineteenth-century debates over evolution, and the relations between a putatively triumphant science and a vanquished religion in particular, the view of the disparity between science and aestheticism articulated by Dowling and others actually expresses the partisan, self-serving perspective of participants such as Huxley, who endeavoured to dissociate evolutionary science from the taint of aestheticism in order to establish the respectability of their own positions. The ostensibly epistemological distinction between a scientific and an aesthetic outlook insisted on in modern scholarship would certainly not have been recognized by many in the nineteenth century, and instead largely replicates the strategic boundary separating the two that was constructed, for contingent local reasons, at the end of the Victorian period.

It was only by clearly distinguishing their scientific position from the alleged iniquities of aestheticism that the proponents of Darwinism could invalidate the charges of immorality made by their adversaries, and the construction of such strategic and contingent boundaries offers a valuable new way of understanding the perpetually shifting relations between science and literature in the final decades of the nineteenth century. In this period, Thomas F. Gieryn has argued, '"science" becomes a space on maps of culture, bounded off from other territories', and these 'cultural cartographies of science-in-culture', as Gieryn puts it, required 'strategic practical action' that would establish 'desired boundaries' to ensure that the epistemic authority of science was not compromised by awkward connections with cultural factors like commerce or religion.[128] In particular,

scientific naturalists such as Tyndall, Gieryn proposes, 'redrew the boundaries of the Victorian cultural landscape that would reconfigure the place
of science in the cultural marketplace' in order to give 'increased attention
to the professional needs of scientists'.[129] While Gieryn does not consider
the contemporaneous boundaries that were drawn between science and
literature, his sociological analysis nevertheless provides a model for how
evolutionary science was strategically separated from aestheticism, as well
as any other manifestations of sexual impropriety, as part of the endeavour
to establish the credibility of Darwinism with both scientific professionals
and the wider Victorian public.

Rather than adhering to Young's schema of the progressive 'fragmentation' of an erstwhile 'common context' as an inevitable result of increasing
scientific specialization, it can instead be seen that more localized boundaries between science and general culture were constructed at various times
across the Victorian period and for particular strategic reasons such as
the need to neutralize accusations of Darwinism's implication with the
transgressive excesses of aesthetic literature and art. This perspective does
not, of course, deny that science and literature are similarly cultural formations with numerous correspondences and shared values, but it does
contest the prevalent assumption that the interrelations between them are
almost always creative and advantageous and that the arts and sciences of
the Victorian age inevitably benefited from a single unified culture whose
eventual fragmentation is only to be lamented. By recognizing the adverse
potential of many cross-disciplinary interconnections in the nineteenth
century, moreover, we also gain an important new insight into how concerns with sexual respectability, focusing particularly on aestheticism as well
as new legal definitions of obscenity, became so integral to the reception of
Darwin's evolutionary theories in Victorian Britain.

Notes

NOTES TO CHAPTER ONE

1 Richard Owen, 'On the Affinities of the *Stereognathus Ooliticus* (Charlesworth), a Mammal from the Oolitic Slate of Stonesfield', *Quarterly Journal of the Geological Society of London* 13 (1856), 1–11 (8).

2 Frederick H. Burkhardt *et al.* (eds.), *The Correspondence of Charles Darwin*, 13 vols. (Cambridge: Cambridge University Press, 1983–), 6:260; see also Adrian Desmond, *Huxley: The Devil's Disciple* (London: Michael Joseph, 1994), 229–30.

3 Leonard Huxley, *Life and Letters of Thomas Henry Huxley*, 2 vols. (London: Macmillan, 1900), 1:151.

4 See Adrian Desmond, *Archetypes and Ancestors: Palaeontology in Victorian London 1850–1875* (Chicago: University of Chicago Press, 1982), 57–8.

5 Quoted in Adrian Desmond, *The Politics of Evolution: Morphology, Medicine, and Reform in Radical London* (Chicago: University of Chicago Press, 1989), 366.

6 Thomas W. Laqueur, *Solitary Sex: A Cultural History of Masturbation* (New York: Zone Books, 2003), 46.

7 See Margaret C. Jacob, 'The Materialist World of Pornography', in *The Invention of Pornography: Obscenity and the Origins of Modernity, 1500–1800*, ed. by Lynn Hunt (New York: Zone Books, 1993), 157–202.

8 See Jack Morrell and Arnold Thackray, *Gentlemen of Science: Early Years of the British Association for the Advancement of Science* (Oxford: Clarendon Press, 1981), 17–29 and passim.

9 See, for instance, Desmond, *Archetypes and Ancestors*, 19–55; and Paul White, *Thomas Huxley: Making the 'Man of Science'* (Cambridge: Cambridge University Press, 2003), 32–66.

10 See, amongst others, Frank Miller Turner, *Between Science and Religion: The Reaction to Scientific Naturalism in Late Victorian England* (New Haven and London: Yale University Press, 1974); Frank M. Turner, 'The Victorian Conflict between Science and Religion: A Professional Dimension', in *Contesting Cultural Authority: Essays in Victorian Intellectual Life* (Cambridge: Cambridge University Press, 1993), 171–200; and Adrian Desmond, 'Redefining the X

Axis: "Professionals", "Amateurs" and the Making of Mid-Victorian Biology – A Progress Report', *Journal of the History of Biology* 34 (2001), 3–50.

11 See Ruth Barton, 'Evolution: The Whitworth Gun in Huxley's War for the Liberation of Science from Theology', in *The Wider Domain of Evolutionary Thought*, ed. by David Oldroyd and Ian Langham (Dordrecht: Reidel, 1983), 261–87; and Adrian Desmond, *Huxley: Evolution's High Priest* (London: Michael Joseph, 1997), 235–61.

12 See James R. Moore, 'Theodicy and Society: The Crisis of the Intelligentsia', in *Victorian Faith in Crisis: Essays on Continuity and Change in Nineteenth-Century Religious Belief*, ed. by Richard J. Helmstadter and Bernard Lightman (London: Macmillan, 1990), 153–86.

13 Adrian Desmond and James Moore, *Darwin* (London: Michael Joseph, 1991), 432.

14 See, for instance, Desmond, *Politics of Evolution*, 398–414; and James Moore, 'Deconstructing Darwinism: The Politics of Evolution in the 1860s', *Journal of the History of Biology* 24 (1991), 353–408.

15 See Mike J. Huggins, 'More Sinful Pleasures?: Leisure, Respectability and the Male Middle Classes in Victorian England', *Journal of Social History* 33 (2000), 585–600 (586–87).

16 Michael Mason, *The Making of Victorian Sexual Attitudes* (Oxford: Oxford University Press, 1994), 174.

17 Martin Myrone, 'Prudery, Pornography and the Victorian Nude', in *Exposed: The Victorian Nude*, ed. by Alison Smith (London: Tate Publishing, 2001), 23–35 (31).

18 See Lynda Nead, *Victorian Babylon: People, Streets and Images in Nineteenth-Century London* (New Haven and London: Yale University Press, 2000), 149–61.

19 Robert Buchanan, *The Fleshly School of Poetry and Other Phenomena of the Day* (London: Strahan, 1872), 2, 3 and 4.

20 Ibid., 1 and 6–7.

21 Peter Bailey, 'Parasexuality and Glamour: The Victorian Barmaid as Cultural Prototype', *Gender and History* 2 (1990), 148–72 (167).

22 See Huggins, 'More Sinful Pleasures?', 585–6; Myrone, 'Victorian Nude', 23–8; and Michael Mason, *The Making of Victorian Sexuality* (Oxford: Oxford University Press, 1994), 1–35.

23 Stefan Collini, *Public Moralists: Political Thought and Intellectual Life in Britain 1850–1930* (Oxford: Clarendon Press, 1991), 63.

24 James A. Secord, 'Knowledge in Transit', *Isis* 95 (2004), 654–72 (661).

25 On the need for historians to be 'responsive to a greater plurality of the sites for the making and reproduction of scientific knowledge', and especially to 'popular prose and non-scientific texts', see Roger Cooter and Stephen Pumfrey, 'Separate Spheres and Public Places: Reflections on the History of Science Popularization and Science in Popular Culture', *History of Science* 32 (1994), 237–67 (255).

26 See George Levine, 'One Culture: Science and Literature', in *One Culture: Essays in Science and Literature*, ed. by George Levine (Madison: University of Wisconsin Press, 1987), 3–32.

27 James E. Strick, *Sparks of Life: Darwinism and the Victorian Debates over Spontaneous Generation* (Cambridge, MA: Harvard University Press, 2000), 93.

28 Burkhardt *et al.* (eds.), *Correspondence of Charles Darwin*, 6:178.

29 Lisa Z. Sigel, *Governing Pleasures: Pornography and Social Change in England, 1815–1914* (New Brunswick: Rutgers University Press, 2002), 67.

30 Ernst Renan, *Souvenirs d'enfance et de jeunesse* (Paris: Calmann-Lévy, 1883), 359; Matthew Arnold, 'Numbers', *Nineteenth Century* 15 (1884), 669–85 (678).

31 Arnold, 'Numbers', 681.

32 Burkhardt *et al.* (eds.), *Correspondence of Charles Darwin*, 6:178.

33 Huggins, 'More Sinful Pleasures?', 587.

34 Hannah Gay and John W. Gay, 'Brothers in Science: Science and Fraternal Culture in Nineteenth-Century Britain', *History of Science* 35 (1997), 425–53 (442–3 and 426).

35 Rebecca Stott, 'Darwin's Barnacles: Mid-Century Victorian Natural History and the Marine Grotesque', in *Transactions and Encounters: Science and Culture in the Nineteenth Century*, ed. by Roger Luckhurst and Josephine McDonagh (Manchester: Manchester University Press, 2002), 151–81 (161 and 164).

36 Introduction to Charles Darwin, *The Origin of Species*, ed. by J. W. Burrow (Harmondsworth: Penguin, 1968), 41.

37 Michael Ruse, *The Darwinian Revolution: Science Red in Tooth and Claw* (Chicago: University of Chicago Press, 1979), 251.

38 Strick, *Sparks of Life*, 53.

39 Ibid., 86.

40 Desmond, *Politics of Evolution*, 404.

41 Ibid., 413.

42 James A. Secord, *Victorian Sensation: The Extraordinary Publication, Reception, and Secret Authorship of* Vestiges of the Natural History of Creation (Chicago: University of Chicago Press, 2000), 415.

43 Strick, *Sparks of Life*, 152. Strick's important account of the Victorian debates over spontaneous generation is a rare exception in actually following Darwinian concerns with maintaining respectability beyond the 1850s.

44 Quoted in Gay and Gay, 'Brothers in Science', 449.

45 C. Lyell to T. H. Huxley, 9 August 1862, Huxley Papers 11.66, Imperial College of Science, Technology, and Medicine Archives, London.

46 Huxley, *Life*, 1:200.

47 Karl Robert V. Wikman, *Letters from Edward B. Tylor and Alfred Russel Wallace to Edward Westermarck* (Åbo: Åbo Akademi, 1940), 7.

48 Ibid., 19–20.

49 See Democritus [Georg von Weissenfeld], *Darwin on Trial at the Old Bailey* (Watford: University Press, [1899]), 20–1 and passim.

50 Ruth Barton, '"Men of Science": Language, Identity and Professionalization in the Mid-Victorian Scientific Community', *History of Science* 41 (2003), 73–119 (81 and 86). See also White, *Huxley*, 2–5 and passim.

51 Lorraine Daston and Peter Galison, 'The Image of Objectivity', *Representations* 40 (1992), 81–128 (82–3).

52 Ibid., 121–2.

53 George Levine, *Dying to Know: Scientific Epistemology and Narrative in Victorian England* (Chicago: University of Chicago Press, 2002), 4.

54 T. H. Huxley, 'On the Advisableness of Improving Natural Knowledge', *Fortnightly Review* 3 (1866), 626–37 (637 and 632); W. K. Clifford, 'The Ethics of Religion', *Fortnightly Review* 22 n.s. (1877), 35–52 (38).

55 See White, *Huxley*, 60–2.

56 Steven Shapin, *A Social History of Truth: Civility and Science in Seventeenth-Century England* (Chicago: University of Chicago Press, 1994), 221.

57 Collini, *Public Moralists*, 105–6.

58 See Patricia Fara, *Sex, Botany and Empire: The Story of Carl Linnaeus and Joseph Banks* (Cambridge: Icon, 2003).

59 Desmond, *Huxley: Evolution's High Priest*, 186.

60 Richard St John Tyrwhitt, 'Hellenic and Christian Views of Beauty', *Contemporary Review* 36 (1880), 474–91 (481–2).

61 Collini, *Public Moralists*, 89.

62 See Dennis Denisoff, *Aestheticism and Sexual Parody 1840–1940* (Cambridge: Cambridge University Press, 2001), 6–7 and passim.

63 See Collini, *Public Moralists*, 60–90 and 185–9.

64 See Josephine M. Guy, *The British Avant-Garde: The Theory and Politics of Tradition* (Hemel Hempstead: Harvester Wheatsheaf, 1991), 37–40.

65 John Morley, *Recollections*, 2 vols. (London: Macmillan, 1917), 1:86.

66 See John Morley, 'Causeries', *Fortnightly Review* 1 n.s. (1867), 100–3.

67 Edwin Mallard Everett, *The Party of Humanity: The* Fortnightly Review *and its Contributors 1865–1874* (Chapel Hill: University of North Carolina Press, 1939), 278–9.

68 John Morley, 'Valedictory', *Fortnightly Review* 32 n.s. (1882), 511–21 (519).

69 Cecil Y. Lang (ed.), *The Swinburne Letters*, 6 vols. (New Haven: Yale University Press, 1959–62), 5:163–4.

70 [Carter Blake], 'Professor Huxley on *Man's Place in Nature*', *Edinburgh Review* 117 (1863), 541–69 (566 and 568).

71 Quoted in Bernard Lightman, *The Origins of Agnosticism: Victorian Unbelief and the Limits of Knowledge* (Baltimore: Johns Hopkins University Press, 1987), 25.

72 Algernon Charles Swinburne, *George Chapman: A Critical Essay* (London: Chatto and Windus, 1875), 82.

73 Thomas Maitland [Robert Buchanan], 'The Fleshly School of Poetry', *Contemporary Review* 18 (1871), 334–50 (335).

74 Ibid., 338.

75 Ibid., 335.

76 [William John Courthope], 'The Latest Development of Literary Poetry', *Quarterly Review* 132 (1872), 59–84 (63).

77 John Tyndall, *Address Delivered Before the British Association Assembled at Belfast* (London: Longmans, Green, 1874), 64, 55, and 54.

78 Robert Buchanan, 'Lucretius and Modern Materialism', *New Quarterly Magazine* 6 (1876), 1–30 (7).

79 [Buchanan], 'Fleshly School', 338; Buchanan, 'Lucretius', 10.

80 Buchanan, 'Lucretius', 2.

81 Buchanan, *Fleshly School*, 85.

82 Buchanan, 'Lucretius', 4–5.

83 See Margot K. Louis, *Swinburne and his Gods: The Roots and Growth of an Agnostic Poetry* (Montreal: McGill–Queen's University Press, 1990), 42–3.

84 Algernon Charles Swinburne, 'Victor Hugo: *Religions et Religion*', *Fortnightly Review* 27 n.s. (1880), 761–8 (762).

85 See Collini, *Public Moralists*, 187–8.

86 Barton, 'Men of Science', 109–10; White, *Huxley*, 94–9.

87 *The Times* (4 May 1881), 13; Huxley, *Life*, 2:337.

88 John Tyndall, 'Personal Recollections of Thomas Carlyle', *Fortnightly Review* 47 n.s. (1890), 5–32 (29); quoted in Hallam Tennyson, *Alfred, Lord Tennyson: A Memoir*, 2 vols. (London: Macmillan, 1897), 2:475.

89 Frank M. Turner, 'Victorian Scientific Naturalism and Thomas Carlyle', in *Contesting Cultural Authority*, 131–50 (136).

90 Quoted in James R. Friday, Roy M. MacLeod and Philippa Shepherd, *John Tyndall, Natural Philosopher, 1820–1893: Catalogue of Correspondence, Journals and Collected Papers* (London: Mansell, 1974), printed guide:11.

91 Janis McLarren Caldwell, *Literature and Medicine in Nineteenth-Century Britain: From Mary Shelley to George Eliot* (Cambridge: Cambridge University Press, 2004), 49.

92 Ibid., 55.

93 John Tyndall, 'On the Relations of Radiant Heat to Chemical Constitution, Colour and Texture', *Fortnightly Review* 4 (1866), 1–15 (9); [Walter Pater], 'Winckelmann', *Westminster Review* 31 n.s. (1867), 80–110 (99).

94 Walter Pater, *Studies in the History of the Renaissance* (London: Macmillan, 1873), 207.

95 Walter Pater, *Plato and Platonism* (London: Macmillan, 1893), 140. See, for instance, Billie Andrew Inman, 'The Intellectual Context of Walter Pater's "Conclusion"', *Prose Studies* 14 (1981), 12–30; Charles S. Blinderman, 'Huxley, Pater and Protoplasm', *Journal of the History of Ideas* 43 (1982), 477–86; Levine, *Dying to Know*, 244–67; and Gowan Dawson, 'Walter Pater's *Marius the Epicurean* and the Discourse of Science in *Macmillan's Magazine*: "A Creature of the Nineteenth Century"', *English Literature in Transition 1880–1920* 48 (2005), 38–54.

96 Lang (ed.), *Swinburne Letters*, 2:334–5.

97 Quoted in Hypatia Bradlaugh Bonner, *Charles Bradlaugh: A Record of his Life and Work*, 2 vols. (London: T. Fisher Unwin, 1902), 2:332.

98 Lang (ed.), *Swinburne Letters*, 5:8.
99 See Helen Small, '"In the Guise of Science": Literature and the Rhetoric of Nineteenth-Century English Psychiatry', *History of the Human Sciences* 7 (1994), 27–55; and Gillian Beer, 'Parable, Professionalization, and Literary Allusion in Victorian Scientific Writing', in *Open Fields: Science in Cultural Encounter* (Oxford: Clarendon Press, 1996), 196–215.

NOTES TO CHAPTER TWO

1 'A New Work by Mr Darwin', *Academy* 1 (1869), 15.
2 Francis Darwin (ed.), *The Life and Letters of Charles Darwin*, 3 vols. (London: John Murray, 1887), 3:126 and 131.
3 See James Moore, 'Deconstructing Darwinism: The Politics of Evolution in the 1860s', *Journal of the History of Biology* 24 (1991), 353–408 (389–98).
4 Darwin (ed.), *Life*, 3:138–9.
5 Adrian Desmond and James Moore, *Darwin* (London: Michael Joseph, 1991), 579; Janet Browne, *Charles Darwin: The Power of Place* (London: Jonathan Cape, 2002), 353.
6 [William Boyd Dawkins], 'Darwin on the *Descent of Man*', *Edinburgh Review* 134 (1871), 195–235 (195).
7 Darwin (ed.), *Life*, 3:138–9.
8 Desmond and Moore, *Darwin*, 581.
9 Darwin (ed.), *Life*, 3:98.
10 Charles Darwin, *The Descent of Man, and Selection in Relation to Sex*, 2 vols. (London: John Murray, 1871), 1:23. Citations will hereafter be made in the text.
11 J. Murray to C. R. Darwin, 28 September [1870], DAR 171:378, Darwin Manuscript Collection, Cambridge University Library.
12 Darwin (ed.), *Life*, 3:99.
13 Patrick Brantlinger, *Dark Vanishings: Discourse on the Extinction of Primitive Races, 1800–1930* (Ithaca: Cornell University Press, 2003), 147.
14 See Rosemary Jann, 'Darwin and the Anthropologists: Sexual Selection and its Discontents', *Victorian Studies* 37 (1994), 287–306.
15 On the sexist assumptions implicit in the theory of sexual selection, see Evelleen Richards, 'Darwin and the Descent of Woman', in *The Wider Domain of Evolutionary Thought*, ed. by David Oldroyd and Ian Langham (Dordrecht: Reidel, 1983), 57–111; and Jann, 'Darwin and the Anthropologists', 294–300.
16 Darwin (ed.), *Life*, 3:96.
17 Charles Darwin, *The Variation of Animals and Plants under Domestication*, 2 vols. (London: John Murray, 1868), 2:202.
18 Charles Darwin, *The Descent of Man, and Selection in Relation to Sex*, 2nd edn. (London: John Murray, 1874), 586.
19 Ruth Bernard Yeazell, *Fictions of Modesty: Women and Courtship in the English Novel* (Chicago: University of Chicago Press, 1991), 219.
20 Frederick H. Burkhardt *et al.* (eds.), *The Correspondence of Charles Darwin*, 13 vols. (Cambridge: Cambridge University Press, 1983–), 7:427.

21 Gillian Beer, *Darwin's Plots: Evolutionary Narrative in Darwin, George Eliot and Nineteenth-Century Fiction* (London: Routledge and Kegan Paul, 1983), 211.

22 Darwin (ed.), *Life*, 3:95.

23 Gillian Beer, 'Four Bodies on the *Beagle*', in *Open Fields: Science in Cultural Encounter* (Oxford: Clarendon Press, 1996), 13–30 (29).

24 See Michael Ruse, *The Darwinian Revolution: Science Red in Tooth and Claw* (Chicago: University of Chicago Press, 1979), 154 and 212–14.

25 Burkhardt *et al.* (eds.), *Correspondence of Charles Darwin*, 11:612 and 621.

26 John Ferguson McLennan, *Studies in Ancient History*, 2nd series (London: Macmillan, 1896), 52.

27 J. Murray to C. R. Darwin, 1 July 1870, DAR 171:376.

28 See Bert Bender, *The Descent of Love: Darwin and the Theory of Sexual Selection in American Fiction, 1871–1926* (Philadelphia: University of Pennsylvania Press, 1996), 35.

29 See Yeazell, *Fictions of Modesty*, 219–28; and Angelique Richardson, *Love and Eugenics in the Late Nineteenth Century: Rational Reproduction and the New Woman* (Oxford: Oxford University Press, 2003), 45–50.

30 Murray to Darwin, 28 September [1870], DAR 171:378.

31 George Paston, *At John Murray's: Records of a Literary Circle 1843–1892* (London: John Murray, 1932), 230. On Hunter's gentlemanly reputation in the nineteenth century, see L. S. Jacyna, 'Images of John Hunter in the Nineteenth Century', *History of Science* 21 (1983), 85–108 (94–100).

32 John Hunter, *Essays and Observations on Natural History, Anatomy, Physiology, Psychology, and Geology*, ed. by Richard Owen, 2 vols. (London: John Van Voorst, 1861), 1:194.

33 Murray to Darwin, 10 October [1870], DAR 171:379.

34 Lynda Nead, 'Bodies of Judgement: Art, Obscenity, and the Connoisseur', in *Law and the Image: The Authority of Art and the Aesthetics of Law*, ed. by Costas Douzinas and Lynda Nead (Chicago: University of Chicago Press, 1999), 203–25 (206–7).

35 The translation is provided in Charles Darwin, *The Descent of Man*, ed. by James Moore and Adrian Desmond (London: Penguin, 2004), 645n.

36 See Frederick Burkhardt and Sydney Smith (eds.), *A Calendar of the Correspondence of Charles Darwin, 1821–1882, with Supplement* (Cambridge: Cambridge University Press, 1994), letter 7312, p. 321.

37 A. Smith to C. R. Darwin, 26 March 1867, DAR 85: A103–A105.

38 See Yeazell, *Fictions of Modesty*, 222; on stereotypes of black women's primitive sexuality, see Sander L. Gilman, *Difference and Pathology: Stereotypes of Sexuality, Race, and Madness* (Ithaca: Cornell University Press, 1985), 79–93.

39 Londa Schiebinger, *Nature's Body: Sexual Politics and the Making of Modern Science* (London: Pandora, 1994), 168.

40 Quoted in ibid.

41 Theodor Waitz, *Introduction to Anthropology*, trans. by J. Frederick Collingwood (London: Longman, Green, 1863), 105–6.

42 Ibid., 106.

43 Quoted in Schiebinger, *Nature's Body*, 167–8.

44 [Richard Grant White], *The Fall of Man: or, The Loves of the Gorillas* (New York: G. W. Carleton, 1871), 6.

45 Ibid., 27n.

46 Ibid., 46; the translation is provided in Darwin, *Descent of Man*, ed. by Moore and Desmond, 25n.

47 R. F. Burton, 'Notes on Waitz's *Anthropology*', *Anthropological Review* 2 (1864), 233–50 (238); on Burton's notoriety, see Evelleen Richards, 'The "Moral Anatomy" of Robert Knox: The Interplay between Biological and Social Thought in Victorian Scientific Naturalism', *Journal of the History of Biology* 22 (1989), 373–436 (430).

48 [John Cuthbert Hedley], 'Evolution and Faith', *Dublin Review* 17 n.s. (1871), 1–40 (3).

49 [William Sweetland Dallas], '*The Descent of Man*', *Westminster Review* 42 n.s. (1872), 378–400 (398).

50 Yeazell, *Fictions of Modesty*, 219; Desmond and Moore, *Darwin*, 579–80; Introduction to Darwin, *Descent of Man*, ed. by Moore and Desmond, xxxix.

51 *The Times* (8 April 1871), 5.

52 Darwin (ed.), *Life*, 3:139.

53 [St George Mivart], 'Darwin's *Descent of Man*', *Quarterly Review* 131 (1871), 47–90 (47 and 90).

54 St George Mivart, 'Evolution and its Consequences', *Contemporary Review* 19 (1872), 168–97 (196).

55 *The Times* (3 June 1871), 12; *The Times* (7 April 1871), 8.

56 See Rupert Christiansen, *Tales of the New Babylon: Paris 1869–1875* (London: Sinclair-Stevenson, 1994), 309–10 and 346–7.

57 Mivart, 'Evolution', 196.

58 St George Mivart, *On the Genesis of Species* (London: Macmillan, 1871), 206.

59 Ibid., 204–5.

60 Ibid., 198.

61 Ibid., 287.

62 [John R. Leifchild], '[Review of] *The Descent of Man and Selection in Relation to Sex* by Charles Darwin', *Athenaeum* (1871), 275–7 (276).

63 See James A. Secord, *Victorian Sensation: The Extraordinary Publication, Reception, and Secret Authorship of* Vestiges of the Natural History of Creation (Chicago: University of Chicago Press, 2000), 164.

64 Burkhardt *et al.* (eds.), *Correspondence of Charles Darwin*, 11:223; [John R. Leifchild], '[Review of] *Evidence as to Man's Place in Nature* by Thomas Henry Huxley', *Athenaeum* (1863), 287–8 (287).

65 Alfred R. Wallace, '[Review of] *The Descent of Man and Selection in Relation to Sex* by Charles Darwin', *Academy* 2 (1871), 177–83 (177).

66 Darwin, *Descent*, 2nd edn., 586.

67 See Adrian Desmond, *Archetypes and Ancestors: Palaeontology in Victorian London 1850–1875* (Chicago: University of Chicago Press, 1982), 181–3.

68 [Dawkins], 'Darwin', 195.

69 Ibid., 217.
70 Ibid., 234–5.
71 Algernon Charles Swinburne, *Poems and Ballads* (London: Edward Moxon, 1866), 79.
72 [John Morley], 'Mr. Swinburne's New Poems', *Saturday Review* 22 (1866), 145–7 (147).
73 [Thomas Spencer Baynes], 'Swinburne's *Poems*', *Edinburgh Review* 134 (1871), 71–99 (75 and 71).
74 See Stephanie Kuduk, '"A Sword of a Song": Swinburne's Republican Aesthetics in *Songs Before Sunrise*', *Victorian Studies* 43 (2001), 253–78.
75 A. C. Swinburne, *Songs Before Sunrise* (London: F. S. Ellis, 1871), 82.
76 [Baynes], 'Swinburne', 97–8.
77 Ibid., 72 and 77.
78 See John Knox Laughton, *Memoirs of the Life and Correspondence of Henry Reeve*, 2 vols. (London: Longmans, Green, 1898), 1:370.
79 [Baynes], 'Swinburne', 71–2; [Thomas Spencer Baynes], 'Darwin on *Expression*', *Edinburgh Review* 137 (1873), 492–528 (494).
80 [Baynes], 'Swinburne', 75; [Baynes], 'Darwin', 492.
81 [Baynes], 'Darwin', 496; [Baynes], 'Swinburne', 71 and 98.
82 [Baynes], 'Swinburne', 72; [Baynes], 'Darwin', 502–3.
83 [Baynes], 'Darwin', 503.
84 Rikky Rooksby, *A. C. Swinburne: A Poet's Life* (Aldershot: Scolar Press, 1997), 135.
85 [Morley], 'Swinburne's New Poems', 145 and 147; [Baynes], 'Swinburne', 72.
86 Edmund Gosse, *The Life of Algernon Charles Swinburne* (London: Macmillan, 1917), 141.
87 See Rooksby, *Swinburne*, 137.
88 Swinburne, *Poems and Ballads*, 29–30; see Nina Auerbach, *Woman and the Demon: The Life of a Victorian Myth* (Cambridge, MA: Harvard University Press, 1982), 104–5.
89 'Books and Reading', *Hours at Home* 9 (1869), 42–50 (47).
90 Richard A. Kaye, *The Flirt's Tragedy: Desire Without End in Victorian and Edwardian Fiction* (Charlottesville: University of Virginia Press, 2002), 98.
91 Richardson, *Love and Eugenics*, 56–7.
92 Roy Porter and Lesley Hall, *The Facts of Life: The Creation of Sexual Knowledge in Britain, 1650–1950* (New Haven: Yale University Press, 1995), 138 and 142.
93 Swinburne, *Poems and Ballads*, 178–9.
94 Ibid., 182.
95 See Judith R. Walkowitz, *City of Dreadful Delight: Narratives of Sexual Danger in Late-Victorian London* (London: Virago, 1992), 22–3.
96 See Gay L. Gullickson, *Unruly Women of Paris: Images of the Commune* (Ithaca: Cornell University Press, 1996), 85–9, 176–9 and passim.
97 *The Times* (29 May 1871), 9–10.
98 Alfred Tennyson, *Idylls of the King* (London: Edward Moxon, 1859), 244–5.
99 Ibid., 250.

100 [Alfred Tennyson], *In Memoriam* (London: Edward Moxon, 1850), 183; [John Chapman], 'Equatorial Africa, and its Inhabitants', *Westminster Review* 20 n.s. (1861), 137–87 (187).

101 Thomas H. Huxley, *Evolution and Ethics* (London: Macmillan, 1894), 52.

102 Burkhardt *et al.* (eds.), *Correspondence of Charles Darwin*, 11:655.

103 Ibid., 13:5.

104 Darwin (ed.), *Life*, 1:100–1.

105 See Browne, *Darwin*, 299–300 and 347.

106 Helen Small, '"In the Guise of Science": Literature and the Rhetoric of Nineteenth-Century English Psychiatry', *History of the Human Sciences* 7 (1994), 27–55 (47).

107 Algernon Charles Swinburne, 'Dethroning Tennyson: A Contribution to the Tennyson–Darwin Controversy', *Nineteenth Century* 23 (1888), 127–9.

108 Darwin (ed.), *Life*, 3:135–6.

109 St George Mivart, 'Contemporary Evolution', *Contemporary Review* 22 (1873), 595–614 (614).

110 Ibid., 608.

111 [James Bucham Brown], 'Ethics and Aesthetics of Modern Poetry', *Cornhill Magazine* 37 (1878), 569–83 (583).

112 Mivart, 'Contemporary Evolution', 614.

113 See Patricia Anderson, *The Printed Image and the Transformation of Popular Culture 1790–1860* (Oxford: Clarendon Press, 1991); James G. Paradis, 'Satire and Science in Victorian Culture', in *Victorian Science in Context*, ed. by Bernard Lightman (Chicago: University of Chicago Press, 1997), 143–75; and Secord, *Victorian Sensation*, 437–70.

114 James D. Hague, 'A Reminiscence of Mr. Darwin', *Harper's New Monthly Magazine* (European edn.) 8 (1884), 759–63 (760).

115 Browne, *Darwin*, 376.

116 'The Development of Dress', *Punch* 60 (1871), 197.

117 G. M. [George Du Maurier], 'A Logical Refutation of Mr. Darwin's Theory', *Punch* 60 (1871), 130.

118 Hague, 'Reminiscence', 760.

119 J. T. [John Tenniel], 'National (Black) Guards', *Punch* 60 (1871), 131.

120 G. M. [George Du Maurier], 'The Descent of Man', *Punch* 64 (1873), 217.

121 Gillian Beer, 'Forging the Missing Link', in *Open Fields*, 115–45 (131–2).

122 'Most Natural Selection', *Punch* 60 (1871), 127.

123 'The Wedding Procession', *Fun* 13 n.s. (1871), 126.

124 See Gilman, *Difference and Pathology*, 79–93.

125 Paul B. Du Chaillu, *Explorations and Adventures in Equatorial Africa* (London: John Murray, 1861), 58.

126 Ibid., 60.

127 On the doubts over Du Chaillu's findings, see Stuart McCook, '"It May be Truth, But it is Not Evidence": Paul Du Chaillu and the Legitimation of Evidence in the Field Sciences', *Osiris* 2nd ser. 11 (1996), 177–97.

128 'With Mr. Gorilla's Compliments', *Temple Bar* 3 (1861), 482–91 (485).

129 Richard F. Burton, *The Book of the Thousand Nights and a Night*, 16 vols. (Benares [London]: Kamashastra Society, 1885–8), Supplemental Nights 4:333n.

130 Du Chaillu, *Explorations*, 59.

131 Ibid., 262.

132 Ibid., 61.

133 Quoted in Peter Raby, *Bright Paradise: Victorian Scientific Travellers* (London: Chatto and Windus, 1996), 189.

134 See H. W. Janson, *Nineteenth-Century Sculpture* (London: Thames and Hudson, 1985), 184–5; Christoph Brockhaus and Hans Albert Peters, *Alfred Kubin: Das zeichnerische Frühwerk bis 1904* (Baden-Baden: Kunsthalle Baden-Baden, 1977), 146.

135 Thomas Henry Huxley, *Evidence as to Man's Place in Nature* (London: Williams and Norgate, 1863), 54.

136 H. W. Janson, *Apes and Ape Lore in the Middle Ages and the Renaissance* (London: The Warburg Institute, 1952), 208.

137 Spenser St John, *Life in the Forests of the Far East*, 2 vols. (London: Smith, Elder, 1862), 1:22; Donna Haraway, *Primate Visions: Gender, Race, and Nature in the World of Modern Science* (New York: Routledge, 1989), 311.

138 On such attributions of sexual licentiousness to male apes, see Londa Schiebinger, 'The Gendered Ape: Early Representations of Primates in Europe', in *A Question of Identity: Women, Science and Literature*, ed. by Marina Benjamin (New Brunswick: Rutgers University Press, 1993), 119–51.

139 Huxley, *Man's Place*, 8 and 12.

140 Ibid., 12.

141 See Janson, *Apes*, 56 and 74–5; Midas Dekkers, *Dearest Pet: On Bestiality*, trans. by Paul Vincent (London: Verso, 1994), 40–2.

142 Du Chaillu, *Explorations*, 304.

143 Huxley, *Man's Place*, 12–13.

144 'Monkeyana', *Punch* 40 (1861), 206.

145 H. G. Wells, *The Island of Doctor Moreau* (London: William Heinemann, 1896), 131 and 136.

146 'Our Monthly Parcel of Books', *Review of Reviews* 13 (1896), 374–6 (374).

147 See Janson, *Apes*, 268; Gustave Flaubert, *Early Writings*, trans. by Robert Griffin (Lincoln: University of Nebraska Press, 1991), 76–102.

148 See Burton, *Thousand Nights*, 4:299n.; 6:54n.; Supplemental Nights 4:331n.

149 Charles Darwin, *On the Origin of Species* (London: John Murray, 1859), 254 and 43.

150 See Richards, 'Moral Anatomy', 432–5.

151 Burton, *Thousand Nights*, Supplemental Nights 4:331n.

152 See Dekkers, *Dearest Pet*, 88–90; and Diana Snigurowicz, 'Sex, Simians, and Spectacle in Nineteenth-Century France: or, How to Tell a "Man" from a Monkey', *Canadian Journal of History* 34 (1999), 51–81 (79n.).

153 See Hélène Védrine, *De l'encre dans l'acide: l'œuvre gravé de Félicien Rops et la littérature de la Décadence* (Paris: Champion, 2002), 253.

154 Baron Alcide de M*** [Alfred de Musset], *Gamiani, or Two Passionate Nights: A Literal Translation* (London: n.p., 1908), 104–5.

155 See Adrian Desmond, *The Politics of Evolution: Morphology, Medicine, and Reform in Radical London* (Chicago: University of Chicago Press, 1989), 45.

156 See Védrine, *L'Encre dans l'acide*, 250.

157 Lisa Z. Sigel, *Governing Pleasures: Pornography and Social Change in England, 1815–1914* (New Brunswick: Rutgers University Press, 2002), 162–3.

158 Gilman, *Difference and Pathology*, 81; see also Anne McClintock, *Imperial Leather: Race, Gender and Sexuality in the Colonial Conquest* (New York: Routledge, 1995), 41–2 and 113.

159 Érastène Ramiro [Eugène Rodrigues], *Catalogue descriptif et analytique de l'œuvre gravé de Félicien Rops* (Paris: Librairie Conquet, 1887), 182. My translation.

160 See Sigel, *Governing Pleasures*, 32.

161 See Richardson, *Love and Eugenics*, 56–7.

162 Quoted in Védrine, *L'Encre dans l'acide*, 262. My translation.

163 [Rodrigues], *Catalogue descriptif*, 181–2. My translation. On Darwin's frequent association with Littré, see Browne, *Darwin*, 379.

164 Sigel, *Governing Pleasures*, 88–9.

165 G. T. [Gordon Thomson], 'That Troubles Our Monkey Again', *Fun* 16 n.s. (1872), 203.

166 Charles Darwin, *The Expression of the Emotions in Man and Animals* (London: John Murray, 1872), 327 and 314–15.

167 Darwin, *Descent*, 2nd edn., v.

168 McLennan, *Studies in Ancient History*, 50–1.

169 Darwin, *Descent*, 2nd edn., 590.

170 Ibid., 594.

171 [St George Mivart], 'Primitive Man: Tylor and Lubbock', *Quarterly Review* 137 (1874), 40–77 (70).

172 George Darwin, 'On Beneficial Restrictions to Liberty of Marriage', *Contemporary Review* 22 (1873), 412–26 (424).

173 [Mivart], 'Primitive Man', 70.

174 St George Mivart, 'Reminiscences of Thomas Henry Huxley', *Nineteenth Century* 42 (1897), 985–98 (997); Mivart, 'Contemporary Evolution', 608.

175 Darwin (ed.), *Life*, 1:89.

176 Charles Darwin, *Autobiographies*, ed. by Michael Neve and Sharon Messenger (London: Penguin, 2002), 76.

177 C. R. Darwin to E. B. Tylor, [January 1875?], MS Add. 50254, British Library.

178 Mivart, 'Reminiscences', 997.

179 C. R. Darwin to G. H. Darwin, 27 July 1874, DAR 210.1:25; 'Note upon the Article "Primitive Man: Tylor and Lubbock" in No. 273', *Quarterly Review* 137 (1874), 587–9 (587).

180 Browne, *Darwin*, 355.

181 See ibid., 356; and Jacob W. Gruber, *A Conscience in Conflict: The Life of St George Jackson Mivart* (New York: Columbia University Press, 1960), 98–114. C. R. Darwin to St G. Mivart, 12 January 1875, DAR 97: C36.
182 C. R. Darwin to G. H. Darwin, 5 August 1874, DAR 210.2:38.
183 C. R. Darwin to T. H. Huxley, 24 December 1874, Huxley Papers 5.311, Imperial College of Science, Technology and Medicine Archives, London.
184 T. H. Huxley, '[Review of] *Anthropogenie* by Ernst Haeckel', *Academy* 7 (1875), 16–18 (16–17).
185 T. H. Huxley, 'Mr. Darwin's Critics', *Contemporary Review* 18 (1871), 443–76 (468).
186 James Marchant, *Alfred Russel Wallace: Letters and Reminiscences*, 2 vols. (London: Cassell, 1916), 1:292; T. H. Huxley to J. D. Hooker, 11 December 1874, Huxley Papers 2.218.
187 J. Tyndall to C. R. Darwin, 28 December 1874, DAR 106: C17–C18.
188 St G. Mivart to T. H. Huxley, 20 December 1874, Huxley Papers 22.263.
189 Huxley, '[Review of] *Anthropogenie*', 17.
190 St G. Mivart to T. H. Huxley, 24 December 1874, Huxley Papers 22.267.
191 Huxley, '[Review of] *Anthropogenie*', 17.
192 Darwin (ed.), *Life*, 3:149.

NOTES TO CHAPTER THREE

1 John Tyndall, *Address Delivered Before the British Association Assembled at Belfast* (London: Longmans, Green, 1874), v and 55. Citations will hereafter be made in the text.
2 Ruth Barton, 'John Tyndall, Pantheist: A Rereading of the Belfast Address', *Osiris* 2nd Ser. 3 (1987), 111–34; Stephen S. Kim, *John Tyndall's Transcendental Materialism and the Conflict between Religion and Science in Victorian England* (New York: Edwin Mellen, 1996).
3 John Tyndall, '"Materialism" and its Opponents', *Fortnightly Review* 22 n.s. (1875), 579–99 (595).
4 Quoted in Barton, 'Tyndall, Pantheist', 116.
5 See C. W. Stokes, *An Inquiry of the Home Secretary as to Whether Professor Tyndall Has Not Subjected Himself to the Penalty of Persons Expressing Blasphemous Opinions* (London: privately printed, 1874), 8.
6 Frank M. Turner, 'John Tyndall and Victorian Scientific Naturalism', in *John Tyndall: Essays on a Natural Philosopher*, ed. by W. H. Brock, N. D. McMillan, and R. C. Mollan (Dublin: Dublin Royal Society, 1981), 169–80 (170).
7 See Barton, 'Tyndall, Pantheist'; Kim, *Tyndall's Transcendental Materialism*; Bernard Lightman, 'Scientists as Materialists in the Periodical Press: Tyndall's Belfast Address', in *Science Serialized: Representations of the Sciences in Nineteenth-Century Periodicals*, ed. by Geoffrey Cantor and Sally Shuttleworth (Cambridge, MA: MIT Press, 2004), 199–237; and David N. Livingstone, 'Darwinism and Calvinism: The Belfast–Princeton Connection', *Isis* 83 (1992), 408–28.

8 Frank M. Turner, 'Ancient Materialism and Modern Science: Lucretius Among the Victorians', in *Contesting Cultural Authority: Essays in Victorian Intellectual Life* (Cambridge: Cambridge University Press, 1993), 262–83 (266).

9 See Frank M. Turner, *The Greek Heritage in Victorian Britain* (New Haven and London: Yale University Press, 1981); and Norman Vance, *The Victorians and Ancient Rome* (Oxford: Blackwell, 1997).

10 F. W. Farrar, *The Early Days of Christianity* (London: Cassell, 1882), 1.

11 Matthew Arnold, 'Pagan and Christian Religious Sentiment', *Cornhill Magazine* 9 (1864), 422–35 (424).

12 Ibid., 432 and 434.

13 Farrar, *Early Days*, 4.

14 [William Rathbone Greg], 'On the Failure of "Natural Selection" in the Case of Man', *Fraser's Magazine* 78 (1868), 353–62 (357); Charles Darwin, *The Descent of Man, and Selection in Relation to Sex*, 2 vols. (London: John Murray, 1871), 1:178.

15 [Lord Byron], *Don Juan* (London: Thomas Davison, 1819), 23.

16 Alfred Tennyson, 'Lucretius', *Macmillan's Magazine* 18 (1868), 1–9 (7).

17 [James Bucham Brown], 'Ethics and Aesthetics of Modern Poetry', *Cornhill Magazine* 37 (1878), 569–83 (569–70).

18 'The Survival of Paganism', *Fraser's Magazine* 12 n.s. (1875), 640–51 (640).

19 Ibid., 651.

20 John Walter Lea, *Christian Marriage: Its Open and Secret Enemies* (London: W. Skeffington, 1881), 11.

21 St George Mivart, 'Contemporary Evolution', *Contemporary Review* 22 (1873), 595–614 (607–8).

22 Ibid., 613.

23 John Tyndall, *Heat Considered as a Mode of Motion* (London: Longmans, Green, 1863), 432; Mivart, 'Contemporary Evolution', 608.

24 Mivart, 'Contemporary Evolution', 607–8.

25 Ibid., 614.

26 J. Tyndall to T. A. Hirst, 5 September 1868, Tyndall Papers RI MS JT/1/T/688, Royal Institution of Great Britain, London.

27 'Mr Tennyson's Death of Lucretius', *Spectator* 41 (1868), 523.

28 See Crosbie Smith, *The Science of Energy: A Cultural History of Energy Physics in Victorian Britain* (London: Athlone Press, 1998), 277–80; and Turner, 'Ancient Materialism', 268–9.

29 [Fleeming Jenkin], 'The Atomic Theory of Lucretius', *North British Review* 9 n.s. (1868), 211–42 (224).

30 J. Tyndall to C. R. Darwin, 5 August 1874, DAR 106: C16, Darwin Manuscript Collection, Cambridge University Library.

31 Katherine Murray Lyell (ed.), *Life, Letters and Journals of Sir Charles Lyell, Bart.*, 2 vols. (London: John Murray, 1881), 2:455.

32 Friedrich Albert Lange, *History of Materialism and Criticism of its Present Importance*, trans. by Ernest Chester Thomas, 3 vols. (London: Trübner, 1877), 1:19.

33 [Jenkin], 'Atomic Theory', 242.

34 [John Tulloch], 'Modern Scientific Materialism', *Blackwood's Edinburgh Magazine* 116 (1874), 519–39 (522).

35 Ibid., 527.

36 [Henry Reeve], 'Mill's *Essays on Theism*', *Edinburgh Review* 141 (1875), 1–31 (4).

37 Ibid., 2–3.

38 *The Times* (20 August 1874), 4.

39 [Reeve], 'Mill's *Essays*', 6.

40 Lyell (ed.), *Life*, 2:455.

41 *The Times* (31 October 1874), 7. On Cullen's fasting, see J. Tyndall to G. H. Wiedemann, 24 September 1874, Tyndall Papers RI MS JT/1/T/1491.

42 Robert Watts, *Atomism: Dr. Tyndall's Atomic Theory of the Universe Examined and Refuted* (Belfast: William Mullan, 1874), 20–1.

43 See Livingstone, 'Darwinism and Calvinism', 412–17.

44 James McCosh, *Ideas in Nature Overlooked by Dr. Tyndall* (New York: Robert Carter, 1875), iii.

45 Ibid., 12.

46 See Lynda Nead, 'Bodies of Judgement: Art, Obscenity, and the Connoisseur', in *Law and the Image: The Authority of Art and the Aesthetics of Law*, ed. by Costas Douzinas and Lynda Nead (Chicago: University of Chicago Press, 1999), 203–25.

47 Darwin, *Descent*, 1:96.

48 George Sexton, *Scientific Materialism Calmly Considered* (London: J. Burns, 1874), 60 and 12–13.

49 See Frank M. Turner, 'The Victorian Conflict between Science and Religion: A Professional Dimension', in *Contesting Cultural Authority*, 171–200.

50 The expression is also found in Isaiah 22:13.

51 Edwin T. J. Marriner, *'The Raising of the Widow's Son at Nain': A Sermon in Reply to Professor Tyndall's Address at Belfast* (London: Simpkin, Marshall, 1874), 16.

52 [James Casey], *Tyndall and Materialism and Gladstone and the Vatican Decrees. Two Epistles in Verse* (Dublin: James Duffy, 1875), 6 and 13–14.

53 Lord Selborne, 'A Modern "Symposium": The Influence upon Morality of a Decline in Religious Belief', *Nineteenth Century* 1 (1877), 333–40 (337–9).

54 Walter Pater, *Studies in the History of the Renaissance* (London: Macmillan, 1873), 212.

55 [Margaret Oliphant], 'New Books', *Blackwood's Edinburgh Magazine* 114 (1873), 604–9 (608).

56 'Modern Cyrenaicism', *Examiner* (1873), 381–2 (381).

57 John Morley, 'Mr. Pater's Essays', *Fortnightly Review* 13 n.s. (1873), 469–77 (474).

58 Quoted in Edmund Gosse, 'Walter Pater: A Portrait', *Contemporary Review* 66 (1894), 795–810 (804).

59 Pater, *Studies*, ix.

60 George Levine, *Dying to Know: Scientific Epistemology and Narrative in Victorian England* (Chicago: University of Chicago Press, 2002), 249.

61 Richard A. Kaye, *The Flirt's Tragedy: Desire Without End in Victorian and Edwardian Fiction* (Charlottesville: University of Virginia Press, 2002), 92.

62 'Literary Notices', *London Quarterly Review* 40 (1873), 505–7 (505–6).

63 [Oliphant], 'New Books', 608.

64 Frederick William Farrar, *The Silence and the Voices of God* (London: Macmillan, 1874), 23.

65 Ibid., 12.

66 Paul White, 'Ministers of Culture: Arnold, Huxley and Liberal Anglican Reform of Learning', *History of Science* 43 (2005), 115–38 (125 and 128).

67 Farrar, *Silence*, 13.

68 Pater, *Studies*, 98.

69 Percy Bysshe Shelley, *Posthumous Poems*, ed. by Mary W. Shelley (London: John and Henry L. Hunt, 1824), 140.

70 See White, 'Ministers of Culture', 121–3.

71 Farrar, *Silence*, 28.

72 Ibid., 62.

73 W. H. Mallock, 'Is Life Worth Living?', *Nineteenth Century* 3 (1878), 146–68 (166–7).

74 Ibid., 153.

75 See John Tyndall, 'A Morning on Alp Lusgen', in *New Fragments* (London: Longmans, Green, 1892), 498–500; and John Tyndall, 'On the Scientific Use of the Imagination', in *Fragments of Science for Unscientific People*, 2nd edn. (London: Longmans, Green, 1871), 127–67.

76 Quoted in Hallam Tennyson, *Alfred, Lord Tennyson: A Memoir*, 2 vols. (London: Macmillan, 1897), 2:470.

77 See Frank M. Turner, 'Victorian Scientific Naturalism and Thomas Carlyle', in *Contesting Cultural Authority*, 131–50.

78 William Hurrell Mallock, *Is Life Worth Living?* (London: Chatto and Windus, 1879), 85.

79 W. H. Mallock, 'A Familiar Colloquy on Recent Art', *Nineteenth Century* 4 (1878), 289–302 (294–5).

80 Quoted in Oscar Wilde, 'The English Renaissance in Art', in *Lectures and Essays* (London: Methuen, 1909), 111–55 (132).

81 See Tim Hilton, *John Ruskin: The Later Years* (New Haven and London: Yale University Press, 2000), 396.

82 Mallock, 'Familiar Colloquy', 294.

83 Mallock, *Is Life Worth Living?*, 210.

84 Jill Howard, '"Physics and Fashion": John Tyndall and his Audiences in Mid-Victorian Britain', *Studies in History and Philosophy of Science* 35 (2004), 729–58 (738).

85 'The Ladies of the Creation', *Punch* 24 (1853), [ii]–[iv]. See also 'An Awful Demonstration', *Punch* 48 (1865), 124.

86 J. Pollock to J. Tyndall, 1 December [1874], Tyndall Papers RI MS JT/1/P/175.

87 Leonard Huxley, *Life and Letters of Thomas Henry Huxley*, 2 vols. (London: Macmillan, 1900), 1:386.

88 J. Tyndall to E. Hamilton, 28 July [aft. 1873], Tyndall Papers MS Add. 63092, British Library; J. Tyndall to T. A. Hirst, 29 December 1855, Tyndall Papers RI MS JT/1/T/615.

89 A. S. Eve and C. H. Creasy, *Life and Work of John Tyndall* (London: Macmillan, 1945), 202.

90 See Gillian Beer, 'Wave Theory and the Rise of Literary Modernism', in *Open Fields: Science in Cultural Encounter* (Oxford: Clarendon Press, 1996), 295–318 (307–8 and 312).

91 Lewis Campbell and William Garnett (eds.), *The Life of James Clerk Maxwell* (London: Macmillan, 1882), 634.

92 *The Times* (24 August 1874), 6.

93 Oliver Lodge, *Advancing Science: Being Personal Reminiscences of the British Association in the Nineteenth Century* (London: Ernest Benn, 1931), 36. On Lodge's relations with Tyndall and Maxwell, see Smith, *Science of Energy*, 290–1.

94 [William Hurrell Mallock], *The New Republic, or Culture, Faith, and Philosophy in an English Country House*, 2 vols. (London: Chatto and Windus, 1877), 1:31.

95 Ibid., 1:71.

96 Ibid., 2:67.

97 'The New Republic', *Contemporary Review* 30 (1877), 1098–1100 (1098).

98 'The New Republic', *Saturday Review* 43 (1877), 554–5; L. S. Bevington, 'Modern Atheism and Mr. Mallock', *Nineteenth Century* 6 (1879), 585–603 (585 and 603).

99 *The Value of Life: A Reply to Mr Mallock's Essay 'Is Life Worth Living?'* (New York: G. P. Puttnam's Sons, 1879), 45.

100 [Mallock], *New Republic*, 1:169.

101 Ibid., 1:230 and 2:75–6.

102 Ibid., 2:61–3.

103 W. H. Mallock, *Memoirs of Life and Literature* (London: Chapman and Hall, 1920), 67; W. H. Mallock, *The New Paul and Virginia, or Positivism on an Island* (London: Chatto and Windus, 1878), 23.

104 Mallock, *New Paul and Virginia*, 43–4 and 109.

105 Frederick Burkhardt and Sydney Smith (eds.), *A Calendar of the Correspondence of Charles Darwin, 1821–1882, with Supplement* (Cambridge: Cambridge University Press, 1994), letter 10382, p. 444.

106 *The Times* (31 October 1874), 9.

107 Turner, 'Ancient Materialism', 271.

108 On the timing of the Address's composition, see C. R. Darwin to J. Tyndall, 12 August 1874, DAR 261.8:21.

109 John Tyndall, 'Crystalline and Molecular Forces', in *Science Lectures for the People. Sixth Series* (Manchester: John Heywood, 1874), 1–13 (6).

110 Quoted in James R. Friday, Roy M. MacLeod and Philippa Shepherd, *John Tyndall, Natural Philosopher, 1820–1893: Catalogue of Correspondence, Journals and Collected Papers* (London: Mansell, 1974), printed guide:12 and 14.

III Tyndall, 'Crystalline', 6; on Carlyle's use of the expression, see Oscar Wilde, 'The True Function and Value of Criticism', *Nineteenth Century* 28 (1890), 435–59 (448).

112 W. K. Clifford, 'Right and Wrong: The Scientific Ground of their Distinction', *Fortnightly Review* 18 n.s. (1875), 770–800 (775–6).

113 W. K. Clifford, 'The First and Last Catastrophe', *Fortnightly Review* 17 n.s. (1875), 465–84 (466).

114 J. Tyndall to H. M. Adair, 11 January [1875], Tyndall Papers RI MS JT/1/T/89.

115 J. Tyndall to T. H. Huxley, 4 November 1874, Huxley Papers 1.30–1, Imperial College of Science, Technology, and Medicine Archives, London; T. H. Huxley to J. Tyndall, 9 November 1874, Huxley Papers 9.88.

116 John Tyndall, 'Science and Man', *Fortnightly Review* 22 n.s. (1877), 593–617 (613).

117 Ibid., 616.

118 Ibid., 614–15.

119 John Tyndall, *Six Lectures on Light* (London: Longmans, Green, 1873), 211–12 and 215.

120 James E. Strick, *Sparks of Life: Darwinism and the Victorian Debates over Spontaneous Generation* (Cambridge, MA: Harvard University Press, 2000), 176.

121 Tyndall, 'Science and Man', 613.

122 John Stuart Mill, *Utilitarianism* (London: Parker, Son, and Bourne, 1863), 10–11.

123 Huxley, *Life*, 1:220.

124 Thomas H. Huxley, *Evolution and Ethics* (London: Macmillan, 1894), 72–3 and 110–11.

125 Walter Pater, *Marius the Epicurean*, 2 vols. (London: Macmillan, 1885), 1:156.

126 Walter Pater, *The Renaissance: Studies in Art and Poetry*, 3rd edn. (London: Macmillan, 1888), 246n.

127 Alfred Tennyson, *Tiresias and Other Poems* (London: Macmillan, 1885), 53 and 65.

128 Quoted in Tennyson, *Memoir*, 2:476–7.

129 John Tyndall, *Fragments of Science*, 5th edn. (London: Longmans, Green, 1876), v.

130 Quoted in Strick, *Sparks of Life*, 179; Francis Darwin (ed.), *The Life and Letters of Charles Darwin*, 3 vols. (London: John Murray, 1887), 3:149.

131 Lightman, 'Scientists as Materialists', 230.

NOTES TO CHAPTER FOUR

1 St G. Mivart to C. R. Darwin, 25 April 1870, DAR 171:187, Darwin Manuscript Collection, Cambridge University Library.

2 See H. W. Janson, *Apes and Ape Lore in the Middle Ages and the Renaissance* (London: The Warburg Institute, 1952), 270–1.

3 Frederick H. Burkhardt *et al.* (eds.), *The Correspondence of Charles Darwin*, 13 vols. (Cambridge: Cambridge University Press, 1983–), 11:179–80.

4 *Law Reports*, 3 Q.B.D. 1867–8, 360–79 (371).

5 T. H. Huxley, 'Mr. Darwin's Critics', *Contemporary Review* 18 (1871), 443–76 (476).

6 Leonard Huxley, *Life and Letters of Thomas Henry Huxley*, 2 vols. (London: Macmillan, 1900), 1:200.

7 See Lynda Nead, *Victorian Babylon: People, Streets and Images in Nineteenth-Century London* (New Haven and London: Yale University Press, 2000), 160.

8 See M. J. D. Roberts, 'Morals, Art, and the Law: The Passing of the Obscene Publications Act, 1857', *Victorian Studies* 28 (1985), 609–29.

9 Lynda Nead, 'Bodies of Judgement: Art, Obscenity, and the Connoisseur', in *Law and the Image: The Authority of Art and the Aesthetics of Law*, ed. by Costas Douzinas and Lynda Nead (Chicago: University of Chicago Press, 1999), 203–25 (212).

10 Quoted in Walter L. Arnstein, *The Bradlaugh Case: A Study in Late Victorian Opinion and Politics* (Oxford: Clarendon Press, 1965), 12.

11 Michael Mason, *The Making of Victorian Sexual Attitudes* (Oxford: Oxford University Press, 1994), 184 and 210.

12 Quoted in G. Astor Singer [Georg von Weissenfeld], *Judicial Scandals and Errors* (Watford: University Press, [1899]), 97.

13 Nead, 'Bodies of Judgement', 214.

14 T. N. Talfourd, *Speech for the Defendant in the Prosecution of the Queen v. Moxon for the Publication of Shelley's Works* (London: Edward Moxon, 1841), 18–19.

15 See M. J. D. Roberts, 'Making Victorian Morals?: The Society for the Suppression of Vice and its Critics, 1802–1886', *Historical Studies* 21 (1984), 157–73; and Roberts, 'Morals, Art, and the Law', 615.

16 *Daily Telegraph* (17 June 1857), 3.

17 Quoted in Roberts, 'Morals, Art, and the Law', 613.

18 Quoted in Nead, 'Bodies of Judgement', 215.

19 See Ian McCalman, *Radical Underworld: Prophets, Revolutionaries and Pornographers in London, 1795–1840* (Oxford: Clarendon Press, 1993), 204–31; and Roberts, 'Making Victorian Morals?', 161–2.

20 'The Indictment', *National Reformer* (1877), 335.

21 Advertisement included in *National Reformer* (1877), 192.

22 Beverly Brown, 'Troubled Vision: Legal Understandings of Obscenity', *New Formations* 19 (1993), 29–44 (35).

23 See Anne Taylor, *Annie Besant: A Biography* (Oxford: Oxford University Press, 1992), 113–14.

24 C. R. Darwin to C. Bradlaugh, 6 June 1877, DAR 202:32.

25 See, for instance, Adrian Desmond and James Moore, *Darwin* (London: Michael Joseph, 1991), 627–8; and Janet Browne, *Charles Darwin: The Power of Place* (London: Jonathan Cape, 2002), 443–4.

26 Annie Besant, 'Notes on the Trial', *National Reformer* (1877), 250–1 (251).

27 Ibid.

28 Alison Winter, 'The Construction of Orthodoxies and Heterodoxies in the Early Victorian Life Sciences', in *Victorian Science in Context*, ed. by

Bernard Lightman (Chicago: University of Chicago Press, 1997), 24–50 (35 and 39).

29 See Adrian Desmond, *Archetypes and Ancestors: Palaeontology in Victorian London 1850–1875* (Chicago: University of Chicago Press, 1982), 92–3; and Adrian Desmond, *The Politics of Evolution: Morphology, Medicine, and Reform in Radical London* (Chicago: University of Chicago Press, 1989), 210–22.

30 See William B. Carpenter, 'Charles Darwin: His Life and Work', *Modern Review* 3 (1882), 500–24; and Roger Smith, 'The Human Significance of Biology: Carpenter, Darwin, and the *vera causa*', in *Nature and the Victorian Imagination*, ed. by U. C. Knoepflmacher and G. B. Tennyson (Berkeley: University of California Press, 1977), 216–30.

31 [Richard Owen], '[Review of] *Introduction to the Study of Foraminifera* by William B. Carpenter', *Athenaeum* (1863), 417–19 (418–19); 'Dr. Carpenter and his Reviewer', *Athenaeum* (1863), 461.

32 'Dr. Carpenter and his Reviewer', 461; Carpenter, 'Darwin', 500.

33 See Frederick Burkhardt and Sydney Smith (eds.), *A Calendar of the Correspondence of Charles Darwin, 1821–1882, with Supplement* (Cambridge: Cambridge University Press, 1994), letter 13681, p. 572 and passim.

34 Quoted in J. Estlin Carpenter, 'William Benjamin Carpenter', in William B. Carpenter, *Nature and Man: Essays Scientific and Philosophical* (London: Kegan, Paul, Trench, 1888), 3–152 (148).

35 Ibid., 16.

36 Desmond, *Politics of Evolution*, 221.

37 Quoted in Doris Langley Moore, *Ada, Countess of Lovelace: Byron's Legitimate Daughter* (London: John Murray, 1977), 202.

38 Quoted in Ibid., 209.

39 Carpenter, 'William Benjamin Carpenter', 29.

40 [Charles Bradlaugh and Annie Besant], *In the High Court of Justice. Queen's Bench Division, June 18th, 1877. The Queen v. Charles Bradlaugh and Annie Besant* (London: Freethought Publishing Company, [1877]), 125.

41 [James Campbell], *The Amatory Experiences of a Surgeon* (Moscow [London]: The Nihilists, 1881), 80 and 55.

42 Steven Marcus, *The Other Victorians: A Study of Sexuality and Pornography in Mid-Nineteenth Century England* (London: Weidenfeld and Nicolson, 1966), 241.

43 See Peter Wagner, 'The Discourse on Sex – or Sex as Discourse: Eighteenth-Century Medical and Paramedical Erotica', in *Sexual Underworlds of the Enlightenment*, ed. by G. S. Rousseau and Roy Porter (Manchester: Manchester University Press, 1987), 46–68. Lisa Z. Sigel, *Governing Pleasures: Pornography and Social Change in England, 1815–1914* (New Brunswick: Rutgers University Press, 2002), 51.

44 [Louis Jacolliot], *Untrodden Fields of Anthropology*, 2 vols. (Paris: Librairie des Bibliophiles, 1896), 1:vi–vii and 2:x and viii.

45 Coral Lansbury, 'Gynaecology, Pornography, and the Antivivisection Movement', *Victorian Studies* 28 (1985), 413–37.

46 George Eliot, *Middlemarch*, 4 vols. (Edinburgh: William Blackwood, 1871–2), 1:255–6.

47 Roy Porter and Lesley Hall, *The Facts of Life: The Creation of Sexual Knowledge in Britain, 1650–1950* (New Haven and London: Yale University Press, 1995), 153.

48 See Adrian Desmond, *Huxley: The Devil's Disciple* (London: Michael Joseph, 1994), 15–17.

49 '[Review of] *On the Curability of Certain Forms of Insanity, Epilepsy, Catalepsy, and Hysteria, in Females* by Baker Brown', *British Medical Journal* (1866), 438–40 (440).

50 'Clitoridectomy', *British Medical Journal* (1866), 664–5 (665).

51 Susan Stewart, *Crimes of Writing: Problems in the Containment of Representation* (New York: Oxford University Press, 1991), 235–6.

52 'Prosecution of Mr. Bradlaugh and Mrs. Annie Besant', *National Reformer* (1877), 257–64 (257).

53 Ibid., 260.

54 Ibid., 264.

55 Quoted in Carpenter, 'William Benjamin Carpenter', 67.

56 William B. Carpenter, *Principles of Human Physiology*, ed. by Henry Power, 8th edn. (London: J. & A. Churchill, 1876), 958.

57 Gillian Beer, *Darwin's Plots: Evolutionary Narrative in Darwin, George Eliot and Nineteenth-Century Fiction* (London: Routledge and Kegan Paul, 1983), 227.

58 'A Grave Social Problem', *British Medical Journal* (1881), 904–5 (904).

59 Carpenter, *Principles*, 958n.

60 [Lord Byron], *Don Juan* (London: Thomas Davison, 1819), 7 and 12.

61 See William B. Carpenter, *Principles of Human Physiology*, 5th edn. (London: John Churchill, 1855), 796–7.

62 'Prosecution of Mr. Bradlaugh', 264.

63 [Campbell], *Amatory Experiences*, 37.

64 'Prosecution of Mr. Bradlaugh', 260.

65 Kate Flint, *The Woman Reader 1837–1914* (Oxford: Clarendon Press, 1993), 85.

66 See Edward B. Aveling, 'At University College', *National Reformer* (1883), 67–9 (67); Edward Lane, 'Home-work for the Medical Missionary', *Medical Press and Circular* 18 n.s. (1875), 71–3 (72).

67 [Bradlaugh and Besant], *In the High Court of Justice*, 127.

68 Annie Besant, 'Does Not the Bible Come Within the Ruling of the Lord Chief Justice as to Obscene Literature?', *National Reformer* (1877), 546–7 (546).

69 Ibid., 546–7.

70 [Bradlaugh and Besant], *In the High Court of Justice*, 267.

71 Ibid., 209.

72 See Roberts, 'Morals, Art, and the Law', 622.

73 W. B. Carpenter to A. R. Wallace, 5 October 1877, Wallace Papers MS Add. 46439, British Library.

74 See James A. Secord, *Victorian Sensation: The Extraordinary Publication, Reception, and Secret Authorship of* Vestiges of the Natural History of Creation (Chicago: University of Chicago Press, 2000), 111–16 and 141–50.

75 [Bradlaugh and Besant], *In the High Court of Justice*, 205.

76 See, for instance, *The Times* (20 June 1877), 11.

77 [Bradlaugh and Besant], *In the High Court of Justice*, 229.

78 Hypatia Bradlaugh Bonner, *Charles Bradlaugh: A Record of his Life and Work*, 2 vols. (London: T. Fisher Unwin, 1902), 2:24.

79 Nead, *Victorian Babylon*, 151.

80 [Sydney Smith], 'Proceedings of the Society for the Suppression of Vice', *Edinburgh Review* 13 (1809), 333–43 (334).

81 'The Suppression of Vice', *Athenaeum* (1875), 720.

82 Carpenter, 'William Benjamin Carpenter', 143–4.

83 *Report of the Forty-Seventh Meeting of the British Association for the Advancement of Science* (London: John Murray, 1878), 229.

84 W. B. Carpenter to A. R. Wallace, 9 October 1877, Wallace Papers MS Add. 46439.

85 *Report of the Forty-Seventh Meeting of the British Association*, 229.

86 W. B. Carpenter to G. C. Robertson, 17 May 1877, Robertson Papers MS Add. 88, University College London Library; W. B. Carpenter to A. R. Wallace, 5 June 1877, Wallace Papers MS Add. 46439.

87 *Report of the Forty-Seventh Meeting of the British Association*, 229.

88 William B. Carpenter, 'The Morality of the Medical Profession', *Modern Review* 2 (1881), 489–532 (495).

89 Ibid., 527 and 532.

90 Ludmilla Jordanova, *Sexual Visions: Images of Gender in Science and Medicine between the Eighteenth and Twentieth Centuries* (London: Harvester Wheatsheaf, 1989), 63.

91 C. R. Darwin to [?] Truelove, 1 July 1878, DAR 202:89.

92 See Lucy Bland, *Banishing the Beast: English Feminism and Sexual Morality 1885–1914* (London: Penguin, 1995), 196.

93 See Mason, *Making of Victorian Sexual Attitudes*, 175–80.

94 See Porter and Hall, *Facts of Life*, 127–8.

95 See Angus McLaren, *Birth Control in Nineteenth-Century England* (London: Croom Helm, 1978), 130.

96 See Mason, *Making of Victorian Sexual Attitudes*, 180–1.

97 T. L. Nichols, *Human Physiology* (London: Trübner, 1872), 301.

98 Annie Besant, *The Law of Population* (London: Freethought Publishing Company, 1878), 33.

99 Carpenter, *Principles*, 8th edn., 959.

100 Ibid., 959–60.

101 Besant, *Law of Population*, 33.

102 Moore, *Ada*, 201.

103 Darwin to Bradlaugh, 6 June 1877, DAR 202:32.

104 Besant, *Law of Population*, 39.

105 Francis Darwin (ed.), *More Letters of Charles Darwin*, 2 vols. (London: John Murray, 1903), 2:50.

106 Besant, *Law of Population*, 39.

107 'Prosecution of Mr. Bradlaugh and Mrs. Annie Besant', *National Reformer* (1877), 401–14 (404).

108 Charles Darwin, *The Descent of Man, and Selection in Relation to Sex*, 2 vols. (London: John Murray, 1871), 1:176.

109 Ibid., 2:403.

110 See 'Prosecution of Mr. Bradlaugh', 412.

111 Ibid., 404.

112 Darwin, *Descent*, 1:134; [St George Mivart], 'Primitive Man: Tylor and Lubbock', *Quarterly Review* 137 (1874), 40–77 (70).

113 Darwin (ed.), *More Letters*, 2:50.

114 'Prosecution of Mr. Bradlaugh', 413.

115 Besant, *Law of Population*, 43.

116 Karl Pearson, *The Life, Letters and Labours of Francis Galton*, 3 vols. (Cambridge: Cambridge University Press, 1914–30), 2:111.

117 See Angelique Richardson, *Love and Eugenics in the Late Nineteenth Century: Rational Reproduction and the New Woman* (Oxford: Oxford University Press, 2003).

118 Bland, *Banishing the Beast*, 199.

119 See Evelleen Richards, 'Redrawing the Boundaries: Darwinian Science and Victorian Women Intellectuals', in *Victorian Science in Context*, ed. by Lightman, 119–42 (137).

120 'Prosecution of Mr. Bradlaugh', 413.

121 Adrian Desmond, *Huxley: Evolution's High Priest* (London: Michael Joseph, 1997), 146.

122 Edward B. Aveling, *Darwinism and Small Families* (London: Bradlaugh and Besant, 1882), 2.

123 Burkhardt *et al.* (eds.), *Correspondence of Charles Darwin*, 8:65.

124 Ibid., 6:416.

125 Browne, *Darwin*, 71.

126 See J. Miriam Benn, *The Predicament of Love* (London: Pluto Press, 1992), 26–7.

127 Quoted in ibid., 28; Mason, *Making of Victorian Sexual Attitudes*, 203.

128 Lane, 'Home-work for the Medical Missionary', 71–2.

129 Benn, *Predicament of Love*, 27.

130 Tomo Sato, 'E. W. Lane's Hydropathic Establishment at Moor Park', *Hitotsubashi Journal of Social Studies* 10 (1978), 45–59 (46).

131 Burkhardt *et al.* (eds.), *Correspondence of Charles Darwin*, 7:119.

132 Ibid., 6:407.

133 See Burkhardt and Smith (eds.), *Calendar of the Correspondence of Charles Darwin*, letter 10354, p. 443.

134 See James E. Strick, *Sparks of Life: Darwinism and the Victorian Debates over Spontaneous Generation* (Cambridge, MA: Harvard University Press, 2000), 119–23.

135 While *The Correspondence of Charles Darwin* states that John James Drysdale was Lady Elizabeth Drysdale's son, Sato and Benn claim that he was actually

the child of Lord Drysdale's second wife (Burkhardt *et al.* (eds.), 10:811; Sato, 'Lane's Hydropathic Establishment', 51; Benn, *Predicament of Love*, 25).

136 Mason, *Making of Victorian Sexual Attitudes*, 201–2.

137 [Herbert Spencer], 'A Theory of Population, Deduced from the General Law of Animal Fertility', *Westminster Review* 1 n.s. (1852), 468–501 (498).

138 [George Drysdale], *Physical, Sexual, and Natural Religion* (London: Edward Truelove, 1855), 82 and 338.

139 Sally Shuttleworth, *Charlotte Brontë and Victorian Psychology* (Cambridge: Cambridge University Press, 1996), 144.

140 [Drysdale], *Natural Religion*, 366.

141 Ibid., 353, 357 and 366.

142 Ibid., 270–1.

143 Mason, *Making of Victorian Sexual Attitudes*, 202.

144 Ibid., 210 and 184.

145 Charles Knowlton, *Fruits of Philosophy* (London: Freethought Publishing Company, 1877), vii.

146 See Edward Royle, *Radicals, Secularists and Republicans: Popular Freethought in Britain, 1866–1915* (Manchester: Manchester University Press, 1980), 18–19.

147 Quoted in Arnstein, *Bradlaugh Case*, 22.

148 M. Foster to C. Bradlaugh, 19 July [1890], Bradlaugh Papers, Bishopsgate Institute, London.

149 Bernard Lightman, 'Ideology, Evolution and Late Victorian Agnostic Popularizers', in *History, Humanity and Evolution*, ed. by James R. Moore (Cambridge: Cambridge University Press, 1989), 285–309 (301).

150 John Tyndall, 'Science and Man', *Fortnightly Review* 22 n.s. (1877), 593–617 (613–14).

151 See A. Gowans Whyte, *The Story of the R.P.A. 1899–1949* (London: Watts, 1949), 22.

152 Quoted in Desmond, *Huxley: Evolution's High Priest*, 118; G. J. Holyoake to L. Huxley, [1895?], Huxley Papers 18.220, Imperial College of Science, Technology, and Medicine Archives, London.

153 'Professor Huxley. A Character Sketch', *Agnostic Journal* 37 (1895), 1–2 (2).

154 See Lightman, 'Agnostic Popularizers', 303; and Desmond, *Huxley: Evolution's High Priest*, 145.

155 Quoted in Lewis S. Feuer, 'Is the "Darwin–Marx Correspondence" Authentic?', *Annals of Science* 32 (1975), 1–12 (2).

156 See James R. Moore, 'Freethought, Secularism, Agnosticism: The Case of Charles Darwin', in *Religion in Victorian Britain: Traditions*, ed. by Gerald Parsons (Manchester: Manchester University Press, 1988), 274–319 (309–13).

157 Quoted in Feuer, 'Darwin–Marx Correspondence', 2.

158 See Ralph Colp Jr., 'The Myth of the Darwin–Marx Letter', *History of Political Economy* 14 (1982), 461–82.

159 Quoted in Taylor, *Annie Besant*, 158.

160 T. H. Huxley to E. B. Aveling, 31 May 1883, Bradlaugh Papers.

161 See AM/C/125, UCL Council Papers, University College London Library.

162 See Feuer, 'Darwin–Marx Correspondence', 11–12.

163 Huxley, *Life*, 2:56.

164 'University College London', *National Reformer* (1883), 429; T. H. Huxley to G. C. Robertson, 10 July 1883, Robertson Papers MS Add. 88/12; Huxley, *Life*, 2:56–7.

165 See Aveling, 'At University College', 67–9.

166 Huxley, *Life*, 2:56–7.

167 Aveling, 'At University College', 67.

168 See ibid., 67–8.

169 Huxley to Robertson, 10 July 1883, Robertson Papers MS Add. 88/12.

170 Quoted in David Tribe, *President Charles Bradlaugh, M.P.* (London: Elek, 1971), 227.

171 Huxley to Robertson, 10 July 1883, Robertson Papers MS Add. 88/12.

172 Quoted in Tribe, *President Charles Bradlaugh*, 227.

173 Gordon S. Haight, *George Eliot and John Chapman, with Chapman's Diaries* (New Haven: Yale University Press, 1940), 131.

174 Quoted in Tribe, *President Charles Bradlaugh*, 227.

175 *The Times* (1 December 1890), 13. See Michael S. Helfand, 'T. H. Huxley's "Evolution and Ethics": The Politics of Evolution and the Evolution of Politics', *Victorian Studies* 20 (1977), 159–77 (170 and 174).

176 Huxley to Robertson, 10 July 1883, Robertson Papers MS Add. 88/12.

177 See Arnstein, *Bradlaugh Case*, 158–9.

178 Quoted in Desmond, *Huxley: Evolution's High Priest*, 146.

179 Bonner, *Charles Bradlaugh*, 2:128.

180 A. Besant to T. H. Huxley, 22 December 1883, Huxley Papers 10.307; Edward B. Aveling, 'The Messrs. Facing-Both-Ways of Science', *Agnostic Annual* 2 (1885), 41–5 (45).

181 Aveling, 'Messrs. Facing-Both-Ways', 41.

182 Huxley, *Life*, 1:323.

183 Quoted in Amy M. King, *Bloom: The Botanical Vernacular in the English Novel* (New York: Oxford University Press, 2003), 18; Londa Schiebinger, 'The Private Life of Plants: Sexual Politics in Carl Linnaeus and Erasmus Darwin', in *Science and Sensibility: Gender and Scientific Enquiry 1780–1945*, ed. by Marina Benjamin (Oxford: Basil Blackwell, 1991), 121–43 (130).

184 [Bradlaugh and Besant], *In the High Court of Justice*, 236.

185 See Mason, *Making of Victorian Sexual Attitudes*, 213.

186 Carpenter, 'Morality of the Medical Profession', 492–3.

187 Desmond, *Huxley: Evolution's High Priest*, 75.

188 See [Weissenfeld], *Judicial Scandals*, 97.

189 Quoted in Phyllis Grosskurth, *Havelock Ellis: A Biography* (London: Allen Lane, 1980), 194.

190 'The Police and the Press', *Review of Reviews* 18 (1898), 162.

191 See Grosskurth, *Havelock Ellis*, 200–1.

192 [Georg von Weissenfeld], 'Danger Ahead', *University Magazine* 10 (1898), 449–62 (449–50).

193 Ibid., 455; 'Police and the Press', 162.
194 Quoted in Grosskurth, *Havelock Ellis*, 196.
195 [Georg von Weissenfeld], *Darwin on Trial at the Old Bailey* (Watford: University Press, [1899]), 4. On Weissenfeld, see Grosskurth, *Havelock Ellis*, 202–3.
196 [Weissenfeld], *Darwin on Trial*, 14–15.
197 Ibid., 20 and 25.
198 Ibid., 35.
199 Ibid., 36.

NOTES TO CHAPTER FIVE

 1 See L. Clifford to A. Macmillan, 19 April 1879, Macmillan Archive MS Add. 54932, British Library; and L. Clifford to K. Pearson, 27 December 1924, Pearson Papers 661, University College London Library.
 2 John W. Bicknell (ed.), *Selected Letters of Leslie Stephen*, 2 vols. (London: Macmillan, 1996), 1:236.
 3 W. K. Clifford to H. Huxley, 25 June 1878, Huxley Papers 12.244, Imperial College of Science, Technology, and Medicine Archives, London.
 4 'Lectures and Essays', *Examiner* (1879), 1123–4 (1123); *The Times* (22 October 1879), 4.
 5 *Jewish Chronicle* (24 December 1897), 14.
 6 Leslie Stephen, *Life of Henry Fawcett* (London: Smith, Elder, 1885), 86.
 7 'The Late Professor Clifford', *National Reformer* (1879), 165; [William Hurrell Mallock], 'The Late Professor Clifford's *Essays*', *Edinburgh Review* 151 (1880), 474–511 (479).
 8 *The Times* (6 March 1879), 9.
 9 See Joan L. Richards, *Mathematical Visions: The Pursuit of Geometry in Victorian England* (London: Academic Press, 1988), 103–11.
10 See Bernard Lightman, *The Origins of Agnosticism: Victorian Unbelief and the Limits of Knowledge* (Baltimore: Johns Hopkins University Press, 1987), 171–2; and Helen Small, 'Science, Liberalism, and the Ethics of Belief: The *Contemporary Review* in 1877', in *Science Serialized: Representations of the Sciences in Nineteenth-Century Periodicals*, ed. by Geoffrey Cantor and Sally Shuttleworth (Cambridge, MA: MIT Press, 2004), 239–57 (240–3).
11 Bicknell (ed.), *Letters of Leslie Stephen*, 1:210.
12 See Stephen, *Henry Fawcett*, 286.
13 See F. Pollock to A. Macmillan, 4 April 1879, Macmillan Archive MS Add. 55083.
14 Lucy Clifford, 'A Remembrance of George Eliot', *Nineteenth Century* 74 (1913), 109–18 (116).
15 See Paul White, *Thomas Huxley: Making the 'Man of Science'* (Cambridge: Cambridge University Press, 2003), 6–31.
16 See Frederick Burkhardt and Sydney Smith (eds.), *A Calendar of the Correspondence of Charles Darwin, 1821–1882, with Supplement* (Cambridge: Cambridge University Press, 1994), letters 11886 and 11883a, pp. 502 and 521.

17 W. Kingdon Clifford, 'On Some Conditions of Mental Development', *Notices of the Proceedings at the Meetings of the Members of the Royal Institution of Great Britain* 5 (1866–9), 311–28 (328).

18 Quoted in Richards, *Mathematical Visions*, 131.

19 See 'On the Education of the People', *Notices of the Proceedings at the Meetings of the Members of the Royal Institution of Great Britain* 7 (1873–5), 314–15; 'The Ethics of Belief', *Contemporary Review* 29 (1877), 289–309 (295); and 'Right and Wrong: The Scientific Ground of Their Distinction', *Fortnightly Review* 18 n.s. (1875), 770–800 (775–6).

20 Moncure Daniel Conway, *Autobiography: Memories and Experiences*, 2 vols. (London: Cassell, 1904), 2:351.

21 W. K. Clifford to H. Huxley, 19 April 1876, Huxley Papers 12.242.

22 See W. K. Clifford to C. Bradlaugh, n.d., Bradlaugh Papers, Bishopsgate Institute, London; and W. K. Clifford to A. Besant, 24 October 1876, MS Misc. 3C, University College London Library.

23 Clifford to Besant, 24 October 1876, MS Misc. 3C.

24 Annie Besant, 'The Ethics of Religion', *National Reformer* (1877), 538–9 (538).

25 J. M. H. Munro, 'Professor Clifford's Essays', *National Reformer* (1879), 804–5 (804).

26 J. Morley to T. H. Huxley, 9 January 1876, Huxley Papers 23.24.

27 See Patricia Thomas Srebrnik, *Alexander Strahan, Victorian Publisher* (Ann Arbor: University of Michigan Press, 1986), 149–77; and Small, 'Science, Liberalism, and the Ethics of Belief', 248.

28 Clifford, 'Ethics of Belief', 299–300.

29 W. K. Clifford, 'The Unseen Universe', *Fortnightly Review* 17 n.s. (1875), 776–93 (779).

30 George Levine, 'Scientific Discourse as an Alternative to Faith', in *Victorian Faith in Crisis: Essays on Continuity and Change in Nineteenth-Century Religious Belief*, ed. by Richard J. Helmstadter and Bernard Lightman (London: Macmillan, 1990), 225–61 (255 and 257).

31 Philip E. Smith and Michael S. Helfand (eds.), *Oscar Wilde's Oxford Notebooks: A Portrait of Mind in the Making* (New York: Oxford University Press, 1989), 29–32.

32 Oscar Wilde, 'The True Function and Value of Criticism', *Nineteenth Century* 28 (1890), 123–47 (138).

33 Clifford, 'Some Conditions of Mental Development', 328.

34 Syllabus for 'The Relations between Science and Some Modern Poetry', 4 May 1873, Proceedings of the Sunday Lecture Society 1869–90, British Library 4355.df.17.

35 'Notes and News', *Academy* 7 (1875), 398–9 (398).

36 Roger W. Peattie (ed.), *Selected Letters of William Michael Rossetti* (University Park: Pennsylvania State University Press, 1990), 322.

37 Clifford, 'Unseen Universe', 791.

38 W. K. Clifford, 'Cosmic Emotion', *Nineteenth Century* 2 (1877), 411–29 (424).

39 A. C. Swinburne, *Songs Before Sunrise* (London: F. S. Ellis, 1871), 172.

40 Conway, *Autobiography*, 2:377–8.

41 [James Bucham Brown], 'Ethics and Aesthetics of Modern Poetry', *Cornhill Magazine* 37 (1878), 569–83 (583); St George Mivart, 'Contemporary Evolution', *Contemporary Review* 22 (1873), 595–614 (608).

42 [Joseph Alfred Hardcastle], 'The *New Republic* and Modern Philosophers', *Quarterly Review* 144 (1877), 515–39 (530).

43 [Richard Holt Hutton], 'Clifford's *Lectures and Essays*', *Spectator* (1879), 1411–14 (1412 and 1413–14).

44 [Mallock], 'Clifford's *Essays*', 483.

45 'Professor Clifford', *Fraser's Magazine* 20 n.s. (1879), 685–701 (697 and 695).

46 See Gillian Beer, 'Parable, Professionalization, and Literary Allusion in Victorian Scientific Writing', in *Open Fields: Science in Cultural Encounter* (Oxford: Clarendon Press, 1996), 196–215 (209); and Clifford, 'Unseen Universe', 776.

47 Oscar Wilde, 'The English Renaissance in Art', in *Lectures and Essays* (London: Methuen, 1909), 111–55 (116).

48 Frederick Pollock, 'William Kingdon Clifford', *Fortnightly Review* 25 n.s. (1879), 667–87 (670).

49 Ibid., 675.

50 Ibid., 676–7.

51 William Kingdon Clifford, *Lectures and Essays*, ed. by Leslie Stephen and Frederick Pollock, 2 vols. (London: Macmillan, 1879), 1:70.

52 Clifford, 'Unseen Universe', 781; *The Times* (22 October 1879), 4.

53 F. Pollock to A. Macmillan, 4 April 1879, Macmillan Archive MS Add. 55083.

54 L. Clifford to K. Pearson, 13 March 1885, Pearson Papers 661.

55 William Kingdon Clifford, *The Common Sense of the Exact Sciences* (London: Kegan Paul, Trench, 1885), viii.

56 [Thomas Spencer Baynes], 'Swinburne's *Poems*', *Edinburgh Review* 134 (1871), 71–99 (71–2).

57 Clifford, *Lectures and Essays*, 1:253n.

58 G. Chrystal, 'Clifford's Mathematical Papers', *Nature* 26 (1882), 217–19 (217).

59 Stefan Collini, *Public Moralists: Political Thought and Intellectual Life in Britain 1850–1930* (Oxford: Clarendon Press, 1991), 97.

60 See Crosbie Smith, *The Science of Energy: A Cultural History of Energy Physics in Victorian Britain* (London: Athlone Press, 1998), 170–91.

61 P. G. Tait, 'Clifford's Exact Sciences', *Nature* 32 (1885), 124–5 (124).

62 Annotated copy of Tait, 'Clifford's Exact Sciences', Pearson Papers 661.

63 L. Clifford to K. Pearson, 17 June 1885, Pearson Papers 661.

64 Clifford to Pearson, 18 June 1885, Pearson Papers 661.

65 Quoted in A. J. Meadows, *Science and Controversy: A Biography of Sir Norman Lockyer* (London: Macmillan, 1972), 37. In response to Pearson's letter of complaint, Tait replied: 'On reperusing my notice . . . I still think that it expresses what I meant to say.' 'Clifford's Common Sense of the Exact Sciences', *Nature* 32 (1885), 196.

66 Marysa Demoor, 'Self-fashioning at the Turn of the Century: The Discursive Life of Lucy Clifford (1846–1929)', *Journal of Victorian Culture* 4 (1999), 276–91.

67 C. K. Paul to L. Clifford, 19 June 1885, Pearson Papers 661.

68 See Marysa Demoor, 'Where No Woman Fears to Tread: The Gossip Column in the *Athenaeum*, 1885–1901', *Barcelona English Language and Literature Studies* 7 (1996), 33–42.

69 'Literary Gossip', *Athenaeum* (1886), 779.

70 The editor's 'marked file' of the *Athenaeum*, which identities nearly all of the anonymous contributors to the journal between 1830 and 1919, is held at City University Library, London.

71 'Science Gossip', *Athenaeum* (1886), 849.

72 [Karl Pearson], '[Review of] *The Elements of Dynamic* by W. K. Clifford', *Athenaeum* (1887), 86–7.

73 Ibid., 86.

74 L. Clifford to K. Pearson, 24 January 1887, Pearson Papers 661.

75 See Judith R. Walkowitz, *City of Dreadful Delight: Narratives of Sexual Danger in Late-Victorian London* (London: Virago, 1992), 135–69.

76 Clifford to Pearson, 22 November 1886, Pearson Papers 661.

77 See M. Blind to K. Pearson, 6 January 1887, Pearson Papers 638/6, University College London Library.

78 Clifford to Pearson, 22 November 1886, Pearson Papers 661.

79 Bertrand Russell and Patricia Russell (eds.), *The Amberley Papers: The Letters and Diaries of Lord and Lady Amberley*, 2 vols. (London: Hogarth Press, 1937), 2:167.

80 Alexander J. Ellis, *On Discussion as a Means of Eliciting Truth* (London: London Dialectical Society, 1879), 13; Michael Mason, *The Making of Victorian Sexual Attitudes* (Oxford: Oxford University Press, 1994), 199.

81 Anne Taylor, *Annie Besant: A Biography* (Oxford: Oxford University Press, 1992), 111.

82 Quoted in Charles Maurice Davies, *Heterodox London*, 2 vols. (London: Tinsley, 1874), 1:181.

83 Conway, *Autobiography*, 2:351.

84 These details are provided on the back wrapper of W. C. Coupland, *The Principle of Individual Liberty* (London: London Dialectical Society, 1878).

85 Clifford to Pearson, 22 November 1886, Pearson Papers 661.

86 Coupland, *Individual Liberty*, 33.

87 [George Drysdale], *Physical, Sexual, and Natural Religion* (London: Edward Truelove, 1855), 355 and 359.

88 Ibid., 367.

89 Clifford to Pearson, 22 November 1886, Pearson Papers 661.

90 Clifford to Pearson, 20 December 1886, Pearson Papers 661.

91 St G. Mivart to T. H. Huxley, 24 December 1874, Huxley Papers 22.267.

92 W. K. Clifford, 'A Modern "Symposium": The Influence upon Morality of a Decline in Religious Belief', *Nineteenth Century* 1 (1877), 353–8 (358); Clifford to Pearson, 22 November 1886, Pearson Papers 661.

93 [William Hurrell Mallock], *The New Republic, or Culture, Faith, and Philosophy in an English Country House*, 2 vols. (London: Chatto and Windus, 1877), 2:99.

94 Ibid., 1:24 and 1:205.

95 Ibid., 2:99–100 and 1:90.

96 Ibid., 1:89–90.

97 [Drysdale], *Natural Religion*, 271 and 409.

98 Russell and Russell (eds.), *Amberley Papers*, 2:116–17.

99 [Mallock], 'Clifford's *Essays*', 482.

100 [Hardcastle], '*New Republic*', 526–7 and 530.

101 See Russell and Russell (eds.), *Amberley Papers*, 2:166–237.

102 F. Pollock to F. Macmillan, 26 May 1886, Macmillan Archive MS Add. 55083.

103 Bicknell (ed.), *Letters of Leslie Stephen*, 2:344; Clifford to Pearson, 24 January 1887, Pearson Papers 661.

104 Clifford to Pearson, 24 January 1887, Pearson Papers 661.

105 See Cecil Y. Lang (ed.), *The Swinburne Letters*, 6 vols. (New Haven: Yale University Press, 1959–62), 6:243; Blind to Pearson, 6 January 1887, Pearson Papers 638/6.

106 'P.' [Karl Pearson], 'Socialism and Sex', *To-Day* 7 (1887), 42–55 (53).

107 Ibid., 53n.

108 Clifford to Pearson, 10 February 1888, Pearson Papers 10/32.

109 William Samuel Lilly, *On Right and Wrong* (London: Chapman and Hall, 1890), 209–10.

110 Ibid., vii, 4 and 7.

111 Alfred W. Benn, '[Review of] *On Right and Wrong* by W. S. Lilly', *Academy* 38 (1890), 33–4 (33).

112 Clifford to Pearson, 24 January 1887, Pearson Papers 661.

113 Clifford to Pearson, 13 March 1885, Pearson Papers 661.

114 Sarah A. Tooley, 'Some Women Novelists', *Woman at Home* 6 (1897), 161–211 (170); Anne Oliver Bell (ed.), *The Diary of Virginia Woolf*, 5 vols. (London: Hogarth Press, 1977–84), 2:12.

115 Clifford to Pearson, 10 February 1888, Pearson Papers 10/32.

116 Clifford, 'Unseen Universe', 782.

117 [Lucy Clifford], 'Lost', *Macmillan's Magazine* 44 (1881), 48–52 (49).

118 Marysa Demoor and Monty Chisholm (eds.), *'Bravest of Women and Finest of Friends': Henry James's Letters to Lucy Clifford* (Victoria, BC: University of Victoria, 1999), 108.

119 Ralph Barton Perry (ed.), *The Thought and Character of William James*, 2 vols. (London: Oxford University Press, 1935), 1:591.

120 Clifford to Pearson, 19 January 1925, Pearson Papers 661.

121 See Lucy Clifford, 'Victoria, Lady Welby. An Ethical Mystic', *Hibbert Journal* 23 (1924), 101–6; and Clifford to Pearson, 22 November 1886, Pearson Papers 661.

122 Irene Cooper Willis (ed.), *Vernon Lee's Letters* (London: privately printed, 1937), 144.

123 See L. Clifford to F. Macmillan, 10 May 1904, Macmillan Archive MS Add. 54932.
124 See Clifford, 'Unseen Universe', 779–80.

NOTES TO CHAPTER SIX

1 Edward Dowden, 'The Scientific Movement and Literature', *Contemporary Review* 30 (1877), 558–78 (573).
2 Ibid., 577–8.
3 Ibid., 578.
4 Ibid., 576.
5 Ibid., 559 and 576.
6 Ibid., 578.
7 Edward Dowden, 'French Aesthetics', *Contemporary Review* 1 (1866), 279–310 (288).
8 Algernon Charles Swinburne, *William Blake: A Critical Essay* (London: J. C. Hotten, 1868), 91; [Walter Pater], 'Poems by William Morris', *Westminster Review* 34 n.s. (1868), 300–12 (312).
9 See L. M. Findlay, 'The Introduction of the Phrase "Art for Art's Sake" into English', *Notes and Queries* 20 n.s. (1973), 246–8.
10 Tess Cosslett, *The 'Scientific Movement' and Victorian Literature* (Brighton: Harvester Press, 1982), 3.
11 See, for instance, George Levine, 'One Culture: Science and Literature', in *One Culture: Essays in Science and Literature*, ed. by George Levine (Madison: University of Wisconsin Press, 1987), 3–32.
12 Richard St John Tyrwhitt, 'The Greek Spirit in Modern Literature', *Contemporary Review* 29 (1877), 552–66 (563 and 558).
13 Ibid., 562 and 557.
14 See Richard Dellamora, *Masculine Desire: The Sexual Politics of Victorian Aestheticism* (Chapel Hill: University of North Carolina Press, 1990), 162–3.
15 Tyrwhitt, 'Greek Spirit', 555.
16 Ibid., 554.
17 Ibid., 560 and 558.
18 See Jay Wood Claiborne, 'Two Secretaries: The Letters of John Ruskin to Charles Augustus Howell and the Rev. Richard St John Tyrwhitt', unpublished PhD thesis, University of Texas (1969), 160–74.
19 John Ruskin, *Modern Painters vol. II*, 2nd edn., 2 vols. (Orpington: George Allen, 1883), 1:21.
20 Ibid., 1:22, 26 and xv.
21 John Ruskin, 'The Three Colours of Pre-Raphaelitism', *Nineteenth Century* 4 (1878), 1072–82 (1072).
22 See Paul Sawyer, 'Ruskin and Tyndall: The Poetry of Matter and the Poetry of Spirit', in *Victorian Science and Victorian Values: Literary Perspectives*, ed. by James Paradis and Thomas Postlewait (New Brunswick: Rutgers University Press, 1985), 217–46.

23 See Claiborne, 'Two Secretaries', 344–5. Richard St John Tyrwhitt, 'Hellenic and Christian Views of Beauty', *Contemporary Review* 36 (1880), 474–91 (481).
24 Tyrwhitt, 'Hellenic and Christian Views', 482.
25 Algernon Charles Swinburne, *Poems and Ballads* (London: Edward Moxon, 1866), 189.
26 Tyrwhitt, 'Hellenic and Christian Views', 480.
27 Tyrwhitt, 'Greek Spirit', 563.
28 Ibid., 562.
29 T. H. Huxley, 'Scientific Education', *Macmillan's Magazine* 20 (1869), 177–84 (180–1 and 183).
30 Ibid., 183.
31 [Robert Buchanan], '[Review of] *Poems and Ballads* by Algernon Charles Swinburne', *Athenaeum* (1866), 137–8.
32 T. H. Huxley, 'Administrative Nihilism', *Fortnightly Review* 10 n.s. (1871), 525–43 (543); [John Morley], 'Mr. Swinburne's New Poems', *Saturday Review* 22 (1866), 145–7 (145 and 147).
33 James G. Paradis, *T. H. Huxley: Man's Place in Nature* (Lincoln: University of Nebraska Press, 1978), 173.
34 T. H. Huxley, 'Joseph Priestley', *Macmillan's Magazine* 30 (1874), 473–85 (480).
35 [Edwin Paxton Hood], 'Mr. Swinburne, his Crimes and Critics', *Eclectic Review* 124 (1866), 493–508 (496 and 505); [Thomas Spencer Baynes], 'Darwin on Expression', *Edinburgh Review* 137 (1873), 492–528 (494).
36 Ronald W. Clark, *The Huxleys* (London: William Heinemann, 1968), 111.
37 W. S. Lilly, 'Materialism and Morality', *Fortnightly Review* 40 n.s. (1886), 575–94 (583).
38 Ibid., 583.
39 T. H. Huxley, 'Science and Morals', *Fortnightly Review* 40 n.s. (1886), 788–802 (792–3).
40 Ibid., 788.
41 Dennis Denisoff, *Aestheticism and Sexual Parody 1840–1940* (Cambridge: Cambridge University Press, 2001), 25; see also Thaïs E. Morgan, 'Mixed Metaphor, Mixed Gender: Swinburne and the Victorian Critics', *Victorian Newsletter* 73 (1988), 16–19.
42 Huxley, 'Science and Morals', 788.
43 See Adrian Desmond, *Huxley: The Devil's Disciple* (London: Michael Joseph, 1994), 214.
44 T. H. Huxley, 'Science and Art in Relation to Education', in *Science and Education: Collected Essays*, 9 vols. (London: Macmillan, 1893), 3:160–88 (178–9).
45 Francis Darwin (ed.), *The Life and Letters of Charles Darwin*, 3 vols. (London: John Murray, 1887), 1:100–2.
46 Oscar Wilde, 'The Soul of Man under Socialism', *Fortnightly Review* 49 n.s. (1891), 292–319 (306).
47 W. S. Lilly, 'The Province of Physics', *Fortnightly Review* 41 n.s. (1887), 276–93 (277–8).

48 T. H. Huxley, 'Yeast', *Contemporary Review* 19 (1872), 23–36 (31).

49 [Charles Bradlaugh and Annie Besant], *In the High Court of Justice. Queen's Bench Division, June 18th, 1877. The Queen v. Charles Bradlaugh and Annie Besant* (London: Freethought Publishing Company, [1877]), 230; A. C. Swinburne, 'The Suppression of Vice', *Athenaeum* (1875), 720.

50 Quoted in Philip McEvansoneya, '"A Libel in Paint": Religious and Artistic Controversy around P. H. Calderon's *The Renunciation of Saint Elizabeth of Hungary*', *Journal of Victorian Culture* 1 (1996), 254–79 (259).

51 *The Times* (16 May 1891), 9.

52 McEvansoneya, 'A Libel in Paint', 265–6.

53 *The Times* (20 May 1891), 13.

54 See Gillian Beer, 'Parable, Professionalization, and Literary Allusion in Victorian Scientific Writing', in *Open Fields: Science in Cultural Encounter* (Oxford: Clarendon Press, 1996), 196–215 (211–12). Leonard Huxley, *Life and Letters of Thomas Henry Huxley*, 2 vols. (London: Macmillan, 1900), 2:338.

55 Quoted in Wilfrid Ward, 'Thomas Henry Huxley: A Reminiscence', *Nineteenth Century* 40 (1896), 274–92 (286–7).

56 Walter Pater, 'The School of Giorgione', *Fortnightly Review* 22 n.s. (1877), 526–38 (528).

57 T. H. Huxley, 'Universities: Actual and Ideal', *Contemporary Review* 23 (1874), 657–79 (665).

58 Paradis, *Huxley*, 192.

59 Huxley, 'Universities', 665; Matthew Arnold, *Culture and Anarchy* (London: Smith, Elder, 1869), 163.

60 Walter Pater, *Studies in the History of the Renaissance* (London: Macmillan, 1873), 213.

61 Quoted in Ward, 'Huxley', 282.

62 William Morris, *The Earthly Paradise* (London: F. S. Ellis, 1868), 2.

63 Ibid., 215.

64 [Pater], 'Poems by William Morris', 309 and 312.

65 Edward B. Aveling, 'The Messrs. Facing-Both-Ways of Science', *Agnostic Annual* 2 (1885), 41–5 (41).

66 T. H. Huxley, 'The School Boards', *Contemporary Review* 16 (1870), 1–15 (13); Ernst Haeckel, *Freedom in Science and Teaching* (London: C. Kegan Paul, 1879), xvii.

67 W. Earl Hodgson, 'The Immorality of Evolutionary Ethics', *National Review* 22 (1893), 46–58 (52).

68 W. Earl Hodgson, *Unrest; or, The Newer Republic* (London: W. H. Allen, 1887), 49–50.

69 Hodgson, 'Immorality', 58.

70 Daniel Pick, *Faces of Degeneration: A European Disorder, c. 1848–c. 1918* (Cambridge: Cambridge University Press, 1989), 7.

71 Ibid., 8.

72 Allon White, *The Uses of Obscurity: The Fiction of Early Modernism* (London: Routledge, 1981), 43.

73 Stephen Arata, *Fictions of Loss in the Victorian Fin de Siècle* (Cambridge: Cambridge University Press, 1996), 18.

74 Quoted in Eugene L. Stelzig, 'Romantic Subjectivity: Disease or Fortunate Fall?', in *English and German Romanticism: Cross Currents and Controversies*, ed. by James Pipkin (Heidelberg: Carl Winter Universitätsverlag, 1985), 153–68 (153).

75 See Arata, *Fictions of Loss*, 18.

76 Cesare Lombroso, *The Man of Genius* (London: Walter Scott, 1891), 359.

77 Max Nordau, *Degeneration* (London: William Heinemann, 1895), vii–viii.

78 Ibid., 94 and 91.

79 Helen Small, '"In the Guise of Science": Literature and the Rhetoric of Nineteenth-Century English Psychiatry', *History of the Human Sciences* 7 (1994), 27–55 (44).

80 Elaine Showalter, *The Female Malady: Women, Madness, and English Culture, 1830–1980* (London: Virago, 1987), 117.

81 Henry Maudsley, *The Physiology and Pathology of the Mind* (London: Macmillan, 1867), 185–6.

82 Henry Maudsley, *Body and Will* (London: Kegan Paul, 1883), 325.

83 Ibid., 326.

84 Ibid., 327.

85 Ibid., 328.

86 Henry Maudsley, *Shakespeare: 'Testimonied in his Own Bringingsforth'* (London: John Bale, 1905), 39.

87 Thomas Maitland [Robert Buchanan], 'The Fleshly School of Poetry', *Contemporary Review* 18 (1871), 334–50 (337); see Arata, *Fictions of Loss*, 13.

88 [Buchanan], 'Fleshly School', 335 and 336.

89 See Linda Dowling, *Language and Decadence in the Victorian Fin de Siècle* (Princeton: Princeton University Press, 1986), 176–8; and Morgan, 'Mixed Metaphor', 17.

90 [Thomas Spencer Baynes], 'Swinburne's *Poems*', *Edinburgh Review* 134 (1871), 71–99 (75).

91 Ibid., 71, 75 and 85.

92 See, in particular, Showalter, *Female Malady*, 122–5.

93 Maudsley, *Body and Will*, 326–7.

94 Nordau, *Degeneration*, 3.

95 William Thomson, 'On the Age of the Sun's Heat', *Macmillan's Magazine* 5 (1862), 388–93 (392).

96 [Alfred Austin], 'The Poetry of the Period', *Temple Bar* 26 (1869), 457–74 (473).

97 [Buchanan], 'Fleshly School', 335.

98 Stefan Collini, *Public Moralists: Political Thought and Intellectual Life in Britain 1850–1930* (Oxford: Clarendon Press, 1991), 107.

99 [Baynes], 'Swinburne's *Poems*', 74.

100 Maudsley, *Body and Will*, 328.

101 Ruskin, *Modern Painters*, 2nd edn., 1:36–7.

102 Lombroso, *Man of Genius*, 5; [Buchanan], 'Fleshly School', 337.

103 Robert A. Nye, *Crime, Madness, and Politics in Modern France: The Medical Concept of National Decline* (Princeton: Princeton University Press, 1984), 48.

104 Ibid., 331.

105 Lombroso, *Man of Genius*, 359, vi, 8, 33, 356–7 and 353.

106 See Gillian Beer, *Darwin's Plots: Evolutionary Narrative in Darwin, George Eliot and Nineteenth-Century Fiction* (London: Routledge and Kegan Paul, 1983), 212.

107 See Frederick Burkhardt and Sydney Smith (eds.), *A Calendar of the Correspondence of Charles Darwin, 1821–1882, with Supplement* (Cambridge: Cambridge University Press, 1994), letters 6749, 6750 and 6752, p. 298. Charles Darwin, *The Descent of Man, and Selection in Relation to Sex*, 2 vols. (London: John Murray, 1871), 1:59; Henry Maudsley, 'Insanity and its Treatment', *Journal of Mental Science* 17 (1871), 311–34 (311).

108 'Our Monthly Parcel of Books', *Review of Reviews* 12 (1895), 183–5 (183).

109 William Greenslade, *Degeneration, Culture and the Novel 1880–1940* (Cambridge: Cambridge University Press, 1994), 120.

110 Nordau, *Degeneration*, 317.

111 Talia Schaffer, '"A Wilde Desire Took Me": The Homoerotic History of *Dracula*', *ELH* 61 (1994), 381–425 (398); Bram Stoker, *Dracula* (Westminster: A. Constable, 1897), 352.

112 See Pick, *Faces of Degeneration*, 171–2; and Schaffer, 'Wilde Desire', 408.

113 Stoker, *Dracula*, 219 and 352.

114 Ibid., 249.

115 H. G. Wells, *The Time Machine* (London: William Heinemann, 1895), 36.

116 Ibid., 54.

117 Harry M. Geduld (ed.), *The Definitive Time Machine: A Critical Edition of H. G. Wells's Scientific Romance* (Bloomington: Indiana University Press, 1987), 21.

118 Thomas H. Huxley, *Evolution and Ethics* (London: Macmillan, 1894), 6 and 13.

119 Ibid., 42.

120 Wells, *Time Machine*, 54.

121 Ibid., 40; Huxley, *Evolution and Ethics*, 9.

122 Harold Bloom, *The Anxiety of Influence: A Theory of Poetry* (New York: Oxford University Press, 1973), 7, 14 and 42.

123 Robert M. Young, 'Natural Theology, Victorian Periodicals, and the Fragmentation of a Common Context', in *Darwin's Metaphor: Nature's Place in Victorian Culture* (Cambridge: Cambridge University Press, 1985), 126–63 (127–8 and 156); Levine, 'One Culture', 5–6.

124 Theodore M. Porter, 'Historicizing the Two Cultures', *History of Science* 43 (2005), 109–14 (109).

125 Helen Small, *Love's Madness: Medicine, the Novel, and Female Insanity 1800–1865* (Oxford: Clarendon Press, 1996), viii. For an earlier critique of the 'One

Culture' model, see E. S. Shaffer, 'The Sphinx and the Muses: The Third Culture', *Comparative Criticism* 13 (1991), xv–xxix.

126 Paul White, *Thomas Huxley: Making the 'Man of Science'* (Cambridge: Cambridge University Press, 2003), 98–9.

127 Linda Dowling, *The Vulgarization of Art: The Victorians and Aesthetic Democracy* (Charlottesville: University Press of Virginia, 1996), 51.

128 Thomas F. Gieryn, *Cultural Boundaries of Science: Credibility on the Line* (Chicago: University of Chicago Press, 1999), x and 23.

129 Ibid., 62.

Bibliography

Unattributed periodical articles, newspaper reports, and cartoons from *Punch* and *Fun* have not been included in this bibliography; full references to these sources are given in the endnotes for individual chapters.

UNPUBLISHED MATERIALS

Bradlaugh Papers, Bishopsgate Institute, London.
Claiborne, Jay Wood, 'Two Secretaries: The Letters of John Ruskin to Charles Augustus Howell and the Rev. Richard St John Tyrwhitt', unpublished PhD thesis, University of Texas (1969).
Darwin Manuscript Collection, Cambridge University Library, Cambridge.
Huxley Papers, Imperial College of Science, Technology, and Medicine Archives, London.
Macmillan Archive, British Library, London.
'Marked File' of the *Athenaeum*, City University Library, London.
Pearson Papers, University College London Library, London.
Proceedings of the Sunday Lecture Society 1869–90, British Library, London.
Robertson Papers, University College London Library, London.
Tyndall Papers, British Library, London.
Tyndall Papers, Royal Institution of Great Britain, London.
UCL Council Papers, University College London Library, London.
Wallace Papers, British Library, London.

PUBLISHED WORKS

Anon., *The Value of Life: A Reply to Mr Mallock's Essay 'Is Life Worth Living?'* (New York: G. P. Puttnam's Sons, 1879).
Anderson, Patricia, *The Printed Image and the Transformation of Popular Culture 1790–1860* (Oxford: Clarendon Press, 1991).
Arata, Stephen, *Fictions of Loss in the Victorian Fin de Siècle* (Cambridge: Cambridge University Press, 1996).
Arnold, Matthew, 'Pagan and Christian Religious Sentiment', *Cornhill Magazine* 9 (1864), 422–35.

Culture and Anarchy (London: Smith, Elder, 1869).

'Numbers', *Nineteenth Century* 15 (1884), 669–85.

Arnstein, Walter L., *The Bradlaugh Case: A Study in Late Victorian Opinion and Politics* (Oxford: Clarendon Press, 1965).

Auerbach, Nina, *Woman and the Demon: The Life of a Victorian Myth* (Cambridge, MA: Harvard University Press, 1982).

[Austin, Alfred], 'The Poetry of the Period', *Temple Bar* 26 (1869), 457–74.

Aveling, Edward B., 'At University College', *National Reformer* (1883), 67–9.

Darwinism and Small Families (London: Bradlaugh and Besant, 1882).

'The Messrs. Facing-Both-Ways of Science', *Agnostic Annual* 2 (1885), 41–5.

Bailey, Peter, 'Parasexuality and Glamour: The Victorian Barmaid as Cultural Prototype', *Gender and History* 2 (1990), 148–72.

Barton, Ruth, 'Evolution: The Whitworth Gun in Huxley's War for the Liberation of Science from Theology', in *The Wider Domain of Evolutionary Thought*, ed. by David Oldroyd and Ian Langham (Dordrecht: Reidel, 1983), 261–87.

'John Tyndall, Pantheist: A Rereading of the Belfast Address', *Osiris* 2nd Ser. 3 (1987), 111–34.

'"Men of Science": Language, Identity and Professionalization in the Mid-Victorian Scientific Community', *History of Science* 41 (2003), 73–119.

[Baynes, Thomas Spencer], 'Swinburne's *Poems*', *Edinburgh Review* 134 (1871), 71–99.

'Darwin on *Expression*', *Edinburgh Review* 137 (1873), 492–528.

Beer, Gillian, *Darwin's Plots: Evolutionary Narrative in Darwin, George Eliot and Nineteenth-Century Fiction* (London: Routledge and Kegan Paul, 1983).

Open Fields: Science in Cultural Encounter (Oxford: Clarendon Press, 1996).

Bell, Anne Oliver, ed., *The Diary of Virginia Woolf*, 5 vols. (London: Hogarth Press, 1977–84).

Bender, Bert, *The Descent of Love: Darwin and the Theory of Sexual Selection in American Fiction, 1871–1926* (Philadelphia: University of Pennsylvania Press, 1996).

Benn, Alfred W., '[Review of] *On Right and Wrong* by W. S. Lilly', *Academy* 38 (1890), 33–4.

Benn, J. Miriam, *The Predicament of Love* (London: Pluto Press, 1992).

Besant, Annie, 'Notes on the Trial', *National Reformer* (1877), 250–1.

'The Ethics of Religion', *National Reformer* (1877), 538–9.

'Does Not the Bible Come Within the Ruling of the Lord Chief Justice as to Obscene Literature?', *National Reformer* (1877), 546–7.

The Law of Population (London: Freethought Publishing Company, 1878).

Bevington, L. S., 'Modern Atheism and Mr. Mallock', *Nineteenth Century* 6 (1879), 585–603.

Bicknell, John W., ed., *Selected Letters of Leslie Stephen*, 2 vols. (London: Macmillan, 1996).

[Blake, Carter], 'Professor Huxley on *Man's Place in Nature*', *Edinburgh Review* 117 (1863), 541–69.

Bland, Lucy, *Banishing the Beast: English Feminism and Sexual Morality 1885–1914* (London: Penguin, 1995).

Blinderman, Charles S., 'Huxley, Pater and Protoplasm', *Journal of the History of Ideas* 43 (1982), 477–86.

Bloom, Harold, *The Anxiety of Influence: A Theory of Poetry* (New York: Oxford University Press, 1973).

Bonner, Hypatia Bradlaugh, *Charles Bradlaugh: A Record of his Life and Work*, 2 vols. (London: T. Fisher Unwin, 1902).

[Bradlaugh, Charles, and Annie Besant], *In the High Court of Justice. Queen's Bench Division, June 18th, 1877. The Queen v. Charles Bradlaugh and Annie Besant* (London: Freethought Publishing Company, [1877]).

Brantlinger, Patrick, *Dark Vanishings: Discourse on the Extinction of Primitive Races, 1800–1930* (Ithaca: Cornell University Press, 2003).

Brockhaus, Christoph, and Hans Albert Peters, *Alfred Kubin: Das zeichnerische Frühwerk bis 1904* (Baden-Baden: Kunsthalle Baden-Baden, 1977).

Brown, Beverly, 'Troubled Vision: Legal Understandings of Obscenity', *New Formations* 19 (1993), 29–44.

[Brown, James Bucham], 'Ethics and Aesthetics of Modern Poetry', *Cornhill Magazine* 37 (1878), 569–83.

Browne, Janet, *Charles Darwin: The Power of Place* (London: Jonathan Cape, 2002).

[Buchanan, Robert], '[Review of] *Poems and Ballads* by Algernon Charles Swinburne', *Athenaeum* (1866), 137–8.

'The Fleshly School of Poetry', *Contemporary Review* 18 (1871), 334–50.

Buchanan, Robert, *The Fleshly School of Poetry and Other Phenomena of the Day* (London: Strahan, 1872).

'Lucretius and Modern Materialism', *New Quarterly Magazine* 6 (1876), 1–30.

Burkhardt, Frederick H., *et al.*, eds., *The Correspondence of Charles Darwin*, 13 vols. (Cambridge: Cambridge University Press, 1983–).

Burkhardt, Frederick, and Sydney Smith, eds., *A Calendar of the Correspondence of Charles Darwin, 1821–1882, with Supplement* (Cambridge: Cambridge University Press, 1994).

Burton, Richard F., 'Notes on Waitz's *Anthropology*', *Anthropological Review* 2 (1864), 233–50.

The Book of the Thousand Nights and a Night, 16 vols. (Benares [London]: Kamashastra Society, 1885–8).

[Byron, Lord], *Don Juan* (London: Thomas Davison, 1819).

Caldwell, Janis McLarren, *Literature and Medicine in Nineteenth-Century Britain: From Mary Shelley to George Eliot* (Cambridge: Cambridge University Press, 2004).

[Campbell, James], *The Amatory Experiences of a Surgeon* (Moscow [London]: The Nihilists, 1881).

Campbell, Lewis, and William Garnett, eds., *The Life of James Clerk Maxwell* (London: Macmillan, 1882).

Carpenter, William Benjamin, *Principles of Human Physiology*, 5th edn. (London: John Churchill, 1855).

Principles of Human Physiology, ed. by Henry Power, 8th edn. (London: J. & A. Churchill, 1876).

'The Morality of the Medical Profession', *Modern Review* 2 (1881), 489–532.

'Charles Darwin: His Life and Work', *Modern Review* 3 (1882), 500–24.

Nature and Man: Essays Scientific and Philosophical, ed. by J. Estlin Carpenter (London: Kegan, Paul, Trench, 1888).

[Casey, James], *Tyndall and Materialism and Gladstone and the Vatican Decrees. Two Epistles in Verse* (Dublin: James Duffy, 1875).

Chaillu, Paul B. Du, *Explorations and Adventures in Equatorial Africa* (London: John Murray, 1861).

[Chapman, John], 'Equatorial Africa, and its Inhabitants', *Westminster Review* 20 n.s. (1861), 137–87.

Christiansen, Rupert, *Tales of the New Babylon: Paris 1869–1875* (London: Sinclair-Stevenson, 1994).

Chrystal, George, 'Clifford's Mathematical Papers', *Nature* 26 (1882), 217–19.

Clark, Ronald W., *The Huxleys* (London: William Heinemann, 1968).

[Clifford, Lucy], 'Lost', *Macmillan's Magazine* 44 (1881), 48–52.

Clifford, Lucy, 'A Remembrance of George Eliot', *Nineteenth Century* 74 (1913), 109–18.

'Victoria, Lady Welby. An Ethical Mystic', *Hibbert Journal* 23 (1924), 101–6.

Clifford, William Kingdon, 'On Some Conditions of Mental Development', *Notices of the Proceedings at the Meetings of the Members of the Royal Institution of Great Britain* 5 (1866–9), 311–28.

'On the Education of the People', *Notices of the Proceedings at the Meetings of the Members of the Royal Institution of Great Britain* 7 (1873–5), 314–15.

'The First and Last Catastrophe', *Fortnightly Review* 17 n.s. (1875), 465–84.

'The Unseen Universe', *Fortnightly Review* 17 n.s. (1875), 776–93.

'Right and Wrong: The Scientific Ground of Their Distinction', *Fortnightly Review* 18 n.s. (1875), 770–800.

'A Modern "Symposium": The Influence upon Morality of a Decline in Religious Belief', *Nineteenth Century* 1 (1877), 353–8.

'Cosmic Emotion', *Nineteenth Century* 2 (1877), 411–29.

'The Ethics of Belief', *Contemporary Review* 29 (1877), 289–309.

'The Ethics of Religion', *Fortnightly Review* 22 n.s. (1877), 35–52.

Lectures and Essays, ed. by Leslie Stephen and Frederick Pollock, 2 vols. (London: Macmillan, 1879).

The Common Sense of the Exact Sciences (London: Kegan Paul, Trench, 1885).

Collini, Stefan, *Public Moralists: Political Thought and Intellectual Life in Britain 1850–1930* (Oxford: Clarendon Press, 1991).

Colp Jr., Ralph, 'The Myth of the Darwin–Marx Letter', *History of Political Economy* 14 (1982), 461–82.

Conway, Moncure Daniel, *Autobiography: Memories and Experiences*, 2 vols. (London: Cassell, 1904).

Cooter, Roger, and Stephen Pumfrey, 'Separate Spheres and Public Places: Reflections on the History of Science Popularization and Science in Popular Culture', *History of Science* 32 (1994), 237–67.

Cosslett, Tess, *The 'Scientific Movement' and Victorian Literature* (Brighton: Harvester Press, 1982).

Coupland, W. C., *The Principle of Individual Liberty* (London: London Dialectical Society, 1878).

[Courthope, William John], 'The Latest Development of Literary Poetry', *Quarterly Review* 132 (1872), 59–84.

[Dallas, William Sweetland], '*The Descent of Man*', *Westminster Review* 42 n.s. (1872), 378–400.

Darwin, Charles, *On the Origin of Species* (London: John Murray, 1859).

    The Variation of Animals and Plants under Domestication, 2 vols. (London: John Murray, 1868).

    The Descent of Man, and Selection in Relation to Sex, 2 vols. (London: John Murray, 1871).

    The Expression of the Emotions in Man and Animals (London: John Murray, 1872).

    The Descent of Man, and Selection in Relation to Sex, 2nd edn. (London: John Murray, 1874).

    The Origin of Species, ed. by J. W. Burrow (Harmondsworth: Penguin, 1968).

    Autobiographies, ed. by Michael Neve and Sharon Messenger (London: Penguin, 2002).

    The Descent of Man, ed. by James Moore and Adrian Desmond (London: Penguin, 2004).

Darwin, Francis, ed., *The Life and Letters of Charles Darwin*, 3 vols. (London: John Murray, 1887).

    ed., *More Letters of Charles Darwin*, 2 vols. (London: John Murray, 1903).

Darwin, George, 'On Beneficial Restrictions to Liberty of Marriage', *Contemporary Review* 22 (1873), 412–26.

Daston, Lorraine, and Peter Galison, 'The Image of Objectivity', *Representations* 40 (1992), 81–128.

Davies, Charles Maurice, *Heterodox London*, 2 vols. (London: Tinsley, 1874).

[Dawkins, William Boyd], 'Darwin on the *Descent of Man*', *Edinburgh Review* 134 (1871), 195–235.

Dawson, Gowan, 'Walter Pater's *Marius the Epicurean* and the Discourse of Science in *Macmillan's Magazine*: "A Creature of the Nineteenth Century"', *English Literature in Transition 1880–1920* 48 (2005), 38–54.

Dekkers, Midas, *Dearest Pet: On Bestiality*, trans. by Paul Vincent (London: Verso, 1994).

Dellamora, Richard, *Masculine Desire: The Sexual Politics of Victorian Aestheticism* (Chapel Hill: University of North Carolina Press, 1990).

Demoor, Marysa, 'Where No Woman Fears to Tread: The Gossip Column in the *Athenaeum*, 1885–1901', *Barcelona English Language and Literature Studies* 7 (1996), 33–42.

'Self-fashioning at the Turn of the Century: The Discursive Life of Lucy Clifford (1846–1929)', *Journal of Victorian Culture* 4 (1999), 276–91.

and Monty Chisholm, eds., *'Bravest of Women and Finest of Friends': Henry James's Letters to Lucy Clifford* (Victoria, BC: University of Victoria, 1999).

Denisoff, Dennis, *Aestheticism and Sexual Parody 1840–1940* (Cambridge: Cambridge University Press, 2001).

Desmond, Adrian, *Archetypes and Ancestors: Palaeontology in Victorian London 1850–1875* (Chicago: University of Chicago Press, 1982).

The Politics of Evolution: Morphology, Medicine, and Reform in Radical London (Chicago: University of Chicago Press, 1989).

and James Moore, *Darwin* (London: Michael Joseph, 1991).

Huxley: The Devil's Disciple (London: Michael Joseph, 1994).

Huxley: Evolution's High Priest (London: Michael Joseph, 1997).

'Redefining the X Axis: "Professionals", "Amateurs" and the Making of Mid-Victorian Biology – A Progress Report', *Journal of the History of Biology* 34 (2001), 3–50.

Dowden, Edward, 'French Aesthetics', *Contemporary Review* 1 (1866), 279–310.

'The Scientific Movement and Literature', *Contemporary Review* 30 (1877), 558–78.

Dowling, Linda, *Language and Decadence in the Victorian Fin de Siècle* (Princeton: Princeton University Press, 1986).

The Vulgarization of Art: The Victorians and Aesthetic Democracy (Charlottesville: University Press of Virginia, 1996).

[Drysdale, George], *Physical, Sexual, and Natural Religion* (London: Edward Truelove, 1855).

Eliot, George, *Middlemarch*, 4 vols. (Edinburgh: William Blackwood, 1871–2).

Ellis, Alexander J., *On Discussion as a Means of Eliciting Truth* (London: London Dialectical Society, 1879).

Eve, A. S., and C. H. Creasy, *Life and Work of John Tyndall* (London: Macmillan, 1945).

Everett, Edwin Mallard, *The Party of Humanity: The* Fortnightly Review *and its Contributors 1865–1874* (Chapel Hill: University of North Carolina Press, 1939).

Fara, Patricia, *Sex, Botany and Empire: The Story of Carl Linnaeus and Joseph Banks* (Cambridge: Icon, 2003).

Farrar, Frederick William, *The Silence and the Voices of God* (London: Macmillan, 1874).

The Early Days of Christianity (London: Cassell, 1882).

Feuer, Lewis S., 'Is the "Darwin–Marx Correspondence" Authentic?', *Annals of Science* 32 (1975), 1–12.

Findlay, L. M., 'The Introduction of the Phrase "Art for Art's Sake" into English', *Notes and Queries* 20 n.s. (1973), 246–8.

Flaubert, Gustave, *Early Writings*, trans. by Robert Griffin (Lincoln: University of Nebraska Press, 1991).

Flint, Kate, *The Woman Reader 1837–1914* (Oxford: Clarendon Press, 1993).

Friday, James R., Roy M. MacLeod and Philippa Shepherd, *John Tyndall, Natural Philosopher, 1820–1893: Catalogue of Correspondence, Journals and Collected Papers* (London: Mansell, 1974).

Gay, Hannah, and John W. Gay, 'Brothers in Science: Science and Fraternal Culture in Nineteenth-Century Britain', *History of Science* 35 (1997), 425–53.

Geduld, Harry M., ed., *The Definitive Time Machine: A Critical Edition of H. G. Wells's Scientific Romance* (Bloomington: Indiana University Press, 1987).

Gieryn, Thomas F., *Cultural Boundaries of Science: Credibility on the Line* (Chicago: University of Chicago Press, 1999).

Gilman, Sander L., *Difference and Pathology: Stereotypes of Sexuality, Race, and Madness* (Ithaca: Cornell University Press, 1985).

Gosse, Edmund, 'Walter Pater: A Portrait', *Contemporary Review* 66 (1894), 795–810.

The Life of Algernon Charles Swinburne (London: Macmillan, 1917).

[Greg, William Rathbone], 'On the Failure of "Natural Selection" in the Case of Man', *Fraser's Magazine* 78 (1868), 353–62.

Greenslade, William, *Degeneration, Culture and the Novel 1880–1940* (Cambridge: Cambridge University Press, 1994).

Grosskurth, Phyllis, *Havelock Ellis: A Biography* (London: Allen Lane, 1980).

Gruber, Jacob W., *A Conscience in Conflict: The Life of St George Jackson Mivart* (New York: Columbia University Press, 1960).

Gullickson, Gay L., *Unruly Women of Paris: Images of the Commune* (Ithaca: Cornell University Press, 1996).

Guy, Josephine M., *The British Avant-Garde: The Theory and Politics of Tradition* (Hemel Hempstead: Harvester Wheatsheaf, 1991).

Haeckel, Ernst, *Freedom in Science and Teaching* (London: C. Kegan Paul, 1879).

Hague, James D., 'A Reminiscence of Mr. Darwin', *Harper's New Monthly Magazine* (European edn.) 8 (1884), 759–63.

Haight, Gordon S., *George Eliot and John Chapman, with Chapman's Diaries* (New Haven: Yale University Press, 1940).

Haraway, Donna, *Primate Visions: Gender, Race, and Nature in the World of Modern Science* (New York: Routledge, 1989).

[Hardcastle, Joseph Alfred], 'The *New Republic* and Modern Philosophers', *Quarterly Review* 144 (1877), 515–39.

[Hedley, John Cuthbert], 'Evolution and Faith', *Dublin Review* 17 n.s. (1871), 1–40.

Helfand, Michael S., 'T. H. Huxley's "Evolution and Ethics": The Politics of Evolution and the Evolution of Politics', *Victorian Studies* 20 (1977), 159–77.

Hilton, Tim, *John Ruskin: The Later Years* (New Haven and London: Yale University Press, 2000).

Hodgson, W. Earl, *Unrest; or, The Newer Republic* (London: W. H. Allen, 1887).
'The Immorality of Evolutionary Ethics', *National Review* 22 (1893), 46–58.

[Hood, Edwin Paxton], 'Mr. Swinburne, his Crimes and Critics', *Eclectic Review* 124 (1866), 493–508.

Houghton, Walter E., ed., *The Wellesley Index to Victorian Periodicals 1824–1900*, 5 vols. (Toronto: University of Toronto Press, 1966–89).

Howard, Jill, '"Physics and Fashion": John Tyndall and his Audiences in Mid-Victorian Britain', *Studies in History and Philosophy of Science* 35 (2004), 729–58.

Huggins, Mike J., 'More Sinful Pleasures?: Leisure, Respectability and the Male Middle Classes in Victorian England', *Journal of Social History* 33 (2000), 585–600.

Hunter, John, *Essays and Observations on Natural History, Anatomy, Physiology, Psychology, and Geology*, ed. by Richard Owen, 2 vols. (London: John Van Voorst, 1861).

[Hutton, Richard Holt], 'Clifford's *Lectures and Essays*', *Spectator* (1879), 1411–14.

Huxley, Leonard, *Life and Letters of Thomas Henry Huxley*, 2 vols. (London: Macmillan, 1900).

Huxley, Thomas Henry, *Evidence as to Man's Place in Nature* (London: Williams and Norgate, 1863).
'On the Advisableness of Improving Natural Knowledge', *Fortnightly Review* 3 (1866), 626–37.
'Scientific Education', *Macmillan's Magazine* 20 (1869), 177–84.
'The School Boards', *Contemporary Review* 16 (1870), 1–15.
'Administrative Nihilism', *Fortnightly Review* 10 n.s. (1871), 525–43.
'Mr. Darwin's Critics', *Contemporary Review* 18 (1871), 443–76.
'Yeast', *Contemporary Review* 19 (1872), 23–36.
'Universities: Actual and Ideal', *Contemporary Review* 23 (1874), 657–79.
'Joseph Priestley', *Macmillan's Magazine* 30 (1874), 473–85.
'[Review of] *Anthropogenie* by Ernst Haeckl', *Academy* 7 (1875), 16–18.
'Science and Morals', *Fortnightly Review* 40 n.s. (1886), 788–802.
'Science and Art in Relation to Education', in *Science and Education: Collected Essays*, 9 vols. (London: Macmillan, 1893), 3:160–88.
Evolution and Ethics (London: Macmillan, 1894).

Inman, Billie Andrew, 'The Intellectual Context of Walter Pater's "Conclusion"', *Prose Studies* 14 (1981), 12–30.

Jacob, Margaret C., 'The Materialist World of Pornography', in *The Invention of Pornography: Obscenity and the Origins of Modernity, 1500–1800*, ed. by Lynn Hunt (New York: Zone Books, 1993), 157–202.

[Jacolliot, Louis], *Untrodden Fields of Anthropology*, 2 vols. (Paris: Librairie des Bibliophiles, 1896).

Jacyna, L. S., 'Images of John Hunter in the Nineteenth Century', *History of Science* 21 (1983), 85–108.

Jann, Rosemary, 'Darwin and the Anthropologists: Sexual Selection and its Discontents', *Victorian Studies* 37 (1994), 287–306.

Janson, H. W., *Apes and Ape Lore in the Middle Ages and the Renaissance* (London: The Warburg Institute, 1952).

Nineteenth-Century Sculpture (London: Thames and Hudson, 1985).

[Jenkin, Fleeming], 'The Atomic Theory of Lucretius', *North British Review* 9 n.s. (1868), 211–42.

Jordanova, Ludmilla, *Sexual Visions: Images of Gender in Science and Medicine between the Eighteenth and Twentieth Centuries* (London: Harvester Wheatsheaf, 1989).

Kaye, Richard A., *The Flirt's Tragedy: Desire Without End in Victorian and Edwardian Fiction* (Charlottesville: University of Virginia Press, 2002).

Kim, Stephen S., *John Tyndall's Transcendental Materialism and the Conflict between Religion and Science in Victorian England* (New York: Edwin Mellen, 1996).

King, Amy M., *Bloom: The Botanical Vernacular in the English Novel* (New York: Oxford University Press, 2003).

Knowlton, Charles, *Fruits of Philosophy* (London: Freethought Publishing Company, 1877).

Kuduk, Stephanie, '"A Sword of a Song": Swinburne's Republican Aesthetics in *Songs Before Sunrise*', *Victorian Studies* 43 (2001), 253–78.

Lane, Edward, 'Home-work for the Medical Missionary', *Medical Press and Circular* 18 n.s. (1875), 71–3.

Lang, Cecil Y., ed., *The Swinburne Letters*, 6 vols. (New Haven: Yale University Press, 1959–62).

Lange, Friedrich Albert, *History of Materialism and Criticism of its Present Importance*, trans. by Ernest Chester Thomas, 3 vols. (London: Trübner, 1877).

Lansbury, Coral, 'Gynaecology, Pornography, and the Antivivisection Movement', *Victorian Studies* 28 (1985), 413–37.

Laqueur, Thomas W., *Solitary Sex: A Cultural History of Masturbation* (New York: Zone Books, 2003).

Laughton, John Knox, *Memoirs of the Life and Correspondence of Henry Reeve*, 2 vols. (London: Longmans, Green, 1898).

Lea, John Walter, *Christian Marriage: Its Open and Secret Enemies* (London: W. Skeffington, 1881).

[Leifchild, John R.], '[Review of] *Evidence as to Man's Place in Nature* by Thomas Henry Huxley', *Athenaeum* (1863), 287–8.

'[Review of] *The Descent of Man and Selection in Relation to Sex* by Charles Darwin', *Athenaeum* (1871), 275–7.

Levine, George, ed., *One Culture: Essays in Science and Literature*, (Madison: University of Wisconsin Press, 1987).

'One Culture: Science and Literature', in *One Culture: Essays in Science and Literature*, ed. by George Levine (Madison: University of Wisconsin Press, 1987), 3–32.

'Scientific Discourse as an Alternative to Faith', in *Victorian Faith in Crisis: Essays on Continuity and Change in Nineteenth-Century Religious Belief*, ed. by

Richard J. Helmstadter and Bernard Lightman (London: Macmillan, 1990), 225–61.

Dying to Know: Scientific Epistemology and Narrative in Victorian England (Chicago: University of Chicago Press, 2002).

Lightman, Bernard, *The Origins of Agnosticism: Victorian Unbelief and the Limits of Knowledge* (Baltimore: Johns Hopkins University Press, 1987).

'Ideology, Evolution and Late Victorian Agnostic Popularizers', in *History, Humanity and Evolution*, ed. by James R. Moore (Cambridge: Cambridge University Press, 1989), 285–309.

ed., *Victorian Science in Context* (Chicago: University of Chicago Press, 1997).

'Scientists as Materialists in the Periodical Press: Tyndall's Belfast Address', in *Science Serialized: Representations of the Sciences in Nineteenth-Century Periodicals*, ed. by Geoffrey Cantor and Sally Shuttleworth (Cambridge, MA: MIT Press, 2004), 199–237.

Lilly, William Samuel, 'Materialism and Morality', *Fortnightly Review* 40 n.s. (1886), 575–94.

'The Province of Physics', *Fortnightly Review* 41 n.s. (1887), 276–93.

On Right and Wrong (London: Chapman and Hall, 1890).

Livingstone, David N., 'Darwinism and Calvinism: The Belfast–Princeton Connection', *Isis* 83 (1992), 408–28.

Lodge, Oliver, *Advancing Science: Being Personal Reminiscences of the British Association in the Nineteenth Century* (London: Ernest Benn, 1931).

Lombroso, Cesare, *The Man of Genius* (London: Walter Scott, 1891).

Louis, Margot K., *Swinburne and his Gods: The Roots and Growth of an Agnostic Poetry* (Montreal: McGill–Queen's University Press, 1990).

Lyell, Katherine Murray, ed., *Life, Letters and Journals of Sir Charles Lyell, Bart.*, 2 vols. (London: John Murray, 1881).

McCalman, Ian, *Radical Underworld: Prophets, Revolutionaries and Pornographers in London, 1795–1840* (Oxford: Clarendon Press, 1993).

McClintock, Anne, *Imperial Leather: Race, Gender and Sexuality in the Colonial Conquest* (New York: Routledge, 1995).

McCook, Stuart, '"It May be Truth, But it is Not Evidence": Paul Du Chaillu and the Legitimation of Evidence in the Field Sciences', *Osiris* 2nd ser. 11 (1996), 177–97.

McCosh, James, *Ideas in Nature Overlooked by Dr. Tyndall* (New York: Robert Carter, 1875).

McEvansoneya, Philip, '"A Libel in Paint": Religious and Artistic Controversy around P. H. Calderon's *The Renunciation of Saint Elizabeth of Hungary*', *Journal of Victorian Culture* 1 (1996), 254–79.

McLaren, Angus, *Birth Control in Nineteenth-Century England* (London: Croom Helm, 1978).

McLennan, John Ferguson, *Studies in Ancient History*, 2nd series (London: Macmillan, 1896).

[Mallock, William Hurrell], *The New Republic, or Culture, Faith, and Philosophy in an English Country House*, 2 vols. (London: Chatto and Windus, 1877).

'The Late Professor Clifford's *Essays*', *Edinburgh Review* 151 (1880), 474–511.

Mallock, William Hurrell, 'Is Life Worth Living?', *Nineteenth Century* 3 (1878), 146–68.

'A Familiar Colloquy on Recent Art', *Nineteenth Century* 4 (1878), 289–302.

The New Paul and Virginia, or Positivism on an Island (London: Chatto and Windus, 1878).

Is Life Worth Living? (London: Chatto and Windus, 1879).

Memoirs of Life and Literature (London: Chapman and Hall, 1920).

Marchant, James, *Alfred Russel Wallace: Letters and Reminiscences*, 2 vols. (London: Cassell, 1916).

Marcus, Steven, *The Other Victorians: A Study of Sexuality and Pornography in Mid-Nineteenth Century England* (London: Weidenfeld and Nicolson, 1966).

Marriner, Edwin T. J., *'The Raising of the Widow's Son at Nain': A Sermon in Reply to Professor Tyndall's Address at Belfast* (London: Simpkin, Marshall, 1874).

Mason, Michael, *The Making of Victorian Sexuality* (Oxford: Oxford University Press, 1994).

The Making of Victorian Sexual Attitudes (Oxford: Oxford University Press, 1994).

Maudsley, Henry, *The Physiology and Pathology of the Mind* (London: Macmillan, 1867).

'Insanity and its Treatment', *Journal of Mental Science* 17 (1871), 311–34.

Body and Will (London: Kegan Paul, 1883).

Shakespeare: 'Testimonied in his Own Bringingsforth' (London: John Bale, 1905).

Meadows, A. J., *Science and Controversy: A Biography of Sir Norman Lockyer* (London: Macmillan, 1972).

Mill, John Stuart, *Utilitarianism* (London: Parker, Son, and Bourne, 1863).

Mivart, St George, *On the Genesis of Species* (London: Macmillan, 1871).

'Evolution and its Consequences', *Contemporary Review* 19 (1872), 168–97.

'Contemporary Evolution', *Contemporary Review* 22 (1873), 595–614.

'Reminiscences of Thomas Henry Huxley', *Nineteenth Century* 42 (1897), 985–98.

[Mivart, St George], 'Darwin's *Descent of Man*', *Quarterly Review* 131 (1871), 47–90.

'Primitive Man: Tylor and Lubbock', *Quarterly Review* 137 (1874), 40–77.

Moore, Doris Langley, *Ada, Countess of Lovelace: Byron's Legitimate Daughter* (London: John Murray, 1977).

Moore, James R., 'Freethought, Secularism, Agnosticism: The Case of Charles Darwin', in *Religion in Victorian Britain: Traditions*, ed. by Gerald Parsons (Manchester: Manchester University Press, 1988), 274–319.

'Theodicy and Society: The Crisis of the Intelligentsia', in *Victorian Faith in Crisis: Essays on Continuity and Change in Nineteenth-Century Religious Belief*, ed. by Richard J. Helmstadter and Bernard Lightman (London: Macmillan, 1990), 153–86.

'Deconstructing Darwinism: The Politics of Evolution in the 1860s', *Journal of the History of Biology* 24 (1991), 353–408.

Morgan, Thaïs E., 'Mixed Metaphor, Mixed Gender: Swinburne and the Victorian Critics', *Victorian Newsletter* 73 (1988), 16–19.

[Morley, John], 'Mr. Swinburne's New Poems', *Saturday Review* 22 (1866), 145–7.

Morley, John, 'Causeries', *Fortnightly Review* 1 n.s. (1867), 100–3.

'Mr. Pater's Essays', *Fortnightly Review* 13 n.s. (1873), 469–77.

'Valedictory', *Fortnightly Review* 32 n.s. (1882), 511–21.

Recollections, 2 vols. (London: Macmillan, 1917).

Morrell, Jack, and Arnold Thackray, *Gentlemen of Science: Early Years of the British Association for the Advancement of Science* (Oxford: Clarendon Press, 1981).

Morris, William, *The Earthly Paradise* (London: F. S. Ellis, 1868).

Munro, J. M. H., 'Professor Clifford's Essays', *National Reformer* (1879), 804–5.

[Musset, Alfred de], *Gamiani, ou Deux nuits d'excès* (Amsterdam [Paris]: n.p., 1840 [1864]).

Gamiani, or Two Passionate Nights: A Literal Translation (London: n.p., 1908).

Myrone, Martin, 'Prudery, Pornography and the Victorian Nude', in *Exposed: The Victorian Nude*, ed. by Alison Smith (London: Tate Publishing, 2001), 23–35.

Nead, Lynda, 'Bodies of Judgement: Art, Obscenity, and the Connoisseur', in *Law and the Image: The Authority of Art and the Aesthetics of Law*, ed. by Costas Douzinas and Lynda Nead (Chicago: University of Chicago Press, 1999), 203–25.

Victorian Babylon: People, Streets and Images in Nineteenth-Century London (New Haven and London: Yale University Press, 2000).

Nichols, T. L., *Human Physiology* (London: Trübner, 1872).

Nordau, Max, *Degeneration* (London: William Heinemann, 1895).

Nye, Robert A., *Crime, Madness, and Politics in Modern France: The Medical Concept of National Decline* (Princeton: Princeton University Press, 1984).

[Oliphant, Margaret], 'New Books', *Blackwood's Edinburgh Magazine* 114 (1873), 604–9.

[Owen, Richard], '[Review of] *Introduction to the Study of Foraminifera* by William B. Carpenter', *Athenaeum* (1863), 417–19.

Owen, Richard, 'On the Affinities of the *Stereognathus Ooliticus* (Charlesworth), a Mammal from the Oolitic Slate of Stonesfield', *Quarterly Journal of the Geological Society of London* 13 (1856), 1–11.

Paradis, James G., *T. H. Huxley: Man's Place in Nature* (Lincoln: University of Nebraska Press, 1978).

'Satire and Science in Victorian Culture', in *Victorian Science in Context*, ed. by Bernard Lightman (Chicago: University of Chicago Press, 1997), 143–75.

Paston, George, *At John Murray's: Records of a Literary Circle 1843–1892* (London: John Murray, 1932).

[Pater, Walter], 'Winckelmann', *Westminster Review* 31 n.s. (1867), 80–110.

'Poems by William Morris', *Westminster Review* 34 n.s. (1868), 300–12.

Pater, Walter, *Studies in the History of the Renaissance* (London: Macmillan, 1873).

'The School of Giorgione', *Fortnightly Review* 22 n.s. (1877), 526–38.

Marius the Epicurean, 2 vols. (London: Macmillan, 1885).

The Renaissance: Studies in Art and Poetry, 3rd edn. (London: Macmillan, 1888).

Plato and Platonism (London: Macmillan, 1893).

[Pearson, Karl], 'Socialism and Sex', *To-Day* 7 (1887), 42–55.

'[Review of] *The Elements of Dynamic* by W. K. Clifford', *Athenaeum* (1887), 86–7.

Pearson, Karl, *The Life, Letters and Labours of Francis Galton*, 3 vols. (Cambridge: Cambridge University Press, 1914–30).

Peattie, Roger W., ed., *Selected Letters of William Michael Rossetti* (University Park: Pennsylvania State University Press, 1990).

Perry, Ralph Barton, ed., *The Thought and Character of William James*, 2 vols. (London: Oxford University Press, 1935).

Pick, Daniel, *Faces of Degeneration: A European Disorder, c. 1848–c. 1918* (Cambridge: Cambridge University Press, 1989).

Pollock, Frederick, 'William Kingdon Clifford', *Fortnightly Review* 25 n.s. (1879), 667–87.

Porter, Roy, and Lesley Hall, *The Facts of Life: The Creation of Sexual Knowledge in Britain, 1650–1950* (New Haven and London: Yale University Press, 1995).

Porter, Theodore M., 'Historicizing the Two Cultures', *History of Science* 43 (2005), 109–14.

Raby, Peter, *Bright Paradise: Victorian Scientific Travellers* (London: Chatto and Windus, 1996).

[Reeve, Henry], 'Mill's *Essays on Theism*', *Edinburgh Review* 141 (1875), 1–31.

Renan, Ernst, *Souvenirs d'enfance et de jeunesse* (Paris: Calmann-Lévy, 1883).

Richards, Evelleen, 'Darwin and the Descent of Woman', in *The Wider Domain of Evolutionary Thought*, ed. by David Oldroyd and Ian Langham (Dordrecht: Reidel, 1983), 57–111.

'The "Moral Anatomy" of Robert Knox: The Interplay between Biological and Social Thought in Victorian Scientific Naturalism', *Journal of the History of Biology* 22 (1989), 373–436.

'Redrawing the Boundaries: Darwinian Science and Victorian Women Intellectuals', in *Victorian Science in Context*, ed. by Bernard Lightman (Chicago: University of Chicago Press, 1997), 119–42.

Richards, Joan L., *Mathematical Visions: The Pursuit of Geometry in Victorian England* (London: Academic Press, 1988).

Richardson, Angelique, *Love and Eugenics in the Late Nineteenth Century: Rational Reproduction and the New Woman* (Oxford: Oxford University Press, 2003).

Roberts, M. J. D., 'Making Victorian Morals?: The Society for the Suppression of Vice and its Critics, 1802–1886', *Historical Studies* 21 (1984), 157–73.

'Morals, Art, and the Law: The Passing of the Obscene Publications Act, 1857', *Victorian Studies* 28 (1985), 609–29.

[Rodrigues, Eugène], *Catalogue descriptif et analytique de l'œuvre gravé de Félicien Rops* (Paris: Librairie Conquet, 1887).

Rooksby, Rikky, *A. C. Swinburne: A Poet's Life* (Aldershot: Scolar Press, 1997).

Royle, Edward, *Radicals, Secularists and Republicans: Popular Freethought in Britain, 1866–1915* (Manchester: Manchester University Press, 1980).

Ruse, Michael, *The Darwinian Revolution: Science Red in Tooth and Claw* (Chicago: University of Chicago Press, 1979).

Ruskin, John, 'The Three Colours of Pre-Raphaelitism', *Nineteenth Century* (1878), 1072–82.

Modern Painters vol. II, 2nd edn. 2 vols. (Orpington: George Allen, 1883).

Russell, Bertrand, and Patricia Russell, eds., *The Amberley Papers: The Letters and Diaries of Lord and Lady Amberley*, 2 vols. (London: Hogarth Press, 1937).

St John, Spenser, *Life in the Forests of the Far East*, 2 vols. (London: Smith, Elder, 1862).

Sato, Tomo, 'E. W. Lane's Hydropathic Establishment at Moor Park', *Hitotsubashi Journal of Social Studies* 10 (1978), 45–59.

Sawyer, Paul, 'Ruskin and Tyndall: The Poetry of Matter and the Poetry of Spirit', in *Victorian Science and Victorian Values: Literary Perspectives*, ed. by James Paradis and Thomas Postlewait (New Brunswick: Rutgers University Press, 1985), 217–46.

Schaffer, Talia, '"A Wilde Desire Took Me": The Homoerotic History of *Dracula*', *ELH* 61 (1994), 381–425.

Schiebinger, Londa, 'The Private Life of Plants: Sexual Politics in Carl Linnaeus and Erasmus Darwin', in *Science and Sensibility: Gender and Scientific Enquiry 1780–1945*, ed. by Marina Benjamin (Oxford: Basil Blackwell, 1991), 121–43.

'The Gendered Ape: Early Representations of Primates in Europe', in *A Question of Identity: Women, Science and Literature*, ed. by Marina Benjamin (New Brunswick: Rutgers University Press, 1993), 119–51.

Nature's Body: Sexual Politics and the Making of Modern Science (London: Pandora, 1994).

Secord, James A., *Victorian Sensation: The Extraordinary Publication, Reception, and Secret Authorship of* Vestiges of the Natural History of Creation (Chicago: University of Chicago Press, 2000).

'Knowledge in Transit', *Isis* 95 (2004), 654–72.

Selborne, Lord, 'A Modern "Symposium": The Influence upon Morality of a Decline in Religious Belief', *Nineteenth Century* 1 (1877), 333–40.

Sexton, George, *Scientific Materialism Calmly Considered* (London: J. Burns, 1874).

Shaffer, E. S., 'The Sphinx and the Muses: The Third Culture', *Comparative Criticism* 13 (1991), xv–xxix.

Shapin, Steven, *A Social History of Truth: Civility and Science in Seventeenth-Century England* (Chicago: University of Chicago Press, 1994).

Shelley, Percy Bysshe, *Posthumous Poems*, ed. by Mary W. Shelley (London: John and Henry L. Hunt, 1824).

Showalter, Elaine, *The Female Malady: Women, Madness, and English Culture, 1830–1980* (London: Virago, 1987).

Shuttleworth, Sally, *Charlotte Brontë and Victorian Psychology* (Cambridge: Cambridge University Press, 1996).

Sigel, Lisa Z., *Governing Pleasures: Pornography and Social Change in England, 1815–1914* (New Brunswick: Rutgers University Press, 2002).

Small, Helen, '"In the Guise of Science": Literature and the Rhetoric of Nineteenth-Century English Psychiatry', *History of the Human Sciences* 7 (1994), 27–55.

Love's Madness: Medicine, the Novel, and Female Insanity 1800–1865 (Oxford: Clarendon Press, 1996).

'Science, Liberalism, and the Ethics of Belief: The *Contemporary Review* in 1877', in *Science Serialized: Representations of the Sciences in Nineteenth-Century Periodicals*, ed. by Geoffrey Cantor and Sally Shuttleworth (Cambridge, MA: MIT Press, 2004), 239–57.

Smith, Crosbie, *The Science of Energy: A Cultural History of Energy Physics in Victorian Britain* (London: Athlone Press, 1998).

Smith, Philip E., and Michael S. Helfand, eds., *Oscar Wilde's Oxford Notebooks: A Portrait of Mind in the Making* (New York: Oxford University Press, 1989).

Smith, Roger, 'The Human Significance of Biology: Carpenter, Darwin, and the *vera causa*', in *Nature and the Victorian Imagination*, ed. by U. C. Knoepflmacher and G. B. Tennyson (Berkeley: University of California Press, 1977), 216–30.

[Smith, Sydney], 'Proceedings of the Society for the Suppression of Vice', *Edinburgh Review* 13 (1809), 333–43.

Snigurowicz, Diana, 'Sex, Simians, and Spectacle in Nineteenth-Century France: or, How to Tell a "Man" from a Monkey', *Canadian Journal of History* 34 (1999), 51–81.

[Spencer, Herbert], 'A Theory of Population, Deduced from the General Law of Animal Fertility', *Westminster Review* 1 n.s. (1852), 468–501.

Srebrnik, Patricia Thomas, *Alexander Strahan, Victorian Publisher* (Ann Arbor: University of Michigan Press, 1986).

Stelzig, Eugene L., 'Romantic Subjectivity: Disease or Fortunate Fall?', in *English and German Romanticism: Cross Currents and Controversies*, ed. by James Pipkin (Heidelberg: Carl Winter Universitätsverlag, 1985), 153–68.

Stephen, Leslie, *Life of Henry Fawcett* (London: Smith, Elder, 1885).

Stewart, Susan, *Crimes of Writing: Problems in the Containment of Representation* (New York: Oxford University Press, 1991).

Stoker, Bram, *Dracula* (Westminster: A. Constable, 1897).

Stokes, C. W., *An Inquiry of the Home Secretary as to Whether Professor Tyndall has Not Subjected Himself to the Penalty of Persons Expressing Blasphemous Opinions* (London: privately printed, 1874).

Stott, Rebecca, 'Darwin's Barnacles: Mid-Century Victorian Natural History and the Marine Grotesque', in *Transactions and Encounters: Science and Culture in the Nineteenth Century*, ed. by Roger Luckhurst and Josephine McDonagh (Manchester: Manchester University Press, 2002), 151–81.

Strick, James E., *Sparks of Life: Darwinism and the Victorian Debates over Spontaneous Generation* (Cambridge, MA: Harvard University Press, 2000).

Swinburne, Algernon Charles, *Poems and Ballads* (London: Edward Moxon, 1866).

William Blake: A Critical Essay (London: J. C. Hotten, 1868).

Songs Before Sunrise (London: F. S. Ellis, 1871).

George Chapman: A Critical Essay, (London: Chatto and Windus, 1875).

'The Suppression of Vice', *Athenaeum* (1875), 720.

'Victor Hugo: *Religions et Religion*', *Fortnightly Review* 27 n.s. (1880), 761–68.

'Dethroning Tennyson: A Contribution to the Tennyson–Darwin Controversy', *Nineteenth Century* 23 (1888), 127–9.

Tait, P. G., 'Clifford's Exact Sciences', *Nature* 32 (1885), 124–5.

Talfourd, T. N., *Speech for the Defendant in the Prosecution of the Queen v. Moxon for the Publication of Shelley's Works* (London: Edward Moxon, 1841).

Taylor, Anne, *Annie Besant: A Biography* (Oxford: Oxford University Press, 1992).

Tennyson, Hallam, *Alfred, Lord Tennyson: A Memoir*, 2 vols. (London: Macmillan, 1897).

[Tennyson, Alfred], *In Memoriam* (London: Edward Moxon, 1850).

Tennyson, Alfred, *Idylls of the King* (London: Edward Moxon, 1859).

'Lucretius', *Macmillan's Magazine* 18 (1868), 1–9.

Tiresias and Other Poems (London: Macmillan, 1885).

Thomson, William, 'On the Age of the Sun's Heat', *Macmillan's Magazine* 5 (1862), 388–93.

Tooley, Sarah A., 'Some Women Novelists', *Woman at Home* 6 (1897), 161–211.

Tribe, David, *President Charles Bradlaugh, M.P.* (London: Elek, 1971).

[Tulloch, John], 'Modern Scientific Materialism', *Blackwood's Edinburgh Magazine* 116 (1874), 519–39.

Turner, Frank Miller, *Between Science and Religion: The Reaction to Scientific Naturalism in Late Victorian England* (New Haven and London: Yale University Press, 1974).

The Greek Heritage in Victorian Britain (New Haven and London: Yale University Press, 1981).

'John Tyndall and Victorian Scientific Naturalism', in *John Tyndall: Essays on a Natural Philosopher*, ed. by W. H. Brock, N. D. McMillan, and R. C. Mollan (Dublin: Dublin Royal Society, 1981), 169–80.

Contesting Cultural Authority: Essays in Victorian Intellectual Life (Cambridge: Cambridge University Press, 1993).

Tyndall, John, *Heat Considered as a Mode of Motion* (London: Longmans, Green, 1863).

'On the Relations of Radiant Heat to Chemical Constitution, Colour and Texture', *Fortnightly Review* 4 (1866), 1–15.

Fragments of Science for Unscientific People, 2nd edn. (London: Longmans, Green, 1871).

Six Lectures on Light (London: Longmans, Green, 1873).

Address Delivered Before the British Association Assembled at Belfast (London: Longmans, Green, 1874).

'Crystalline and Molecular Forces', in *Science Lectures for the People. Sixth Series* (Manchester: John Heywood, 1874).

'"Materialism" and its Opponents', *Fortnightly Review* 22 n.s. (1875), 579–99.

Fragments of Science, 5th edn. (London: Longmans, Green, 1876).

'Science and Man', *Fortnightly Review* 22 n.s. (1877), 593–617.

'Personal Recollections of Thomas Carlyle', *Fortnightly Review* 47 n.s. (1890), 5–32.

New Fragments (London: Longmans, Green, 1892).

Tyrwhitt, Richard St John, 'The Greek Spirit in Modern Literature', *Contemporary Review* 29 (1877), 552–66.

'Hellenic and Christian Views of Beauty', *Contemporary Review* 36 (1880), 474–91.

Vance, Norman, *The Victorians and Ancient Rome* (Oxford: Blackwell, 1997).

Védrine, Hélène, *De l'encre dans l'acide: l'œuvre gravé de Félicien Rops et la littérature de la Décadence* (Paris: Champion, 2002).

Wagner, Peter, 'The Discourse on Sex – or Sex as Discourse: Eighteenth-Century Medical and Paramedical Erotica', in *Sexual Underworlds of the Enlightenment*, ed. by G. S. Rousseau and Roy Porter (Manchester: Manchester University Press, 1987), 46–68.

Waitz, Theodor, *Introduction to Anthropology*, trans. by J. Frederick Collingwood (London: Longman, Green, 1863).

Walkowitz, Judith R., *City of Dreadful Delight: Narratives of Sexual Danger in Late-Victorian London* (London: Virago, 1992).

Wallace, Alfred R., '[Review of] *The Descent of Man and Selection in Relation to Sex* by Charles Darwin', *Academy* 2 (1871), 177–83.

Ward, Wilfrid, 'Thomas Henry Huxley: A Reminiscence', *Nineteenth Century* 40 (1896), 274–92.

Watts, Robert, *Atomism: Dr. Tyndall's Atomic Theory of the Universe Examined and Refuted* (Belfast: William Mullan, 1874).

[Weissenfeld, Georg von], 'Danger Ahead', *University Magazine* 10 (1898), 449–62.

Darwin on Trial at the Old Bailey (Watford: University Press, [1899]).

Judicial Scandals and Errors (Watford: University Press, [1899]).

Wells, H. G., *The Time Machine* (London: William Heinemann, 1895).

The Island of Doctor Moreau (London: William Heinemann, 1896).

White, Allon, *The Uses of Obscurity: The Fiction of Early Modernism* (London: Routledge, 1981).

White, Paul, *Thomas Huxley: Making the 'Man of Science'* (Cambridge: Cambridge University Press, 2003).

'Ministers of Culture: Arnold, Huxley and Liberal Anglican Reform of Learning', *History of Science* 43 (2005), 115–38.

[White, Richard Grant], *The Fall of Man: or, The Loves of the Gorillas* (New York: G. W. Carleton, 1871).

Whyte, A. Gowans, *The Story of the R.P.A. 1899–1949* (London: Watts, 1949).

Wikman, Karl Robert V., *Letters from Edward B. Tylor and Alfred Russel Wallace to Edward Westermarck* (Åbo: Åbo Akademi, 1940).

Wilde, Oscar, 'The True Function and Value of Criticism', *Nineteenth Century* 28 (1890), 123–47 and 435–59.

'The Soul of Man under Socialism', *Fortnightly Review* 49 n.s. (1891), 292–319.

'The English Renaissance in Art', in *Lectures and Essays* (London: Methuen, 1909), 111–55.

Willis, Irene Cooper, ed., *Vernon Lee's Letters* (London: privately printed, 1937).

Winter, Alison, 'The Construction of Orthodoxies and Heterodoxies in the Early Victorian Life Sciences', in *Victorian Science in Context*, ed. by Bernard Lightman (Chicago: University of Chicago Press, 1997), 24–50.

Yeazell, Ruth Bernard, *Fictions of Modesty: Women and Courtship in the English Novel* (Chicago: University of Chicago Press, 1991).

Young, Robert M., *Darwin's Metaphor: Nature's Place in Victorian Culture* (Cambridge: Cambridge University Press, 1985).

Index

276

CAMBRIDGE STUDIES IN NINETEENTH-CENTURY
LITERATURE AND CULTURE

General editor
Gillian Beer, *University of Cambridge*

Titles published